MARSHAL OF FRANCE

THE LIFE AND TIMES

OF

MAURICE, COMTE DE SAXE

[1696-1750]

Maurice de Saxe
Duc de Curlande et de Semigallie
Marechal de France

MAURICE DE SAXE
Portrait by Rigaud

MARSHAL
OF FRANCE

THE LIFE AND TIMES

OF

MAURICE, COMTE DE SAXE

[1696-1750]

BY

JON MANCHIP WHITE

RAND McNALLY & COMPANY
Chicago · New York · San Francisco
PRINTED IN GREAT BRITAIN

Printed in Great Britain by
Northumberland Press Limited
Gateshead on Tyne

TO

T. R. HENN

Scholar and Soldier

CONTENTS

ILLUSTRATIONS

Plates

Tables

Figures

AUTHOR'S FOREWORD

MAURICE DE SAXE was the brilliant adornment of a brilliant age, one of the most renowned and admired men in the Europe of his day. It is not surprising that the writing of the biography of this vivid, talented and entertaining figure should have provided the author with a genial and absorbing task.

He came of extraordinary stock; the circumstances of his birth were remarkable; he was the lover of many celebrated women; he won the lifelong friendship of men of the stature of Voltaire; he aspired to a crown, and nearly became the Czar of Russia; his activities spanned a whole continent, from Paris to Dresden, from Dresden to Warsaw, from Warsaw to Moscow. Yet he was more, much more, than an energetic and flamboyant adventurer: he was acknowledged to be the outstanding general of his era, a military genius who linked the epoch of Marlborough with the epoch of Frederick the Great. He led great armies and won great victories.

It is part of the purpose of this book to restore him to the pre-eminent place in social and military history to which his achievements entitle him. The study of his campaigns has proved no dutiful or dreary labour, for he was among the wittiest and most elegant military practitioners who have ever lived. There was a touch of *diablerie* about the manner in which he gained his spectacular triumphs that set him apart from the other great captains of his era.

His claim to a due measure of re-assessment does not reside in his professional success alone. He was a deeply interesting person in his own right, and in many ways a sad one. His essential core of hard good sense was embedded in a strange romantic temperament. The practical soldier was also a dreamer and an idealist. Nor did his victories come to him cheaply or easily: they had to be brought about in the teeth of adversity, animosity, and mental and physical distress. He was compelled to fulfil his ultimate destiny and realize the purpose of his life in spite of sickness, self-mistrust, and the most bitter and ruthless opposition.

It is, I think, true to say that this is the first comprehensive biography of Saxe. With the exception of one or two short and sensational studies, the only serious attempts at biography were those that appeared during the closing years of the *ancien régime*, and the book by René Taillandier, published over ninety years ago. Taillandier, however, was not interested in military affairs; and the monumental researches of Colonel Colin on Saxe's campaigns were terminated by Colin's death in battle at Verdun. It has therefore been my particular privilege to try to bring together the two halves —private and professional—of Maurice's life, and to examine them much more fully than has been done hitherto. The actual biographies of Saxe have not in fact constituted my main sources of printed material. In this field such miscellanies as that of Vitzthum d'Eckstaedt, published in 1867, containing Maurice's correspondence with the Saxon court, have been especially useful: and above all there are the five packed volumes of the *Lettres et Mémoires choisis parmi les Papiers originaux du Maréchal de Saxe*, published in Paris in 1794—curiously enough, at the height of the Revolution that was sweeping away the Old Order of which Saxe had been a notable pillar. These volumes, haphazard and chaotically organized as they are, are a mine of information about the conduct of the Wars of the Polish and Austrian Succession, and appear to have remained almost untouched in the study of those wars.

The available materials relating to the career of this remarkable and important figure have not previously been sifted. At first glance it seems strange that such a rich and glowing personality should not have been the subject of a full-scale modern work: but paradoxically his very glamour may have been responsible for this omission. He is that rare creature whom historians are always glad to treat in a marginal fashion, but whom they do not like to encounter head on: the colourful character. It is the economists and diplomats who provide the historian with his safer and more respectable matter. Maurice was different: he loved noise, excitement, rewards, women, wine, and glory—especially glory, a defunct attribute of human existence whose sheen dulls and dies as swiftly as the sheen on the scales of a splendid dying fish. It is not surprising that a professional historian has not cared to embroil himself with a man as extravagant as Maurice, whose achievements are so individual that it is a temptation to treat them far less seriously than they merit. For this reason it is perhaps no bad thing that it should be left to a writer of novels and imaginative literature to write the life of Maurice, for he can revel in an unashamed and uninhibited way in the contradictions of Maurice's character and the eccentric outline of his career. It would, of course, be absurd to put forward grandiose claims on behalf of Maurice. But it would be equally foolish to underrate him, since his contemporaries clearly regarded him as a person of supreme importance. And it is in any case often the more peripheral personalities who enable one to glimpse with unusual clarity the true nature of an age. They are more human, more representative, and swim closer to the median current of their time.

Although history never repeats itself, it is notorious that historians do. Maurice's character and career have been subjected to reiterated inaccuracies. This is particularly true in the personal domain, where a legendary, one might almost say fantastic atmosphere surrounds his father's and mother's families and his own quasi-heroic exploits. Here it has been of special importance to disentangle fact from fiction. Where his military campaigns are concerned, it has not been so necessary to separate the true from the false as to collate the contemporary narratives and the writings of later military historians. In the numerous accounts of what happened at even such a well-known battle as Fontenoy, lavishly documented on both the French and British sides, there are wide differences concerning every detail of the encounter. The accounts of Maurice's campaigns which I have given, though based primarily on his field-correspondence with his own officers and on the French military archives, are therefore largely a matter of intelligent interpretation, supplemented by a long-cultivated study of eighteenth-century warfare in general and a careful personal survey of the actual ground over which the engagements were fought, so far as its original conformation can be discerned.

The figures which I have drawn of the main battles and the identity of the individual regiments are, like the genealogical table of the Königsmarcks, a unique feature. I would also respectfully beg my readers to follow the wider progress of the successive campaigns on the end-papers and on the maps which I have provided, where the towns and fortresses have been marked. If the accounts of the campaigns seem long, this is because I felt that there was no point in stating that Maurice de Saxe was the greatest general of his day unless I undertook to prove it by quoting chapter and verse. This accordingly I have done. At the same time my interest in Saxe has not been, as I have indicated, exclusively martial: my interest in him stems from the fact that he led a life that was notably varied and universal, and which touched the heights and depths of human experience. Few men have lived as fully as Maurice de Saxe. His life is by turns bizarre, comic, touching and tragic—but always compelling.

The biography stems from an article on Saxe which appeared in *History Today*: and it is pleasant to acknowledge here my wider indebtedness to the editors of that journal, Mr. Alan Hodge and Mr. Peter Quennell. My chief acknowledgement is to my friend and former colleague in the Foreign Office, Mr. John Tyrer Egg. Without his encouragement and active help the book would not exist. In its first state it was twice as long as it is now, and it was Mr. Egg who shouldered the responsibility of reducing it to its present proportions. Without his assistance it would have degenerated into an encyclopaedia of the wars, armies and commanders of the eighteenth century. He also made skilful excisions in the sections relating to the political background, although it was not possible to reduce these with too drastic a hand, as part of Saxe's importance resides in the manner in which his career is linked simultaneously with events in Eastern and Western Europe. Mr. Egg's specialist knowledge of the period has also been of incalculable help to me.

Among the many librarians and museum officials who have rendered service, I must first thank those of the Invalides, who allowed me to work for many happy hours in their beautiful library, with the records of the French army spread out around me. The love and care with which these records have been maintained must be seen to be appreciated, and they were made available to me with the greatest readiness and courtesy. I hope that this book will be regarded at the Invalides as a not wholly negligible tribute to a man who shed much lustre on the arms of France.

Next I should like to thank the staff of the London Library, an institution which has recently been subjected to crude and philistine treatment. Its staff were as tireless as ever in their anxiety to further the work of learning. I am also indebted to the staffs of the Musée Carnavalet in Paris and of the museum at Strasbourg, and also of the Staatsbibliotek in East Berlin. I was unable, however, to secure from the Communist authorities permission to travel to Saxony and its capital, Dresden.

Finally I must thank Mr. H. D. Lyon, the antiquarian bookseller, who secured for me many of the items in my now extensive collection of Saxeiana; M. Morssen, who allowed me to inspect private autograph material; Mr. David Farrell, who provided me with the photographs of the illustrations; Miss Veronica Vernon and Mrs. Winifred Walker, who typed the successive drafts of the manuscript; and the host of archivists, municipal officials, policemen, taxi-drivers, hoteliers, farmers and others who made visits to battlefields or châteaux in France, Belgium and along the length of the Rhine an exciting and rewarding undertaking.

Minsterworth Court,
Gloucester.

*The very substance of the ambitious is
merely the shadow of a dream*

PROLOGUE

GOSLAR, 1696

De toutes les resveries du monde, la plus receue et plus
universelle est le soing de la reputation et de la gloire,
que nous espousons iusques à quitter les richesses, le repos,
la vie et la santé, qui sont biens intellectuels et substan-
tiaux, pour suyvre cette vaine image et cette simple voix
qui n'a ny corps, ny prinse.

MONTAIGNE

THE birth of Maurice de Saxe occurred in circumstances wholly out of key with the brilliant rôle which he was to play in later life. The illegitimate son of a great German prince and a high-born Swedish adventuress, the prodigy, who was to become one of the outstanding generals of his age, was brought into the world in secrecy, shame and anguish.

In the autumn of 1696 the Lutheran pastor of the city of Goslar, an obscure town in northern Germany, recorded in his parish register that:

> Today, October 28, a male child was born to a noble and high-born lady in the house of Heinrich Christoph Winkel, and was christened Moritz.

The boy appears to have been given the dual christian name of Moritz-Hermann, and it was under the appropriately bastard style of 'Arminius-Maurice de Saxe' that his name was to be entered forty-seven years later in the proud roll of the Marshals of France.

Why the remote and crumbling imperial free city of Goslar should have been chosen as his birthplace is a mystery. It had no particular association with either his father or his mother, and neither Goslar nor Heinrich Christoph Winkel were to play any part in his later career. The choice of this particular township may have been accidental; he may have been born while his distracted mother was journeying towards another destination. But it was not inappropriate that this old Hanseatic town, the birthplace of great Emperors and a former centre of the Hohenstaufen power, should have been the birthplace

1

of such a fiery soul. His daemonic spirit was cradled among the wild splendour of the Hartz mountains, in the shadow of the Brocken, where the witches dance on Walpurgisnacht.

His mother was a Swedish noblewoman, the Countess Maria Aurora von Königsmarck. Voltaire was later to call her 'the most famous woman of two centuries, celebrated throughout the world for her wit and beauty', and his father was no less a person than Frederick August I, Elector of Saxony, soon to be renowned as Augustus the Strong, King of Poland. Through his father, Maurice would be able to trace his illicit descent from Hermann I, the founder of the house of Wettin, who had ruled in Saxony as count palatine at the close of the twelfth century. The boy was part of that clan of warriors and princes whose Albertine branch provided kings for Poland and Saxony in the eighteenth and nineteenth centuries, and whose Ernestine line was destined in modern times to rule in Great Britain, Belgium, Portugal and Bulgaria. The men of the house of Wettin were by nature dynasts; Maurice was to be no exception to the rule.

Yet it was not as an Albertine, but as the last heir of the restless and eccentric family of Königsmarck, that Maurice would prefer to think of himself. It was the exploits of this extraordinary breed that he would strive to emulate. He had inherited many of the qualities of his mother's ancestors; and when blended with those that he derived from the house of Wettin, they would produce an explosive mixture.

The Königsmarcks, originally of Brandenburger origin, were Swedish by adoption [vide Table 1]. Maurice's great-grandfather, Hans Christoph, was later celebrated as the Old Königsmarck. He deserted the Catholic armies of the Emperor early in his military career, and espoused instead the Lutheran cause of the young Swedish king, Gustavus Adolphus, under whom he fought at Lützen. After the premature deaths of the king and his general Banér, Königsmarck was entrusted with temporary command of the disorganized and dispirited Swedes. He was immediately successful, and in the short space of a month he had led the Protestant forces to victory over the Imperial troops at Wolfenbüttel. Seven years later he was to perform an even greater feat of arms. In 1648, while the main Swedish and French forces under Wrangel and Turenne were subduing Bavaria, Königsmarck led a flying column into the heart of the Habsburg domains and laid siege to Prague. His troops were already burning and looting in the outskirts of the Bohemian capital when the Peace of Westphalia was concluded, and it was this treaty alone, which concluded the terrible Thirty Years' War, that saved the ancient city from falling to the furious Swedes. Old Königsmarck's investment of Prague

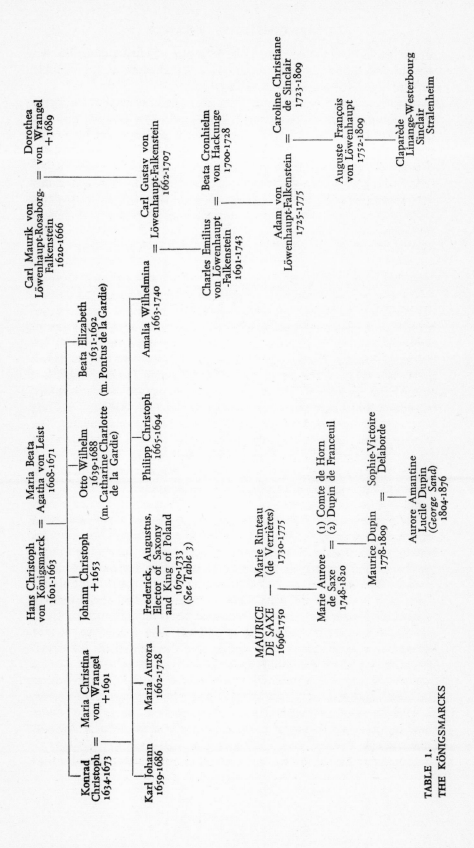

TABLE 1.
THE KÖNIGSMARCKS

was an exploit worthy of Maurice de Saxe himself : and indeed Maurice was to re-enact his great-grandfather's action with greater success and less bloodshed ninety years later.

In the ensuing years of peace, Old Königsmarck became Governor of the Swedish fiefs of Bremen and Verden. On the occasion of Queen Christina's coronation in 1650, he was ennobled as a count and promoted to field marshal. Later he fought in the Polish campaigns of Charles X, and passed several bitter years in captivity at Danzig before dying at Stockholm in 1663. With Horn and Wrangel, Banér and Torstenssen, Maurice's gallant ancestor took his place in effigy among the generals who adorn the monument of Gustavus Adolphus in Stockholm.

The old general's two sons were worthy of their sire.

The elder, Maurice's grandfather Karl Christoph, distinguished himself as a commander of artillery, and was killed at the siege of Bonn in 1673. His four young children were then adopted by his dynamic younger brother, Otto Wilhelm, who early in life had fallen under the spell of the great French commander Turenne, and had entered the service of France. He was among the three hundred volunteers who shared in La Feuillade's amateur crusade to save Crete from the Turks, and later he served in Turenne's last campaign and was personally commended for gallantry by the old Marshal before Maastricht. He fought with such distinction at the battle of Senef, where he commanded the *Royal-Étranger* regiment, that Louis XIV presented him with a sword of honour and promoted him *maréchal de camp*.

The Swedes made a strenuous attempt to regain Otto Wilhelm's services by offering him the Governorship of Pomerania, but his innate restlessness drove him instead to seek service once more against the Turks. He enlisted in the army of the Most Serene Republic of Venice, then engaged in a deadly struggle with the Most Sublime Porte, and in 1686 he was made Generalissimo of the Venetian Armies, and sent to Greece to reinforce the native Venetian Commander, Francesco Morosini. He landed in the Peloponnese, fought his way down the isthmus of Corinth, and carried Athens by storm. It was during these operations that the Parthenon, which was being used by the Turks as an arsenal, was almost destroyed by a shell from the Venetian batteries. Otto Wilhelm and Morosini were undeterred. If Venetian soldiers could sack Constantinople in 1204, they could shoulder the lesser odium of blowing up the temple of Pallas Athene. Königsmarck is usually saddled with the blame for the mishap, although it was Morosini who was the real culprit. It was also Morosini who later hacked the temple to pieces in his efforts to steal the figures of Poseidon and the horses of Pallas Athene as spoils of war. He had to be content with the great marble lion which still guards the Arsenal of Venice, the oldest and loveliest of naval bases.

Otto Wilhelm died shortly afterwards of wounds. In 1688 his body was interred in the Königsmarck mausoleum at Stade, the town near Hamburg which had become the family seat.

Otto Wilhelm's turbulent nephews were to become Maurice's notorious uncles. Karl Johann was fair, with blue eyes set in a strong face, while his younger brother Philipp Christoph was darker, and had more delicate features. Their foolhardy adventures in battlefield and bedchamber were to become the talk of Europe.

In 1681, Karl Johann, fresh from campaigning at Malta with the Knights of Saint John, was deputed to escort Philipp Christoph to London. The older boy was then eighteen, and it was hoped that he and his brother would benefit from the rigours of an English education. Karl Johann soon established himself as a personal favourite of King Charles II, and within a matter of months he had fallen deeply in love with the young Lady Elizabeth Percy, the widowed Countess of Ogle and the richest heiress in the three kingdoms. His request for her hand was brusquely rejected by the lady's mother, for the unfortunate girl, who had been widowed at fifteen, was destined for a more lucrative match. Instead of marrying the ardent and accomplished Königsmarck, she was given in marriage to a wealthy young rake called Thomas Thynne of Longleat, better known as 'Tom of Ten Thousand'. But within a few days of marriage, repelled by the manner of her husband's advances, she had fled to The Hague, and on February 12th, 1686, Thynne was murdered in his coach by three horsemen as he was being driven along Pall Mall. The lady's rejected suitor, Karl Johann, immediately fell under suspicion of conspiracy to murder, and was summoned before the Privy Council. Together with another Swedish officer and two Poles, all of them his hirelings, he was subsequently tried at the Old Bailey. He was almost certainly guilty, but although his three accomplices were sentenced to death he was acquitted. The royal favour had stood him in good stead.

Nevertheless, the two young Swedes were compelled to remove themselves to France. The elder brother was soon fighting with distinction for Louis XIV, as colonel of the Fürstemberg regiment, but his career in the French Army was cut short by the revocation of the Edict of Nantes, a blow against Protestantism which as a Lutheran he could not accept. He therefore offered his sword to the less bigoted Venetians and joined his uncle in Greece. He fought there with fierce courage; but while campaigning on the island of Euboea he died of pleurisy. He was twenty-seven.

His young brother, Philipp Christoph, was fated to be the last man to bear the name of Königsmarck.

His education, which had begun so inauspiciously in London, was eventually completed at Dresden, capital of the Electorate of Saxony. There the young Count Königsmarck became a firm friend of Prince Frederick Augustus, the heir presumptive, a youth five years his junior and the future father of Maurice de Saxe. Frederick Augustus had not yet come into his inheritance, so Philipp Christoph could not immediately achieve his aim of entering the service of Saxony, and retired instead to his Pomeranian estates. There he lived with typical Königsmarck extravagance, galloping about the north German plain with an escort of regal proportions. His style of life was undoubtedly impressive: and among those whose attention it attracted was the Elector of Hanover's ugly mistress, the Countess Platen. This lady, whose influence at the court of Herrenhausen was paramount, persuaded the Elector to appoint the handsome Swede to a colonelcy in the Hanoverian guards.

Once installed at the court of Hanover, Philipp's attention wandered away from the middle-aged Platen in a fatal and forbidden direction. He fell in love with the Elector's daughter-in-law, the young and beautiful Electoral Princess, Sophia Dorothea. He was soon entangled with her as dangerously as his elder brother had been entangled with Elizabeth Percy.

The affair, which began in the summer of 1691, when Philipp was twenty-five and Sophia Dorothea was two years his senior, was at first a well-kept secret. The lovers had a trusted *confidante* in the person of Maurice de Saxe's future mother, the elder of Philipp's two sisters, Maria Aurora. When Philipp was absent at the wars, it was Maria Aurora who ensured that he received Sophia's distraught letters, and ultimately it was Maria Aurora who retained possession of the incriminating but moving correspondence which the pair had exchanged, and which is now in the keeping of the University of Lund.

In 1692, while campaigning against the French in Flanders, Philipp was able to resume his friendship with the Saxon Crown Prince, Frederick Augustus. During bouts of enforced inactivity, the two young officers had ample opportunity to indulge a common taste for heavy gambling, as a result of which the prince found himself in Philipp's debt to the tune of thirty thousand crowns. The latter, who had squandered his own fortune at a prodigious rate, badly needed the money, for in those days the field expenses of officers with extravagant tastes were as heavy as their expenses at home. Frederick Augustus, who had not yet succeeded to the Electoral cap, was reluctant to pay up. Yet it was a debt which was to yield very curious dividends.

By the winter of 1693, Philipp's passion for Sophia was stronger than ever, but his finances were now in an utterly ruinous condition. His repeated attempts to enlist the aid of the bankers of Hamburg had proved fruitless. In addition, he knew that suspicions of his affair with Sophia Dorothea were growing daily, and that the risk of discovery was becoming acute. Maria Aurora, the go-between, had already been packed off to Sweden, and it was obvious that the jilted Platen only waited a suitable opportunity for revenge. The lovers were even contemplating fleeing from Hanover altogether. There is pathos in Sophia Dorothea's delusion that she might yet escape from her morose husband, the Electoral Prince George Louis, and fly with Königsmarck from her father-in-law's court.

In April 1694, their one ally, Prince Frederick Augustus, succeeded to the throne of Saxony on the premature death of his elder brother, John George IV. Philipp immediately posted to Dresden in pursuit of his thirty thousand crowns. But although the new Elector had overnight become inordinately wealthy, he was not in the giving vein; the richest of princes are not necessarily, as Philipp discovered, the most generous. Königsmarck was fobbed off with promises. Then he was offered a major-generalship in the Saxon army, an offer which in due course he accepted, although as a serving officer in the service of Hanover he had no legal right to do. No doubt he was aware that the discovery of his love for Sophia Dorothea was now but a matter of time, and that if he and his royal mistress were ever to live outside Hanover, he must first be able to provide a secure and relatively prosperous refuge for her.

Unfortunately, once he had shaken off the cramped and furtive restrictions of his life in Hanover, the young count grew over-expansive. He responded to the easy-going debauchery of Dresden by openly gossiping about the scandals of Hanover. He regaled his friend Frederick Augustus with anecdotes about the Platen's avarice, and talked freely of his own affair with the Electoral Princess. In a mattter of days the news of his indiscretions had reached Hanover.

This most sad of royal *affaires de coeur* now reached its dénouement with the relentlessness of a Greek drama. The boorish George Louis, who had plenty of mistresses of his own, overacted the part of

7

outraged husband, burst into his wife's apartments, and almost strangled her. Sophia fled to her native Celle, where her father, Duke George William of Brunswick-Lüneburg-Celle, refused to shelter her. Fearfully, she crept back to Hanover: to be greeted, as she entered the Leine Schloss, with the astonishing news that Philipp had returned for some inexplicable reason to Hanover, and had shut himself in his lodging, aloof and enigmatic. He had deliberately left Dresden in order to share her fate.

On the night of July 1st, he went to the Leine Schloss in obedience to a summons purporting to come from Sophia Dorothea. He had armed himself with nothing more lethal than a short court sword; and after a last meeting with his mistress, in her apartments, he walked into a nice little ambush of halberdiers arranged by the jealous Countess Platen. He put up the kind of fight expected of a Königsmarck, killing one of his four assailants and disabling another. But at last he was chopped down: and there on the floor of the Hall of the Knights they murdered the last of the Königsmarcks. As he lay dying, the Countess Platen waddled down the Hall and stamped on his mouth with her foot.

Sophia Dorothea, who might under other circumstances have become the Queen of England, was doomed to spend the long remainder of her life—thirty-three years—in close confinement in the remote schloss of Ahlden. She was summarily divorced, forcibly separated from her children and deprived of her estates. In 1698, her former husband succeeeded his father as Elector of Hanover and sixteen years later became King of Great Britain and Ireland. King George I, happy with his hideous mistresses, never abated in the least degree the sufferings of the prisoner of Ahlden. Lord Acton asserted that he had been the moving spirit behind the assassination of Königsmarck, and that the proper destination of this King of England

> should have been not St. James but Newgate, and indeed not Newgate but Tyburn.[1]

The reputation of the Königsmarcks was now entrusted to a woman, Countess Maria Aurora von Königsmarck, who keenly felt the shame of her brother's murder. She was never to succeed in her efforts to avenge his death, but she was to become, during the course of her efforts to vindicate him, the mother of Maurice de Saxe.

The news of Königsmarck's disappearance was received with great concern at the court of Dresden. There was at first no suspicion that he had been murdered. The young Elector of Saxony wrote in pungent terms to the old Elector of Hanover, urging that if Königsmarck was in prison he should instantly be released, for as an officer in the Saxon army he was under orders to join the Saxon forces on the Rhine. Hanover's answer was not unnaturally evasive, and the Saxon Elector pressed the matter more forcefully by despatching a special messenger to make an unequivocal demand for the release of his friend. In July 1694, the British Minister at Dresden informed his counterpart at Hanover that:

> Our Elector has sent one of his Adjutants to Hanover, I believe with a design to stop the blow if it was not yet given. But I suppose the Corps by this time is in the common shore, and our Elector by the accident has cleared the 30,000 Dollar debt he had lost to him two years ago at play. I have been told his sister raves like Cassandra, and will know what is become of her brother; but at Hanover they answer, like Cain, that they are not her brother's keeper.[2]

The Elector of Hanover could hardly be expected to admit that Philipp had been murdered, and his body interred hugger-mugger in the basement of the Royal palace. He was therefore compelled to issue a series of denials which sounded with every repetition increasingly hollow. His discomfiture was increased by the clamour of the dead man's sister, Maria Aurora, who bombarded him with shrill appeals. Similar entreaties issued from other German princes, including the Elector of Brandenburg, and even from the Emperor Leopold in distant Vienna.

Maria Aurora automatically turned for aid and comfort to her brother's closest friend, Frederick Augustus of Saxony. Not only did he owe a small fortune to the dead man, but by virtue of his position he was one of the most important princes in the Empire. She hoped to persuade him to convey to the Council of the Lower Saxon Circle, a cumbrous administrative lever in the Imperial machine, her complaints against the court of Hanover and the bankers of Hamburg, who had seized her brother's remaining possessions in part payment of his debts. If Philipp were alive, she would secure his release; if he were dead, she would see his death was revenged; and if revenge were denied her, she would at least lay hands on her thirty thousand dollars. 'I am persuaded,' observed Lord Stepney, the British minister at Dresden, 'that she will not take her brother's death to heart when she had got her hand on his inheritance.'[3]

She was thirty-two, and an adventuress of fame and beauty. In Hanover, she had been the mistress of Klaus Gustav Horn, a flamboyant soldier ten years younger than herself. In appearance she was splendid in a voluptuous full-breasted way, with dark brown eyes and a mass of curling black hair [Plate 1]. Her great-great-grand-daughter, George Sand, has described her portrait in the Carnavalet as that of:

> a woman of striking beauty. She is extremely dark, and her tresses, as black as ink, are caught up by ruby clips. Her smooth high forehead gives her a bold appearance. She wears the gown of gold brocade and the red velvet mantle with which she was found clad in her coffin.[4]

Her figure was not perfect, nor were her features flawless, yet her warmth and vitality were almost irresistible. They would have aroused a far less ardent man than the future Augustus the Strong. It was no wonder that, when he heard of the arrival of the beautiful Cassandra-cum-Antigone, he cut short his visit to the annual Leipzig Fair and hastened back to Dresden.

At the age of twenty-four, Frederick Augustus was well launched on his astonishing career. He was handsome, cultured, hedonistic and ambitious. The stockiness of his build was offset by his powerful head and massive shoulders and he was fair-complexioned and with eyes of a penetrating light blue [Plate 2]. He was proud of his resemblance to Louis XIV, the grandest monarch of the age, and he was determined to make Dresden the most brilliant capital in Europe after Versailles.

To an agreeable and charming character, he united a legendary strength. He is said to have courted some of his women by holding a bag of ducats in his left hand and crushing a horseshoe in his right, a highly original and impressive gambit. He is also supposed to have enlivened the deadly formality of state banquets by twisting the bars of iron balustrades, and lifting armour-clad men-at-arms high above his head and dropping them with a crash into the courtyard below.

> The goodness of his constitution permitted him to take his full swing, without endangering his health; for he had a strong and healthful body, that could withstand excesses of any kind.[5]

As soon as he reached the age of puberty, he began to devote much of his immense physical vitality to the art of love: with such success that, long before his accession to the throne, he had begun to accumulate that tally of bastards which was eventually to break the record previously held by his great-grandfather, Christian IV of Denmark. Towards the end of his life, when his chancellor compiled a list of his illegitimate progeny for fiscal purposes, the tentative total had reached three hundred and fifty-five. As the British minister at Dresden said of him:

> Constancy is not in his nature and he may be called in the literal sense a father of his people, as good King Charles the Second was, for he is an impartial distributor of his bounty, and while he is in the humour, the first woman that offers is sure of his caresses.[6]

MARIA AURORA, COUNTESS VON KÖNIGSMARCK
An Engraving by Schenk

Frederick Augustus also possessed the instincts, though not much of the skill, of a warrior. He was determined to restore the faded glories of Saxon arms. He was acutely aware that during the Thirty Years' War the martial reputation of his countrymen had reached the nadir. At the first battle of Breitenfeld, in 1631, the Saxons had fled the field at the onset of a mob of unruly Croats, an act of cowardice that had made them the laughing-stock of Europe. Her new young Elector burned to restore to her the prestige and position of power which she had enjoyed fifty years before, and the intense pleasure which he subsequently derived from the military career of his most famous son, Maurice, stemmed largely from the lustre which it shed on Saxon arms.

In 1694, the Elector restrained his military ardour in order to stay at Dresden and lay siege to Maria Aurora.[7] At first she was lodged as a royal guest in the palace of Augustenburg; but when the Elector's infatuation for her began to infringe the bounds of modesty, she was installed instead in the distant Moritzburg, a famous hunting-lodge originally built by the great Elector Maurice in 1542 beside a lake among the mountains. Here she was fêted with a succession of masked balls and hunting parties, and was finally seduced during the course of a spectacular pageant in which the Elector personated the Grand Turk in the midst of his harem.

The Elector had a wife, a Hohenzollern, whom he had married only the previous year. Christine Eberhardine, daughter of the Margrave of Bayreuth, was a plain and dignified girl of devout Lutheran principles. She was already inured to her husband's *fredaines*. Together with her mother-in-law, Anna Sophia of Denmark, she went out of her way to be kind to her husband's new mistress, who was at least better than her immediate predecessor, a rapacious woman whom he had recently married off. The Electress was even more attentive to Maria Aurora than Frederick Augustus himself, for in the spring of 1695 he finally tore himself away from the delights of Dresden to fight with the Imperial armies against the Turks. The campaign was far from successful, and largely as a result of the Elector's ineptitude the Imperial forces in Transylvania were routed. It was a chastened Frederick Augustus who rode back, at the beginning of winter, to his comfortable capital and his complaisant womenfolk.

In January 1696, within a fortnight of each other, Maria Aurora and Christine Eberhardine became pregnant. Christine Eberhardine was to bear the Elector his only legitimate child, the future Augustus the Weak. Maria Aurora was to bear him the prodigious Maurice. Unfortunately, the Swedish Countess had grown importunate and demanding, and had even played him false during his tedious absence in the Danubian provinces. When he reproached her with her infidelity, and told her that Caesar's wife should be above suspicion, she replied tartly, with Königsmarck arrogance, that he was not Caesar nor was she his wife. *Enceinte*, and out of favour, she withdrew from Dresden, and it was probably when she was on the high road to her native Hamburg that she was compelled to halt at Goslar to bring her child to birth. Maurice was a large and lusty infant, and contemporary writers state that he caused his mother such an agonizing confinement that she was incapable thereafter of making love. She would therefore have no chance whatever of regaining her ascendancy over a man like Frederick Augustus. None the less she is said to have remained 'the only one of his mistresses for whom he ever retained any lasting trace of affection'.[8]

CHAPTER I

DRESDEN, 1696-1709

> 'Ay,' quoth Sancho, 'you rake-helly fellows have a saying
> that is pat to your purpose: "Never cringe nor creep for
> what you by force may reap."'
>
> DON QUIXOTE

MARIA AURORA'S instinct was to keep the boy at her side. She was quite willing if need be to rear him in near-poverty: but she quickly realized that for Maurice's own good she must surrender him to his father. Frederick Augustus would only agree to have the child at his court on condition that he was removed from the influence of his mother; and it was obvious to Maria Aurora, with her negligible resources, that if Maurice was to receive a start in life worthy of his heritage, she would have to give him up. Moreover, his twenty-seven-year-old father had just brought off a resounding diplomatic coup: he had mounted the throne of Poland as King Augustus II. So when Maurice was taken from his mother he was sent not to Dresden, but to the new royal capital of Warsaw. He shared his father's elevation in rank. Was it not more illustrious to be the bastard of a King than the bastard of a mere Elector?

Frederick Augustus was crowned King of Poland and Grand Duke of Lithuania on September 15th 1697. There had been a trifling detail to attend to before the solemn ceremony took place: his reception into the Church of Rome. He had promised his chief supporters, foremost among them the Primate of Poland, to renounce the Lutheranism of his baptism on his election as king. It was a remarkable step for the reigning prince of a traditionally Protestant house to take— a case of *cujus regio ejus religio* with a vengeance. It was certainly not motivated by conscience. As the wits now said of him, he was a Lutheran by birth, a Moslem by appetite, and a Catholic by ambition. The change was not absolutely without precedent, for the great Sigismund Vasa had also renounced Lutheranism to become King of

Poland. But although the age was not an age of faith, it was still an age of strong religious loyalties, and Frederick Augustus's defection was abhorrent to the bulk of his Saxon subjects. His wife Christine refused to follow his example, and she was never crowned Queen of Poland.

At this period the kingdom of Poland was moribund. Frederick Augustus found it rent by civil war. In recent years Swedes and Russians had marched unimpeded about the country, and the last great Polish feat of arms, King John Sobieski's impulsive dash to the rescue of the Emperor when the Turks were at the gates of Vienna, had long ago faded into history. Sobieski had died in 1696, and the Polish crown, aptly described as the 'challenge cup of Europe',[9] at once became the object of covetous glances from all over Europe. Sobieski himself had wished to be succeeded by a French Bourbon, the Prince de Conti: but Conti was only one of eighteen candidates, including Frederick Augustus, who rushed forward to claim the crown.

Poland was in theory a crowned republic, but in reality an oligarchy. It was laid down that the Diet, dominated by the great nobles, should elect the king, and that their choice must be unanimous. The veto of a single deputy could quash any decision. Under this remarkable and unworkable constitution, corruption was the natural order of the day. The deputies sold their votes to the highest bidder, and it is only fair to add that, if they had insisted on remaining honest, no act would have been passed, and the business of the state would have come to a halt. The highest bidders in the coronation stakes were often foreign powers, and the actual candidates usually foreigners. It was fondly hoped that outsiders would incline towards neutrality in internal issues, and would bring with them the wealth and benevolent protection of their own country. The contest between Frederick Augustus and Conti was brief. Conti had the initial advantage that Louis XIV had purchased the bulk of the votes in the Diet, but Frederick Augustus was the man on the spot. He despatched a flying column of ten thousand men under the command of Count Flemming to seize Warsaw. Conti, whose heart was not really in the business, trailed off homewards. The election lighted on Saxony.

The new King at once embarked on a policy of aggrandisement. As ambitious for his adopted country as he was for his native land, he resolved to oust the Swedes from northern Poland and Livonia, where they had remained since the Treaty of Oliva in 1660. He entered a triple alliance with his cousin Frederick IV of Denmark and the Tsar Peter the Great, and the self-styled Great Northern League at once declared war on the Swedes. The moment seemed propitious. The King of Sweden, another cousin of Frederick August, was a mere

AUGUSTUS II, ELECTOR OF SAXONY AND KING OF POLAND

boy of seventeen, barely free from the tutelage of his royal grandmother and her six co-regents. Unfortunately for the aggressors, the
youthful King was Charles XII.

Meanwhile, Maria Aurora languished in enforced retirement. Her
career as *maîtresse en titre* at the court of Dresden had lasted in all
a mere two winters. Now she was banished to the little town of
Quedlinburg, thirty miles south of Goslar and just within the juris-
diction of Saxony. Here, as near to her young son as she was at first
allowed to approach, she became, by the whimsical favour of her
former lover, the Co-adjutrix of the secularized nunnery of Quedlinburg. In this pleasant retreat she had ample leisure to compose her
verses and her plays, and address an almost unending stream of
letters to Maurice and his father. She had at least fared better than
her former friend, Sophia Dorothea, and in later years she was allowed
to travel freely, and was able to spend most of her time in Berlin,
Hamburg, even Dresden itself. And in 1702 she was to make a famous
journey to Courland, to visit the redoubtable King of Sweden
himself.

When Charles XII had descended on Poland as liberator, he made
it abundantly clear to nobility and peasantry alike that his quarrel
was not with them, but with the foreign usurper who had bought
their throne. His argument was well received. Not only were the
Polish nobles quarrelling as usual among themselves, but the faction
opposed to Frederick Augustus had recently grown in strength. It
was not long before Charles induced the Diet to depose Frederick
Augustus and elect Prince James Sobieski in his stead.

By now the Great Northern League lay in ruins. The boy king had
led his Swedes across the Baltic in August 1700 (he was never again
to see Stockholm), and swiftly showed himself to be a military genius.
In six weeks Denmark was over-run and Holstein saved, and
Frederick Augustus' attempt to counterattack by seizing Riga ended
in a humiliating failure. In his anxiety, Frederick Augustus hastened
to Lithuania to consult with Peter the Great and conclude a new
treaty of mutual aid. Voltaire tells us that, at this perilous juncture,
the two sovereigns spent a lively and abandoned fortnight together,
'for the Tsar, who had set himself to reform his kingdom, could not
restrain his own dangerous inclination to riotous living'.[10]

The subsequent agreement between them was never translated
from parchment into reality, for at this juncture the Russians were
temporarily demoralized, in November 1700, by a crushing defeat at
Narva. It seemed that Frederick Augustus' crown was in the hazard.
Not only were the Poles suing for peace, but in order to pay for his

wars he had pawned huge tracts of Saxon territory and drained the Electorate of men and money.

He therefore hit upon the stratagem of trying to negotiate personally with Charles, as one king to another. To make preliminary soundings, he decided to employ the talents of Maria Aurora—a woman, as Voltaire says, 'more capable than any minister of bringing a negotiation to a successful issue'. She was moreover a Swedish noblewoman by birth. Voltaire continues:

> The countess, among the gifts which made her one of the most delightful persons in Europe, had the ability to speak several languages like a native, and would sometimes amuse herself by making French verses which might have been written at Versailles. She made some for Charles XII: but all her wit and charm were lost on such a man as the King of Sweden. He obstinately refused to see her. She planned to intercept him when he was taking his usual exercise on horseback. Thus meeting him one day in a very narrow lane she alighted as soon as she saw him. The King bowed without a word, turned his horse and rode straight back. So that the only satisfaction the Countess got from her journey was the conviction that she was the only person of whom this King was afraid.[11]

Her mission had been a fiasco. If she had entertained hopes that her mature beauty might charm the heart of this gauche and boorish youth, they were foredoomed to failure. There would be no prize to lay at the feet of a grateful Elector. Charles was interested neither in peace nor women, and he despised good manners. On his return to his tent, he gave the cruel order that 'all disreputable women' were to be drummed out of the camp immediately. Maria Aurora left Courland that same night. Thirty years later her brilliant son Maurice would return there in very different circumstances.

The cause of Frederick Augustus was only saved from total annihilation by the timely emergence of a first-class general. Johann Matthias von Schulenburg, like 'Old Königsmarck' was a mercenary soldier of Brandenburg extraction. He speedily rallied the demoralized Saxons and managed to stem the Swedish advance. It was a brilliant feat of arms by a famous master of the art of retreat, but it could hardly serve to turn defeat into victory. And Frederick Augustus' crowning mortification was to see his Saxon subjects welcome his Swedish conquerors with open arms.

After a confused period of painful defiance, he finally acknowledged the inevitable. In 1706 he signed the Peace of Altranstadt. It was a very harsh treaty. He was allowed to retain the throne of Saxony, but Charles forced him to renounce even the bare claim to the throne of Poland. When the two princes finally met, Charles admitted that his defeated rival was a good loser. 'He is not very tall, but strongly built and rather fat, and wears his own hair which is quite dark.'[12]

Voltaire wrote of the Elector that 'he was a prince still more famed for his courage and chivalrous ideals than for his incredible physical strength. There was never a prince more generous nor liberal, nor one who gave with so good a grace'.[13] And, at Altranstadt, the former King of Poland was required to give a great deal.

At last the Swedish prodigy withdrew from Saxon soil, to prepare for his final attack on Peter the Great, the ally whom Frederick Augustus had calmly betrayed in order to regain Saxony. The Elector crept back to Dresden to lick his wounds, burying himself there in the soothing tasks of embellishing his capital and reorganizing his army. Thwarted in his desire to expland to the north and east, he allowed himself, after a breathing-space, to turn his attention to the west, and duly entered the War of the Spanish Succession on the side of the Grand Alliance. A Saxon contingent of 4,500 men was formed for service in Flanders under Schulenburg. To Schulenburg's care the King now entrusted that eager fledgling, his twelve-year-old son Maurice.

The boy had been reared among wars and rumours of wars. Deprived during his formative years of the influence and affection of his mother, he had seen even less of his father, and had been continuously dragged from place to place, in victory and defeat, by uncongenial tutors. Frederick Augustus' concern for his son was at best fitful. Maurice was seven before a regular grant of 3,000 Saxon dollars a year was made towards his upkeep, which until then had been principally maintained by the diminishing revenues of the surviving Königsmarck estates in Sweden and Germany.

It was the fate of Maurice de Saxe to have been reared in relative poverty and insecurity, without abiding loyalty to any one country, and under the stigma of illegitimacy. True, he had dozens of equally uneasy bastard brothers and sisters, but they did not bolster his morale so much as compete with him for the paternal bounty. Even in an age notorious for its lax morals, at a court famed for its sexual licence, the boy seems to have felt his condition acutely. His bastardy engendered in him ill-assorted sentiments of defiance, ambition, and occasional self-pity, although he was endowed with a saving sense of fun and with indestructible good nature. And if his vanity and ambition arose from his irregular birth, so did the determination that enabled him to harness them to constructive ends.

His inner conflicts were echoed by the external battles that raged about him. An intelligent boy, bred to the sound of the drumfire and cannonade of the Great Northern War, he was bound to become either a whole-hearted pacifist or a devoted soldier. It must have seemed to him in his earliest years that the bustle and brutality of the wars were simply the normal condition of humanity.

Warfare was the *métier* of his house. The princes of the house of Wettin had been fighters almost to a man. The Augustenburg Palace at Dresden, where much of his childhood was spent, was adorned with great martial trophies: the armour of Charles Emmanuel of Savoy; the tournament records of René of Anjou; the bâtons of Tilly and Pappenheim; the silken tents captured from the Turks by John Sobieski. There were other objects in the Augustenburg which appealed as strongly to a boyish taste. There were crystal goblets, golden reliquaries, Nuremburg eggs, Tuscan chalices, and rings, cups and necklaces of chalcedony, onyx and lapis lazuli.[14] His father's wonderful collection of precious stones further implanted in him a lifelong passion for rich objects. The collection included Saxon pearls, sapphires from Peter the Great, Peruvian emeralds from the Emperor Rudolph, and a profusion of diamonds, including the forty-carat 'Green Brilliant'.[15]

To all these marvels the boy stood in a curious relationship. He could move among them, even handle them, yet they could never belong to him. His position with respect to them was parallel to his position in Saxon society. He could play on the very steps of the throne, but he would always remain a fixed and inalienable distance away from it. Only a few days separated his birth from that of his legitimate brother: but when crowns, bâtons, jewels and decorations were being poured into the lap of the indolent and pudgy heir-apparent, Maurice would be sweating to earn them in the blood and din of battle.

He was no fop or dilettante. Even at twelve, he was a replica of his father, certainly more so than that fat booby, the Hereditary Prince. Like his father, he was impulsive, active and unruly. What he wanted, he had to have. Like his father too he was blue-eyed, fresh-complexioned, and possessed an extraordinary physique. Already at the tender age of five he had decided to be a soldier; and to the despair of his tutors, his subsequent interest in learning was strictly subordinated to the demands of his chosen career. He regarded languages as superfluous, and although he was destined to spend over half of his life in France he would never learn to speak or write the French tongue correctly. Other foreign languages he would not deign to grapple with at all, and for such abstruse subjects as philosophy he had not the slightest inclination. But where mathematics and engineering were concerned the case was quite different. Were not these the kind of subjects which no future general could afford to neglect?

His chief pleasure as a boy was to attend military parades in the company of his mentor, a Frenchman of Huguenot persuasion called

Captain d'Alençon. We are told that on returning to his apartments
he would often have

> children of his own age brought to him with whom he imitated in
> miniature what he had seen executed at full length. He had always in
> his hand a stick, a pistol or a sword. He had such an extraordinary
> liking for horses that the moment he could walk, he went among them;
> and this familiarity grew upon him so much that to the day of his
> death he was passionately fond of them.[16]

For what it was worth, he was reared in the Protestant faith.
Religion was to play as little part in his life as it had in his father's:
but unlike his father, no subsequent inducement would ever prove
strong enough to make him abandon his formal profession of Lutheranism. Maurice was proud and, in his own way, he was loyal.

It was on a cold evening, in January 1709, that Schulenburg called
on the boy to invest him with the royal commission. The fortunes
of Charles XII had recently been faring so badly that the buoyant
Frederick Augustus had already resumed the title of King of Poland.
Maurice was reading a dull book in his draughty room when all at
once the door opened, and the commanding figure of Schulenburg
entered. He listened to the news the General brought him.
'He told me in the King's name,' Maurice later wrote,

> that His Majesty wished to make me a soldier, that I was greatly
> indebted to him and that we would leave the next morning. I was
> to take with me only one of my own servants, my valet. I was drunk
> with joy, above all because I thought I was finished with tutors.
> Schulenburg had brought me a uniform which I put on. A big belt
> with a huge sword was buckled round my waist and my outfit was
> completed by an enormous pair of Saxon boots. I was then led before
> the King to kiss his hand and found myself dining at his own table,
> where all present cheerfully drank my health. The conversation next
> turned on my studies, and I was questioned about my knowledge of
> geometry, my facility at drawing and my ability to make plans. The
> King said to Schulenburg, 'I want every plan that you send me drawn
> by his own hand.' He went on, 'Keep him on his toes and don't coddle
> him. Toughen him up. I want you to make him march on foot to
> Flanders.' This last notion did not please me. Footslogging did not
> appeal to me because I wanted to be a cavalryman; and I was summon-
> ing up courage to broach the matter when I was pulled up short. 'I
> don't want anyone else to carry his weapons on the march', said the
> King; 'his shoulders are broad enough for him to carry them himself.
> And don't let him pay other soldiers to do his guard duty for him,
> unless he is seriously ill.' This made me prick up my ears, for the King,

who usually treated me with geniality, was now talking like a real Turk. But I comforted myself with the thought that I was free forever from tutors and considered myself the happiest mortal alive. After saying my farewells, next day I left Dresden.[17]

At the age of twelve, a future Marshal of France went off to trail his musket in the ranks. Many other famous commanders had done so before him, including the greatest soldier produced until that time by the country he was later to serve: the hero of the earlier generation of Königsmarcks, the vicomte de Turenne.

CHAPTER II

MALPLAQUET, 1709

*One man is no more than another, if he do no more
than what another does.*

DON QUIXOTE

THE following day, Maurice and Schulenburg reached Leipzig, where the Saxon expeditionary force had been assembled. Here Maurice was joined by the personal retinue presented to him by his father. It consisted of a campaigning coach, a dozen mules, four horses, and a number of servants: and to his dismay it also included a tutor.

After a week's drilling the contingent was ready to march. A final review was held on the battlefield of Lützen. Maurice was marched to his battalion, nominated an ensign, handed a musket, and sworn in. Then he was summoned from the ranks, and kissed on both cheeks by Schulenburg in front of four thousand men. With one hand on the stone monument which commemorated the death of Gustavus Adolphus eighty years before, Schulenburg declared:

> I should like this battlefield to be a happy augury for you. May you inherit the spirit of the great man who died here. Let all your actions be inspired by his gentleness, severity and justice. Never relax discipline in the slightest degree, even when prompted by friendship. Above all, be sure that your personal conduct is above reproach, for that is the only way to ensure respect.[18]

Next day, the contingent broke camp. Maurice wrote later:

> I marched continuously on foot, and my colonel, Herr von Preuss, although he was elderly, kept me company with several of his officers. To entertain me, a bag-piper and some soldiers who knew many comic songs were put at the head of the column. Their comrades roared out the choruses. I have never since known such cheerful marching, and there were no deserters. We were lucky that there were heavy frosts which dried the mud. But I could hardly stand the rigours of the march; my feet were blistered, my shoulders black and blue from the weight of the musket. For several days I had to ride a horse, but, when the men jeered at me, I dismounted and returned to the column.

21

Schulenburg joined us at Wolfenbüttel, and there I dined with him at the table of the old Duke Anton Ulrich, who was very gracious. From there we made our way to Hanover, where I was well received, in spite of what had happened to my uncle Philipp: and on the very day of my arrival I was invited to stay with the Prince Elector.[19]

It must have been a macabre meal. Maurice was dining in the palace where he knew that his uncle Philipp had been murdered fifteen years before. The oddity of the occasion was enhanced by the presence of Schulenburg's scrawny sister, Ehrengard Melusina, the Elector's favourite mistress. She was nicknamed 'The Maypole', while her fat rival, the Baroness Kilmansegge, was popularly known as 'The Elephant'. After the Elector became King of Great Britain, the Maypole was created Duchess of Kendal, and ultimately a Princess of the Holy Roman Empire.

By the end of January 1709, Schulenburg and his young charge had reached Flanders. There Maurice was to witness the final act of the bitter struggle which had begun eight years earlier, when Louis XIV had ordered Villars to invade the Spanish Netherlands in the name of his grandson, the future Philip V of Spain. It was Maurice's baptism of fire: and his opponents would be those French armies which he was one day to lead.

Louis XIV and the War of the Spanish Succession had dominated the age in which Maurice grew to manhood.

The guiding principle of the great Sun King was absolutism; the natural foreign policy of the absolutist is aggressive war. The King was ably abetted in his policy of conquest by Michel le Tellier, marquis de Louvois, one of the greatest war ministers of modern times. Louvois was the founder of the army which Maurice later took into battle: and after seventy years it would still remain the mightiest war machine of the age.

Louvois was war minister of France for twenty-three years. When he assumed power, there were 175,000 Frenchmen under arms; when he died, the number had risen to 400,000. Except for a few brief months during Maurice's period of command, the latter figure was not to be exceeded before the era of Napoleon.

Nine hundred volumes of despatches show how Louvois continued Colbert's policy of expanding the armed services of France. Colbert had been a man of peace, and Louvois was a man of war: yet paradoxically it was to be the crowning achievement of Louvois that he 'civilianized' the army. His introduction of a vast civilian apparatus enabled the armed forces to undergo an unparalleled expansion. Not only were transport and supply revolutionized, but recruitment was regularized, pay was increased, and conditions of service were generally improved. A corps of engineers was raised, the artillery arm was expanded, cadet schools were created. Medical services were established for the wounded, and the Hôtel des Invalides was founded. Richelieu's policy of opening the upper echelons of the army to those promoted from the ranks was revived, and the only commissions which could still be purchased were those of colonel and captain. This healthy trend, with which Maurice was strongly to sympathize, was not reversed until 1781, in a perverse attempt to put the clock back that brought the dynasty ever closer to disaster. Louvois also continued Richelieu's attempt to reform the high command. The feudal post of Constable of France was abolished, and the beginning of a general staff instituted under a *Maréchal-Général des Armées*. This exalted position, first enjoyed by Turenne and subsequently by Villars, was to be held by Maurice himself.

Having forged this huge war machine, and equipped it with such novel weapons as bayonets and hand-grenades, *le plus grand et le plus brutal des commis* lusted to employ it. In his guise of War Minister, he encouraged the king's dynastic and territorial ambitions; and as Minister of Public Works he pandered to Louis' megalomania by superintending the construction of the gigantic château of Versailles. Nor was his zeal exclusively political, for he was a religious bigot as well. When he was not promoting a ruinous *politique d'orgueil*, he was successfully persuading Louis to persecute the Huguenots.

Louvois died in 1691. His ideas persisted, and his army thrived; but his ability and skill were irreplaceable. The three great commanders of the first half of Louis's reign, Condé, Turenne and Luxembourg, had predeceased him. France still possessed many commanders of skill and daring—such as Villars, Vendôme, Boufflers and Catinat; but when war came, the Sun King was foolish enough to entrust Louvois' army to the pliant and incompetent Villeroi, a man better known for his dancing than his fighting. At Blenheim, in 1704, Marlborough was confronted with generals of the indifferent quality of Tallard and Marsin, both of whom he duly took prisoner. And as the coach carrying Tallard rumbled through Nottingham, carrying him into exile, a genial butcher called out: 'Welcome to England, sir! We hope to see your master here next year!'[20]

The butcher's prediction seemed very likely to come true. There were times when Louis was desperate, when Paris itself was in danger. Slowly but surely the Grand Alliance between Great Britain and the Empire had gathered strength; and from the moment when Marlborough and Eugène first clasped hands in Swabia in 1704, the cause of France seemed doomed. The Schellenberg, Blenheim, the forcing of the Lines of Brabant, Ramillies, Oudenard, Lille: the progress of the war was a roll-call of Allied victories. The French had already been decisively beaten at sea; and when Maurice arrived in Flanders in 1709 it seemed that the *coup de grâce* was about to be administered.

The young Saxon was welcomed warmly at headquarters. Schulenburg was an old friend of Eugène, and only a year previously Maurice's father had visited Flanders and entered Brussels at Marlborough's side. The King of Poland had no doubt informed 'The Princes' at that time that he intended to send his son to the wars: and we are told that 'the reputation of Prince Eugène and the Duke of Marlborough had already inspired Maurice with a desire of fighting under two such great men,' and that he wanted to be 'a witness of their noble actions, with a desire one day to imitate them'.[21]

Nevertheless the war had nearly ended by negotiation before Maurice's arrival. France was bankrupt, and her King had almost had enough. But by a diplomatic blunder, the Allies required him not merely to surrender valuable territory, but also summoned him to help them to drive his own grandson from the throne of Spain in the interests of the Imperial candidate. 'I would rather,' Louis declared, 'fight my enemies than my children.' He called on his sorely-tried but proud people to fight to the end, placing his last army under the command of the fire-eating Louis-Hector de Villars.

Maurice may well have felt more at home with Eugène than with Marlborough. Eugène, in spite of his exalted rank, was at bottom a soldier of fortune, such as Maurice was to become. Moreover, the forty-six-year-old Savoyard had also had in Olympia Mancini, a niece of Cardinal Mazarin, an adventuress for a mother. His career was a glittering model for Maurice to follow. He had been a colonel at twenty-one, a general at twenty-four, a field-marshal at thirty, and commander-in-chief at thirty-one; he was the saviour of Vienna, the victor of Zenta and Cremona.

In the seventeenth and eighteenth centuries the career of arms was to a great extent dominated by men like Eugène. The type had been made familiar by Wallenstein, Mansfeld, Christian of Brunswick, Bernard of Saxe-Weimar, and by Old Königsmarck himself. For the most part, they were men without any marked loyalty to one country or one religion; their principles, like their swords, were for sale; yet restless as they were, they all nourished dynastic ambitions. Since ancient times, of course, successful generals have sought to carve out prominent niches for themselves; but in the modern epoch the line of dynastic generals may be said to begin with red-plumed Wallenstein, who became Grand Duke of Mecklenburg and planned to be Elector of Bohemia, and to end with Marshal Bernadotte, who became King Charles XIV of Sweden. To this category belonged the great Protestant general Ernst von Mansfeld, a bastard son of a governor of Luxembourg, whose career has close similarities with that of Maurice. Mansfeld, like Maurice, was sensitive about his illegitimacy; and again like Maurice his dearest ambition was to obtain a principality. The former's reward for his mighty exertions during the Thirty Years' War was the coronet of the tiny Rhenish county of Hagenau; and the latter was to covet to distraction the crown of the barren little duchy of Courland.

The personal lives of these generals were usually irreproachable, despite their harsh reputation in the field. They were sober and industrious. Wallenstein was a model husband; the Belgian Tilly, the notorious Butcher of Magdeburg, was known to his men as 'the Saint in Armour'. 'Let your character be above reproach,' Schulenburg had urged Maurice, 'for that is the way to earn men's obedience.' Whatever their failings, Schulenburg and his master Eugène tried to live by this stern precept. In his own way, Maurice too was to hold true to it.

The boy received his introduction to warfare at the siege of Tournai in July 1709. It was a sombre experience. The rain poured down incessantly, and to the normal hazards of siege warfare were added the anxieties of mining and counter-mining. Tournai was one of Vauban's most impressive essays in fortification, and was therefore a considerable stronghold. Marlborough, conducting the siege in person, had cleverly screened his movement from Villars, and had been able to bring forward sixty battalions to reduce the town, whose capture would secure the approaches to Brussels. Three distinct attacks were launched, two against the gates and one against the citadel. The Prussian general Lottum commanded the first, Schulenburg the second, the Dutchman Fagel the last. Rivalry among the three commanders was intense, but Schulenburg's attack was the most furious; in breaking down the Sainte-Fontaine Gate he lost 1,200 men, which was nearly twice the number of his two rivals put together. On July 28, the French commander surrendered the outer precincts. After dining ceremoniously with Prince Eugène, he then retired into the citadel. There he held out for a further six weeks, until shortage of food and the prospect of a final attack in which it was announced that no quarter would be given induced him to surrender. On September 5, the French garrison beat the *chamade* and marched out with the honours of war.

> Upon the capitulation of Tournai, an access of mental rage seems to have taken possession of both sides simultaneously. They discarded their cold calculations. They flung caution to the winds. The King gave Villars full freedom. He used it to court an encounter battle.[22]

Villars was now reinforced by a general as skilled and rough-hewn as himself. A spy reported to Marlborough from Paris that: 'M. de Boufflers has left for Flanders. *He has brought his cuirass and his weapons with him.*' The crucial encounter of the war was imminent.

It was a thrilling spectacle for young Maurice to watch, on the misty morning of September 11, the battalions of Villars and Boufflers square off to those of Marlborough and Eugène in front of the village of Malplaquet [Fig. 1].

Villars' army, protected at intervals by entrenchments, was drawn up opposite the Trouée d'Aulnois, a wide gap between two thick woods. The French commander took it for granted that his flanks were secure, for it was an article of faith among generals of the period that woods and rivers constituted insuperable barriers. Villars expected to see the opposing infantry decimated as they struggled to advance across the constricted terrain of the Trouée. He therefore posted five brigades in a forward position along the southern neck of the wood to his right, and confidently awaited the attack.

Marlborough was never a man to oblige an opponent by doing the obvious or the expected. He despatched Lottum with twenty-two battalions to deal with Villars' five forward brigades, and ordered Schulenburg, at the head of no less than forty battalions, to force his way through the wood and attack the French left flank. Almost simultaneously, the Dutch and Scots were sent forward to assail the French right.

A fearful battle developed in the wood. Two of Schulenburg's three major-generals and all the colonels in the first line were killed or wounded. Eugène led up the second line in person. Villars, realizing that Schulenburg had been sent to outflank him, resolved to cut the Saxons to ribbons in the forest. At the same time he had the satisfaction of seeing the enemy left wing floundering and wavering, as with only thirty battalions they sought to make an impression on sixty battalions of Frenchmen under the fiery Boufflers. Dutch, Scots and Hanoverians battled bravely, but after losing 5,000 men in the space of half an hour they were forced to retreat.

On the other wing, the Allies were faring no better. It took Schulenburg, Lottum and an English contingent under Withers three punishing hours before they could push their way clear of the trees. They left behind them 7,000 killed and wounded in an area of 600 square yards. The shattered remnant of Schulenburg's force were then drawn up on open ground, ready for another attack. The imperturbable Saxon general had somehow contrived to manhandle through the inferno of the wood seven large cannon which, more than any other factor, were to disconcert the French and contribute to their eventual defeat. Marlborough rode out to consult Schulenburg, and they were soon joined by Eugène, suffering from a wound in the face which he did not bother to dress. The triumvirs held a tense conference. With their left in check, and suffering from such appalling losses, their situation was quite as perilous as that of the French. To add to their troubles, Villars was now unleashing a vigorous counter-attack against the exhausted Saxons.

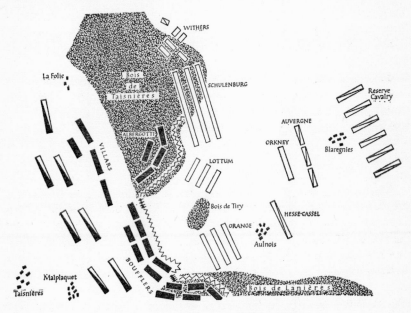

FIG. 1. THE BATTLE OF MALPLAQUET

To make this attack possible, Villars had been compelled to call for reserves from his centre. But Boufflers too had been drawing battalions from the centre, to strengthen his position on the right wing. As a result, the middle of the French line was being gradually thinned down: and, as at Blenheim, Marlborough had held in reserve a force sufficient to exploit just such an opportunity. The Englishman saw his chance and seized it. With superb judgement, he launched Orkney's little force of eleven British and two foreign battalions into the Trouée, and backed them by thirty squadrons of Dutch cavalry. Swiftly he ordered the British, Prussian and Hanoverian cavalry to follow them: and in a matter of minutes 30,000 horsemen were charging the crumbling French centre. And, at this critical moment, fate decided that a bullet should smash Villars' knee just when he was thrusting home a successful attack on the enemy right. A chair was brought for him from a near-by cottage; but after gallant efforts to continue the direction of the battle, he fainted, and was carried off the field.

Boufflers had been too busily engaged away on the right to have any clear idea of the general progress of the battle. But he realized, as soon as he assumed command, that the only way to bolster the French centre was to prevent the enemy cavalry from concentrating for a fresh assault. Placing himself at the head of the *Maison du Roi*, he made six separate charges, and for the next two hours the bulk of the fighting was done with the naked sword. Eventually he was compelled to realize that he could not prevail; none of his charges had gone fully home. And as he withdrew with his cavalry, he saw that his two wings were falling back. The Allied line was rolling triumphantly forward.

Yet the advancing Allies were in no condition to deliver the *miséricorde*. 'Marlborough and Eugène were both convinced that they could ask no further sacrifice of their troops. The battle was won, and the victors camped upon the bloody field.'[23]

Maurice was not, in spite of his own assertions in later life, in the forefront of that terrible encounter. The Saxon stripling did not, as a pretty legend later put it, shout: 'I have lived long enough!', and hurl himself pistol in hand upon the French. He had been placed by the prudent Schulenburg well to the rear, in the care of the baggage-master. Nevertheless, he had never at any time been more than a short mile away from one of the great battles of modern times, the bloodiest engagement of the entire eighteenth century. He had witnessed, at an age when most boys are playing football, the 'blood-red blossom of war with the heart of fire'. He had been the spectator of a battle in which a quarter of a million men had fought, and nearly 40,000 of them had been killed or wounded. Not until Borodino in 1812 was the 'butcher's bill' of Malplaquet to be surpassed. It was no wonder that all Europe was horrified when the details of the carnage were known.

Malplaquet, and the earlier operations around Tournai, made an ineffacable impression on Maurice's mind. Two years later, he returned to Flanders to attend the dogged sieges of Douai and Aire; but it was Tournai and Malplaquet that had made the most searing impression. At Tournai, he had witnessed a prime example of what he later anathematized as the 'rage for sieges', where whole armies were immobilized while rival commanders carried out ceremonious evolutions which may have been logical, Cartesian, and expressive of the *esprit géometrique* of the age, but which were also tedious, wasteful, and sterile. There he had watched the rigid theories of siege warfare, perfected forty years before at Maastricht and Luxemburg, put into practice. He had watched the methodical digging of trenches, saps and parallels; the establishing of the *place d'armes*; the erection of the *cavaliers de tranchées*: and all this in the lashing rain. And his lively young mind had revolted against the whole laborious process. There must surely, he asked himself, be a better method of taking fortresses.

As for Malplaquet, there must surely be a better way of winning battles. The disposition of Villars and his opponents gave him endless food for thought. Incessantly he was to brood, write, and argue about the lessons of that devastating day. Its problems obsessed him as though they were problems in chess. Twenty years later, he would not only make a careful analysis of the battle, but at the climax of his career he would virtually fight the whole thing over again, and be called upon in literal earnest to try and improve on Villars' performance. Although the parallel has not previously been drawn, it is not an exaggeration to claim that one cannot understand the course of Maurice's greatest battle without first understanding the progress of Malplaquet. Much as he admired Marlborough and Eugène, the fact that their sophisticated early manoeuvres before Tournai had degenerated into the brutal slogging match of Malplaquet had horrified him. He made up his mind to try, when he himself became a general, to conduct his battles in such a way as to avoid the grosser errors of his illustrious predecessors. War, of course, is such an unpredictable and haphazard business that he could not hope to avoid them all. But he would try.

CHAPTER III

BELGRADE, 1709-1720

*Chacun disait: Voyez donc comme
Il est grand, comme il est beau!
Le bel habit! Le beau chapeau!
Morbleu, qu'un soldat est bel homme!*
                                        FRANCOEUR

AT the beginning of 1711, with two campaigns in Flanders behind him, the fifteen-year-old veteran returned in triumph to Saxony. He called first on his mother at Leipzig, where she was enjoying a temporary respite from the enforced seclusion of Quedlinburg. Proudly she accompanied her son to Dresden, to be accorded the friendliest of welcomes. Once again, if only for a few weeks, she basked in the glow of Frederick Augustus' approval, not this time in the dubious rôle of courtesan but in the impeccable rôle of matron. And to her joy, Frederick Augustus at last agreed to her ceaselessly reiterated request to acknowledge Maurice as his son. Not only did the King circulate to his chancelleries an official decree proclaiming Maurice as his child, but he also raised the boy's annual allowance from three to ten thousand thalers. More than that, although the titles of duke of Saxony and prince of Poland were reserved for his legitimate son, he gave Maurice the rank of *Graf von Sachsen*, Count of Saxony. It was under the French form of this title, *comte de Saxe*, that Maurice was to become famous.

Encouraged by these outward and visible signs of paternal grace, Maurice was soon in the field again, this time in the north, where the embers of the Great Northern War still smouldered. The war there had reached its turning point. In 1709, Charles XII had rashly decided to join forces with the boyar Mazeppa, hetman of the Cossacks of the Ukraine. The Swedish King marched the grim battalions of the *karolinerna* six hundred miles into southern Russia, with the intention of turning Peter the Great's flank. Then, reinforced by Mazeppa, by Lübecker from Ingria, and by Maurice's cousin Löwenhaupt from Livonia, he would advance on Moscow itself. The plan miscarried from the start. Lübecker was held up; Löwenhaupt made slow progress; Mazeppa proved a broken reed; and Charles's own

30

army was half destroyed by the Muscovites' faithful ally, General Winter. With mad obstinacy Charles pushed on with his plan. In January 1709 he ordered his starving troops to attack the town of Poltava, and there, after a bloody and historic encounter, the Swedes were utterly routed by a huge Russian army.

Wounded and raging, Charles fled far to the south, where he was eventually captured by the Turks and imprisoned at Dimotika in Thrace. For forty-three weeks, he sulked in his tent, brooding on the debâcle and blaming it on the innocent Löwenhaupt. As for his countrymen, with their king in Turkish hands, their army broken, their economy shattered, they had difficulty in maintaining as much as a toehold on the southern shores of the Baltic. Frederick Augustus lost no time in declaring void the humiliating Treaty of Altranstadt which Charles had forced on him three years before. After renewing the Northern Alliance, he tumbled Stanislas Leczinski from the Polish throne and entered once again into his kingdom. Secure in Warsaw, he turned on the Swedes to his north. The Swedes fought back with wonderful tenacity, and it was against a single army under General Steinbock that Maurice fought in Pomerania throughout 1711 and 1712. He was to learn a great deal from the swift, clever, mobile exchanges, practically amounting to guerilla operations, which formed the preliminaries to the bitter sieges which terminated the Great Northern War. He took an active part in the capture of Treptow and Peenemunde, two of the strongpoints which the Swedes defended desperately in the vain hope of retaining their grip on the southern Baltic.

The main Swedish gateway into Germany was the ancient city of Stralsund in Pomerania. It was situated just across the straits from Scania, the province at the southern tip of Sweden. As the principal Swedish entrepôt, it was heavily fortified: and as long as the Swedes held Stralsund they could never be completely dislodged from Germany. This had been clearly demonstrated during the Thirty Years' War when Wallenstein had failed to capture the city after the most ferocious efforts.

The Saxons and their allies began their siege operations in a spirited fashion, but their initial attempts to hammer a breach were failures. Attack after attack was mounted, and in one of them Maurice swam pistol in hand across the freezing river in full view of the garrison, losing thirty men in the process. It was then decided to switch the campaign to another sector, thus granting the beleaguered city a temporary respite. Maurice therefore went off with his regiment to western Pomerania. There he headed a victorious assault on the town of Stade, in which stood the family mausoleum of his Königsmarck forebears.

After subduing the whole of western Pomerania the Saxons

resumed the siege of Stralsund. But that battered city was about to secure another unexpected reprieve. In December 1712 Steinbock sallied out from its defences, engaged the besiegers head on, and brought off a remarkable but bloody victory near the village of Gadebusch. On this occasion Maurice and the Saxon cavalry, under their commander Count Flemming, were well to the fore. Three times the young soldier led his cuirassiers against the Swedish host and had his horse shot under him. At the end of the day ten thousand dead and dying were strewn on the plain of Gadebusch. The Saxons and their Danish allies withdrew, compelled yet again to raise the sieges of Stralsund and its dependency Wismar. For Steinbock it none the less proved a pyrrhic victory, for his exhausted troops were unable to follow up their advantage and advance into Poland.

Maurice returned on leave to Dresden. Here he received a further sign of paternal approval in the shape of an appointment to command the King's own regiment of cuirassiers. The delighted youth at once set out to transform them into the smartest regiment in Europe, an effort that quickly swallowed up his annual allowance and plunged him up to the ears in debt. But his father, himself a practised spendthrift, believed that he had hit upon an excellent remedy for Maurice's inherited restlessness and chronic insolvency. He summoned the boy to his presence and told him to prepare himself for marriage. The bride had already been chosen. The nuptials would be celebrated immediately.

Maurice was sixteen. His future bride, the pretty Countess Johanna-Victoria von Löben, was a year younger. Marriage was no new experience for her. As the sole heiress to one of the largest private fortunes in Saxony, she had long attracted the attention of an unsavoury horde of fortune-hunters. She had been betrothed at the age of eight to Count Friesen, the son of a court official; but when she was nine her father had died, her mother married again, and her stepfather saw no reason why so much money should leave the family. He therefore arranged for a nephew of his own, a lieutenant of cavalry, to abduct the girl and carry her off to Silesia. There, with the connivance of a complaisant priest, she was forced to undergo a form of wedding.

The lamentations of Count Friesen were piteous to hear. He promptly appealed to Frederick Augustus. It proved to be an appeal to Caesar—for the King decreed that Johanna-Victoria should be brought back and groomed for marriage with Maurice. Friesen was paid off; the lieutenant of cavalry was posted to the back of beyond; the girl's venal mother was told brusquely that her daughter would be taken from her care and reared at court.

Maurice was not grateful to his father for all the thought and trouble that had been taken on his behalf. As a soldier he approved of the example of Charles XII, to whom marriage was a weakness and an irrelevance: but as a man he responded to the sensual example of his royal father. He had therefore decided early in life to have the best of both worlds: to despise marriage—and to pursue women. In his precocious fashion he had already resolved that a wife was 'a useless piece of furniture for a soldier'.[24]

It was hardly the frame of mind in which to enter into the estate of matrimony. Johanna-Victoria, for her part, was eager to swear everlasting fidelity. Shortly after their betrothal she penned a pathetic little plea to her fiancé to assure him that

> as far as I am concerned, I shall be eternally attached to you. I shall never lose this attachment, however long the periods during which I am deprived of your presence. Please keep a little affection in your heart for me, and I promise that I will never abuse it. I rely on the constancy of your friendship, and remain, monsieur le comte, your faithful
>
> Johanna-Victoria von Löben.[25]

The pair were married at the Moritzburg on March 12th, 1714, and their nuptials were made the excuse for a series of spectacular fêtes. As it had been at the Moritzburg that the King had seduced the bride-groom's mother, twenty years before, it is evident that Frederick Augustus possessed a somewhat misplaced sense of occasion.

Maurice was naturally expected to prove his virility at the earliest possible moment. The son of the leading satyr in Europe needed no prompting, and by midsummer Johanna-Victoria was pregnant. But if Maurice had thought of a wife as a useless piece of furniture, he had even less concern for his future offspring. His one desire was to return to active service: and Johanna-Victoria was foolish enough to frustrate his wish by prevailing on her royal father-in-law to keep him in Saxony, at least until the birth of their child. For twelve long months, he was forced to cool his heels in Dresden, diverting himself as best he could by squandering his wife's money on his own pleasures, or on his beloved regiment of cuirassiers.

'A soldier's time,' said Dr. Johnson, 'is passed in distress and danger or in idleness and corruption.'[26] Maurice learned, very early in life, the truth of this dictum. The violent swings of the military pendulum exactly matched the pattern of his own moods; and the alternating intensities and *longueurs* of his profession tended to unsettle still further a nature already disturbed by an unstable inheritance. During the difficult emotional period between his fifteenth and twenty-first years, when most young men can count on the steadying influence of parents or schooling, he was deprived of such advantages. His education, which had been intermittent and exclusively military, ceased when he went off to the wars. His parents were not only separated, but his mother was growing increasingly eccentric as the years passed, while his father was an ogre of self-indulgence who regarded the debauching of his brilliant son's character with positive complacency. Like many vicious men, Frederick Augustus delighted to excuse his own self-indulgence by encouraging the weaknesses of those around him. He was unable wholly to corrupt his son, and many of the princely qualities of Maurice's nature survived intact. He retained to the end of his life the energy, magnanimity and gusto that made him so attractive a person. But his formative years at the cultivated and madcap court of Dresden fostered in him the strain of fantasy and exaggeration that was to haunt his career, colour all his thoughts and ambitions, and finally bring him to the brink of madness—or at least to that shadowy frontier of the mind where sanity and insanity are fused together. While his personality was still unformed, it might have been possible to restrain these baleful tendencies, to impose restraint upon the imperious and strong-willed boy. But there was no one on hand to undertake the task.

Perhaps it was just as well. A more conventional introduction to manhood might have bred a more docile Maurice de Saxe.

His son was born on January 21st, 1715. The sole legitimate offspring of Maurice de Saxe lived for only a few days. On the day of the baby's death the father was not at his wife's side, but was rollicking with a sledging party on the frozen Elbe. In the middle of a wild race the ice gave way, and plunged horses, sledges and riders into the freezing water. Maurice and his companions almost drowned.

The death of his boy freed him from family ties, and soon he was heading once more for the fighting that was still devastating his father's dominions. One evening the young count, with his suite of five officers and a dozen servants, arrived at a remote Polish inn while on their way to join the main Saxon army at Sandomierz on the Vistula. While they were at supper, a band of enemy cavalry attacked the village in which the inn stood. In later years Maurice used to say that there were eight hundred of them; but as he grew older he was increasingly given to Falstaffian embroidery. At any rate, there were at least eighty or ninety, and Maurice and his score of companions hastily barricaded themselves inside the inn. In the fight that followed three of the defenders were killed, and Maurice himself received a wound in the thigh. By nightfall it seemed that their chances of surviving until dawn were slim. Maurice decided to risk a break-out. He and his men ran for the stables, saddled up, and made a dash for the forest. A few sabre-slashes and they were through.

Next day they joined the Saxon detachment that was marching to besiege Usedom, a small fortress on an island off the Pomeranian coast. After many weeks of hard fighting, it fell to Frederick Augustus' troops. Usedom had been the town where Gustavus Adolphus, the Lion of the North, had landed from Sweden seventy-five years before. Its loss in 1715 was an indication of the rapid collapse of the Swedish empire, the downward spiral towards disintegration.

Maurice and his regiment were next transferred to Stralsund, where events had taken a suddenly dramatic turn. After five years in captivity, Charles XII had escaped from his captors and, accompanied by only a single companion had traversed the eleven hundred miles between Thrace and Pomerania. After seven weeks in the saddle and a series of extraordinary adventures, the mud-encrusted pair presented themselves to the astounded garrison of Stralsund at midnight at November 11th, 1714. Charles stood once more on what was technically Swedish soil.

Inspired by the return of their king, the Swedish defenders beat off the storming parties of five nations: Saxony, Denmark, Hanover, Russia, and Prussia. But as the months went by, the walls and installations of the port were reduced to heaps of useless rubble. Stralsund became indefensible. In December 1715, the Swedes were forced to take their last desperate measures. Charles evacuated the survivors of his forces at dead of night and pushed out to sea in a rowing boat with his senior officers. The departure from reeking Stralsund was symbolic of his whole career. It was the ruin of his ambitions; it was the end of the Great Northern War; it wrote finis to the imperial greatness of Sweden. Within three years Charles was dead, killed by a dubious hand before the petty fortress of Frederikshald in Norway. 'Voilà la pièce finie,' observed a cynical French military engineer who witnessed the event: 'Allons souper.'

For Charles' cousin, Frederick Augustus, the death of the hero was the end of a long nightmare. When they had met to conclude the Peace of Altranstadt (Frederick Augustus had been the only sovereign whom Charles had ever deigned to meet), the Swedish king seemed 'like a newly enlisted peasant youth beside a handsome knight'. Yet it was the handsome knight who had lost his throne and his peace of mind. After December 1718, however, the King of Poland was free to slumber out the rest of his life in comparative quietude.

In 1716, Maurice was again compelled to return to Dresden to eat out his heart in more idleness and corruption. Although his estrangement from his wife was complete, he generously consented to squander what remained of her fortune. He was very young, very spoiled, very bored. To add to his sense of frustration, he was deprived of his regiment, and expressly forbidden to leave the court for the Turkish front, where another war was raging.

His great enemy at court was Count Flemming, the first minister of Saxony. Flemming, who plays the part of villain in every account of Maurice's early life, was arrogant and sly. Yet he was a sagacious politician, and he is hardly to be blamed for counselling wise and pacific policies that were not to the taste of the immature and belligerent Maurice. If he was secretly responsible for the disbanding of Maurice's cuirassiers, it was no mere act of spite, as Maurice asserted, but a sensible step in a general policy of financial retrenchment. This is not to deny that it may have given him, of course, a certain quiet satisfaction.

It is true that Flemming had no affection for Maria Aurora or her bumptious son. Maria Aurora had long wearied him by her unsolicited advice and incessant complaints. As for Maurice, he did not endear himself to his masters by his frequent displays of uncontrolled temper. When Frederick Augustus refused to listen to his remonstrances about the disbandment of his regiment, Maurice so far forgot himself as to storm and shout in the royal presence: conduct which nearly landed him in the dreaded fortress of Königstein.

On the whole, Flemming was commendably tolerant of Maurice's wild behaviour. When Maria Aurora's sister, the wife of General Löwenhaupt, defended her nephew's part in an unsavoury brawl, Flemming bluntly told her that 'by flattering and indulging him in the way that you do, you will wreck and destroy whatever good qualities he may still possess'.[27] Such good advice made little impression on the clique of doting women who surrounded Maurice. 'Since the count's infancy,' his mother indignantly informed Frederick Augustus, 'I have studied him closely. Never have I seen any trace of any bad inclination or heard of any bad action which he has performed.'[28]

To another of Maurice's female champions, Countess Dönhof, Flemming wrote early in 1718:

> Count Saxe maintains that it is my fault that he cannot go to Hungary, although I have constantly told him that I am perfectly willing that he should do so, and that he need only ask his father's permission. He wants to go there as colonel of a regiment; but he has no regiment, and am I really justified in taking one away from another officer in order to give him one? In any case, it is a matter for the King to decide.[29]

Unfortunately for Maurice, Augustus the Strong was no longer seriously interested in the business of warfare, although he retained a latent taste for glory. Maurice's pleas therefore fell upon indifferent

ears. Like most restored monarchs, the King of Poland had no wish
to have to go on his travels again. He had found to his cost that the
trouble with war is the uncertainty of victory. Moreover, he had by
now convinced himself of his own greatness, a belief which coincided
conveniently with his relapse into almost total indolence. He considered that his reign had reached its gleaming meridian, and saw
himself as the dispenser of universal peace and benevolence. He could
not understand why Maurice, at the height of his youth and vigour,
pined for the danger and discomfort of the wars instead of staying at
home and exploring the delights of Dresden. Why could the gifted
boy not interest himself in women, in the new porcelain process stolen
from the Chinese, in his father's great vision of transforming Dresden
until its baroque magnificence outshone Versailles itself? Poppelmann
had already remodelled the Moritzburg and was engaged in designing
the fabulous palace of the Zwinger; Baehr was about to start work
on the elaborate Frauenkirche. Who would exchange all this for the
dusty uncertainties of war?

Frederick Augustus had come to prefer his baubles to his army, his
buildings to his people. The riches of Saxony and Poland were being
consumed in providing a lavish setting for a kindly and corpulent
autocrat. As Thackeray wrote of the King of Poland's great idol, Louis
XIV:

> It is incalculable how much that royal bigwig cost Germany. Every
> prince imitated the French King and had his Versailles, his Wilhelms-
> höhe and his Ludwigslust; his court and its splendours; his gardens laid
> out with statues; his fountains and waterworks and tritons; his actors,
> his dancers and singers and fiddlers; his harem with its inhabitants; his
> diamonds and duchies for these latter; his enormous festivals, his
> gaming-tables, tournaments, masquerades and banquets lasting a week
> long, for which the people paid their money when the poor wretches had
> it, with their bodies and their blood when they had none; being sold in
> thousands by their lords and masters, who gaily dealt in soldiers, staked
> a regiment upon the red at the gaming-table, swapped a battalion against
> a girl's diamond necklace; and, as it were, pocketed the people.[30]

Augustus was just such a German prince. At a review at Mühlberg
a few years later he was to 'swap a battalion' in exactly this fashion
for some choice pieces of porcelain. King Frederick William I of
Prussia possessed some precious vases which had inflamed the King
of Poland's collector's itch, and at Mühlberg he finally acquired them
in exchange for his best regiment of dragoons. The private thoughts
of Maurice de Saxe and of the future Frederick the Great, who were
both witnesses of the transaction, may easily be imagined.

In 1717 Maurice had no 'Dragoon Vases' or other aesthetic trifles
with which to tempt his father: so he had to do without his regiment.
But at least he managed at last to obtain permission to leave the

capital on active service. The presence at court of the harum-scarum and improvident princeling had eventually proved too much for the royal nerves.

War was raging in the Danube valley and the eastern Mediterranean. While Schulenburg, who had been seconded by Frederick Augustus to the Venetians, pinned down the Turks along the Adriatic, Prince Eugène had marched to strike at the Sultan's troops along the Danube. Between them the Empire and Venice had caught the Turks between a pair of pincers. In August 1716, Eugène engaged the Turkish forces at Petrovaradin, where his sixty-two thousand troops routed one hundred and fifty thousand Turks. For the loss of three thousand Austrian dead and wounded, he slaughtered six thousand of the enemy, including the Grand Vizier himself. And while the demoralized Turks recoiled on Belgrade, he seized the citadel of Temesvár, a hundred miles to the east. It was at the moment when Eugène paused to rest the Imperial forces, before administering the *coup de grâce*, that the twenty-one-year-old Maurice came bustling into camp in the guise of a plain volunteer.

The task of rebuilding the Imperial Army continued throughout the winter. Eugène had even amassed a sizeable fleet, by bringing down the Danube and the lesser rivers of eastern Europe the well-organized flotilla of transports which had served him so well on the Rhine. In the spring of 1717, he led out his troops to the supreme task of taking Belgrade: and was promptly overtaken by disaster. As Maurice later recalled:

> When we left our quarters and encamped before Belgrade we were fifty thousand strong. We were at a high altitude, the air was sweet, the water we drank was untainted, we had an abundance of everything we required. Yet on August 18, the day of the battle, we had only twenty-two thousand men. The rest were dead or sick.[31]

Epidemic disease, the scourge of the armies of the epoch, had decimated Eugène's battalions. None the less, the great general girded himself for battle.

The siege that followed was regarded by contemporaries as one of the epic encounters of the eighteenth century. The small Imperial force surged forward for the grand assault. The battle swayed backwards and forwards. By the end of it, Eugène's men had killed twenty thousand Turks, for the loss of fifteen hundred of themselves, and had captured Belgrade. In his imperturbable way, Eugène had once more brought the whole of Hungary under the control of the Emperor. The task he had begun at Zenta in 1697 was complete, and the Turks had been deprived of most of the northern conquests of

Suleiman the Magnificent and his successors. The significance of this achievement was far from lost on Maurice. He saw clearly that the outlying lands of Europe could still be conquered by any general with sufficient nerve to covet them.

Eugène now retired to his estates, notably to his beloved Schönbrunn, and there remained for the space of seventeen years. It seemed as though his active military career was over. Yet he would one day emerge, at the age of seventy-one, to engage a younger man whom he had instructed in the art of war: his disciple at Belgrade, the aptest of all his pupils, Maurice de Saxe.

On his return from Serbia, Maurice was invested by his father with the Order of the White Eagle of Poland, an order of great antiquity which had been revived by Augustus in 1705. Its bestowal on a man so young, even though he was the king's own son, was a rare distinction. Yet Maurice's reluctant return to court life was rendered intolerable by the domestic imbroglio in which he was quickly plunged.

His neglect of his wife was by now habitual. After he had ignored her for a whole year, Johanna-Victoria, who sincerely loved him, had recourse to a fatal expedient in an attempt to gain his affection. She took refuge with her mother-in-law at Quedlinburg. There for a few short weeks it seemed as though heaven had bestowed on her the friend she had so long needed. At first Maria Aurora was in a mood to sympathize with the complaints of her son's boorishness with which Johanna-Victoria regaled her; the mother had suffered in this respect at least as long as the wife; but it was not long before her protective obsession reasserted itself. Her jealous desire to oust her daughter-in-law from her son's affections soon reached pathological, even maniacal proportions. Maurice was after all the sole source and solace of his mother's multiple frustrations, sexual, social and economic. The brilliant, handsome, mettlesome and now renowned youth was her one unique and indisputable achievement. Why should she surrender her proprietory rights in his golden future to a girl whom he did not even like?

With characteristic recklessness, she began to poison Maurice's mind against his unoffending wife. Only Maurice and Maria Aurora's biographers could have believed the lies she spread about poor Johanna-Victoria. Maurice, who had now drained the Löben fortune to the lees, was only too willing to believe his mother's neurotic fantasies. She began by telling him that at Quedlinburg the girl had frequently committed adultery; and Maurice thereupon addressed pompous remonstrances to Johanna-Victoria, upbraiding her for con-

39

duct that might reflect on his own reputation—which, of course, was spotless. Emboldened by her success, Maria Aurora next accused her daughter-in-law of conspiring with a lady-in-waiting to poison Maurice with a white powder from Italy. Maria Aurora herself, ran the tale, was eventually to be killed by the same method. As this fabrication proved too much even for the court of Dresden to swallow, the mother next despatched a letter to Frederick Augustus, purporting to give details of Johanna-Victoria's affair with a page, appropriately named Iago, with whom it was alleged she was openly living.

Johanna-Victoria was no innocent babe—but equally she was incapable of real villainy. Her morals were of necessity better than those of most of her father-in-law's family. Like Desdemona, she protested that the page had come to her in disgrace, begging her to use her influence with his master, Maurice. She told the King that she had realized too late that Maria Aurora was not a friend but an enemy, a malignant woman whose main aim was to dominate those round her. 'Rather than become the countess's slave,' she declared, 'I will live on bread and water.' Frederick Augustus, who knew Maria Aurora's ways only too well, dealt gently with the girl, and she was encouraged to seek his help in effecting a reconciliation with Maurice. This was to be concealed not only from Maurice, but especially from Maria Aurora. 'Your Majesty knows full well,' wrote Johanna-Victoria, 'how cunning the Countess von Königsmarck can be, and how she can ferret out the profoundest secrets.' She urged the King to let Maurice know that she still loved him, and longed to be reunited to him. 'Being bound to him by so strong a tie,' she wrote,

> I desire vehemently to dwell in harmony with him, if only he would show me a little pity. I should be completely content if he would bring himself to treat me with some sort of respect, instead of behaving towards me as though I were a nonentity. For the rest, I assure Your Majesty that I shall always conduct myself in a manner which will give no one any possible grounds for reproach.[32]

Her efforts to save her marriage were wasted. Maurice would no more let himself be tied to Johanna-Victoria than he would to any other woman, now or later. In fact, the din of female squabbling and supplication had risen to such a crescendo that he decided to break completely away from Dresden. He would frankly accept his destined career as an adventurer. He would search for the crown and the kingdom that he felt to be his due. He did not yet know where that kingdom lay: he was only certain that it was not to be found within the borders of Saxony.

In the spring of 1720, he set out on the high road for Paris. For all but the last few years of his troubled life, Paris would be his home—as much as any place could be home for so wayward a spirit.

CHAPTER IV

PARIS, 1720-1725

Love draws me one and glory the other way.
Don Quixote

PARIS was a home from home for a young man like Maurice, who had been bred at a francophile court. The city was close to Versailles; it was the intellectual centre of the civilized world. Maurice had chosen an excellent base for his coming raids on fortune.

France was not, of course, the power she had been during the *Grand Siècle*. The reign of Louis XIV, which had ended five years before Maurice set out from Dresden, had brought disaster as well as glory to the nation. Louis' reign had reached its zenith at the time of the Peace of Nymegen in 1678; but the remaining thirty-seven years had been marred by military setbacks, and by the increasing impoverishment of the common people. Fénélon (whom Louis had exiled) had declared that 'the whole of France is become a huge, desolate, hungry hospital'; Vauban (whom Louis had disgraced) had observed that 'one man in ten is now a beggar, and another five in ten are in want'. To add to the distress caused by incessant waging of war, the new century opened with a run of poor harvests. The peasants were reduced to eating acorns and ferns; the artisans in the towns rioted for bread; there were mutinies among the troops at Versailles. The whole nation groaned under the weight of royal extravagance and despotism, and Louis' death in 1715 was the signal for universal rejoicing.

The accession of his great-grandson, Louis XV, a child of five, brought France a respite. It also released a new spirit of optimism which appealed greatly to Maurice. The duc d'Orléans, the middle-aged Regent, was an easy going debauchee after Maurice's own heart. The Regent was fond of attending Mass with the works of Rabelais bound inside the covers of his missal. Indolent, witty, and probably incestuous, he was none the less no foe of change. A liberal as well as a libertine, he patronized the intelligentsia and made a genuine effort to introduce a measure of religious toleration and a form of government less rigorous than the pure absolutism of his late uncle. His

41

foreign policy was one of easy peace and cheap victories; and with the aid of his chief minister, the abbé Dubois, a clergyman as capable and as corrupt as himself, he secured the peace of western Europe by entering into an alliance with France's old adversaries, Great Britain and the United Provinces. In 1719 this unexpected Triple Alliance was transformed into an even more astonishing Quadruple Alliance, when Dubois secured the adherence of the head of the hated house of Habsburg, the Emperor Charles VI. The abbé's reward was a cardinal's hat, and the knowledge that the body of Louis XIV was turning in its grave. He was now ready for a quick triumph. The British were already at war with Spain, and the French seized a pretext for declaring war in January 1719. An army led by James FitzJames, duc de Berwick, a natural son of James II of England and Marlborough's sister Arabella Churchill, entered Spanish territory in April. Within eight months the Spanish fleets and armies had been broken. Philip V hastily dismissed Cardinal Alberoni and sued for peace.

Maurice reached Paris at the moment when the French were jubilant at Berwick's success. It was also the moment when they had been driven crazy by a speculative boom of lunatic proportions. The streets were jammed with thousands of men and women all rushing towards the Bourse—rushing, did they but know it, towards financial ruin. During the few weeks before Maurice's arrival, the population of the city increased by over a quarter of a million. It was a Gold Rush.

Louis XIV had left France bankrupt, with a national debt amounting to a hundred million livres, a sum equivalent to the entire national income for four years. The Regent knew that drastic measures had to be taken to reduce the debt and restore the value of the currency. To this end he enlisted the aid of an imaginative Scots banker, John Law of Lauriston, who had already built up a vast private fortune by his speculative operations in London and Amsterdam. Law was neither a knave nor a fool; in fact he was a brilliant financier and economist, and many of his revolutionary ideas are today axioms of modern economics. For example, he advocated the development of an un-backed and managed paper currency of the kind which we take for granted in the twentieth century. Unfortunately for France, he was a long way ahead of his time—a sort of rococo Keynes. His attempt to foist modern principles of credit on a feudal society with mercantilist ideals was to prove disastrous.

Law was authorized by the Regent to introduce into France what was supposed to be the system of credit obtaining in Holland. He established a bank which proved so successful that in 1718 it became the Royal Bank of France. Its credulous investors, who regarded the Scotsman as a kind of thaumaturgist, were offered increasingly heady brews: a Company of the Occident which issued Mississippi stock, and a Bank of the Indies which controlled France's entire foreign trade. The trouble was that the volume of trade on which this vast edifice of credit had been erected was actually dwindling. Law was doing nothing more than print bank-notes. In January 1720, six months before the crash, Law was appointed Controller-General of Finance.

Maurice was infected by the prevailing mood of extravagance. Fortunately he also had more sober interests. When he arrived in France in 1720 it was with the original intention of pursuing the study of mathematics, but he also wished to launch himself in a regular career of arms. His father agreed to this. A royal equerry wrote to Count Flemming to ask whether he would approve of Maurice entering the military service of France: 'for there he can learn the business of war better than he can in Saxony, which is not at war, and which hopes to remain at peace'. Flemming replied that he saw no objection, 'provided that Count Maurice applies himself, for although he has great natural aptitude he lacks concentration'.[33] The chief minister was probably delighted at the prospect of seeing the back of Maurice—and certainly Frederick Augustus was flattered at the notion of having a son in the army of France. The King ignored a hint from the Saxon minister at Paris that his son was already behaving badly and ought to be recalled, and Maurice was given permission to apply for a French commission and granted indefinite leave to stay in Paris. Frederick Augustus also enjoined him, with a perfectly straight face, to avoid all gambling and lewd company.

Maurice had already made friends with two cadets of the royal house of France. While at Belgrade he had been a close companion of two young French soldiers, cousins and dependents of Louis XIV's favourite bastard, the duc de Maine. The elder, the prince de Dombes, was Maine's son by a princesse de Condé; the other, who was in Paris when Maurice arrived, was the comte de Charolais. Nor was it long before Maurice had secured another and more powerful friend at court. This was the Regent's mother, Elizabeth of the Rhine, a daughter of Charles Louis, Elector Palatine. A haughty, vinegary old woman, the second wife of Louis XIV's degenerate brother Philippe, the dowager duchess of Orléans had endured much unhappiness during her long sojourn in France. The good-looking young German scapegrace, who spoke her native tongue and shared her Lutheran background, soon became a firm favourite of the stiff and pious duchess.

The Regent was easily persuaded to engage Maurice's services. Quite apart from the prestige of his paternity, the young man's Königsmarck forebears had served France well in their time. On August 9th 1720, Maurice received his brevet as *maréchal de camp*, a post which carried with it an annual salary of ten thousand livres. The relatively minor duties of this rank were not enough to keep an energetic young officer sufficiently occupied: so Maurice promptly offered to purchase the colonelcy of the *Régiment Greder*. And when the news of this offer reached Dresden, there was a positive uproar.

Maurice had family precedent on his side. Karl Johann von Königsmarck had once commanded the *Régiment Fürstemberg*, which had been the *Régiment Greder* under an older name. Later, when it became known as the *Régiment Salm-Salm*, it drew the bulk of its recruits from the predominantly German and Lutheran province of Alsace, and was therefore particularly attractive to Maurice.[34] Indeed, the regiment was tailor-made for him. The only drawback was the expense of buying it, for one did not purchase a crack French regiment cheaply. Its colonel wanted thirty-five thousand thalers for it, a sum far beyond the scope of Maurice's own resources. 'Thirty-five thousand thalers!', exclaimed Flemming,

> I suppose Count Saxe expects the money to come from the privy purse? That might be done if it could be paid in livres, three to the thaler. But pay it in our own good specie! Why don't we just make him a Saxon lieutenant-general, and throw in a couple of regiments for good measure?[35]

It was not just Flemming's instinct for economy that was offended: the Chief Minister suspected that he was being paid out for the way in which he had deprived Maurice of his Saxon cuirassiers four years previously. He opposed the project with such obstinacy that it seemed as though Maurice would have to withdraw. But Maurice, whose option on the regiment was already public knowledge, refused to be made to look a fool in the eyes of Paris. He hastened to Dresden and personally begged his father to make the money available. Although the sum in question was considerable, Maurice had rightly divined that the King was in benevolent mood. It was agreed that the Saxon exchequer should put up the bulk of the purchase money, the rest being drawn from the sale of part of the remaining Königsmarck estates.

On March 1st, 1721, the *Régiment Greder* became the *Régiment Saxe*. Within a few weeks its displays of drill were helping to divert a Paris newly depressed by the total collapse of 'Law's system'. For the Company of the Indies had finally gone bankrupt in the summer of 1720, and thousands of holders of Mississippi stock were irretrievably ruined. Law himself had to be smuggled over the French border to escape the fury of the mob. Fortunately Maurice, who at this time had no money to spare, does not seem to have been greatly affected by the pricking of the bubble. Perhaps it was borne in upon him that there was no easy money to be made in Paris; and at last he had the security of a regiment of his own and a settled career.

The men of the *Régiment Saxe* carried out their complicated evolutions with astonishing precision. Maurice was, like all German commanders, an accomplished drillmaster, inheriting the tradition of Frundsberg, whose Landsknechts had sacked Rome. But Maurice was no mere martinet. He was to become famous as an innovator in the technique of moving troops on the ground, and as the inventor of new weapons and tactics. He therefore wanted, even at this early stage, to discipline his men in such a way that they would be able to execute his novel dispositions in the field with speed and accuracy, and handle improved or unfamiliar firearms with assurance. Maurice was the very last of men to regard the troops under his command as automata. His system of drill had a serious purpose.

We know from his portrait by Rigaud [Frontispiece], although it dates from a few years later, what Maurice looked like as he caracoled up and down the lines of his legionnaires as they stood drawn up on the Champ-de-Mars.[36] And a flashing, *farouche* image he presented to the excited eyes of the Parisians. Across the black steel cuirass, on which reposed the blue moiré sash of his Polish order, lay the silk-lined, leopard-skin pélisse worn by Polish officers of the period. The rich pelt was fastened at the right shoulder by one of the fine jewels which he loved to collect. Upon the pélisse was pinned the white-and-red cross of the White Eagle, with its sheaf of golden rays. His *tenue* was completed by soft white gauntlets of Spanish leather and a Polish sword with a hilt wrought in the shape of an eagle. The Polish element in his appearance is worth noting, for he was to bring to the French scene not merely an amusing touch of colour, but certain unorthodox military ideas he had garnered in his campaigns in Eastern Europe. In the portrait even the wig he wears is an expression of his vivid uninhibited character, for it resembles less a wig than his own hair, worn in the style of his family, the famous curling fair hair of the Königsmarcks, prodigiously long, twisted into a tight yellow braid falling half-way down his back.

The famous French military theorist, the chevalier Folard, was soon writing of Maurice's regiment in eulogistic terms. ' Troops should be trained,' he asserted, ' to carry out firing orders on the lines laid down in the *Régiment Saxe*. The comte de Saxe is one of the most promising commanders I have ever encountered, and the next war will prove the correctness of my forecast.'[37]

Folard soon became a firm friend and mentor to Maurice. The

young *maréchal de camp* could boast, and doubtless did, that at the age of twenty-four he had served in no less than eleven campaigns—but they had taught him more about the business of swinging a sabre than the mysteries of directing a bombardment. Maurice now returned to his studies, attacking mathematics, geometry, mechanics and the study of fortification with a zeal that would have astonished his frustrated tutors of former days. In this work he was greatly assisted by Folard, whose rare military intelligence Maurice had divined beneath the chevalier's spiky facade of eccentricity.

Folard was certainly odd. On all occasions he expected his olympian advice to be instantly accepted. Although he had been gravely wounded at Malplaquet, he had refused to become *hors de combat*, and had continued to follow the campaign in his coach, showering the various French commanders in the field with unasked-for advice. Boufflers and Villars both breathed a sigh of relief when the voluble pedant eventually blundered, coach and all, behind the enemy lines. Prince Eugène quickly invited the captured chevalier to enter the Imperial service; but Folard chose instead to retire to Malta in order to instruct the Knights of St. John in the art of war. His attempts to explain their military shortcomings to the Hospitallers met with a rebuff; so the peppery pundit spent the next two years showing the ruined Charles XII how to regain his empire across the Baltic; and on Charles' death, he returned to France to devote himself to purely academic pursuits. He had by now turned fifty, and thought that it was time that he began to record the fruits of a lifetime's experience for the benefit of posterity. The works that flowed from his facile pen were voluminous in scope and revolutionary in character. They were also sensational, for the chevalier could seldom resist the temptation to illustrate the mistakes of the generals of antiquity by drawing analogies with recent campaigns. It was not surprising that he became in consequence unpopular and disregarded; but at least in his old age he had the consolation of becoming an intimate of Maurice, never a man to be alarmed by unorthodoxy. Folard saw in Maurice the promise of a very great general; and Maurice found in Folard an inspiring and exciting mentor.

The young Saxon count soon became notorious among the ladies of Paris.

He was short, even stocky, and his complexion was rather too *basané*, or swarthy, to be quite in fashion: but the appeal of the golden earrings which he wore was hard to resist. As early as April 1720, the duchesse d'Orléans had written to the Princess of Wales to retail the latest gossip: how the British ambassador, Lord Stair, had fallen in love with a certain Mme Raymond, and how Mme Raymond, the former mistress of the Elector of Bavaria,

> . . . has just taken another lover who causes my Lord Stair a great deal of heartburning. This is Count Saxe, who is not particularly handsome, but who is young, seductive and possesses fine manners.[38]

This particular liaison was short-lived; but later in the same year Maurice was to form the overwhelming attachment which was to dominate much of his life. It was to be an *affaire de coeur* marred by cruelty and betrayal, but it was to bring him a posthumous fame greater than that earned by all his battles.

In a letter to an English friend at this time, the abbé d'Allainval enumerated the four marvels of contemporary Paris. In order of precedence, they were the Tuileries, the acting of Mlle Lecouvreur, the dancing of Camargo, and the singing of Mlle Le Maure.

It was in the autumn of 1720 that Maurice visited the Théâtre-français to view the second of these marvels for himself. The theatre, situated in Saint-Germain-des-Prés, was mean, musty and uncomfortable. Enthusiastic playgoer though he was, the young Saxon may well have taken his chair upon the stage with a lively sense of the contrast between this cramped place and the sumptuous playhouses of Dresden. The play was Racine's *Phèdre*; yet it was only when the tragic princess herself had made her entrance that his attention was aroused. As she spoke her tremendous opening lines, a shiver went through him.

> N'allons point plus avant. Demeurons, chère Œnone,
> Je ne me soutiens plus, ma force m'abandonne.
> Mes yeux sont éblouis du jour que je revoi,
> Et mes genoux tremblants se dérobent sous moi.

The rôle of Phèdre displayed the genius of Adrienne Lecouvreur to perfection. The secret of her art, and of her approach to life, was a radiant naturalness and simplicity. She was quite explicit, in this age of artifice, about the kind of effect that she wanted to produce. Writing towards the end of her life to a young Breton noble who sought closer acquaintance with her, on the pretext of learning the art of rhetoric, she gracefully excused herself with the words,

> You say you would like me to teach you the art of declamation, which would be useful to you in your political pursuits. Have you not overlooked the fact that I never declaim? The unique and feeble merit of my playing resides in its naturalness.[39]

Naturalness and simplicity. These were the qualities that captivated Maurice, as earlier they had captivated the French public. Adrienne tried to moderate and purify the bombastic style of her predecessor, Mlle Duclos. Her most powerful dramatic strokes were produced in moments of repose; yet she was also capable of displaying fiery passion. As one of her rivals cattily observed, she was often audible in the cafés outside the theatre; but she never allowed her technique to obscure the meaning of her lines, and the lucidity of her interpretation was so remarkable for her time as to be hailed as innovation. She was experimental in the matter of costume, for her natural style of delivery required less formal trappings than the huge wigs, hooped skirts and high red heels that were the order of the day. It was Adrienne who introduced the graceful garb *à la romaine* to supplement her style of acting, though privately she delighted in rich and curious gowns that no doubt endeared her to Maurice, himself a sartorial innovator. She also originated the practice of varying her costume from scene to scene; and altogether her theatrical reforms heralded the onset of a less severe approach to the drama in general.[40]

Her rise to the position of the leading actress in France had been neither rapid nor easy. The daughter of a village hatmaker, she was already appearing in amateur productions at the age of thirteen. She showed such promise that she was given an audition by Mlle Fonpré, the directress of the theatre at Lille. There she became the mistress of a young officer in the crack *Régiment de Picardie*, and when he died in battle she passed under the protection of Philippe le Roy, an officer on the staff of the Duke of Lorraine. In 1710 she bore him a daughter and accompanied him to the ducal court at Lunéville. Later she performed at Metz, Nancy and Verdun, and eventually joined the Duke's principal company at Strasbourg.

During her sojourn in Strasbourg, the *prédestinée de l'amour*, as Cécile Sorel called her,[41] fell passionately in love with François de Klinglin, the son of the Prêteur-Royal or governor of the city. He seduced Adrienne after proposing marriage, and it would indeed have been a brilliant match for an actress. In 1716 their daughter Françoise was born, and shortly afterwards her lover abandoned her. In her disappointment she decided to leave Strasbourg, and eagerly accepted an offer to join the *Comédie-française*.[42]

She made her Parisian *début* in the rôle of Electra in March 1717. It was a triumph. Both the Regent and the Tsar of Russia attended the second performance. In the remaining nine months of the year she played a hundred and thirty-nine times, in twenty different rôles, a greater number of performances than she had made in any previous year, or than she was ever to make again. Her constitution had never been robust, and one is not surprised to learn that already, in 1717, she was *poitrinaire*, or suffering from incipient tuberculosis.

'Without being tall,' pronounced an eye-witness,

> she is extremely well proportioned, and has a distinct air of nobility. She is the most graceful person imaginable, commands great pathos,

ADRIENNE LE COUVREUR
Actrice du Théatre François
Neé à Fimes en 1690 Morte à Paris le 20 Mars 1730.

ADRIENNE LE COUVREUR
Portrait by Fontaine

and delivers her lines in a manner that reveals that she has carefully studied and fully understands them. Her eyes are as expressive as her lips, and often supply the force that is lacking in her voice. I cannot do more, in conclusion, than compare her with a miniature, for she has all a miniature's charm. . . . [Plate 3].[43]

So unusual a creature was certain to attract a large circle of admirers. She had not been in Paris for many months before malicious tongues had begun to credit her with a dozen lovers. One was said to be the eccentric English soldier Lord Peterborough, who is alleged to have exclaimed at their first meeting: 'Come on, show me plenty of spirit and plenty of love!' In fact, she showed him the door. Certainly she had, from the first, two constant companions whose regard outlasted her life, Voltaire and the marquis d'Argental. With Argental her relationship, although intense, was probably platonic; but Voltaire was her lover. He always spoke of her with reverence, and greatly disliked the vulgar habit of calling her 'La Lecouvreur', referring to her punctiliously when in company as 'Mademoiselle Lecouvreur'. She in her turn appeared in his plays. In 1719 she struggled valiantly to prevent the early demise of *Artémire*; and when the play was recast six years later, as *Mariamne*, she secured for it a distinct if temporary triumph. She also appeared in his first comedy, *L'Indiscret*.

Curiously enough, Voltaire and Maurice, who soon became rivals for her affections, always remained on the best of terms with one another. Shortly before Voltaire sought refuge in England in 1727, after his second spell inside the Bastille, he consulted Maurice about the *Vie de Charles XII*, which he was then preparing. One of the later editions of this brilliant work contained a handsome tribute to Maurice, *le plus grand général de nos jours*.

Part of the fascination which Maurice held for Adrienne was that, unlike Voltaire and Argental, he was in no obvious sense an intellectual but a man of action. Her temperament, behind the outward simplicity of her dramatic technique, was intrinsically theatrical. Like many actresses of our own age, when naturalism is again the fashion in the playhouse, Adrienne was more theatrical off the stage than on. In Maurice she discerned a real-life hero with the soul of an artist, the living embodiment of the fantastic characters who were regularly enacted on the boards of the *Comédie*. To Adrienne he was Lord Essex and the Cid, he was Antiochus, Coriolanus and Bajazet.

He also attracted her for another reason. In spite of his courtly origins, his rudimentary education and his long campaigns in some of the less civilized corners of Europe had left him ill-equipped for Parisian society. He was therefore a promising subject for any woman who had a taste for polishing rough diamonds.

> Beneath the guise of Sarmatius she had detected the lineaments of a hero, and undertook to soften the lines of the soldier. She was thirty, an age favourable to experience and passion, an age which makes a woman as clever at pleasing as ready for love. As in the days of chivalry, her tact, tenderness and counsel were to initiate him into a gracious, virtuous and courtly way of life that would eventually make him, together with his military victories, a true Frenchman. In this gentle school the Achilles of Homer would become the Achilles of Racine. . . . She was to teach him our language and our literature, inspire in him a taste for poetry, music and books, and nurture that passion for the theatre which he would take with him even into camp. It was to be said of the future victor of Fontenoy that his beautiful mistress had taught him everything he knew except the art of war (which he knew already) and the art of spelling (which he was never to learn).[44]

The first of her surviving letters to Maurice is dated September 13th, 1720. It initiated a justly famous correspondence. Her prose style has often been admired, and no less a judge than Sainte-Beuve was to write:

> We find in her letters that excellent, restrained language which I have more than once attempted to define. It is the language of the early eighteenth century, remarkable above all for its shapeliness, exactitude and clarity. It was the language employed by Mme de Maintenon, which every woman of sensibility was to use henceforward—Caylus, Staël, Aïssé. . . . In life, Adrienne Lecouvreur possessed great charm; and, what is given to very few, something of that charm has survived her death, and still continues to be felt.[45]

The lovers met either at Adrienne's house or at the town house and country estates which Maurice had by now acquired. She lived at the Hôtel de Rannes, in the narrow rue de Marais, now the rue Visconti; it was an historic house, for Racine had lived in it with Mlle Champmeslé, and had died there in 1699. We know that it was richly furnished and that the main room was hung with satin and velvet and furnished with Chinese screens and day-beds of damask; that it had a spinet, a clavichord and a chiming clock; that there were tapestries and pier-glasses and, amidst the generous profusion, a splendid lit de repos à la duchesse, on which Adrienne would lie with Maurice beneath a sumptuous bedspread given her by the wistful Voltaire.

Maurice's town house was on the near-by quai Malaquais, which had not then been spoiled by the grey bulk of the Ecole des Beaux Arts. As neither the pont des Arts nor the pont du Carrousel existed at that time, he enjoyed an uninterrupted view across the Seine to the Louvre. According to another tradition, he also lived at one period at what is today No. 12 rue Bonaparte. In the country he had a fine château, still unspoilt, at La Grange, in the woods beyond the suburb of Villeneuve Saint Georges; and close by was his hunting-box of La Piple.

But their life together in Paris or at La Grange was never idyllic. Maurice was too mercurial to be satisfied with an equable relationship; Adrienne was too prone to the luxury of introspection and self-torture to accept the rough with the smooth. He had already begun to ill-treat her, and she was soon complaining that: 'I keep telling myself that you were not made to love me in the way that I want to be loved.' It was a mere six months after she first became his mistress that he left her for a prolonged visit to Saxony. The cause was not romantic. He wished to sue his neglected wife for divorce.

Johanna-Victoria had decided to cut her losses, to retreat from the battle while some reserves of strength and fortune remained to her. She filed a suit before the consistory court of the state church, demanding the annulment of her marriage on the grounds that he had neglected his duties as a husband and broken his marriage vows. With commendable restraint she cited only one woman as co-respondent— her own waiting woman, with whom, perhaps by prearrangement, he 'had been fairly taken in bed'.[46]

Maurice, who had been summoned to the court, did not trouble to make a defence. When asked what he had to say in rebuttal of the allegations, he answered 'absolutely nothing', adding, 'I admit that we have never had much affection for one another, but she has not exaggerated. The facts are as she has stated, and are perfectly true.'[47] The president of the court thereupon declared the union void in the eyes of the law and in the sight of God. 'His wife did not part with him,' noted the editor of his memoirs forty years after his death, 'without great reluctance', adding shrewdly:

> The proud and independent character of Count Saxe did not allow him to study the modes of how to please. He preferred to command love rather than to merit it.[48]

Johanna-Victoria gratefully relapsed into decent obscurity, and three years later married a certain Herr von Runkel, by whom she bore a large family. She died in 1747. 'After this divorce,' we are told,

> Count Saxe was so far from forgetting her that he never went to Saxony without going to see her; and the complaisance he still had for her gave room to believe that he regretted her loss. He had given her his promise that he would never marry again, and he kept his word, for although he had several opportunities of marrying to advantage, he always declined them.[49]

His disillusionment with marriage was permanent. Shortly after the divorce, his father suggested an engagement to a princess of Holstein-Sonderburg. The alliance was diplomatically desirable, and the king offered him the inducement most likely to attract him: elevation to princely rank. But even this prospect could not cure him of his deep aversion from further matrimonial entanglements.

Maurice returned to Paris and Adrienne. For a while he was even persuaded to adopt intellectual pursuits, and he became a dutiful member of Adrienne's *salon*, discussing history with Voltaire and metaphysics with Fontenelle, Marsais and his friend the marquis de Rochemore.

But these learned diversions did not occupy him for long. On Christmas Eve 1721 he became involved in a major scandal. On that night young François-Louis de Bourbon, prince de Conti, burst sword in hand into the bedroom of his wife, Louise Elizabeth de Bourbon-Condé.[50] At first it was believed that he had discovered Maurice in bed with the lady and had killed him on the spot; later reports suggested that he had found the room empty and that the princess had told him, with all the self-possession of a descendant of Henry IV, that 'if he had suspected that she had a man in her room, then he should have taken care to keep out'. Next morning she left her husband's house. At about the same time it was noticed that the comte de Saxe had begun to limp, for which his explanation was that he had spent the previous evening with the Regent at the Palais Royal, and had been unlucky enough to trip on the stairs.

Count Hoym, the Saxon minister at Paris, anxiously wrote to Dresden to explain away the affair. But Augustus the Strong was delighted. The boy had only been maintaining family tradition, and he had also made a cuckold of the son of his old rival for the throne of Poland. Augustus told Hoym that he was far more interested in the princess's alleged declaration to her jealous husband that she knew seven different ways of being unfaithful to him, six of which she revealed on the spot, but kept the seventh a secret. The most diligent researches of the Saxon minister failed to discover this tantalizing secret for Augustus. Perhaps, in course of time, he wormed it out of Maurice.

'Your long journey,' wrote Adrienne after his next departure for Saxony,

> has made me very sad. I tried to be sensible about it at the time, and told myself that it would be advantageous to you. I feel so deeply the horror of a prolonged absence from you that the present seems to be insupportable. Day in and day out I hunger for you. I say to myself, 'no doubt he is whipping up his horses, and does not spare me a thought. . . .'

Maurice was famous for the fury with which his coach bowled along the roads of Europe; such journeys consumed some of his surplus energy. His travelling companion was usually old Folard, who had too often faced the hazards of war to fear Maurice's coachmen. Not even the rattle of the berlin could still the flow of the chevalier's ideas, to which Maurice, still very much the student of the art of war, paid great attention.

Despite the lingering hostility of Flemming, Maurice was once again *persona grata* at his father's court, and in 1723 he was entrusted with some confidential mission that he discharged greatly to the king's satisfaction. 'You have conducted yourself with the greatest ability and adroitness,' Augustus informed Maurice, 'and I shall remember your zeal on my behalf and will know how to reward it.'

It was another secret mission that seems to have taken him to London early in 1724. He gave two different but not irreconcilable explanations of his two-month visit. Dresden was told that he was going to England to buy horses; Lecoq, the Saxon minister at the court of St. James', was merely informed that his regiment had been posted to Amiens, and that he had been unable to resist crossing the Channel. Both these assertions were probably true. Yet that there was something mysterious about the adventure is suggested by the fact that he travelled *incognito*. And in spite of the incomplete state of his wardrobe—he claimed that he had made the journey only in the clothes he stood up in—he was received by King George I in private audience on May 23rd, and made so favourable an impression on the murderer of his Uncle Philipp that he was invited to hunt at Windsor.

The clue to this visit may have been that Maurice was seeking George Louis' blessing for a certain large scheme then maturing in his restless brain. Great Britain had long had important commercial ties with those Baltic states in which Maurice had recently become interested, and an ambitious man could not afford to ignore the advantages which British prestige and the British fleet bestowed on England's friends.

The truth was that Maurice was in search of new worlds to conquer. He was temporarily out of love with Paris, just as in years gone by he had become bored with Dresden. What had he achieved in France in the past four years, apart from a moderately high rank in a peace-time army? He had begun to look eastwards again, towards the Baltic littoral.

There had developed in Paris an emotional situation similar to that which had driven him from Dresden. Adrienne, like Johanna-Victoria before her, had become reproachful. 'Once more, my dear count,' she wrote to him in London,

> I am saddened at not seeing you. Since you went away I have been oppressed by the most dismal and pitiable notions. I have no other thought in my mind except your return. You never write, and that provokes me. How can you say you love me and then neglect me so? Is it really so difficult to put a few words on paper? A line from you would do much to dispel my uneasiness.

Adrienne called this letter *une epître chagrine*, and she sent many more like it. She must have known that to scold so proud and volatile a man would be fatal, but she loved him. 'I was so happy before your departure,' she wrote; 'will you not try to bring to me something of the happiness which we once enjoyed?'

These elegant, querulous missives taxed Maurice's uncertain patience. From pointed reminders about the precarious state of her health, for which she made him tacitly responsible, she would progress to more lacerating topics. She would recall that the leading princes of the realm, indeed of the world, were still competing for her favours. She would rail at him for the Saxon coarseness that underlay his fine manners. She reproached him for his unfaithfulness, and for his absorption in what she called his 'seraglio'. But above all she harped on his deficiencies as a correspondent.

It is no accident that not a single letter from Maurice to Adrienne is extant. As a writer on military and diplomatic topics he was indefatigable, for these matters had a direct bearing on his material advancement. In affairs of the heart, however, he was curt and circumspect. Adrienne, like most women, delighted to receive love letters; Maurice, whose Uncle Philipp was a horrid example of what might happen to a man foolish enough to set down his amatory feelings on paper, had no inclination to write them. Besides, he could not spell. Here, for example, is a letter written towards the end of his life, at a period when he was a marshal of France and had lived in Paris for over a quarter of a century. The handwriting is firm, large and well-spaced—a handsome, hurried hand. The style flows elegantly and easily. But the spelling, even by the lax standards of the time, is atrocious.

> Madame, j'aime M. de Walfons d'einclination, eindepandanmant de son merite pour la guerre. Je l'ay ecrit a M. le comte d'argenson et luy ay declares que j'an feres mon amis. Je ne fais gere de ses declarations et lon ne maquse pas d'aitre louangeur; einsi vous pouvez aitre assures que j'ores fait pour M. de Walfons se que vous aves eu la bontes de desires pour lui s'il mavet etes possible. Je ne conais sertenement gere se luy que j'ay envoies avec de drapos et n'ay nulle lieson evec luy, mais je n'ai pas oeu faire otrement pour fermer la porte a une cantites de protexion et de soliciteurs tres apres avec qui je me seres fait des querelles si j'aves dones la preference a quelqu'un que l'on sait que j'aimme. J'espere que sais resons vous pareteront bonnes, Madame, et que vous une renderes la justice d'aitre persuades de mon attachement et de mon respect.
>
> M. de Saxe.[51]

It was for letters written in this barbarous French, by a man who spelt the words *je t'aime* as imperfectly as he felt them, that Adrienne longed. And privately she was growing desperate.

She was very ill. In September she told Argental that the doctor had given her only three months to live, adding bitterly that 'one doesn't die of unhappiness'. She appealed to Maurice's friends, particularly Rochemore, to persuade him to treat her more gently. At the same time her private recriminations became more vehement.

> Is this the way you deal with your friends, monsieur? I tell you frankly that I do not like such behaviour. When I have once, after long deliberation, allowed someone to number himself among those whom I love, I cannot bear either to neglect or be neglected. . . . I want you to come to me and to come quickly. Have you forgotten the promises you made to me the last time we were together? . . . If I had written in this way to someone vain and conceited, I should be filled with fear and shame; but, thank God, you I know I can trust. . . .

He ignored her. He was tired of it all. He was tired of watching plays in dingy theatres; tired of half-hearted discussions with *philosophes*; tired of France itself. He was bored by endless inspections of a regiment which was never summoned to war; weary of amusing courtiers at picnics by bending nails into bottle-openers; weary even of hunting the stag and the boar. It was time to move on, to abandon the quagmire of idleness and bankruptcy into which his life in France had sunk. An ambition, a grand design, was surging within him. The diplomatic manoeuvres of recent months had been directed towards a definite end; a tremendous, outrageous opportunity was beckoning him in the east.

He was not yet thirty. He was at the floodtide of his energy and audacity. He was so eager to seize his chance, so sure of it, that he offered to sell his cherished regiment to one of his numerous half-brothers, Count Rutowski. And even before the terms had been properly agreed, he was already lashing his horses into a lather on the snowbound roads to the Baltic.

A throne was vacant. He wanted it.

CHAPTER V

MITAU, 1725-1727

The lives of knight-errants are subject to a thousand
hazards and misfortunes; but on the other side, they may
at any time suddenly become kings and emperors.
                                            DON QUIXOTE

THE vacant throne was that of the duchy of Courland, with its
dependent province of Semigallia or Zemgale, in what is now called
Latvia. The territory was about a hundred miles deep by two
hundred miles wide, and occupied a narrow strip of country south of
the Gulf of Riga. To the west was the Baltic, to the north Livonia and
Estonia; eastwards lay White Russia; Lithuania and Prussia were to
the south [Fig. 2]. It was very small, very bleak and very barren, but
it offered him the prospect of a sceptre and a crown. As soon as he
reached Warsaw, in December 1725, he opened clandestine negotia-

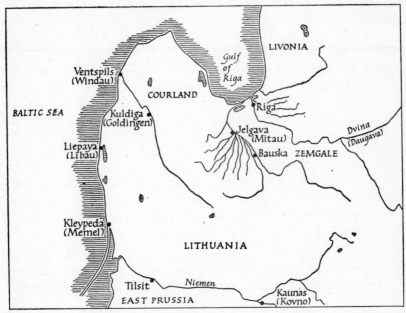

FIG. 2. COURLAND AND SEMIGALLIA

57

tions with the Courlanders in earnest; and clearly at that stage he was receiving tacit encouragement from Augustus.

Since 1561, the duchy of Courland had been an hereditary principality under the suzerainty of the kings of Poland. It was originally colonized, in the middle of the twelfth century, by German merchants from Bremen: and after they succumbed to the Danes, a century later, the three Baltic provinces of Courland, Estonia and Livonia were purchased by a military order, the *Schwert Brüder* or Brethren of the Sword. This order was subsequently merged with the equally rapacious but even more powerful Teutonic Knights.

In 1271, the grand master of the day founded Mitau (Jelgava), later to become the capital of Courland. There he built himself a sombre castle on one of the many islands in the river Aa. But the power of the knights waned in its turn; they suffered a disastrous defeat at Tannenberg in 1410; and eventually, pressed on all sides, their order finally disintegrated in 1560. Their kingdom was then divided. Sweden seized the whole of Estonia, and halved Livonia with the Grand Duchy of Muscovy, while Lithuania went to a Poland which had not yet come to fear the word partition. Gotthard Kettlar, the last grand master, was allowed to become the first Duke of Courland, after acknowledging the suzerainty of King Sigismund of Poland by a *pacta subiectionis*. The era of knightly opportunism was over—at least, until Maurice tried to revive it, by means of his own quaint brand of chivalry.

The dynasty of the Kettlars managed to survive into the eighteenth century, although, with the passage of time, the nominal independence of the small duchy had become precarious. As Polish fortunes ebbed, so did those of Courland; and thus the irony of Courland's plight was that while a powerful Poland would have swallowed her up, a weak Poland could not even protect her. The former prosperity of the rulers of Courland, the 'Dukes of Kurzeme' as the English had called them, had once been based on a lucrative trade with western Europe; but this had now become a thing of the past, and a series of bloody wars began to be fought over the prostrate body politic of the little state.

In 1706 the Russians, after a brief occupation, evacuated the country to the incoming Swedes under Charles XII, devastating the land behind them as they retreated. With unctuous brutality, Marshal Sheremetev informed Peter the Great,

> I beg to inform you that Almighty God and our most Merciful Lady have granted your wish. There is nothing left here for further demolition. From Riga to Balka, everything has been razed to the ground.

It was no wonder that the Courlanders resolved that, whoever ruled them, they did not want it to be the Russians.

A major crisis in the affairs of the unhappy little country occurred in 1711. In that year the last representative of the Kettlar dynasty, Duke Frederick William, died without issue. He left a widow, the former Grand Duchess Anna Ivanovna of Russia, and an old and childless uncle, Duke Ferdinand, whose reign was certain to be brief. The family was not quite extinct, and in fact the last male Kettlar lingered on until 1737, but its days of powers were clearly numbered. It was apparent that the neighbouring states would soon have to choose a new and mutually agreeable candidate for the duchy. The hold of the cantankerous Duke Ferdinand over his territory was uncertain; a Catholic, he had so offended his Lutheran subjects that at one stage they expelled him and forced him to reside at Danzig.

There was much jockeying for position among the interested powers. Russia's interest was well represented by the Duchess Anna, who, although only eighteen, was a niece of the reigning Tsar. Peter the Great had designs on Courland for personal as well as political reasons. It was the native land of his ugly peasant wife, Catherine Alexayevna, who was to succeed him as Catherine I. He termed the other women of his ill-favoured harem his 'aunts', but this woman, whom he loved, he called his 'mother'; and certainly she was one of the few people who could calm him after his maniacal outbursts. But the duchy also had considerable strategic importance, threatening as it did the approaches to his new naval base at Kronstadt and his splendid new capital of St. Petersburg. He therefore instructed his favourite, Prince Menchikov, to sue for the hand of his niece, the young Duchess Anna; and their eventual union would consolidate the Russian grip on the Baltic.

The arrogant and avaricious Menchikov regarded the proposed match as the climax of his spectacular career. He had already risen from baker's boy to the position of chief adviser to the Autocrat of All the Russias; and although he could neither read nor write, he had been gazetted admiral, field marshal, and a prince of the empire. Other pretenders to the throne of Courland would find in him an implacable rival.

For a while, however, the Russians were content to bide their time. In 1717, when the benevolent Augustus of Poland was making a number of 'general settlements', Peter even agreed to the betrothal of Anna Ivanovna and the prince of Saxe-Weissenfels, a cadet of the house of Wettin. But Augustus' best laid plans had a habit of ending where they began, on paper; for although he was himself no stranger to deviousness, the Polish King was no match for the *Realpolitik* of Tsar Peter.

An unexpected rapprochement between Sweden and Russia, the vanquished and the victor, soon prompted Peter to change his mind and to offer the vacancy to a Prussian prince: and he and his new allies also decided that, at the first possible moment, Augustus should again be ejected from the throne of Poland to make way for his old adversary, Stanislas Leczinski.

It was at this delicate moment that Augustus first thought of his son. A warrior and a Lutheran, who could possibly be a better candidate for the duchy than Maurice? The twenty-two-year-old soldier, then living apart from his wife, was surely just the man to win the hot-blooded Anna after a lightning courtship. The Tsar could then be presented with a *fait accompli*. But it was not to be. The auspices were not yet favourable; other candidates, princes of Würtemburg, Anhalt-Zerbst and Hesse-Homburg, were not slow in coming forward, and Maurice disdained to join in the vulgar scramble. Shortly afterwards he left for Paris, for the *Régiment Saxe*, and for Adrienne.

Then, in 1725, the crisis was renewed. The aged Duke Ferdinand fell critically ill at Danzig, and a successor had to be found without delay. And, at this precise moment, there occurred a freakish opportunity to circumvent the all-powerful Russians. The Duchess Anna stated privately but quite unequivocally that she would like to marry the legendary Count Saxe. And since troubles seldom come singly, her sixteen-year-old cousin Elizabeth Petrovna came to the same conclusion at about the same time.

Maurice had as yet met neither of these passionate and peremptory ladies. It was truly an *embarras de princesses*. Whom should he choose —the Tsar's niece or his daughter? Elizabeth was younger, senior in rank, and altogether more attractive. Her Muscovite vivacity was tempered by a Gallic restraint, for she had been bred by a French governess and instructed by a French dancing master. Her proud father had even suggested her as a possible wife for Louis XV; but though she might pass for a Frenchwoman at St. Petersburg, she would have seemed absurdly uncouth to the denizens of Versailles. Still, she clearly represented a promising match [Table 2].

Her cousin Anna, on the other hand, had a duchy to offer. She was the sitting tenant. A great huntswoman, with a passion for wild animals, she evinced a notorious fondness for conducting sexual orgies, naked except for a turban, in her private apartments. Maurice's first impression may well have been favourable. Although her indolence and gluttony had given her a tendency towards fleshiness, she was not without physical charm. Indeed, he may even have feared she might prove too intellectual for his tastes, for she liked to alternate her bouts of self-indulgence with interludes of metaphysical piety. She had also a vein of humour that showed itself in a taste for shooting wild animals from the windows of her palace, and a baroque delight in freaks and monsters. She once decreed that a marriage between a Prince Galitzine and a Kalmuk dwarf should be consummated inside an igloo.

Maurice decided to hasten to Mitau in order to woo Anna. At the same time he shrewdly hedged his bet by sending his portrait to Elizabeth Petrovna, and exhorting the Saxon envoy at St. Petersburg to sustain her interest in him. His prospects here were further enhanced by the fact that the Tsarina Catherine, who had recently ascended the throne of Russia at her husband's death, was known to be sympathetically inclined towards the young Saxon.

In truth Maurice cared little for either Anna or Elizabeth. It was Courland that was the real goal of his desires. The duchy would accord him handsome privileges. As its ruler he would exchange envoys almost on equal terms with his father. He would be licensed to recruit an army of eighteen thousand men, and to raise a navy of forty ships of the line. To the King of France he would be *mon cousin*, and the Emperor of Austria would address him as 'Most Illustrious'. It was a glittering prospect. Mitau was worth an orgy.

On the morning of May 21st 1726, he was on the point of leaving Warsaw for Mitau. Booted and spurred, he was just pulling on his gloves when one of his father's ministers, Count Manteuffel, entered his room hurriedly with the news that permission to embark on the venture had been withdrawn; he was forbidden to proceed to Courland. Maurice stoutly replied that, although he had no wish to disobey the king, if he did not go then and there his plans would be ruined. To the minister's consternation, he thereupon bustled off, and in a matter of minutes, accompanied by a special escort of Lithuanian noblemen, he was on the road to Mitau.

The cause of Augustus' abrupt change of front lay in the steadfast opposition to the venture of most sections of the Polish nobility. It had long been their plan to carve up Courland into palatinates or *voyevodes*. Moreover, the wily Primate of Poland and his episcopal colleagues were strenuously opposed to the enthronement of a Lutheran in the place of the Catholic Duke Ferdinand. Augustus, as usual, was on indifferent terms with both the Roman Church and his nobles. His hold on his Polish throne, even with Charles XII in his grave, was at best shaky, and the Polish estates were only awaiting an opportunity to rid themselves of a king and council to whom Polish was an unknown tongue, and who had to converse with their proud subjects in French or Latin. The Courland issue might endanger Augustus' tenure of his Polish throne; he began to fear that his affectionate support for Maurice might have been extremely ill-advised. Maurice, for his part, tried to placate the Polish Primate in a letter despatched from Mitau on June 30:

I beg you, monsignor, to put yourself for a moment in the place of a nation threatened with the loss of a liberty which it has long enjoyed, and which it does not deserve to lose.

But the Archbishop was quite unmoved by this appeal.[52]

It was made quite plain to Maurice that, if he persisted in his plans, a dismal fate awaited him. His half-brother, the Electoral Prince, the future Augustus the Weak, wrote him a letter which reached him at Kovno in Lithuania.

'I share your sentiment,' wrote the Electoral Prince,

> about a glorious death being preferable to a shameful one; but do you really imagine that the death you will suffer for this present exploit will be particularly glorious?[53]

Maurice, who had pledged his word to the plenipotentiaries from Mitau who had greeted him on his arrival in Warsaw, answered his brother in heady terms.

> I cannot betray a people to whom I have given my promise. I cannot dishonour myself in the eyes of a nation which has placed its trust in me.[54]

He was not, in fact, afraid to fight either a paper war or a real war against the Poles. He clearly supposed at that date that his new friends in Moscow would support his cause, since any attempt on the part of the Courlanders to free themselves from the Poles would surely be to the Russian advantage. He even went so far as to reckon on the assistance of the Russian garrison at Riga.

His entry into his kingdom was a triumph. He was greeted at the border of Courland by hundreds of nobles, headed by the Grand Marshal of Lithuania, and thence escorted to Mitau. A personal regiment of hussars and uhlans was at once placed at his disposal. His first encounter with Anna Ivanovna was a complete success. The Duchess found him even more gallant and personable than report had alleged. His broad physique enchanted the young double-chinned dowager. On June 26th, the great day of his nomination as Duke-Elect, she staged a magnificent banquet for him.

To the Courlanders, noble and peasant alike, he was a saviour and a protector. They liked him for his spirit as much as he admired them for their determination. In spite of Augustus' ban on their assembly, their thirty-two leaders gathered in Mitau to acclaim him as their Duke. 'These Courlanders,' Maurice wrote to Count Friesen,

> are as fiery as the French, and I consider them very valiant. I have no idea how this affair will end; the only certain thing is that I have no intention of backing out. If the Poles attack me, I hope that the Muscovites or the Prussians will lend me twelve or fifteen thousand men. At the moment I am occupied in raising a militia, which could

easily number ten or twenty thousand. There is no lack of officers; the place is crawling with them. At present I am recruiting only Courlanders, but if any Prussians or Germans care to join me I shall be in a splendid position to resist attack. The Russians will certainly help if I marry their princess, although I am not altogether keen on asking for their assistance.[55]

His reservations about Russian intentions were fully justified. The day after his election as ruler-designate, General Sentrovitch rode over with his adjutant to warn him of the imminent arrival of Prince Menchikov, Peter the Great's nominee for the post, with a force of twelve thousand men. At first Maurice was unimpressed; he was busily engaged in despatching fraternal messages to the heads of neighbouring states. It was possibly the happiest week of his entire life. He wrote to the humourless King of Prussia to demand his friendship, irritating that self-important monarch by his condescending tone. He also wrote to the Tsarina, apparently with more success. When the news of his election reached St. Petersburg, the Saxon minister had noted that 'all the females were unable to sleep for joy'. He urged Maurice to strike while the iron was hot, advising him to hasten to the Tsarina's side and ask for the hand of Elizabeth Petrovna. If he wanted to maintain his position in Courland, he had to make up his mind to marry one Grand Duchess or the other without delay.

But Maurice was too deeply involved in affairs at Mitau to seize this opportunity. It was to prove an irreparable blunder. For almost the only time in his life he failed to act promptly and boldly. Meanwhile Menchikov, with that insolent contempt for all authority that had characterized his behaviour since the death of his master, was already sending agents into the duchy with bags of gold to bully and bribe the local magnates. Maurice's principal supporters proved incorruptible. They set their names unanimously to the grand charter of July 5th 1726, by which his election was ratified. This charter enjoined Maurice—and he took its provisions very seriously—to 'conserve the privileges, immunities, prerogatives, liberties, ancient customs and contracts of Courland', and to 'assist, aid and protect the country in every need, necessity and hazard which might arise.'

Legally his position was unassailable; in cold reality it was highly precarious. Two days after the ratification, Menchikov sent Prince Dolgorouki to Mitau with orders to reassemble the Diet and compel it to annul the election. The magnates and deputies refused. Anna Ivanovna, who still had designs on Maurice's person, hurried to Menchikov at Riga and begged him to spare her duchy and its unrepentant Duke-Elect. She managed to win no more than a short postponement. On July 10th, Menchikov himself arrived in Mitau with an escort of three hundred dragoons. His reception by Maurice was marvellously cool, for when it came to masquerades the two men were equally proficient. Maurice drove to Menchikov's lodging in a cavalcade of twelve coaches, magnificently arrayed as Duke-Elect, and was conducted with all due pomp into the Russian's presence. The subsequent interview was both protracted and acrimonious. As Maurice wrote later to the Austrian ambassador at St. Petersburg:

> Menchikov came here posing as the arbiter of human destiny. He was very surprised that such wretched creatures as the Courlanders were so ungrateful and heedless of their own interests as to refuse the honour of being ruled by him, thereby atoning for their sin in choosing me to begin with. In vain did they tell him politely that they were not at liberty to receive his orders. He merely retorted that they did not know what they were saying, and sought to prove it by laying about him with his cane.[56]

The main victims of his blows were the chancellor of Courland and the Grand Marshal of Lithuania. He raved at them, beat them, and threatened to exile them to Siberia. He announced that unless they disposed of their Duke-Elect within ten days, he would devastate their country as his countrymen had devastated it twenty years before him. But they stood firm. That night Maurice and his friends barricaded themselves in his palace at Mitau and made ready to receive the onslaught of the Russian dragoons. As he afterwards told Friesen,

> My little party was not in the least intimidated. The dispositions I made, and the resolute bearing of my companions, convinced me that we would not be attacked with impunity. Luckily it turned out that the Russians had been placed at the ready primarily for their own protection and that of their leader.[57]

Menchikov's bluff had been called, and he retired next day to Riga, where he worked off his frustration by thrashing his servants and lambasting his *aides-de-camp*. Maurice retaliated by astutely urging the Chancellor and the Grand Marshal to complain to their supreme protector, Augustus of Poland, of the Russian prince's infamous behaviour. He also sent a full account of the incident to Baron Ostermann, the Russian foreign minister, whom he knew to be jealous of Menchikov. Neither Augustus nor Ostermann were slow in raising the matter with the Tsarina.

Catherine was angry. Prompted by her daughter Elizabeth and by Anna Ivanovna, who had journeyed from Mitau to St. Petersburg to plead Maurice's cause, the Tsarina disowned Menchikov. Maurice was therefore reprieved, not for the first time, by female intervention, and meanwhile at Mitau his determination was beginning to infect his followers and well-wishers. His father, for example, was increasingly delighted by his bastard's bravado. Whatever his public embarrassment, Augustus was greatly amused in private by the anguish which Maurice's exploits were causing the prelates and magnificoes of War-saw. 'It is contrary to my express wishes,' as he told his advisers, 'that Maurice has embarked on this enterprise; all the same, now that he is in the middle of it, I wish him success with all my heart, provided that he does not damage the fundamental interests of the Polish Republic.'[58]

In September 1726, Maurice's future seemed almost secure. He still enjoyed support at St. Petersburg, where the Saxon minister had persuaded Ostermann to agree to the eventual marriage of the comte de Saxe with either 'Nan' (Anna) or 'Lisa' (Elizabeth); it had even been suggested that he might marry a daughter of Menchikov him-self, if the prospect of union with either Grand Duchess came to nothing.

But all this lay in the future; and under the benign influence of the Baltic autumn his mood had become expansive. At the age of twenty-nine, it really seemed that he had achieved his overriding ambition to make himself acceptable to the crowned heads of Europe. He was a Prince, with Courland as his fief. He wrote in lyrical, im-perial vein to Friesen of his future plans:

> I intend to follow to the letter the advice you gave me, namely to establish a corps of cadets to act as a seedbed for the upper echelons. I shall also reinforce the ranks of the nobility, organise a militia, build schools, and maintain towards my country the attitude which you recommend. I propose to live very simply, for my domains are plunged in debt and ravaged by disease and warfare. It may be possible to revive them in a few years by means of industry and economy, and I shall give this task my undivided attention. Whatever I do shall be done without ostentation. I have always abhorred the display of small courts. Nothing is more ridiculous than misplaced grandeur that is greeted with a snigger by the lower, and with scorn by the upper, part of society. My watchword shall be 'plenty of bayonets and muskets in the armoury, and only a handful of courtiers in the ante-chamber.' But in writing all this to you, my dear count, I am aware that I am still merely dreaming. I have not yet reached my goal, and what I have set down here may be called, with justice, the building of castles in Spain.[59]

A dream, alas, it proved to be. Yet like all the other dreams of this strange man, it was not totally unreal. None of his *rêveries* were complete chimaeras. If he had been left to himself he might well have turned Courland into a model duchy, and have ruled as a benevolent despot. In these few sunny weeks of sovereignty he seemed to be almost on the point of providing unhappy Courland with a stable and intelligent government. He would have made an excellent ruler. He not only possessed the external attributes of a leader of men, but also a distinct natural ability to govern. In the words of Taillandier, 'in a century where there were few real kings, Maurice was a king by vocation'.[60] He possessed energy, optimism, good nature, the capacity to make bold and imaginative decisions, and an incomparable gift for organization. It was part of his personal tragedy that an accident of birth prevented him from developing these constructive talents to the full.

On October 11th, 1726, a council was convened at Dresden to resolve the crisis in Courland. A decree was drafted for the royal signature, enjoining Maurice to quit his duchy immediately, and to surrender to the Polish chancellery the diploma of his election.

Augustus had bowed to the inevitable. It would have been useful and entertaining to have had as vassal a fellow Saxon and a favourite son, but the opposition of the Polish nobility was by now irresistible. The decree was unequivocal: 'We have sent orders to Count Saxe to retire forthwith from the duchy, and to concern himself no further with its affairs under any pretext, pretension, or title whatsoever.' The king signed the document, adding in his own hand, 'I am sorry that I have to ask you for your diploma, but I will make up the sacrifice later in some other fashion.'[61]

The decree took Maurice by surprise. It reached him as he was on his way to Grodno, where he had high hopes of successfully thrashing out the Courland question with the Polish Diet. To deaden the clamour of his opponents, he had provided himself with, as he told Friesen, 'plenty of cotton wool to stuff in his ears'; but he counted confidently on winning over the Diet to his cause. After all, under its rules a single dissident vote could thwart the will of the majority, and it was not unreasonable to suppose that a dramatic personal appearance before the Diet would at least secure him a breathing space.

His reply to his father's summons was succinct.

> Sire, on my arrival here I was given the letter with which your Majesty has honoured me. It is with extreme sorrow that I find myself compelled either to disobey you or dishonour myself. I beg your Majesty to appreciate my predicament, if your Majesty can bring yourself to do so. I shall meet my fate with composure.[62]

He pointed out that he had the honour to hold 'a very distinguished position in the armies of his Most Christian Majesty (i.e., the King of France), where disgraceful conduct is allowed no excuse, extenuation or concealment'.[63]

A worse disappointment was to come. His presence at Grodno had no effect at all on the swift and prearranged deliberations of the Diet. The duchy of Courland was declared to be henceforward indissolubly

united with Poland. On November 9th, the Diet declared his election
to be null, branding his supporters as traitors.[64] His attempt to play
off Russia against Poland had been a total failure.

True to his nature, he still refused to admit defeat. He hastened to
Mitau, and there assumed a posture of defiance. On November 25th,
he wrote to Friesen,

> Well, my dear count, here I am an outlaw with a price on my head.
> God help me if I am caught; I should get less mercy than a wolf. To
> say that I am profoundly wounded is simply the truth, for a splendid
> career was opening out before me. In any case, it is quite intolerable to
> treat me in such a manner. What have I done to be hunted down like a
> criminal? Do they really want to drive me into defending myself? Very
> well then, I shall do so. As long as I can grip the hilt of my sword, I
> shall seek to destroy my adversaries. The alternatives are to conquer
> or to die. I have only four hundred men, but I shall use them, and when
> they are killed I shall try to find more. I shall fight as long as I can still
> draw breath. If you should know how I can get hold of any officers
> or soldiers, send them to me; they will share my fortunes, good or bad.[65]

He wrote to his mother, who had eagerly followed the course
of the struggle from Quedlinburg, and who had sold most of
her jewels to raise money for his cause, to ask her to persuade a
Swedish cousin, Count Löwenhaupt, to join him at Mitau. He recalled
that many years before, his uncle, General Löwenhaupt, had earned
the title of 'defender of Riga'; and his son would be a useful man to
have beside him if Mitau were under siege. 'I have too much on
hand,' he wrote; 'I cannot supervise military and political matters at
the same time. Löwenhaupt can share the burden with me. It will not
be necessary for him to send in his papers to the Swedish Government,
as no one will reproach him for going to the aid of a kinsman.'[66] He
had remembered in his predicament that he was half Swedish. Surely
the Swedes would help him now?

In another letter to Maria Aurora, he declared that he would resist
any force despatched by the Poles. 'Who knows,' he exclaimed, 'if
the world will not see in me another Coriolanus?' In similar mood, he
assured her that in him 'she would see reborn the soul of "Old
Königsmark" who had once held in check all the armies of
Germany.'[67]

Löwenhaupt never came. A circumspect man, who eventually
became head of the Swedish Diet, he preferred to send in his stead a
relation by marriage, Count Axel Cronhielm. Cronhielm, an impressionable youth, set sail eagerly for Mitau, expecting to find Maurice
at the head of a nation in arms. His enthusiasm was considerably
dampened when he discovered that the ducal cohorts consisted of no
more than a hundred badly-equipped men-at-arms, bored and immobilized by the northern winter. Cronhielm reported to Maria Aurora that

her son was now 'reduced to spending most of the day reading in bed', adding that his favourite book was *The History of the Ingenuous Knight, Don Quixote of La Mancha.*

In his extremity, Maurice had begun to hatch any number of crazy diplomatic schemes. He considered enlisting the aid of George I, by offering the British navy a permanent base in Courland. This plan threatened to bring down on the heads of the new Coriolanus and his father the military coalition of Prussia, Sweden, and Russia. In great alarm Augustus and his ministers urged Maurice to retire from Mitau while he was still a free agent, before the Russians sent him 'to write his memoirs in some part of Siberia'. They offered him a thousand ducats in cash to pay his fare back to Paris.

Maurice's rejoinder was to blockade himself in Mitau. He could still count, he thought, on the good offices of his Romanov admirers. But in January 1727 even this last prop was kicked away.

He had quarrelled with the Duchess Anna. According to report, she had caught him late one night carrying one of her ladies-in-waiting on his shoulders across the snowy courtyard of her royal palace, in an attempt to prevent her footsteps betraying the fact that they had been together. The truth is probably more commonplace. The Duchess' infatuation had begun to cool some months earlier, when it became clear that Maurice would never be anything but a political liability. She was a hard-headed woman: she need never want for men, but she possessed only one duchy. Courland was a beggarly sort of place, yet at that time she could hardly have guessed that fate intended to place her within three years on the throne of Russia itself. In 1727 she was merely anxious to keep Courland out of the hands of Menchikov, a tussle in which Maurice was no longer a useful ally.

And Menchikov's star was now at its zenith. The Tsarina had wavered for many months over the problem of Courland. She had not been able to make up her mind whether to give it to Maurice, or to one of her peasant relations, or to Menchikov's son. Then, very suddenly, she died, leaving as her successor Peter II, a mere child of twelve. And as leader of the High Council, Menchikov overnight became the real ruler of Russia.

Maurice was far away from Mitau when this blow fell. He had slipped away from Courland some days before, and was busily travelling round Europe *incognito* in an effort to drum up recruits for his cause. After a fruitless meeting with his colourless brother, the Electoral Prince, he was called to Bialystok for a meeting with his sick father. Frederick Augustus welcomed the prodigal with all his old affection. As Maurice wrote to his mother, 'I am still in good standing with the King. Everything passed off as though nothing had happened, and he behaved as though there was no such place as Courland. It was never even mentioned.'[68]

He sent a shady operator at Liége every sou he could raise to enlist in his service every deserter from every army in Europe. Three thousand men were needed, but less than half that number were forthcoming. They were shipped from Lübeck to Mitau, and on the way half even of that rascally battalion decamped—deserters from an army of deserters.

By midsummer he was back at Mitau, ready to perform the last act of the tragi-comedy. He did not have long to wait. Already deposed by Poland, he was now to be destroyed by Russia. The almighty Menchikov, whose daughter was now betrothed to the young Tsar, gave a Russian army instructions to expel Maurice from Courland without ceremony. General Lascy thereupon sent Maurice an abrupt message to leave Mitau 'before he was transported to a landscape with a wider horizon'.

Maurice's army consisted of twelve officers, four hundred infantry-men, ninety-eight cavalrymen, and thirty-two servants, augmented by his handful of vagabonds from the Low Countries. With these five hundred men, he made ready to resist Lascy's eight thousand trained troops. He ferried his curious force across a lake to an island near Windau, where they dug themselves in. Playing for time, he asked Lascy for ten days' grace. He was given forty-eight hours to surrender.

Even Maurice could see that the game was up. Vainglorious he may have been, but he would never be so vain as to throw away the life of a single soldier unnecessarily. In later years, when he was a Marshal of France, he once overheard a lieutenant-general urge an assault upon an enemy post on the grounds that it would only cost the lives of half a dozen grenadiers. He rounded on the speaker, and declared that he only wished it would cost the lives of half a dozen lieutenant-generals. True to these principles, he now paraded his little garrison and gave them permission to lay down their arms, trusting, with a confidence that was not misplaced, that Lascy would prove a man of honour and deal with them leniently. He told them that, as a man with a price on his head, he could not risk falling into Russian hands. 'They will never take me,' he declared, 'neither today nor tomorrow.'

On August 19th 1727, Duke Maurice set off towards Windau, the modern Ventspils, in search of a ship that could carry him to safety. The only personal possession he retained was the case containing the diploma of his election, which the Polish Diet had already impounded but never obtained. This document was guarded through bog and brake by Beauvais, his faithful body-servant. It was to be sedulously preserved by Maurice for the rest of his life. Neither threats nor cajolery, not flattery nor money, could induce him to part with it. In after years he was fond of taking out the useless document and poring over it; and to the end of his days he maintained his claim to the ducal crown of Courland, insisting always on receiving the honours befitting a ruling prince. He always styled himself 'Duke-Elect of Courland and Semigallia', the title that appeared on his official papers issued in Flanders over twenty years later. It figured on the commemorative medal issued three years before his death. It was chiselled on his monument in Strasbourg.

Menchikov had won; but his triumph was short-lived. After four months of supreme power, during which he submitted Russia to a reign of terror, he fell from grace and was banished to Siberia only three weeks after Maurice had fled from Courland.

As for Maurice, there are aspects of his failure at Mitau which are not easy to explain. At the beginning he could almost certainly have consolidated his position by marrying Anna Ivanovna. His refusal to do so was partly a result of the double game he was playing, holding her at arm's length while his allies at St. Petersburg strove to conclude a match with Elizabeth Petrovna. But perhaps he had never had any real intention of marrying anyone. His early experience of marriage had been dismal. And, although he was anything but a puritan, the palace at Mitau was clearly an unsavoury place. His own tastes may have been a little over-emphatic by Parisian standards, but the libidinous nastiness of the Russian royal family was too much even for him.

It is also possible that he had been secretly planning to make Adrienne his duchess. He had thought of her fondly in his northern exile, and she had supported him nobly in his bid for power. She had not rebuked him for leaving Paris, even though she may have suspected that he had done so partly in order to get away from her. Instead, she had pawned her jewels, just as Maria Aurora had done, in order to provide him with forty thousand livres. Other women, including two Polish countesses, had made a similar sacrifice—but Adrienne was not rich, and her gift was therefore the more magnanimous. It put her to considerable embarrassment. In April 1728, she was forced to tell a creditor that she was bankrupt and could not repay him. 'I had had hopes of doing so,' she explained, 'and I could have done, had it not been for this affair of M. de Saxe.'

As for Courland, without Maurice she was doomed. First she became a satellite of the Russian empire, and eventually, when the Third Partition destroyed Poland altogether, an insignificant satrapy.

CHAPTER VI

PARIS, 1727-1730

On mourra seul.
PASCAL

MAURICE could not bring himself to return immediately to Adrienne, and resume his employment in France as *maréchal de camp*. She had to contain her impatience for more than a year while Maurice, depressed and tormented, wandered about Europe. For some weeks after his expulsion from Courland, he was obsessed with the idea of raising enough mercenary troops to return and drive out Lascy. He went to the Low Countries to engage them; and he was in Holland when a further blow struck him.

On February 16th 1728, his mother died at Quedlinburg, her end hastened by the excitements of the previous year. She had run hither and thither on his behalf; she had undertaken a vast burden of correspondence with those who might have been remotely useful to her son. His failure assisted her decline. In her last letter to her old antagonist Count Flemming, she declared, 'If Count Saxe has done wrong, I beg you to remember that he is driven by the spur of honour and ambition that ever goads him.'[69] Whatever her faults, she had understood Maurice as no one else ever had, or ever would. In April he arrived at Quedlinburg to pay his last respects to *l'Adventurière*. She lay in her coffin in a white brocade dress, wearing a pearl-embroidered cap *à la Marie Stuart*, just as King Frederick William IV of Prussia was to see her when he ordered her tomb to be opened in 1843. She had bequeathed to Maurice all that she had. It amounted to fifty-two *écus*.

Part of the summer he passed at Danzig; still possessed by his dream of glory, he rented a house there as a *point d'appui* for Courland. As a diversion, his sympathetic father, who had also suffered deposition in his time, took him to Berlin on a state visit to the King of Prussia. There he found temporary alleviation for his depression in banquets, in hunting, and in military discussions with the Prussian Crown Prince, the future Frederick the Great. A minor satisfaction in these sorry months was the news of the death at Vienna of his old

71

tormentor, Flemming. He was at the Moritzburg with his father when they heard the news. The despatch related that owing to carelessness the coffin had been made a foot short, and Countess Flemming, as avaricious as her late husband, had ordered the corpse's legs to be broken rather than have the expense of paying for a new coffin. Maurice, with a rare flash of malice, remarked that she had only done in death what his father should have done in life. Augustus rebuked him. 'Count,' he said, 'one should never revenge oneself on a dead enemy.'[70]

By autumn his distemper had abated, and he was ready to return to France. In October 1728, after his coach had broken down thirty leagues away, he entered Paris as a conquering hero. If he had put off his return from fear of public ridicule he had no need to be apprehensive. His exploits in Courland had only added piquancy to the legends already clustered about his name. He was delighted; he felt that he had come home.

After the first excitement was over, he resigned himself to enforced idleness. Life must have been stale and unprofitable after the furious activity of previous months. He thought to stop his mind from dwelling on his misfortunes by occupying himself with practical concerns. He threw himself into his old pastime of designing new weapons of war, or adapting old ones to novel uses. He turned too to civilian problems, devising a barge with a revolutionary system of propulsion that was intended to bring water traffic to Paris from the Channel more rapidly and economically than ever before. Later in the year, he patented the design with the *Académie des Sciences*. He possessed his full share of the spirit of scientific enquiry characteristic of his age, proving himself if not a son, then at least a natural son, of the Enlightenment.

Many of the projects that he developed during his second period in Paris were to be incorporated in his book, *Mes Rêveries*. Written at about this time, it was circulated privately in his lifetime, and only published after his death. Some of his ideas were decidedly odd, but many were based on sound knowledge. In these months he more than made amends for the scholastic shortcomings of his youth. This was recognized when he was elected a fellow of the Royal Society of London. It is unfortunate that the fantastic and airy element in his spirit sometimes concealed the real cogency of his thought. He was often held up to ridicule on this account, both in his own lifetime and after. Carlyle, for example, was to dismiss the remarkable *Mes Rêveries* as 'a strange military farrago dictated, as I should think, under opium'.[71] This was quite unjust. When, in later life, he was given an opportunity to put some of the book's ideas into practice on the battlefield, the laughter of his contemporaries quickly petered out.

Voltaire too was guilty of injustice, when he observed in a letter to Maurice's physician, the celebrated Sénac de Meilhan, that 'it is strange that Count Saxe makes war with such superior intelligence, when he is so chimerical in everything else'.[72] Certainly Maurice little resembled his friends the *savants*, with their dry and detached attitude to life. His brooding mind was alternately occluded and illuminated by the passionate resentments and fiery ambitions which spurred him on. Learned and sophisticated scholars of the stamp of Fontenelle and Marsais often marvelled, as they listened to his highly original conversations, that so intelligent a man, albeit a German, should be so much the prey of romantic obsessions. As he tried to interest the salons of Paris in the glories of Mitau, his listeners may well have felt as the curate and the barber did when Don Quixote delivered his great rodomontade about knight errantry.

> Take him but off from his romantic humour, discourse with him of any other subject, and you will find him to handle it with a great deal of reason, and show himself, by his conversation, to have very clear and entertaining conceptions: insomuch, that if knight errantry bears no relation to his discourse, there is no man but will esteem him for his vivacity of wit, and strength of judgment.[73]

Soon after his return to Paris, his scientific investigations were interrupted by another of the comic interludes that constantly plagued him. His recent adventures had so much enhanced his already considerable physical attractions that women found it difficult to keep away from him. One of them was the celebrated Louise-Henriette-Françoise de Guise-Lorraine, fourth wife of the duc de Bouillon. She had been married two years previously, at the age of seventeen, to a groom of sixty. It had not proved an ideal match. Mme de Bouillon had already become famous for the number of her affairs, most of which were with actors and opera singers; but it is only fair to add that she had also become the mistress of the comte de Clermont.

At Easter 1729, Mme de Bouillon was a guest at Maurice's hunting-lodge. Because the theatres were always closed during Holy Week, Adrienne was already in residence. The young duchess promptly made overtures to Maurice, and was put out when he failed to respond. Like herself, he also had close relations with the *Comédie* and the *Opéra*—with the former in the person of Adrienne, with the latter in the shape of a pretty soprano called Marie-Claude-Nicole Cartou.

His affair with Marie Cartou caused Adrienne acute distress. In July 1729, she received an anonymous letter.

> Mademoiselle, you will be surprised that someone unknown to you should write to beg you to go tomorrow to the terrace of the Luxembourg at half past five; but if you do so, you will find a person who will give you a full explanation. You will recognize him by this sign. He will tap his hat four times on approaching you.

Accompanied by two friends, Adrienne did as she was instructed. She discovered that the hat-tapper was a small hunch-backed priest, the abbé Bouret. He told her, with the utmost politeness, that there was a plot to murder her, and that he himself had been hired to poison her. Her thoughts flew to the *Opéra*: it must be La Cartou who wanted to kill her. 'No, madame,' replied Bouret; 'the person responsible is the duchesse de Bouillon.'

Adrienne at once consulted Maurice. They decided to let the matter drop, and advised Bouret to do the same. Evidently they took his story with a grain of salt; but two days later he returned with the news that the night before he had been waylaid by two masked men, thrashed for betraying the plot to Adrienne, and then offered an even larger sum to carry on with the original plan. He was told to go next day to the garden of the Tuileries, and there collect a packet of lozenges from a certain yew hedge. At the instigation of Maurice and Adrienne, he did so, returning with the lozenges. The smell of three of them was particularly pungent, and the whole matter was laid straightaway before the lieutenant of police.

When the government analyst tried to determine the properties of the lozenges, by the time-honoured method of giving them to the dog, the animal survived. None the less the little priest was bundled off to gaol, and held there under a *lettre de cachet*. In the interrogation that followed, he told a curious story. He said that he possessed a talent for painting miniatures, and that a chance introduction had led to a commission from the duchesse de Bouillon. At the first interview she had confided in him her passion for Maurice, and had dictated to him a letter for Adrienne. Purporting to come from a prince of the blood, it suggested that Adrienne should end her liaison with the Saxon. At a second meeting, the duchesse proposed a course of action that was far more radical. She asked him to insinuate himself into Adrienne's company and poison her.

The rest of his story pursued the same odd course. On the following evening, he said, he had been asked to meet two of the duchesse's retainers near the Pont Royal. They were masked. He was then escorted to the *quai des Théatins*, where they found the duchesse sitting on the cobblestones, dressed in ball attire, and accompanied by her step-daughter. She was in tears. She offered him six thousand livres if he would administer some lozenges to Adrienne which would render her indifferent to Maurice. He decided to accept this offer, on the definite understanding that nothing more lethal would be required of him. Next morning, he was summoned to the Hôtel de Bouillon. The duchesse showed him an engraving of Apollo and a goddess, naked and in the act of love, and asked him to paint a similar portrait of Maurice and herself. The little priest eventually agreed, but before he had time to set brush to canvas he was ordered to meet the two masked men again. They told him in peremptory terms to hurry on with the affair of the lozenges. Yes, he asked them uneasily, but what if he killed his victim? He was assured that in that case he had nothing to fear, and that a fast chaise would be at hand to whirl him away to another country. Thoroughly scared by this sinister turn of events, he hurried home and penned his anonymous note to Adrienne.

The authorities did everything in their power to hush up the scandal, but without success. Soon all Paris had heard the rumour that the duchesse had tried to poison Adrienne. The wretched Bouret was quickly transferred from Saint-Lazare to the Bastille, where he remained for two whole years. He was allowed neither fresh linen nor painting materials; characteristically, the only person to remember his existence was Adrienne. She wrote to him often, and occasionally sent him welcome presents, which included *louis d'or*, books, and Queen of Hungary water.

The principals in this small tragi-comedy have kept their own counsel. It is now almost impossible to distinguish fact from fiction. It is clear that the duchesse was impulsive enough to contemplate rash, even madcap actions in order to achieve her ends. Equally, much of Bouret's story was probably nonsense, though by no means all of it. In any case, whatever his actual part in the episode, he paid for it dearly.

In the end the duchesse had her way. Maurice made her his mistress. Adrienne, diseased and *épuisée*, touched total despair. The joy with which she had greeted Maurice's return the previous winter had now turned almost to hatred. It is sad to have to chronicle the last darkened months of their relationship. By now increasingly hysterical, she was unable to prevent herself from creating embarrassing scenes in public. During a performance of *Phèdre*, the play which had originally brought them together, she rounded on Maurice as he sat in his usual place on the stage. It was the moment when Phèdre begs Hippolyte: '*au défaut de ton bras, prête-moi ton épée.*' Instead of seizing the weapon of Hippolyte, she rushed at Maurice, snatched his sword, and improved on Racine by trying to stab him in the stomach. It was altogether an unforgettable performance.[74]

Three weeks later, again in the character of Phèdre, she gave the now expectant spectators another thrill. Before an audience of twelve hundred people, who immediately grasped her meaning and applauded her to the echo, she turned to where the duchesse de Bouillon was watching from a box and spat out the lines:

Je ne suis point de ces femmes hardies
Qui, goûtant dans le crime une tranquille paix,
Ont su se faire un front qui ne rougit jamais.

It was all very pathetic and very theatrical: but Adrienne had not very long to live. When he realized the truth, Maurice left the duchesse to return to Adrienne. In his own rough way he had truly loved her, and as the end approached he was determined to prove his devotion.

In December 1729, shortly before her death, Adrienne wrote a moving letter to an unknown friend. 'Do you think,' she asked gently,

that you are the only person suffering from a cold? The mishap is wide-spread and I too am not exempt. Yesterday I came home with a fever. The audience could hardly hear me speak, yet this morning I have to rehearse *Ino*. As soon as I return, I shall retire to bed. I am sorry that your ill-health will rob me of the pleasure of seeing you. I never feel that I am alive at all unless I can be with my friends, and that life is too short to be deprived of this, the one real pleasure which it affords. M. le comte de Saxe has also been ill. He has been bled, and has had fever. He believes he is better, and insists on going out soon because of the barge. It is finished now, and tomorrow will be a great day—except, I imagine, for me. Try to come to see us, but wrap up carefully and take care of yourself. Our friend Argental is also indisposed, and M. de Foncemagne is very ill. What a catalogue of misfortunes!

The barge of which Adrienne wrote was the craft which Maurice had designed on a revolutionary principle of propulsion. The day of the launching was a fiasco, as the vessel proved an utter failure. It had cost Maurice 10,000 *écus*.

Adrienne appeared on the stage for the last time three days before her death. Mlle Aïssé, who was also in the cast that night, says that she was in great pain, and afterwards took to her bed with a severe stomach disorder. After much suffering, she died in a final violent paroxysm at eleven o'clock on the morning of March 20th, 1730.

Accounts differ as to whether Maurice was present or not at her death bed. According to a hostile witness, when she lay dying he was outside in the stables, arranging for the sale of her horses. It seems certain that he never left her side. The most reliable authority states categorically that Maurice, Voltaire, and a surgeon called Faget were with her at the moment of death.

It seemed suspicious that a woman known to have been in an advanced stage of pulmonary consumption should have succumbed to an intestinal haemorrhage. Mlle Aïssé at once launched a whispering campaign against the duchesse de Bouillon. The rumour was promptly scotched by Voltaire, who wrote and signed the following record:

> Mlle Lecouvreur died in my arms of an inflammation of the entrails, and it was I myself who suggested a post-mortem. The accusations of Mlle Aïssé are popular suppositions without any basis.[75]

The rumours were revived by the subsequent actions of authority, because for some reason Adrienne was denied a decent burial. At midnight on the day after her death, her body was bundled into a cab and trundled off to an anonymous resting-place. The incident was not unprecedented, but it roused the curiosity of many of those who had followed the Bouret affair.

From time immemorial the burial of actors in France had been subject to stringent regulations. The Church, which controlled all the cemeteries, had ordained that if an actor or actress were dying and expressed a wish to receive Christian burial, he or she must first abjure the acting profession in the presence of a notary as well as a priest. He or she was then required to make a solemn undertaking in the event of recovery not to return to the stage.

Adrienne had long ago shown much anxiety about the disposal of her remains. She had promised her parish priest, M. Languet of Saint-Sulpice, the gift of a diamond and six thousand livres if he would bury her in consecrated ground. He may have been offended by the offer, for although on her death bed she repeatedly sent for him, he failed to appear.[76] (One apologist maintains that he came but could do nothing, as she refused to give 'any promise to repent of her scandalous profession'.[77]) Yet her will revealed that she had left a thousand livres for the poor of the parish, another thousand livres to the nuns of the convent where she had been educated, and a further two hundred livres to the *Petits-Augustins* to pay for masses for the repose of her soul. There is no evidence that any of these godly people refused to share in the wages of her sin.

In practice, although actors were often refused the ministrations of a priest, few eminent members of the profession were denied proper burial. Such actors as Rosimond, Champmeslé, Lavoy, Le Grand, and Molière himself, were decently interred. Why, then, was the Church's supreme contempt reserved for the fragile remains of Adrienne? It is said that the Archbishop of Paris upheld Languet's action, and that M. de Maurepas, the Minister of the Interior, had told the lieutenant of police that Cardinal Fleury, the Prime Minister, was also in agreement. One is at a loss to know why. Neither Fleury nor the young

Louis XV were in the slightest degree bigoted. This was not the France of Mme de Maintenon.

According to Voltaire, the place of the burial was a pit filled with quicklime at the end of the rue de Bourgogne. When he was sixty-five, and Adrienne had been dead for over thirty years, he could still write with horror of the events of that cold March night. Indeed, there is a tradition that three days after the disposal of the body he addressed a protest meeting of actors, at which he urged them to strike until they received the right to enjoy civilized burial. It is said that they gave a promise to do so, but failed to keep it. It was Voltaire who composed her funeral oration, hailing her as 'that inimitable actress who practically invented the art of speaking from the heart, and who put sentiment and truth where before there had been merely pomposity and rhetoric'.

Adrienne's death was a searing experience for the great mocker of religion. For the rest of his life he was to harp on it. He referred to it in a bitter passage in *Candide*;[78] and his great dread in old age was that he too would be 'thrown into the gutter, like poor Lecouvreur'. It was to be one reason which prompted him at Ferney to superintend the construction of his own tomb. He claimed that he had become so frail in old age that two little boys would be able to carry him to his sepulchre, adding that he 'hoped to hop into it without permission from the ecclesiastics'.

Maurice, who had already witnessed many terrible sights in his life and would witness many more, was also ineradicably impressed by the circumstances of Adrienne's death. When he too lay dying, he was to leave a last instruction that his body was to be 'consumed by quicklime', just as Adrienne's had been. This simple request is instinct with pathos. *Sunt lacrimae rerum et mentem mortalia tangunt*. It was a long, long time since the moment when a youth of twenty-four, sitting on the stage of the *Comédie-française*, had watched the Queen of Athens come stepping into the soft light of the chandeliers.

> *N'allons point plus avant. Demeurons, chère Œnone,*
> *Je ne me soutiens plus, ma force m'abandonne.*

CHAPTER VII

———

PHILIPPSBURG, 1730-1735

La guerre est ma patrie,
Mon harnais, ma maison,
Et en toute saison
Combattre, c'est me vie.
LE SOLDAT FRANÇOIS

SEVEN weeks after Adrienne's death in 1730 Maurice went to Saxony to attend the festivities at Mühlberg. Here, in a huge military encampment on the banks of the Elbe, was to be celebrated one of the most memorable fêtes of the *ancien régime*. It had been devised by Augustus II of Poland to honour Frederick William I of Prussia, whose alliance he was at that time soliciting. A friendship had sprung up between them when the Prussian king had recently visited Dresden *incognito* to attend the festivities that accompanied the wedding of one of Augustus' favourite mistresses, the Countess von Cosel. Augustus hoped for great things from Mühlberg. He urgently needed an ally to forestall the dismemberment of Poland which an unexpected *entente* between Vienna and St. Petersburg seemed to presage.

The camp was fitted out with an almost oriental splendour, in an attempt to impress the parsimonious Prussians with the wealth of their new friends. It was to be an eighteenth-century Field of Cloth-of-Gold. The Saxon and Prussian armies marched into camp at the end of May, and throughout the whole of June there followed a succession of balls, pageants, manoeuvres and tournaments. It was estimated that over three hundred thousand people were involved, all of them eating, carousing and roistering at the expense of the King of Poland. The gala uniform of the humblest Saxon subaltern cost a thousand crowns. The silken tents set aside for Augustus' personal use were valued at ten million livres, and every evening supper was served at tables laden with twenty-four covers in gold and three hundred in silver. It was on this occasion that Augustus was to trade a regiment of horse for the coveted 'dragoon vases' from Berlin. The whole affair was an outstanding example of what a modern economist would call conspicuous waste.

79

Augustus had bestowed on Maurice an equipage as expensive as that of his legitimate heir. Maurice signified his appreciation of this handsome gesture by excelling at the various contests and exercises in which the scions of the houses of Hohenzollern and Wettin were expected to compete. He particularly shone in the great hunt with which the festivities ended. On this occasion no fewer than eleven hundred wild animals were killed.

Maurice did not travel to Mühlberg alone. He took with him the little singer from the *Opéra* of whom the scarcely dead Adrienne had been so jealous. Perhaps he was callous; perhaps he was unsentimental; perhaps he was lonely. In the words of a contemporary biographer, 'He was the most gallant prince of the age, and love is a necessary ingredient in the character of a hero.'[79] Maurice's need for women did not necessarily detract from the genuineness of his grief for Adrienne. And Marie was as sympathetic as she was entertaining, famous for her vivacity and repartee. Adrienne, we are told, had been 'extremely sought after in the best houses of Paris, and even at Court'.[80] But even Adrienne had not enjoyed the distinction now bestowed on Marie, a distinction denied to most courtesans except the *maîtresses en titre*, of supping at the same table as two kings and their heirs apparent.

The bond between Augustus and Maurice had become very close. During the years 1730-1732, the latter passed more time at Dresden than he had during the whole of the previous decade. In 1730 his father settled on him the estate of Tautenburg, which his mother had unsuccessfully sought for him at the time of his formal recognition as count of Saxony in 1711. It was an excellent property, worth ten thousand crowns a year. It was also an earnest of his parent's tender regard.

'This king,' as the author of *La Saxe Galante* observed, 'was without real feeling; paternal affection took the place of love in him.'[81] In his old age Augustus delighted to honour the half-dozen of his three hundred children whom he had consented to recognize. They were his favourites, the handsomest, cleverest and least docile of his progeny, the fruit of his most celebrated passions. First came Maurice himself, a stocky replica of his prepotent sire. Eight years his junior was George, the chevalier de Saxe, Augustus' son by a Duchess of Saxe-Teschen. At first a knight of the order of St. John of Jerusalem, the chevalier later left Malta to become a Saxon general. Third came Maurice's special friend, Count Augustus Rutowski. Commonly supposed to be the son of a Turkish girl called Fatima, he was actually the offspring of the beautiful but tiresome Countess Spiegel, by whom the King later had a fourth official child, the Countess Maria Rutowska. Count Rutowski followed Maurice into the career of arms and rose to become commander-in-chief of the Saxon army before he was forty. Fifth came the dashing Frederick Augustus, Count von Cosel, also a soldier, and a general of infantry in his twenties. And finally there was the beautiful dark-haired Countess Orzelska, reputed to be the King's daughter by Henriette Duval, wife of a French wine merchant in Warsaw.

By August 1731 Maurice was again in Saxony, attending a review of his father's army, this time accompanied by Marie's successor, the famous dancer Mlle Sallé. She was a woman of rare charm, and in later years evoked the praise of the Abbé Prévost, a considerable connoisseur of fine women.[82]

Augustus had at last begun to appreciate the outstanding military aptitude of his son. He employed every means at his disposal to tempt Maurice away from the French service. In May 1732 he sent the young *maréchal de camp* a flattering letter, begging for his advice on the subject of light cavalry; it was in fact a thinly-veiled invitation to take a more active interest in the Saxon army. Maurice returned a careful reply, discoursing learnedly on the relative merits of hussars and skirmishers, and embellishing his argument with examples from ancient and modern campaigns. Ten years later he was to annotate his own copy of this letter with marginal comments on subsequent campaigns, and the notes show that many of the theories which he had communicated to his father were later vindicated on the field of battle.[83]

In the summer of 1732 he spent three weeks in Poland at his father's request, writing a report on the state of the army, and immediately on returning to Paris he fell seriously ill. Writing from Versailles, in December, he told a friend that he had been suffering from an affected lung which had given him great pain and hampered his breathing. He boasted that in the thirteen feverish nights that had followed the crisis of the illness he had composed his only book, *Mes Rêveries*, the fruit of a decade of brooding on military affairs. Even sickness could not stem his activity.

At this juncture he pondered long and earnestly on the problem of whether to resign his French commission and return to the service of Saxony. The inducements were considerable. His father would promote him immediately to lieutenant-general, and the dearth of military talent in Saxony was so acute that at the first serious crisis he would inevitably become supreme commander. He had served in the French army for twelve years without rising higher than his original rank, and with little prospect of rising higher. As a foreigner and a Protestant, he was regarded by most French senior officers as an interloper. On the death of Regent Orléans he had also lost his chief patron.

But there were other considerations. His Saxon countrymen had not rallied to his cause in Courland. He owed them nothing. In any case, what self-respecting professional soldier would serve as a field marshal in the Saxon army when he could be a captain in the army of France? The army of France was still the army of Louvois, the admiration of Europe even after twenty years of peace. Slackness and disuse had made their inroads; its general staff was decrepit; its numbers had shrunk from over four hundred thousand to a quarter of a million: but it was still the army which had given birth to the *siècle français*. It was still an army in which any soldier would be proud to serve.

The kingdom of France and Navarre had altered considerably since Maurice, fighting in the ranks of her enemies, had first set foot on her soil a quarter of a century before.

Louis XV, who was soon to reach his majority, symbolized in his own person the coming disintegration of the *ancien régime*. He was the incarnation of the reluctance to face reality which afflicted so many of the ministries over which he gracefully presided. His kindly and cynical mind was one of the points of origin of the fatal paralysis which infected society and the organs of the state like a fashionable disease. Even his inordinate sexuality reflected the failing vitality of France. Behind the handsome exterior lay the canker of decay.

Yet, as Sainte-Beuve pointed out, 'although he was contemptible in character, Louis was lacking neither in spirit nor good sense'.[84] What he needed was a Richelieu. It was unfortunate that the ruling element in his nature was an ironic, negative detachment, amounting almost to indifference. According to Dufort de Cheverny, 'he made it a habit never to interfere, and spoke of affairs as though someone else were at the head of the state'.[85] As another historian observed, 'he appeared to view his own reign like a spectator at a play, watching the spectacle with lazy curiosity'.[86]

This hebetude could be blamed in part on the circumstances of his youth. He had become king at the age of five, and for as long as he could remember he had been the recipient of the most sickly reverence and flattery. He was the last legitimate representative of Louis XIV, the sole obstacle to the succession of the ducs d'Orléans. Losing both parents at the age of two, he never knew true family affection and found it difficult in later life to develop a lasting attachment to any other living creature.

High hopes had been entertained of him. His intellectual abilities were attested by Fleury, first his tutor and then his prime minister. But it soon became apparent that he was frigid in temperament and afraid of responsibility. In his adolescence a certain fondness for other young men was viewed by his mentors with alarm. As he fondled the young duc de Trémouille, unpleasant references were made to Henry III and Louis XIII; and his predilection for embroidery and cooking chocolate soufflés gave rise to anxieties that like Louis XIV's brother, Philippe d'Orléans, he was destined to be effeminate as well as perverted.

The courtiers need not have worried. When he grew to manhood he developed to the full the virile passions for hunting and lechery which were the distinguishing marks of the house of Bourbon, in France as in Spain and Naples. He became the most lascivious monarch ever to sit upon the throne of France, not excepting Henry IV.

In 1725, after a bout of fever had given rise to a paroxysm of anxiety about the royal health, it was decided to marry him off as quickly as possible to some woman capable of childbearing. Ninety-nine princesses were considered, and seventeen of them were placed on the short list. The final choice was made by the duc de Bourbon and his ambitious mistress, Mme de Prie. They wanted to select an impoverished and insignificant candidate who would remain permanently in their debt. They therefore chose Marie Leczinska, daughter of Stanislas Leczinski, the man who had occupied the Polish throne alternately with Augustus II.

The choice was greeted with astonishment. To the French, the Poles were little better that barbarians. Even a Russian grand duchess would have been preferable, for such a marriage would at least have represented some diplomatic advantage. But Mme de Prie was adamant, and the marriage was made.

At the time Stanislas Leczinski, who had been the pawn of the ill-fated Charles XII, was an obscure exile, a boarder at the Hotel Weber at Wissembourg in Alsace. He was the recipient of a small, irregular French pension bestowed on him by the Regent Orléans. His court had shrunk to a handful of indigent gentlemen, his crown jewels were in pawn to Jewish bankers at Frankfort, and he was even short of underclothes. At this extreme point in his personal fortunes he had nearly been persuaded to marry his only daughter to a local colonel of cavalry. She was saved for a worse fate, to be the queen of Louis XV.

In the first eleven years of their marriage, Queen Marie bore her husband ten children, most of them ailing. 'I am tired,' she groaned, 'of being always in bed, always pregnant, always in the throes of childbirth.' Her martyrdom continued even after he became repugnant to her, and when she employed every possible subterfuge to keep him at bay. Gradually she came to adopt a secluded and pietistic way of life, seldom emerging from her apartments, and finding an additional antidote to her unhappiness in gluttony. As early as 1726 she was seriously ill as a result of consuming one hundred and eighty oysters and two quarts of beer at a single sitting.

She had two other consolations. One was her correspondence with her father, now magnificently established at the château de Chambord, the great residence on the banks of the Loire where Maurice de Saxe himself was later to live. The other was the respite from her husband's demands which resulted from his emerging interest in mistresses. Although Louis had been curiously slow to shed his early prudery, he embarked in 1732 on an amatory career of staggering depravity. It lasted over thirty years, and carried him down the scale from duchesses to servant girls, the latter purchased from their families and installed in his private brothel in the Parc aux Cerfs at Versailles.

The condition of his kingdom grew annually worse. The king did little but hunt, fornicate and conspire against his own ministers. Eventually he went so far as to conduct a private foreign policy, the so-called *secret du roi*, the purpose of which no one in his entourage ever discovered. His ministers for their part struggled, some ably and others incompetently, against the rising tide of ills.

The nation grew restless. The frustration of the artisan and middle classes was soon matched by the intellectual ferment in the minds of the philosophers, many of whom were personal friends of Maurice de Saxe. Some of them were already propagating the libertarian ideas that in time were to help to undermine the order in which Maurice had been reared and which, as an officer of the king, he was pledged to defend. Voltaire and Diderot, Malesherbes and Rousseau could see, with a clarity denied to Maurice, the approaching death of the old order in France. They may well have regarded their friend, the self-styled Duke of Courland, with sympathetic amusement: a gallant anachronism, a refugee from the age of chivalry. Yet they would also live to acknowledge him as a great general, the equal of Turenne and Villars, a man of a totally different calibre to the foppish commanders of their own generation. It would be Maurice's misfortune that, born to serve a Gustavus Adolphus, he would be compelled to serve a Louis XV.

The long period of quietude which France had enjoyed since the death of Louis XIV was now drawing to a close. These were to prove the years which the locust had eaten. Fleury, the Nestor of European politics, was emphatically a man of peace, but he had not been sufficiently wise to utilize the epoch of calm to reform and revitalize the exhausted country. Another era of warfare was now at hand, and it would last, with only the rarest of intervals, almost until the advent of Napoleon.

In the campaigns that lay ahead, it was to be Maurice de Saxe who would give the house of Bourbon its last taste of glory. And the spark that touched off the new conflagration was the death of Maurice's father, the King of Poland.

After spending a few days at Versailles early in 1733, Maurice had set out to rejoin his father at Warsaw. When he reached Dresden he was greeted with the news that Augustus was dead. The king had been taken ill on the way to Poland, and when he had arrived at his eastern capital,

> the Heydukes being come to take him out of his coach and carry him into his palace, he intangled his right foot in his cloak and bruised his leg so severely that the blood sprung out; he gave a great cry, and the excess of pain which he felt threw him into a fainting fit.[87]

An old wound in the foot, which had already caused the amputation of two toes, refused to heal. The ox-like constitution of Augustus the Strong had at last been overtaxed. Gangrene set in, and he died on February 1st, 1733, aged sixty-three, fortified by the last rites of his adopted church. His dying words are reputed to have been: 'My whole life has been one ceaseless sin.'[88]

Maurice, who was very upset by his father's death, was also anxious lest his brother, the new Elector Frederick Augustus II, should prove less generous than their father. Indeed, all the members of the late king's enormous brood of natural children were fearful that his successor might cancel their allowances with a stroke of the pen. Their fears were quickly allayed, for the new ruler actually increased their stipends. In this the thirty-seven-year-old Elector showed great foresight. In a matter of weeks, the throne of Poland, to which he was immediately elected as Augustus III, would have urgent need of such experienced defenders as his father's martial progeny.

The old king had been a lazy but by no means maladroit politician. He had managed to fight off every challenge, external and internal, to his Polish throne, and his last years had been devoted to an attempt to making the crown of Poland, though elective in form, in practice hereditary in the house of Saxony. The bulk of the Polish nobility were resolutely opposed to this course, and were equally opposed to allowing the crown to be worn by a Pole who was identified with any powerful faction. On the old king's death the problem of the succession produced a stalemate that closely resembled the crisis of forty years before. Again the *liberum veto* was used. The deputies seemed set on destroying their ancient liberties by interminable wrangling, and as the power and prestige of the once great Republic declined, so the Habsburgs and Romanovs began to make plans for its eventual dismemberment.

Six months before the death of Augustus II, the chancelleries of Vienna and St. Petersburg had secretly agreed to put a Portuguese prince on the Polish throne as soon as it fell vacant. By the spring of 1733 they concluded that the Republic was disintegrating so rapidly that it might be as well to allow the Saxons to retain the Polish crown for what was expected to be a very brief period.

The government of France was not inclined to protest at these high-handed arrangements; it was not Fleury's way. But the authorities, wedded to a policy of peace at almost any price, soon found themselves under pressure from a highly vociferous war party that clung to the traditional French policy of opposition to the Habsburgs. This group, many of them partisans of their Polish Queen, was led by such men as old Villars, Chauvelin, and the remarkable Charles-Louis-Auguste Fouquet, duc de Belle-Isle. They hoped to make the coming War of the Polish Succession a great trial of strength between the Bourbons and the Habsburgs, and they made skilful use of the sense of shame felt by many of their countrymen for France's slavish dependence on the policy of Great Britain.

Like Fleury, Robert Walpole, the British Prime Minister, was a man of peace. His first aim was to keep his country out of foreign wars; his second was to maintain the balance of power in Europe; and for many years his administration had been able to achieve both these ends by remaining on friendly terms with France. This was not difficult so long as France and Spain were at loggerheads; but with the renewal of the Bourbon family compact between Versailles and Madrid in 1732, the British government was forced, in order to maintain the diplomatic balance, to swing over to the support of the Empire. At first Walpole was able to keep his fretful country, eager to fight on the Austrian side, out of actual hostilities. He considered, despite the belligerent attitude of George II and many of his own Whig supporters, that the succession to the crown of Poland was not worth the loss of a single British soldier. As he told Queen Caroline in 1734: 'Madame, there were 50,000 men slain in Europe this year, and not one of them an Englishman.'

Fleury was less successful than Walpole in his attempt to contain his own war party. Inflamed by Elizabeth Farnese, the wife of Philip V of Spain, that party was determined to seize the opportunity presented by the death of Frederick Augustus to revive the alliance of France and Poland. They carried the day. Their plan was a simple one: to restore Stanislas Leczinski once more to the throne of Poland, and to fight the Austrians at the same time. They had the advantage of the support of Louis XV, who supposed that his fellow sovereigns would be less inclined to scoff at his *mésalliance* once his wife had been transformed at a single stroke into the heiress of a reigning king.

Primed with three million francs, Stanislas set out from Chambord to regain his former throne. The money had been reluctantly provided by a harassed Fleury, who hated throwing good money after bad but hoped in the last resort to be able to bridle the Belle-Isle faction. Stanislas travelled through Germany disguised as a merchant, and a decoy in the shape of a French nobleman who bore a physical resemblance to him set sail from Brest in Stanislas's court clothes. On September 12th 1733, Stanislas was duly re-elected King of Poland at Warsaw.

The Saxon reaction was uncommonly energetic. Supported by the Empire and by the Russians, they occupied Poland and ejected Stanis-las. On October 25th a servile Diet ratified the succession of the new Elector of Saxony to his father's throne. Stanislas and his more loyal supporters including the Princes Czartoryski, Sapieha and Poniatow-ski, withdrew to Danzig. Like Maurice at Mitau, they resolved to hold at bay the hosts of their adversaries until help should come. They supposed that they had only to display fortitude and the French army would invade Saxony, while the French navy would bring them reinforcements. They vowed to prevent their candidate succumbing to Augustus III in the way that long years before he had succumbed to Augustus II. They argued that Fleury, even though he had not wanted this conflict, neither could nor would stop the French army from bringing this War of the Polish Succession to a victorious con-clusion.

At this critical moment, the generals of France differed widely in talent and experience. At the declaration of war the duc de Belle-Isle was sent to command in the north, the duc de Berwick to command in the centre, and the duc de Villars to command on the Italian front.

At the age of forty-nine, Belle-Isle was regarded by the future Frederick the Great as another Alexander. In youth he had dis-tinguished himself under Boufflers in Flanders, where he was per-manently disabled by a wound in the chest received before Lille. He then served on Berwick's staff in Spain in 1719, and manifested a taste for intrigue by spying on Berwick on behalf of the Regent and Dubois. Berwick himself, dry and reserved, was now aged seventy-three; and although his physical energy was unimpaired, it was soon apparent that his generalship had hardened into inflexibility. Yet the same charge could by no means be levelled against the indestructible Villars, now in his eightieth year. Sporting the cockades of the Queens of France, Spain and Sardinia, the sprightly veteran was accorded an ovation in every town through which he passed on his way south-wards; and in double-quick time he had swept through the fortresses of the defence system known as the Quadrilateral to establish himself as the master of Lombardy.

On the Rhine, the French cause was less successful. There Berwick was confronted with a general as bowed by age as himself but infinitely more sagacious. Prince Eugène had been summoned from retirement to save the Empire, though not until the crisis had reached its height. Reaching the Rhine seven months after the outbreak of war, he found himself facing the French at a time when the Imperial Treasury was almost empty, its armies depleted, and its allies hesitant. The Emperor could offer him only twenty thousand men with which to hold the east bank of the Rhine against the expected onslaught of a hundred thousand French. His only advantage was that he would be fighting over terrain which he knew intimately. His paramount fear was that the French would strike a blow at the heart of the straggling Empire before he could bar the highway to Vienna.

This might already have happened had Berwick been a commander of Maurice's stamp. Not long before, Maurice had advocated in his *Rêveries* just such a *Blitzkrieg*. Berwick, to give him his due, did make some attempt to strike home quickly. Within two days of the declaration of war on October 10th, he defied the lateness of the season and marched out of Strasbourg with the main French army to force a crossing of the Rhine. Maurice, who was in the van, and who was still only a *maréchal de camp*, was about to take part in his first battle for France after a dozen years in her service. He was certain that his hour had come, and that he would not remain in subordinate rank for much longer. Indeed, at thirty-seven he could not afford to, if he wished to fulfil his ambition of becoming one of the great captains of the age.

There was, of course, an element of gambling in these calculations. Three months earlier he had refused an offer to command the Saxon army, in order to retain his chance of promotion in the alien army of France. At Warsaw, in July 1733,

> The Elector of Saxony did all he could to engage Count Saxe, his brother, to accept of the command of his army; but this last, informed of what passed in France and assured of being employed there, excused himself, choosing rather to go and join his regiment; and accordingly taking leave of the court, he set out for Paris on the 28th day of July 1733. People will no doubt be surprised at the conduct of Count Saxe, who being only a camp-marshal in France, refused to be commander-in-chief of the Saxon troops; but this is perhaps one of the most glorious parts of his life; and from that moment naturalized him in every Frenchman's heart.[89]

Maurice had realized that it was in the western rather than the eastern theatre of war that commanders would make their names.

The Rhine would bear him more swiftly to fame than the Danube. In any case, he regarded himself as bound in honour and duty to France. He must have foreseen that this late-flowering loyalty, compounded partly of love and partly of self-interest, would produce many embarrassments. He would be fighting against his native country, which was leagued with the Empire; and since he still retained his Saxon citizenship he would be technically a traitor. More, he would be fighting to oppose the candidacy of his own brother, for the throne which his own father had adorned.

The siege of Kehl, in which he was promptly plunged, was a harsh initiation into French service. This fortress, a star-shaped stronghold on the German bank of the Rhine, covered and neutralized the precisely similar star-shaped fort on the French bank and constituted an eastward extension of the city of Strasbourg. The French fort guarded one end of the Rhine bridge, the German the other. The *pont de Kehl* had long been a vital junction in Franco-German wars.[90]

Berwick used much skill and imagination in planning the downfall of this Imperial stronghold. He sent Maurice with a sizeable force of twenty companies of grenadiers and two thousand fusiliers across the river in boats. They camped on German soil during the night, and at seven o'clock the next morning they began to build a pontoon bridge. The bridge was finished in five hours, an impressive achievement even by the standards of modern military engineers. The main body of the French immediately began to pass the river.

It is possible to detect the hand of Maurice in the inception of this smart manoeuvre. We know from the *Rêveries* that he took the keenest interest in engineering, and that he had invented a special kind of hinged pontoon bridge designed for use in emergencies. He also possessed allies on Berwick's staff, champions of his energetic and original approach to military problems. Among them was the prince de Dombes, his old companion-in-arms at Belgrade in the days when both of them were pupils of Eugène.

After a day spent in manufacturing fascines and gabions from the reed beds of the Rhine, the main body of the French army opened their trenches in front of the fort of Kehl. The saps and parallels were pushed hurriedly forward, and soon came under brisk fire from the garrison. Three days later Maurice himself narrowly escaped death during the course of the first general assault. The attack itself was a failure, and so the French regrouped for a second attempt: but before they were ready, the Austrian commandant suddenly capitulated, and the fortress was theirs.

Unfortunately, the season was already far advanced. Even if Berwick had been sprightly enough to exploit his advantage, he was defeated by the torrential rains which had plagued him almost from the outset of operations. He was compelled to recross the Rhine, encamp his armies, and await the coming of the spring.

In later years Maurice was to become famous for entering the field earlier in the season, and leaving it later, than had previously been the practice, He was now compelled to spend four mortal months in unendurable idleness, for the army of France would not re-enter the field until early in April. Meanwhile the enforced delay brought closer and closer the salvation of the Empire, whose meagre forces would soon be augmented by the regiments of their allies.

Berwick now decided to divide his army into three parts. He sent Belle-Isle with twenty thousand men northwards to the Moselle, with orders to take Trier, the old Roman township between Luxembourg and Koblenz. At the same time Noailles was detached with a second force of thirty thousand men, and instructed to invest Kaiserslautern. Berwick himself, as commander-in-chief, was to advance eastwards with the bulk of his troops [Fig. 3].

Maurice accompanied Belle-Isle, the most adventurous of the French generals. Trier was swiftly taken by a brilliant manoeuvre as early as April 6th, and the northern army then set out up the serpentine valley towards Koblenz, the city at the junction of the Moselle and the Rhine. On the highway above the celebrated wine town of Bern-kastel they encountered their first opposition. The Imperial commander at Trarbach, on the south bank of the river, bravely disputed their passage. He placed his mediaeval castle, which had been in French hands before the Peace of Ryswick, in a state of defence, spurning the French summons to surrender. The siege lasted from April 13th until May 2nd, a tribute to the architects of the fortress and to the courage of its Austrian garrison, who were bombarded almost continuously with a new type of missile, the *comminge*, each of which weighed over five hundred pounds. On the evening of April 27th Maurice headed two major attacks, in the second of which seven of his grenadiers were killed at his side. The attacks failed, and the deafened defenders battled on grimly for another week before yielding.

The way to Koblenz was open, but before Belle-Isle began his advance towards it, Maurice sought and obtained permission to ride southwards. He saw clearly that Belle-Isle would be required to perform little more than a holding operation against the Danish, Hessian, Hanoverian and Prussian levies then advancing into the upper Rhineland. The decisive encounter would inevitably take place further south, probably in the area between Speyer and Ettlingen where Noailles' advance guard was already established, awaiting the arrival of the main army under Berwick. For once there was little prospect of

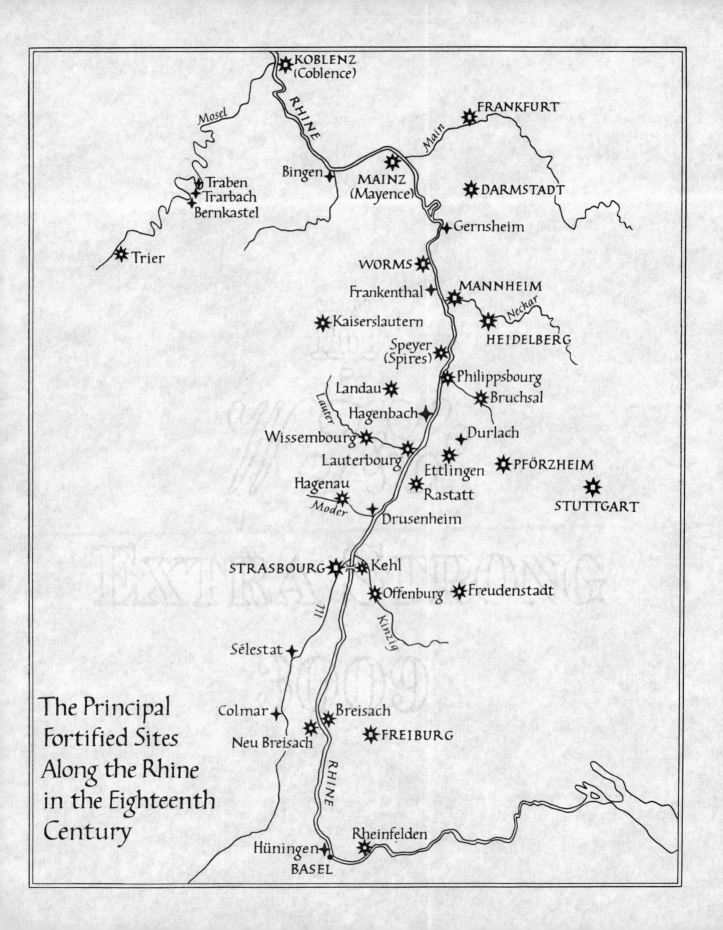

KOBLENZ
(Coblence)

Mosel

RHINE

FRANKFURT

Main

Traben
Trarbach
Bernkastel

Bingen

MAINZ
(Mayence)

DARMSTADT

Trier

Gernsheim

WORMS

Frankenthal

MANNHEIM

Neckar

Kaiserslautern

HEIDELBERG

Speyer
(Spires)

Landau

Philippsbourg

Lauter

Bruchsal

Hagenbach

Wissembourg

Durlach

Lauterbourg

PFÖRZHEIM

Hagenau

Ettlingen

Moder

Rastatt

STUTTGART

Drusenheim

STRASBOURG

Kehl

Offenburg

Freudenstadt

Ill

Kinzig

Sélestat

Colmar

Breisach

The Principal
Fortified Sites
Along the Rhine
in the Eighteenth
Century

Neu Breisach

FREIBURG

RHINE

Rheinfelden

Hüningen

BASEL

excitement to be had at Belle-Isle's side, and Maurice thought that it would be more profitable to hasten to the likely seat of operations. Belle-Isle, a commander of the same stamp as Maurice, fully understood his subordinate's viewpoint and readily released him.

Maurice had already cultivated the friendship of the duc de Noailles. Four months previously he had sent Noailles a copy of *Mes Rêveries*, complete with a flattering inscription. The warmth and closeness of the relationship that had developed between them was remarkable in that Noailles, a prim and reserved man of fifty-five, was the last man who might have been expected to approve of the dissolute young Saxon. Noailles' aloofness was in part inherited from his father, a Marshal of France noted for the enthusiasm with which he had prosecuted the inhuman dragonnades. Father and son had served together in the War of the Spanish Succession, just as Noailles' own son was now serving under his father before Ettlingen. Noailles had fought under Villars, Catinat, and Tallard, and had reached the rank of lieutenant-general at the age of twenty-eight; but it was as a courtier and diplomatist that he was to make his principal mark. When he was little more than a boy he had become a confidant of the old Louis XIV, had married a niece of Mme de Maintenon, and on the Sun King's death had acted as a resourceful Controller-General of Finance until his replacement by the ill-fated John Law. Maurice was fortunate in securing the regard of one of the most versatile and respected men in the realm.

As soon as he joined his new commander, Maurice immediately realized that Noailles' corps ought not to wait until Berwick joined them. Their best course was to lunge straight forward. He saw at once that a unique opportunity had presented itself, a chance to force the Lines of Ettlingen and burst through them at the precise point where they were skimpily protected. Once the lines were pierced, the road to Vienna would lie wide open.

It is easy to see why the Lines were regarded as the nodal point of the middle Rhine. From Darmstadt to Freiburg the mountains rise sheer and straight from the green plain, a barrier of black rock, fronting the Vosges and the Hardt on the opposite side. But between Heidelberg and Ettlingen, between the Odenwald to the north and the Black Forest to the south, there comes a sudden gap, a mist-shrouded plain that arches its way back to the Neckar. To strike through that gap would be to cut the jugular vein of the Empire.

Needless to say, the Lines were normally defended heavily and in depth. Concentric rows of trenches and redoubts had been thrown up to command the narrow defiles, and should have constituted an almost impregnable defence. They did not deter Maurice and Noailles from effecting a useful reconnaissance, after leaving Rastadt on May 3rd: and by nightfall of that day the irrepressible Maurice had detected a possible route through the forest. When midnight came, fifteen companies of grenadiers with Maurice at their head were creeping through the forest. At dawn they were ranged in battle formation, ready to puncture the vital entrenchments manned by a still unsuspecting enemy. Noailles launched two dozen men in a feint attack. Before the sleepy Austrians could rub their eyes or snatch up their muskets, Maurice

> marched to within sixty paces of the enemy trenches, where he ordered a halt. He ordered the infantrymen to take off their haversacks and fix their bayonets, take the covers off their drums, and told the drummers to beat up and everyone to move forward when he gave them the word. There was then a moment of complete silence, after which Count Saxe quickly placed himself sword in hand at the head of the grenadiers and cried: 'March! Charge!' It was a splendid moment.[91]

Maurice and his troops flung themselves on the Austrians. The dark woods were filled with the crackle of arms and the cries of the wounded. After half an hour's stiff fighting, the Imperial troops broke and ran. Maurice and Noailles had only to press on towards the pine-fringed heights in front of them, to capture the remaining strong-points, and they could signal back to Berwick and his men that the way was open, that the armies of France were free to pour through the gap. Admittedly, it would not be easy. After a short march, they came up against a second and stronger Austrian line, this time reinforced with ' citadels and redoubts, well garnished with infantry with flags fluttering'. Maurice was undeterred. He considered that it was still more than possible to carry the day. All that was needed was a spirit of resolution and enterprise. But at the critical moment Noailles reverted to his habitual caution. He refused to move forward without artillery support. Yet how did he imagine that heavy guns would be brought up through such wooded terrain? Maurice begged that at least he should be allowed to attempt an outflanking movement, and to try to take the enemy in the rear. He was overruled.

None the less the Lines of Ettlingen had definitely been penetrated, even if only partially. It could plainly be seen that the French armies were half-way through the gates of the Empire. When Eugène finally reached the scene of operations, on May 26th, he found that the situation was almost irretrievable. The main Imperial army had fallen back on Heilbronn in confusion, and the French were steadily advancing in three columns, one of them under the command of Maurice. For the venerable Austrian commander it was one of the most dangerous crises of his long career. His reaction was characteristically quick and cool. With the utmost assurance, and within a mere hour of his arrival, he was mustering the largest available contingent of horse and foot and marching them to Eppingen, midway between Heilbronn and Durlach. It was pure bluff: a show of pretended force, a stroke of calculated *bravura*. And it worked. Berwick, encountering this small scratch force, decided to play safe. He withdrew. More, he crowned this initial error with an error of even greater magnitude: he now decreed that the whole of his vast army should concentrate not on a direct advance on Vienna, but on the final reduction of a fortress of Philippsburg. He refused to commit his forces to a leap forward until Philippsburg was in French hands.

Philippsburg, now a small village on a secondary road between Spires and Neudorf, was once one of the principal western strong-points of the Empire. Bristling with artillery, garrisoned by nearly five thousand front-line troops, it lay in the margravate of Baden. Its importance was that it covered a vulnerable gap in the forest barrier. Berwick passionately desired its reduction, but at the same time he felt that he must at all costs secure his rear from harassing sallies mounted by its garrison. He was not influenced by the fact that his troops were so numerous that the Austrians in Philippsburg could easily have been neutralized without affecting the pace of his advance. He could have delivered a blow at Eugène's flimsy army that might well have shaken the Empire itself. Maurice, by his fire and daring, had already shown the way. But the aged Berwick was a soldier of the old school; he was siege-minded; he suffered from fortress-phobia.

The siege of Philippsburg duly developed into the grim centrepiece of the war [*vide* Fig. 4]. The French strove to eliminate the Austrian commander and his besieged garrison before Eugène could scrape together enough battalions to succour them. From the French point of view, the siege was not merely irrelevant, but also exceedingly hazardous to mount. The fortress was situated in the middle of huge bog formed by the Rhine, and the French engineers were subjected to continuous cannonading. That rain, which had sorely afflicted the French during the previous winter, again poured ceaselessly down. Two hundred French infantrymen were actually drowned in their own trenches, in addition to the hundreds who died of exposure.

Maurice was soon in the thick of this damp and depressing affair. As usual, he was indefatigable, riding hither and thither, building bridges, preventing the enemy from constructing pontoons and attending to the supply of fodder and armaments. On June 7th, the day after the trenches were opened, six hundred Austrians launched a counter-attack. It was Maurice who was responsible for driving them back. He was becoming indispensable. Berwick had told the truth when he had said to Maurice on the latter's arrival in camp: ' Count,

I had intended sending for three thousand of M. de Noailles' men, but you alone are worth more than that to me.' Count Asfeldt, the able officer in charge of the actual siege operations, did not hesitate to term Maurice his 'right-hand man'.

Maurice was chasing promotion for all he was worth. In the previous month he had written an unusual letter to Noailles, after their skirmishes on the heights of the Odenwald. 'Monsieur,' he had written,

> although good actions are said to speak for themselves, I find myself obliged to sound my own praises. I have neither parents nor friends at court who can do it for me, and false modesty can degenerate into stupidity. It will be clear to you that I am not content to serve the king in any perfunctory manner. I have already been lucky enough to perform a striking action which has advanced the honour of the king's arms. Without me, the flower of our troops might have perished needlessly, and we might have been compelled to retreat. As it was, it was Prince Eugène who retired, acknowledging the supremacy of the forces under your command. And it was I, Monsieur, who acted as your guide. It was I who found a way into that inaccessible region, made the necessary dispositions, and attacked. I led and conquered at the head of your grenadiers. It was I who drew up the plans that enabled you to triumph and carried them into action by exposing myself to perils which made all who saw them shudder. You could not do better than reward such activities, Monsieur, for rewards promote valour. . . . It is fourteen years, Monsieur, since I had the honour to enter the king's service as a *maréchal de camp*. I am now nearing forty, and I am anxious not to be thwarted by the usual rules of promotion. I do not want to remain a *maréchal de camp* forever. I have ignored the claims of my own blood, my interests, even perhaps my honour, in order to serve His Majesty. You will recall, too, that I am a foreigner; and you will understand that this fact makes me doubly eager to secure promotion. Will you please speak to the king on my behalf?[92]

For the time being he had to content himself with his present rank. It was not for want of room at the top. On June 12th, 1734, the septuagenarian Berwick was killed by a cannonball in a forward trench; and five days later the aged Villars died at Turin, in the same bed and in the same room in which he had been born over eighty years before. On this occasion it was not Maurice but his patrons, Noailles and Asfeldt, who secured promotion. They were gazetted Marshals of France, with joint command of the army of the Rhine in succession to Berwick.

The war was not without its pleasant interludes. In June, Maurice accompanied Noailles on a visit to Mannheim, where they dined with the Elector Palatine, Charles Philip, and discussed with him the progress of the war. Towards the end of the same month Maurice was

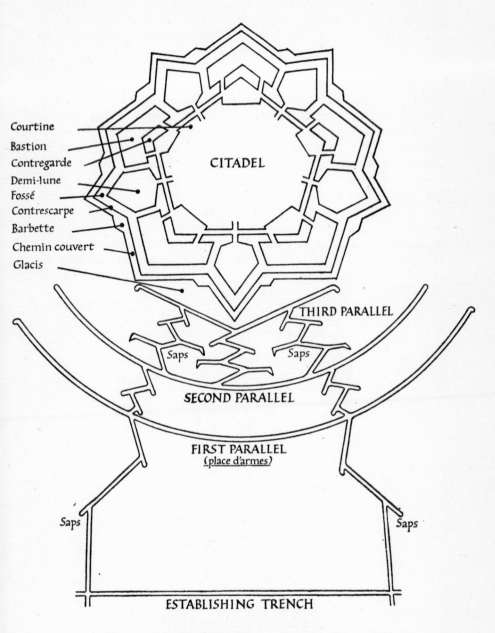

Courtine
Bastion
Contregarde
Demi-lune
Fossé
Contrescarpe
Barbette
Chemin couvert
Glacis

CITADEL

THIRD PARALLEL

Saps

Saps

SECOND PARALLEL

FIRST PARALLEL
(place d'armes)

Saps

Saps

ESTABLISHING TRENCH

FIG. 4. A TYPICAL STAR-SHAPED FORT, OF THE VAUBAN
PATTERN, UNDER ATTACK IN FORM

cheered by the arrival in camp of one of his oldest friends, Voltaire, never the man to skulk in philosophical retirement when history was in the making. At Philippsburg, Voltaire saw Maurice for the first time in his real setting. He was impressed.

A visit to the Rhine was a welcome distraction for Voltaire. Some weeks earlier his *Lettres philosophiques* had been seized by the authorities, and burned by the public hangman, and he himself had been placed under technical arrest. He had prudently withdrawn first to Lorraine, and then to Philippsburg. Soon he would install himself at near-by Cirey, at the beginning of his five years of residence at the château of Mme du Châtelet. His mood at Philippsburg was therefore a strange combination of the sardonic and the exalted, and it happily gave rise to one of his shortest but also one of his very finest poems. This poem is the work of a man admirably fitted to understand not only his friend Maurice, and not only the age in which they lived, but the condition of man itself. It reveals a Voltaire torn between his affection for the France of the *ancien régime*, and his longing for that heavenly city of the eighteenth-century philosophers in which, they believed, war and warriors would be superfluous.

> C'est ici que l'on dort sans lit,
> Et qu'on prend ses repas par terre.
> Je vois et j'entends l'atmosphère
> Qui s'embrase et qui retentit
> De cent décharges de tonnerre.
> Et, dans ces horreurs de la guerre,
> Le Français chante, boit et rit.
> Bellone va réduire en cendres
> Les courtines de Philipsbourg
> Par cinquante mille Alexandres
> Payés à quatre sous par jour:
> Je les vois, prodiguant leur vie,
> Chercher ces combats meurtriers,
> Couverts de fange et de lauriers,
> Et pleins d'honneur et de folie;
> Je vois briller au milieu d'eux
> Ce fantôme nommé la Gloire,
> A l'oeil superbe, au front poudreux,
> Portant au cou cravate noire,
> Ayant sa trompette en sa main,
> Sonnant la charge et la victoire
> En chantant quelques airs à boire
> Dont ils répètent le refrain.
> O nation brillante et vaine!
> Illustres fous, peuple charmant,
> Que la Gloire à son char entraîne,
> Il est beau d'affronter gaiement
> Le trépas et le prince Eugène.[93]

The *trépas* in question was the looming threat of counter-attack by the Imperial forces. The Austrians, now at last joined by the Hanoverians and Prussians, had achieved parity with the French. Eugène wasted no time in recrossing the Neckar and marching to the relief of Wutgenau at Philippsburg, before the French could launch their long-awaited grand assault. On July 1st, 1734, after re-occupying his traditional headquarters at Bruchsal, Eugène advanced to Wiesental, only five kilometres from Philippsburg, and deployed his men in battle order. It was still in doubt who would attack whom first: whether Asfeldt would attack Wutgenau, or whether Eugène would attack Asfeldt.

The sorely-tried Wutgenau could not hold out much longer. He had already lost nearly two thousand men; his supplies were running short. He made an unsuccessful attempt to break out of his beleaguered fortress in the direction of Eugène, then beat off an attack mounted by Maurice on July 14th. He still expected that the Austrian main army could force the French to raise the siege: but—quite unaccountably—Prince Eugène's famous resolution deserted him. At the last moment he vacillated. Like Wellington in the Peninsula, he simply could not afford to risk the destruction of his one and only army in an attempt to rescue three thousand exhausted men. He stood inert while Wutgenau, who deserved a better fate, surrendered on July 17th. The Austrian main army fell back on Bruchsal.

With Philippsburg in his hands, Asfeldt promptly shifted operations northwards, sending forty thousand men to join Belle-Isle at Worms. The plan was that this force should march on Mainz, with the object of stopping Eugène from sending reinforcements to Italy, where the Imperial armies under Mercy had just scored an unexpected success against the duc de Broglie.

Maurice was in the van of the drive on Mainz. On August 1st he captured the castle of Niederulm, an outpost twelve kilometres south of the target, by means of a swift attack. And, on this very day the king at Versailles was signing the patent that raised him, at long last, to the coveted rank of lieutenant-general.

Eugène withdrew quietly to Heidelberg, leaving the French generals to wear down their men with futile marches and counter-marches up and down the middle Rhine.

The French cavalry were seriously embarrassed by lack of fodder. It was in the capacity of quartermaster that Maurice, between skirmishes, now showed himself in a new and welcome light, artfully wheedling supplies out of reluctant German burghers without

H

threatening their lives or damaging their property. On one of these expeditions he fell in with a body of Austrian hussars in the middle of a wood. A hot little encounter ensued, during which he succeeded in cutting down the enemy commander with his own hand after receiving a cut from a sabre full upon the head. The blow seems to have done him no harm, for he was always careful to wear a helmet of his own design, probably a modification of the ideal helmet which he had already illustrated in *Mes Rêveries*. It was characteristic of him that in the field he should contrive to combine the reckless ardour of the Königsmarcks with sensible Saxon precautions against sudden death.

This skirmish occurred on September 19th, after the French army had begun to withdraw once more to its winter quarters. The men were footsore and discouraged. The high hopes with which they had entered upon the campaign of 1733 had not been realized. For purposes of propaganda the capture of Philippsburg had been represented as an epic victory, and Maurice and his companions had been fêted at Versailles as conquering heroes. But these charades had failed to dissipate the prevailing gloom. There had been excellent news from Italy, where Coigny had killed Mercy and eight thousand of his men, and from Parma, where Broglie had thrashed Königsegg at Guastalla, and where the Spaniards had overrun Naples and Sicily: but these triumphs were largely offset by the fiasco in Poland itself. There King Stanislas, abandoned by Fleury, had been forced to flee from Danzig and escape across Prussia in a farm-cart. His supporters, headed by the Czartoryskis, had capitulated after a siege lasting four terrible months, and had been compelled to swear fealty to Augustus III. Eventually, Stanislas, with a sigh of relief, signed his final abdication at Königsberg.

It was therefore in chastened mood that the principal combatants prepared for the campaign of 1735. They had reached a position of stalemate. The French armies were strong, but the Empire had survived, and it was highly unlikely that either Habsburg or Bourbon could deal the other a knockout blow. Noailles, who had been sent to command in Italy, did not trouble to open his campaign until the middle of May, and for their part Eugène and his generals were equally quiescent and content to remain on the defensive. Eugène himself chose to remain at Bruchsal for most of the summer. His health was failing, and he may not have been sorry to linger in this pleasant little town, with its noble baroque church set on a hill, in which the devout little field marshal loved to worship.

It was not until September that he finally bestirred himself and attempted a half-hearted crossing of the Rhine above Mannheim. Coigny, now in command of the main French force in Germany, hurriedly detached Maurice with ten squadrons of cavalry and fourteen battalions of infantry to counter the Austrian move. Maurice chose his ground so adroitly that he was able with his token force to hold Eugène in check and compel him to abandon his design. Eugène was thus frustrated by the ablest of his former pupils. Maurice, who had long ago taken the advice which Eugène had given him as a boy at Lille 'not to confuse courage with recklessness', coolly allowed the leading files of the Austrian columns to advance right up to him. Eugène knew that once Maurice had grappled with them on ground of his own choosing, they would not escape without a serious mauling. Accordingly he withdrew to his original position. Why, he reasoned, should he shed blood at a time when the peace which he had been urging upon his emperor at last seemed imminent?

Maurice also disliked unnecessary blood-letting; but on this occasion he was not particularly grateful for such a tame ending to a general European war. It was his ardent wish to prove his title to his new rank in the field, and he was irked when he discovered that his superiors were as cautious on his side as Eugène was on his. If Maurice had a reputation to gain, they had reputations to lose. In his impatience, he gave way to unwonted rashness. Early in October he was nearly surrounded and cut off while participating in the single engagement which took place during the entire course of the summer, when Coigny and Belle-Isle were attempting a surprise attack on Seckendorff's headquarters near Trier. Pursuing the retreating Austrians with a small force of thirty-six companies of grenadiers, Maurice became reckless and almost fell into a trap.

It was by now perfectly obvious that neither army intended to provoke a major engagement. The Austrians remained impassive even after a contingent of Maurice's old adversaries, the Russians, arrived on the banks of the Neckar in support of Eugène. This was the first time that Russian troops had appeared so far west in Europe: and the more prescient generals and politicians regarded the event with well-founded misgivings.

On November 5th, 1735, an armistice was proclaimed on the Rhine. Ten days later hostilities were also suspended in Italy. The War of the Polish Succession was over. The armies marched homewards from the trampled valleys of the Moselle and the Rhine, the Neckar and the Main. Maurice returned to Paris with his usual precipitancy, while his old master Eugène folded away his much-creased maps with stiff fingers and made his way by easy stages to his beloved Schönbrunn. Here he died on the evening of April 21st, 1736, after a quiet game of piquet. He had served the Empire for fifty-three years, and had been a general officer for half a century. He had been wounded thirteen times. At his funeral, sixteen field marshals bore his small coffin to its vault.

The passing of Villars and Eugène marked the end of the tradition of warfare inherited from Turenne, Luxembourg, Condé and Marlborough. In future, war would be subtly different in conduct and in scope. There would be many radical innovations. The next large-scale clash of arms would lack the over-refinement that had characterized most of the campaigning of the preceding century. Without becoming in any way more crude or slapdash, warfare would be more fluid, more enterprising, more resourceful, and in many ways less brutal.

The man who was to be primarily responsible for the innovations which were now about to be introduced was Maurice de Saxe.

CHAPTER VIII

PRAGUE, 1735-1742

Frederick the Great asked me the names of the people who were present. I told him the names of a number of princes of distinguished blood who were entering upon a military career, some of whom showed great promise. ' Yes,' he said, ' but I think an empire needs a certain amount of cross-breeding. I am all in favour of bastards. Look, for example, at Marshal Saxe.'

PRINCE DE LIGNE: *Memoirs*

NAPOLEON asked of his generals not whether they were able, but whether they were lucky. Maurice had now proved himself to be a lucky general. His forays usually turned out to be successful; he exuded confidence and could communicate it to his subordinates. It was certain that he would be assured of immediate and important command in any future war.

In the meantime, the settlement of the War of the Polish Succession proved almost as lengthy as the war itself. It was finally agreed that the Emperor Charles VI would be allowed to leave his protégé, the Elector of Saxony, on the throne of Poland; but he was compelled to cede Naples and Sicily to a son of Philip V of Spain and Elizabeth Farnese. In addition he was forced to grant to the French the long-coveted reversion to the duchy of Lorraine: and by one of the topsy-turvy arrangements habitual to eighteenth-century diplomacy, the reigning duke of Lorraine, Francis III, the Emperor's son-in-law, was transferred to the grand duchy of Tuscany and his duchy of Lorraine bestowed on Stanislas Leczinski as a consolation prize for the lost throne of Poland.

Stanislas regarded himself as very fortunate to be installed in the small twin duchies of Lorraine and Bar. Fleury would have been content with Bar alone, and only the threats of Chauvelin, the keeper of the Seals, to retain the fortresses of Philippsburg, Kehl and Trier won for France the valuable gift of the province of Lorraine. The mild and unmilitary Stanislas, who had known the extremes of poverty and disappointment in his peripatetic career, was happy enough to settle down at his provincial court at Lunéville, where he proved a happier and more useful ruler than he could ever have been in his native Poland. To this day the splendours of the city of Nancy remain as his abiding monument to posterity. His son-in-law, Louis XV, was not greatly exercised by these diplomatic arrangements. The King of France was content to leave these important affairs in the enfeebled hands of Fleury, while he amused himself at the chase and in the bedchamber.

What of Saxony? During the five crucial years that were to supervene between the ending of the late war and the beginning of the next, state business in Dresden and Warsaw was to be conducted in a manner fully as supine as that of France. Like Louis XV, Augustus III was indifferent to any matter that did not directly affect his own pleasures. His way of life was similar to that of the French king. Sir Charles Hanbury-Williams, the British minister at Dresden, spoke of the king's

> absolute and avowed hatred to all business, and his known love for idleness and low pleasures (which) prevent both him and his country from making that figure in Europe which this noble Electorate ought to do and often has done. . . . He is seldom seen when at Dresden, but at dinner. He always dines with company, and his buffoons make a great noise, and fight with one another during the whole repast. . . . He has had a great loss in the Electress of Bavaria being married for she often came to him in the afternoon, and they have been surprised together in very indecent postures. The Queen knew this and was furious about it. . . . The King is excessively fond of hunting, and 'tis reckoned that the game of all sorts (which is strictly preserved to him) do £50,000 *per annum* of damage to this country. I have myself seen fifty stags in one cornfield; and to take care of all his game and forests there are no less than 4000 persons in constant pay. . . . The expenses of this court of every sort are proportionate with that of the chase. . . . The debts of this Electorate (all incurred since this King came into possession of it) are near four millions sterling, and their credit is quite ruined, but the King will not hear of the expenses of the court being lessened. He has no idea of the state of his country; but as he finds himself easy, he thinks and wishes his people to be so too. He is not beloved or respected. . . . Their fine country, which I believe produces more to its sovereign than any other district of the same size in Europe, grows daily poorer, which is very visible by the decay of the Leipsick Fair.[94]

As Frederick the Great rightly said, empires need cross-breeding; but of all Augustus the Strong's unnumbered brood, his sole legitimate heir was the least fitted to govern Saxony and Poland. Maurice would have done incomparably better than Augustus the Weak, who was incapable of indulging his appetites without impoverishing his domains. His one saving grace was his discernment as a connoisseur of paintings, which procured for Dresden such wonders as the Sistine

Madonna of Raphael. Gross and sybaritic in appearance, he was dominated in later years by his chief minister, Count Brühl, a third-rate boot-licker who even hastened to renounce his Protestant religion in order to please his Roman Catholic master. It was a disaster for Saxony that Brühl, as cynical and rapacious as Flemming but without the latter's ability and patriotism, should have exercised power for over a quarter of a century. He emptied the coffers of the state in order to line his own pockets and pay for the pastimes of his master. Frederick the Great despised him, dismissing him as 'the man of our age with the most suits, watches, ruffles, boots, shoes and breeches'. He maintained over three hundred servants, a private bodyguard larger than his master's, and built a Palais Brühl at Dresden that became the largest and most sumptuous private residence in the whole electorate.

It was with the spineless Brühl that Maurice, who in spite of his own dissipations increasingly resembled a survivor from a sterner era, now had to deal during his visits to Dresden. Soon after the end of the Polish War, he had made his way thither with considerable apprehension, doubtful of the reception he would receive after his refusal to command the army of Saxony and his vigorous service in the ranks of his native country's enemies. He was relieved to be greeted with every sign of warmth and affection. Unlike his fellow sovereigns, during the recent war Augustus had succeeded in achieving all his principal aims, and his new régime was altogether too easygoing to bear fraternal ill-will. Maurice, the last man to play the skeleton at the feast, required little persuasion to spend the whole of 1737 at this congenial court. With fifty stags to the cornfield, and plenty of women available, he was never likely to be bored. His enjoyment was only disturbed by the unexpected revival of his dormant hopes for Courland.

He suddenly received news that the lingering ghost of the Kettlars, the titular Duke William, had finally drawn his last belated breath. Without waiting for word from Russia, Maurice, as legitimate duke-elect, lost no time in claiming the vacant throne as his own. He wrote at once to commiserate with the nobles at Mitau:

> You foresaw this lamentable situation, and passed in my favour an act of eventual election which would have been valid at the present time, if there were any element of stability in human affairs. . . . As for me, I flatter myself that you will do me the justice of believing me happy to die fighting for you, if the question of fighting should arise. I should thus be able to repay you something of what I owe to you.[95]

Unfortunately the Russians still retained their habit of disposing of whatever Maurice had proposed. It made not the slightest difference that a full decade had passed since Lascy's troopers had chased him through the mire to Windau. It mattered not at all to them that he had never abandoned his dream of eventual reinstatement in Courland. Matters might have worn another aspect if he had chosen to reciprocate the fitful ardour of the Duchess Anna Ivanovna, for until 1730 he could have returned to Mitau at any time by surrendering to her desire for him. In 1730, however, Anna's fortunes had changed dramatically. In that year the young Tsar Peter II had died of small-pox, and with the help of the Galitzine family she had been sum-moned from her poverty-stricken capital to St. Petersburg to assume the imperial diadem. The officers and nobles who were responsible for placing the obscure and supposedly malleable young duchess on such a dizzy eminence soon realized their error. Anna was no cipher. Worse, she brought with her to the banks of the Neva the depraved and avaricious intimates who had eased her languors at Mitau, foremost among them Ernst Johann Bühren or Biren, the forty-year-old son of a groom in the ducal service. This course and arrogant man was her principal lover, and after her succession to the throne of Russia, he at once became a power in the land. On the death of the last duke of Courland in 1737, his imperial mistress nominated him to the empty throne of his native province.

Biren was not slow to make his fellow Courlanders feel the weight of his hand. The long-suffering Russians had already experienced the rigours of the 'era of Biren', when tens of thousands of them were tortured, killed, or exiled in a senseless reign of terror. He now cemented his position in Courland by similar methods, after bullying the electoral college into voting him into power by a blatant mixture of intimidation and bribery. The latter practice he could well afford; his establishment at St. Petersburg rivalled that of the Tsarina, and he was probably the wealthiest man in the empire. Public money had a habit of sticking to his fingers; a special department of state was created to look after his brood mares and stallions alone. His wife's diamonds were worth over half a million pounds, and blinded even the jaded eyes of the French ambassador. He had the effrontery to adopt the name and arms of the Navarrese family of Biron, dukes of Périgord, and offered the head of that illustrious family the Russian order of St. Andrew in an attempt to persuade him to condone this affront to his house.

Biren had obtained for himself the order of the White Eagle for the part he had played in establishing Augustus III on the Polish throne. Augustus the Weak was by now little better than a Russian pawn, and Poland a Russian satellite. It suited Russia to maintain Saxony as a pliant and bankrupt buffer-state between herself and the Prussians and Austrians, a *cordon sanitaire* in reverse. Augustus, desiring merely the outward trappings of kingship, and neither speaking Polish nor caring for the country, was content to be maintained in his kingdom by Russian arms. For Courland, he cared not a straw. He made no pretence of backing Maurice, and in any event his obligation to Biren was so great that he could not have supported any other candidate for Courland, even had he been minded to do so. Moreover, by the terms of the Pacification Diet of June 1736, he had undertaken not to appoint any ruler in Courland who was unacceptable to the Russians. This meant that he had no alternative but to underwrite the candidature of the Russian ruler.

Maurice was compelled for the second time to bow to the inevitable. In any case, having recently fought for France on behalf of Stanislas Leczinski, he can hardly have supposed that he would be acceptable either to the Russians or to the victorious party in Poland. Augustus attempted to soften the blow by bestowing on him the considerable French estates of Count Hoym, a former Saxon minister at Versailles who had fallen into disgrace; but it was nevertheless deeply galling to Maurice to have to return to Paris in the late autumn of 1737 in the knowledge that his rightful realm and rightful throne were in the clutch of Biren, an upstart adorned with his beloved White Eagle, and sporting a bogus French ancestry. But there was nothing at all that he could do about it. Biren was to reign in Courland from 1737 until 1740, and again from 1763 until his death in 1772.

Early in 1737, Maurice had received from Voltaire a copy of the latter's *Défense du mondain*, together with a warm personal inscription. Now, out of sheer boredom and frustration, Maurice was again constrained to indulge the *mondain*, even *grivois* bent for which he had so marked a capacity. Voltaire considered the growth of luxurious living to be a testimony to the progress of civilized society, and in hailing Maurice as an outstanding exponent of high living he was not, for once, indulging in irony. It was a mark of genuine respect, a token of Maurice's new standing among the *philosophes*, that Voltaire should have honoured him with one of the precious copies of this entertaining and impudent book, that made even distant Cirey too hot for him and forced him to seek refuge in the Low Countries. Amid much genial apostrophe, Voltaire eulogized the hero of Philippsburg as

> not only an agreeable worldling, but a philosopher of war, as ready to sleep in a bivouac as in the splendid bed of the most beautiful of his mistresses; a man now making a Lucullan repast, now eating the hard rations of a hussar.[96]

Even the life of pleasure, however, is subject to vicissitudes, and the hours hung heavily upon the hero of Philippsburg in the years 1738 and 1739. He was forty-three; he was unemployed; and there was no Adrienne to add a touch of genuine tenderness to his existence. Some of his surplus energies were consumed in compiling a private newsletter, packed with Parisian scandal, for the delectation of King Augustus and his court. This was in the nature of a small return for his financial dependence on Dresden, at a time when newsletters of this kind were all the rage. His periodical vapourings were wholly frivolous, and shed little light on his own life and ambitions. Nor did he content himself with purveying tittle-tattle, for in these years he was even willing to act as unofficial agent for Brühl and Augustus, and we find him reporting on the reception of a gift of tokay by Louis XV, and of a case of porcelain from the Meissen factory by Fleury.

In the winter of 1739 he paid yet another visit to Dresden. Once again he was financially embarrassed. His increased allowance from Augustus had been of little relief to him, and he had been compelled to borrow 50,000 livres on the security of the brevet of retention granted him by Louis XV in 1735. To add to his woes, he now met with a severe accident. While hunting near the Moritzburg, he was thrown from his horse and broke his knee, and the damage was aggravated by the re-opening of the wound which he had received in his youth during the romantic ambush at the inn at Crachnitz. He was forced to spend many weary weeks in bed, and was still very much an invalid when he was helped into his coach and driven southwards by easy stages to recuperate at the Mediterranean spa of Balaruc-les-Bains, twenty-five miles south of Montpellier. He made this journey in April 1740, and proceeded with commendable conscientiousness to take the cure. Although so many of his forbears had served in the Mediterranean and Aegean, Maurice had never in his life been so far south before, and he would never go so far south again. Probably he was happier in the bleak wastes of Courland.

He had not only visited the mineral springs of Balaruc for direct medical relief: the little town was also so far removed from Paris that it provided his exhausted frame with a welcome respite from the temptations of the capital. The prolonged and accumulated strain of hard campaigning, and equally hard debauchery, had weakened even his hardy constitution. The solid frame which he had inherited from Augustus the Strong had already begun, in his early middle age, to fail him.

By midsummer, he felt sufficiently restored to be able to leave his sleepy backwater for a tour of the neighbouring countryside. He visited Montpellier, Avignon and Aix, and was everywhere accorded the honours due to one of France's leading generals. Off Toulon was

anchored the British Mediterranean fleet, and Maurice was invited
aboard the flagship by Admiral Matthews. The admiral and Maurice
were soon employed in downing bulky bumpers to their respective
sovereigns, the ship's guns roaring out cannonades between toasts. It
was an enjoyable occasion, but as one of Maurice's eighteenth-century
biographers later remarked:

> If Admiral Matthews could have foreseen Count Saxe should one day
> give his nation such a bone to pick as he afterwards did, he would
> have sent him to Gibraltar, instead of back to Toulon.[97]

The autumn of 1740 was enlivened for Maurice, after his return to
Paris, by the welcome news that Biren had been disgraced and thrown
with his entire family into the notorious fortress of Schlüsselburg.
The reason for his downfall was that the Tsarina Anna had died unexpectedly in October, leaving as successor her infant great-nephew
Ivan VI. Biren survived his mistress' death as chief minister for less
than a month, when he was arrested by General Münnich as unsere-
moniously as Henry IV of France had once arrested a much greater
duc de Biron.

Maurice knew by now that his chances of regaining the throne of
Courland, temporarily relinquished by Biren, were exceedingly slim.
None the less he hastened to Dresden to take what steps he could. On
reaching Saxony, he learned that the young Tsar, whose father was a
prince of Brunswick-Wolfenbüttel, had been prevailed upon to
nominate a cadet of the house of Brunswick in Biren's place. There
was no alternative for Maurice but to return in a disconsolate mood
to Paris, where in May 1741 he penned a letter to the nobles of Courland. In it he declared that after the events of 1726:

> We had no means now left of opposing an involuntary election, into
> which the Courlanders were dragooned by the Russians, but by pro-
> testations, the only resource of the weak; yet even that course was
> closed to us by the power of our enemies. As it would in some measure
> be giving our sanction to the injustice already done us, and now
> ready to be confirmed by another, were we to remain silent, we
> should be deficient in what we owe to ourselves, and to the solemn
> act which reciprocally binds Courland to us for ever. It would be
> giving up the most lawful of our titles, which no forced consent can
> annihilate, and no tract of time proscribe. It is for these reasons that,
> till it pleases God to cause justice to be rendered to us, which is our
> due, we here protest in the face of the whole world against all election
> made, or to be made, of a duke of Courland to our prejudice and
> contrary to our right. In fine, we declare that our enemies shall be
> alone answerable for the violence which they offer to Courland and

to us; reserving to ourselves all our rights, which still subsist, and will forever subsist, entire. We have set to these presents the seal of our arms, and joined the diploma of our election, that the whole may be published wherever it may be thought necessary.[98]

This curious document, Maurice *contra mundum*, was taken to Mitau by a personal courier, his old friend Dieskau, who volunteered to make the journey at his own risk. Maurice was in a fever of anxiety on behalf of his faithful servant as the day of the letter's delivery approached. In fact, Dieskau was promptly arrested; but while the authorities were debating the form of death which he should suffer, he escaped and returned to France. There, thanks to Maurice's favour, he soon afterwards became colonel of a crack regiment of horse.

In June the prince of Brunswick was formally elected to the duchy of Courland. Maurice received the news calmly: for by that time the edge of the blow had been blunted by something more immediate and equally exciting. On August 11th, 1741, he was once more on the high road to Strasbourg, and the wars.

The death of the Tsarina Anna, on October 17th, 1740, had been an event of no more than domestic importance to Russia. But the death, three days later, of the Emperor Charles VI, was destined to set the whole of Europe ablaze.

Charles was the last male heir of the house of Habsburg. His only son had died in infancy, leaving him with two daughters, Maria Theresa and Maria Anna, both of whom had married into the house of Lorraine. The Empire was elective, and no woman could expect legal election as empress: but it had been the old emperor's obsession that, whatever might be the fate of the main portion of his Empire, at least the hereditary domains of the house of Habsburg in Austria and Hungary should pass at his death to the elder of his daughters. Twenty-seven years earlier, his wish had been embodied in the Pragmatic Sanction of 1713, and endorsed by the Electors of the Empire; and much of the Emperor's subsequent life had been devoted to securing the adherence of the great powers of Europe to this simple plan. Great Britain, for example, had agreed to guarantee the Pragmatic Sanction by the terms of the Second Treaty of Vienna in 1731, but only on condition that the Archduchess Maria Theresa would never marry a Bourbon prince; and France had recognized the Sanction as part of the general settlement that closed the War of the Polish Succession. By the time of his death, Charles was confident that he would bequeath his Empire intact, and with general consent, to his twenty-three-year-old elder daughter. And if the Habsburg dominions had only been in as good heart as the Archduchess, there would have been no difficulty.

During his long reign, Charles VI had seen Vienna outpace Paris in artistic and architectural achievement. But the splendours of *hochbarock* Vienna had not been reflected in the polyglot provinces of which Vienna was the capital; and the imperial treasury had been drained by bad management and by constant war. Charles's closing years had been overcast by the shadow of revolt in Hungary, and by unsuccessful campaigns against the Turks. After the death of Eugène, the Imperial army had few outstanding generals, with the exception of Königsegg and the Emperor's younger son-in-law, Prince Charles of Lorraine; and the military reforms which Eugène had instituted had never been completed. By 1740, the Imperial patrimony was ripe for dismemberment, and the signatories to his Pragmatic Sanction were eyeing his dominions covetously.

Maria Theresa duly succeeded her father as Queen of Hungary, but immediately found herself faced with a hostile coalition of Prussia, France, Spain, Bavaria and Sardinia, against whom the young Queen could count on only one ally, Great Britain. Even the loyalty of her Hungarian subjects was in question. She had been ruling in Vienna for less than two months when, in December 1740, Frederick of Prussia precipitated the War of the Austrian Succession by the abrupt seizure of Silesia. Frederick II was not much older than Maria Theresa; like her, he had only just inherited his throne. He had lost no time whatever in embarking on the treacherous and aggressive policies which were to help earn for him the title of 'the Great'. Compounding his felony by resorting to warfare at a time of the year when, by gentlemanly and immemorial agreement, campaigning should cease, he completed the annexation of Silesia within a matter of weeks. It was the spring of 1741, before the Austrians could mount their counter-attack, and at the subsequent battle of Mollwitz, his first major engagement, the twenty-eight-year-old Frederick was as raw as most of his troops. Completely unprepared for the brutal shock of war, he lost his head and galloped precipitately from the field, and it was left to Field Marshal Schwerin to rally the Prussians and defeat the enemy. Many thousands of Prussian soldiers would die in the years ahead as a result of Frederick's efforts to live down this episode, that provoked the mirth of Europe and would always rankle deeply in his heart.

The Austrian reverse at Mollwitz gave rise to great satisfaction at Paris. The French now hastened to intensify their diplomatic offensive against the Empire, while they prepared for vigorous physical measures. In May, the leader of the war party, who was still Frederick of Prussia's hero, Belle-Isle, went to Bavaria to conclude the Treaty of Nymphenburg with the Elector Charles Albert. In return for various friendly pledges, France agreed at Nymphenburg to support the candidature of the Elector of Bavaria in the coming election for the Imperial throne: and when Maria Theresa was being crowned Queen of Hungary at Pressburg, in June 1741, Belle-Isle was already travelling around the Courts of Europe to drum up support for the Elector of Bavaria. In theory, there was no reason why the Wittelsbachs of Bavaria should not have attained the Imperial dignity, leaving the Habsburgs to enjoy their ancestral privileges in Austria, Bohemia and Hungary. But in practice, as everyone very well knew, the Habsburgs were aware that in order to retain even their ancestral possessions, they must keep the Imperial dignity in their own hands: if not in the hands of Maria Theresa herself, then in the hands of her husband, Francis of Lorraine. Equally, the purpose of the Bourbons in backing the Elector of Bavaria was not merely to raise him to the Imperial title, but to use him as the principal instrument for wrenching apart the Habsburg domains.

Maria Theresa's situation appeared almost hopeless. Great Britain was far away. Russia, divided by internal strife, and preoccupied by a war with Sweden, could offer no aid. Belle-Isle saw clearly that, with Prussia holding down the Austrian army in the north, the time had arrived for France to strike in the west. As a result of his advice, the French forces were therefore divided into two main armies. The first, under the command of the marquis de Maillebois, was sent to guard the northern frontiers of France against a possible invasion by the British, Hanoverians or Dutch. Such a task was perfectly congenial to Maillebois, who is known to history as one of the most amiably inactive of France's generals. The second army, actually under the command of Belle-Isle himself, but nominally under the command of his superior, the duc de Broglie, invaded southern Germany on July 31st. It was in this army that Lieutenant-general the comte de Saxe was appointed to serve as commander of the first division of cavalry.

Maurice had sensed that the coming war would provide the chance for which he had been waiting all his life. 'Here is the general muddle,' he wrote exultantly to Brühl, 'and I have a part to play in it.'[99] He had already offered his services to his former chief, Belle-Isle. 'If I could,' he had written to Belle-Isle in August,

> I should like to go to Saxony, and also to Silesia. I believe that I could bring these two kings to an agreement in a very few days. The King of Prussia has a very great liking for me. I think he would have more confidence in me than in anyone else whom the King of Poland could send him. Then I should come back and manage the King of Poland, whether he liked it or not.[100]

Maurice was in excellent fettle. Spas and cures were forgotten. He was therefore disgusted when the French expeditionary force squandered more than six valuable weeks of summer before beginning its march on Vienna. There was absolutely nothing to prevent the French from marching straight into the city. The roads ahead were already filled with refugees, and the great city itself was stricken with panic.

When at last the French started to move, there was a great sense of elation. Maurice led the vanguard with two squadrons of horse and twelve companies of infantry—rolling along down the high road to Vienna, as they should have been seven years before. And this time there was no Berwick and no Noailles to restrain them. By the Waldsee, south of Ulm, the confident little force brushed aside a defensive screen of eighteen thousand Austrians and continued their brisk advance. Behind them the main body was also making good speed, and by the middle of October the whole French army was encamped at St. Polten, where their ally the Elector of Bavaria joined them. In the celebrations that followed, the Elector went out of his way to flatter and compliment Maurice. He commiserated with him about the loss of Courland, but declared that his position as Lieutenant-General in the army of France was incomparably superior to that of a mere reigning duke. Maurice would privately have disagreed; yet it was a flattering remark, and he remembered that, after all, the Elector would shortly become the Emperor.

St. Polten is only thirty miles from Vienna. The Hofburg was two days' march away across an undefended plain. It was a wonderful, breath-taking, totally unique opportunity. And amazingly enough, it was simply not taken. On October 23rd, 1741, the French broke camp: and instead of falling on Vienna, they marched northwards into Bohemia.

The culprit was the Elector of Bavaria. He was greedy for the Habsburg domains—but he wanted them intact. Silesia had already been lost to the Prussians: now the Saxons were advancing into Bohemia. At that moment the Elector of Bavaria became almost as solicitous for the Habsburg possession as the Queen of Hungary herself. Although the march of the Franco-Bavarian forces to the northwards was ostensibly to join forces with their allies, it was chiefly intended to prevent the Saxons from establishing themselves in Bohemia and Upper Austria.

In addition, the French generals were uneasy about the strength of their army. It was efficient and well-equipped, but thanks to Fleury it was scarcely fifty thousand strong. Foolishly, they reckoned that the better part of valour was discretion.

It is surprising how many armies, finding themselves in sudden possession of the full initiative, cannot nerve themselves to deliver the decisive blow. The unexpected chance of a quick, bloodless victory usually seems too good to be true. There must be a catch in it. It was so now: and instead of riding in triumph through Vienna, Maurice found himself side-tracked into the tedious business of investing the town of Budweis on the right bank of the Vltava.

He was determined not to linger. He lusted for action. At the beginning of November, 1741, he appeared outside the gates of Prague. If his superiors would not allow him to capture the capital of Austria, he would capture the capital of Bohemia.

Encircled by its craggy ramparts, rising sheer above the broad expanse of the Vltava, Prague appeared to be impregnable. As soon as the Elector of Bavaria arrived, he sent a summons to its governor, the Irish Count Ogilvie, calling on him to surrender. Nobody was surprised by his cheerful refusal. The Austrian garrison, over three thousand strong, was backed by a hundred pieces of ordnance. Ogilvie had only to sit tight until the arrival of the main Austrian army under Grand Duke Francis of Tuscany, Maria Theresa's husband, and Field Marshal Neipperg. The two generals were a mere five leagues away.

The French forces were far from ready for a major assault after the long march from St. Polten. Alone of the French officers, Maurice had suffered no diminution of enthusiasm and energy. He had had a long experience of siege warfare, and he thought that its problems were over-rated. On November 25th, he rode round to the Saxon camp on the far side of the city, where he convened a council of war with three of the senior Saxon commanders. They happened to be his own half-brothers, Count Rutowski, Count Cosel, and the chevalier de Saxe. The exuberant quartet hammered out a method of forcing the city.

An attempt was planned for that same night, and one of Maurice's staff officers was disguised as a peasant, and sent into the besieged city to seek out vulnerable points in the fortifications. Maurice then rode back to the French camp to overcome the opposition which his stratagem was bound to arouse. Belle-Isle's younger brother, the most jealous of his rivals, was bitterly scornful, and the jittery and always unreliable Bavarians refused flatly to co-operate. Undaunted, Maurice went ahead with his plans for conquering a stoutly-defended city of over a hundred thousand inhabitants. In a matter of hours he had got together special equipment, in the form of ladders, ropes and planks; with equal despatch, he assembled a hand-picked assault group. It consisted of four companies of grenadiers of his favourite Beauce and Alsatian regiments, with a thousand infantry and twelve hundred dragoons in reserve. Among his principal lieutenants was the young duc de Biron, fresh from campaigning in Italy.

He later recalled the Prague affair for the benefit of his old mentor Folard. 'The marquis de Mirepoix,' he wrote,

> joined my cavalrymen at nine o'clock with his thousand infantrymen, and we set out immediately in the direction of the city. As the sector which I had selected was the citadel, which was extremely strong, we crept along the whole length of the outer moat as far as the *Neue Thor*, the only unfortified gate in this quarter of the town. Although it had been pointed out to me that this was unusually high, I none the less resolved to make it the focus of my attack, for I was poorly supplied with infantry and needed a point of entry through which my cavalry could pour without hindrance. Moreover, the city was so immense that I counted on the cavalry to prevent the enemy posts from linking up with one another. So I came as close to this gate as I could—the second one, facing the Lower Moldau or Vltava—with the object of escalading it. I made my dispositions while we were creeping forward.[101]

At one o'clock on a freezing November morning, the Saxon troops on the far side of the city started up a noisy diversionary attack. After various feints, they made a headlong attack on the great Charles Gate. Simultaneously Maurice halted his columns, distributed powder and shot, and went forward in person with M. de Chevert to observe the lie of the land. Creeping along an exposed section of the moat, the two men inspected the thirty-five-foot high bastion outside the gate, and noticed beside it a ledge of rubble whose top seemed to be almost level with the top of the bastion itself. There was no time for further reconnaissance. Maurice there and then decided to plant his ladders against the polygonal tower on the far side of the bastion of the gate. He would make some of his men climb the pile of rubble, from which vantage point they could shoot at the defenders of the gate and draw their fire. As soon as the musketry duel was under way, he himself would head for the drawbridge with the main force.

> 'All this,' as he told Folard later, 'took place in such a profound silence that the sentries on the rampart did not catch any hint of it. I ordered six hundred dragoons and four hundred carabiniers to dismount, leaving myself with twenty-four troops of cavalry to send through the gate once I had forced it. The grenadiers were ready with their ladders, and I ordered the leading sergeant to ascend with eight of his comrades. He was under no circumstances to let off his musket. He was to try and surprise the sentries and to stab them; if they defended themselves, he was to use the bayonet and the bayonet alone. He would be followed by M. de Chevert (lieutenant-colonel in the *Régiment de Beauce*), at the head of four companies of grenadiers, and by the young Comte de Broglie at the head of four hundred dragoons

or fusiliers. . . . When the sergeant reached the top of the rampart with his eight grenadiers, the sentries gave the alarm. I was stationed beside the moat, near the ledge of rubble, opposite the bastion which M. de Chevert was due to attack. Eight troops of dragoons were hidden thirty paces behind me. I jumped to my feet and shouted, " Come on, dragoons ! " They rushed up, and when the men on the polygonal tower spotted them, these opened fire on us. We replied with a heavy volley, and while we were doing so, M. de Chevert was scaling the bastion. There was a whole company of grenadiers on the rampart before the sentries realized it. . . . Soon M. de Broglie arrived on the scene with three more companies of grenadiers and a number of picquets : but as they were crowding one another so closely, some of the ladders gave way under their weight. . . . Then I charged with my eight troops of dragoons, and no sooner had we arrived at the edge of the moat then M. de Chevert, having over-come the enemy guard, let down the drawbridge for us. Once across it, we galloped hard for the main bridge that cuts the city into two. I found it barricaded, and bristling with cannon and defenders. The officer in charge was about to give us some nasty moments, when his ears caught the sound of the Saxons advancing from the *other* direction. Caught between two fires, he surrendered, and after the rest of the garrison had done likewise, we locked up the whole lot in their own barracks.'[102]

When the French and Saxons joined hands at dawn inside the city, Maurice and his half-brothers embraced each other ecstatically. It was an occasion on which their Saxon effusiveness was justified. A handful of men had captured one of the oldest cities of Europe at a cost of fourteen killed and twenty-two wounded.

Ogilvie delivered up the keys of Prague to Maurice, and next day Maurice presented them to the Elector of Bavaria during his solemn entry into his new capital. Maurice's authority and popularity were so great that there was little or no looting on the part of the con-querors—a state of affairs that compared very favourably with the havoc that was caused when his great-grandfather, Old Königsmarck, had terrorized the outskirts of Prague in 1648. The aldermen of the city were so grateful to Maurice for the discipline which he main-tained over his troops that they sent a deputation to his headquarters in the Coloredo Palace to present him with a magnificent diamond— a tribute nicely calculated to delight a son of Augustus the Strong.

At last he was famous. Single-handed, he had given France and her allies a buoyant sense of victory.

On December 7th 1741, the Elector of Bavaria was solemnly crowned King of Bohemia at Prague. In January 1742, he was formally elected Emperor as Charles VII. The French had thus achieved not only their current war aims, but seemed also to have realized the traditional ambition of the Bourbons: to bring about the downfall of the Habsburg ascendancy, and to secure the election of a client Emperor under the control of Versailles.

From the moment of his coronation, their regal puppet showed that he carried his new dignities without conviction. When Maurice offered his personal congratulations, Charles told him: 'True, I am King of Bohemia: but in much the same way that you are Duke of Courland.' Secretly, Maurice shared Charles' pessimism. By failing to seize Vienna three months earlier, the French had allowed the Queen of Hungary to consolidate her forces. In the previous autumn, Maria Theresa had appealed to the chivalry of the Hungarian nobles, appearing before them with her infant son in her arms. Moved by her courage, Count Battyany had spoken for the other members of the Estates when he cried: 'Let us die for Maria Theresa—our King!' While Hungary's precious levies were being raised and trained, the ranks of the Austrians had been stiffened by the arrival from Italy of many seasoned battalions. Maria Theresa's forces took fresh heart: and when the Emperor Charles, escorted by Maurice and Rutowski, returned to his Bavarian capital, he was quickly challenged by the resurgent Austrians. In a matter of days Charles was in full flight from Munich to Frankfort. As he fled, he may well have reflected on the fate of another member of his house, the Elector Palatine Frederick V, who in 1619 had also been foolhardy enough to flout the Habsburgs by accepting the crown of Bohemia, and who had later died a terrible death in exile, bereft even of his native Palatinate.

The proclamation at Frankfort of the Elector of Bavaria as head of the Empire was purely a sham. The assembled representatives of the European powers were unimpressed when the crown of Charlemagne was placed, in the presence of Maurice and Belle-Isle, on a head already crushed by the weight of the crown of Wenceslas.

Further blows fell speedily. While old Marshal Broglie was dithering, the Austrian general Khevenhüller overwhelmed Ségur's garrison at Linz, thereby snapping a vital link in the French chain of communications between their main armies and their garrison in Prague. By February, 1742, the Bavarian and Saxon armies were already facing the full-blooded wrath of the Austrians.

Maurice himself was by no means idle. When the Frankfort ceremonies were over, he retired for a period to Dresden, before leaving for Prague. Broglie, who shared the growing jealousy of the upper echelons of the French army against the irrepressible foreign interloper, at first refused to provide a post for Maurice. By March, 1742, even Broglie had realized that he could not do without Maurice's services. He ordered Maurice to take charge of the siege of Egra

(Cheb), a town of great strategic importance on the river Eger. Broglie, who had his own headquarters at near-by Pilsen, regarded the capture of Egra as a major objective, and had originally entrusted the task to the marquis de Leuville. The siege had gone wrong from the start. Leuville succumbed to fever, and Maurice was rushed in to take command instead.

The siege was difficult. The town, where Wallenstein had met his death a hundred years before, was an arsenal which the Austrians were determined to retain. The garrison, consisting of thirteen hundred first line troops, was amply provisioned, and supported by thirty pieces of artillery. It considered itself almost impregnable.

The garrison of Prague had held the same opinion four months before. Maurice was in an aggressive mood. In a letter to Augustus of Poland, he reported that: 'since this morning, the governor has been firing cannonballs at us like bullets: but we shall soon stop his noise.'[103] Within four nights, in spite of intense cold, the siege-works had reached the glacis. Then, just as the engineers were about to penetrate the ravelin, the work was disorganized by flooding. The sappers stuck manfully to their task. Soon they had managed to effect a lodgement. Maurice's artillerymen began to batter at the wall in order to effect a breach. The Austrians started to lose confidence as they watched gaps being breached in their counterscarp and saw that the besiegers were deterred neither by arctic conditions nor by a deadly fire from masked batteries. They realized that the siege operations were being directed by an expert hand. On the morning of April 19th, the Austrian commander, seeing French troops busily slithering into his ditch in utter disregard of shot and blizzard, hastened to surrender. Terms were arranged the same day, and the garrison was allowed to march out with the honours of war. In accordance with usage, the Austrian battalions undertook not to serve again against France until they were exchanged or ransomed for an equivalent number of Frenchmen. As at Prague, Maurice's moderation in victory was widely praised.

With the capture of Egra to add to the capture of Prague, Maurice had effected the two outstanding French successes of the war. He fully deserved the congratulatory note which the Emperor Charles sent him from Frankfort on April 25th. The message concluded with the wistful words: 'My dear Count Saxe, why can you not be everywhere?'

It was a pity that not all Maurice's superiors shared the Emperor's view. In spite of his success at Egra, the rift between Saxe and Marshal Broglie was rapidly widening. Maurice was aggrieved. He felt completely justified, even at this critical juncture, in asking for leave of absence. It was an extraordinary request—but he wished to pursue yet another of his urgent personal projects.

CHAPTER IX

MOSCOW AND BREISACH, 1742-1743

*Well, friend Sancho, what thinkest thou now? Dost thou
not hear how matters go? Did I not tell thee so before? See
now, whether we have not a kingdom we may command,
and a queen whom we may espouse?*

DON QUIXOTE

W HILE Charles of Bavaria was making empty gestures at Frankfort,
St. Petersburg was experiencing a second palace revolution within
fourteen months. In December 1741, the Grand Duchess Elizabeth
Petrovna, in concert with the Preobrazhenski Guards, had arrested
Anna Leopoldovna and her son, the young Tsar Ivan VI. The
wretched boy was to grow up in captivity, and would eventually die
in the fortress of Schlüsselburg at the age of twenty-four. Elizabeth
reigned as Tsarina in his stead.

The news of the Russian *coup* revived Maurice's interest in the
blonde Elizabeth and in Courland. He was prevented from journeying
at once to Russia by events in Bohemia, but he lost no time in soliciting the support of his royal brother at Dresden.

'I have learned from Marshal Belle-Isle, Sire,' he wrote to Augustus
'that there has been a change of ruler in Russia. It seems to me
impossible that you have already made arrangements about Courland.
Dare I flatter myself that you will think of me, and change my fortune
for me? You have no more tender, respectful, or longstanding friend
than myself; and since everything that you do has the touch of magnanimity, I pray you be generous to me. All Europe would applaud
you, and perhaps one day, Sire, fortune would enable me to show
you that your favour could not have been better bestowed.'[104]

It was unfortunate for the garrison of Egra that Maurice was
anxious to conclude the siege so swiftly. Without waiting for
Augustus' reply, he set off hot foot for Moscow.

Twelve years earlier he had ignored the urgent appeals of his
Saxon advisers to visit St. Petersburg and propose to Elizabeth
Petrovna. Now he was galled by the few days' delay that prevented
him from seeing her immediately. He recalled how, as a girl, she had

117

become infatuated with the idea of marrying him. There might still be a chance of recovering Courland by marrying her—and not merely Courland. Maurice de Saxe might be on the verge of becoming Tsar of Russia. Elizabeth, moreover, was good-looking. She was still only thirty-three, and resembled Maurice in that her impulsive, boisterous temperament united the native wildness of eastern Europe with the acquired elegance of Versailles. The pair of them might well have been admirably suited to one another. Certainly the marquis de la Chétardie, the principal French agent in Russia, thought so, and he voiced his opinion so strongly that Maurice eagerly absented himself from the wars in order to test his chances.

Maurice arrived in Moscow on the night of June 10th and went immediately to La Chétardie's palace. An experienced adventurer and accomplished secret diplomatist, La Chétardie knew just how to impress his guest with a telling display of magnificence. Maurice was as much a pawn in La Chétardie's game as La Chétardie in Maurice's: both stood to gain by Maurice's elevation. The two professional gamblers caroused until dawn, drinking to the success of their enterprise with much laughter, boasting, and breaking of glasses. At dawn, after an hour's rest, Maurice set off for the royal palace for his first interview with the new Tsarina, accompanied by La Chétardie and his own faithful majordomo, the Courlander Dieskau. The son of Augustus the Strong was graciously received by the daughter of Peter the Great. As if the twelve hundred miles' journey from Egra to Moscow and the junketings of the previous night were not enough, he was straightaway plunged into a round of balls and festivities. Elizabeth Petrovna not only possessed a profligate energy similar to his, but also the formidable advantage of youth and bounding health. That evening she gave a grand ball in his honour. Forty-eight hours later it was La Chétardie's turn to entertain her, with all the lavishness that had often astonished Europe, and which was the basis of his position as diplomatic *entrepreneur*. To this ball Elizabeth Petrovna came dressed as a man, a favourite trick of hers. She liked to give balls at which the sexes changed clothes, and her passion for costumes was so extravagant that at her death she was said to have left fifteen thousand outfits in her wardrobe.

On June 18th, at a sumptuous *déjeuner à la Russe*, she appeared in the guise of an Amazon, and galloped in a scanty tunic at Maurice's side through the streets of Moscow. The ride must have been an ordeal for a man with a disordered liver and a smashed knee, particularly as the exuberance of the Tsarina's horsemanship was widely celebrated. During the ride a torrential downpour began, but the drenched covey pelted on until the violence of the storm compelled even the royal Amazon to seek shelter. She ordered her companions to make for the Kremlin, where she amused herself by showing Maurice over the imperial apartments and playfully festooning him with the Russian crown jewels. They then left for another night of feasting at La Chétardie's palace, which lasted, with fireworks and fountains flowing with wine, until Elizabeth Petrovna left at dawn.

That brief acquaintance with the royal regalia was the closest Maurice came to enjoying them. It was soon made apparent that, much as Elizabeth enjoyed his company, her youthful yearning for the celebrated Saxon adventurer had passed. The dashing hero of her adolescence had become an ailing, middle-aged general, a caricature of the virile youth who had galloped away to seek his fortune in Poland, Germany, France and Courland. True, he had come to her at last: but he had come too late. She now preferred her Cossack favourites. Alexis Razoumovski had never needed to take a cure at a Mediterranean spa.

Maurice had badly misjudged the political as well as the purely personal situation. The Tsarina had certainly been under an obligation to La Chétardie for supporting her in the *coup d'état* of the previous December, but she quickly found his arrogance insupportable. Very soon afterwards he was to be driven from Russia. Maurice only fully realized the truth about her real feelings towards La Chétardie and himself when she informed him that, sympathetic though she was to his claim in Courland, she had unfortunately promised her support to another claimant, the Landgrave of Hesse-Cassel.

The expedition to Russia had been a complete fiasco. Maurice decided to cut his losses and return at once to Bohemia. Within three weeks of his first arrival in Russia, he was again on the long road to Warsaw. The road must have seemed intolerably flat and mournful. The illusion that had been sedulously, lovingly, obstinately nourished for fourteen years had been shattered. He felt ill, and old. Then, in his despair, cheerfulness broke in, as it always did. He took comfort at the thought of the campaign ahead.

The duke-elect of Courland was returning to his post as lieutenant-general in the armies of the king of France.

As matters stood at that moment in Bohemia, a French general seemed less likely to earn fame than terrible disgrace. By July 1742, the position of the French armies in central Europe had become utterly untenable.

France had been deserted by her principal allies. Frederick of Prussia, after a string of victories over the Austrians, had basely concluded a separate peace with Maria Theresa, by the terms of which he had secured the incorporation of Silesia in Prussia. When Belle-Isle hastened to Potsdam to protest against this act of perfidy, Frederick calmly showed the angry Frenchman copies of a secret correspondence between France's chief minister and the Queen of Hungary that clearly showed that Fleury had been contemplating a similar betrayal. Belle-Isle was taken completely by surprise: he had not guessed that his war party had already been sold out by Fleury and the partisans of peace.

Had Belle-Isle himself been in command in Bohemia, Frederick might have been willing to continue the war for a few months longer, at least until the effects of his crowning victory of Chotusitz had exerted some benefit on the French military position. Frederick regarded Broglie, the actual commander in Bohemia, as a hopeless incompetent: and Frederick was right. Moreover the King of Prussia certainly did not regard himself as in any way beholden to the King of France. His main desire was to rest his hard-tried men by ending the present campaign as soon as possible. That was precisely what he did.

Deserted by Prussia and Prussia's Saxon allies, the central French armies under Broglie were soon floundering aimlessly. In a matter of weeks the whole force was cornered by the Austrians and shut up in Prague. Broglie attempted to treat with the enemy, asking to be allowed to make an honourable withdrawal from the trap in which he now found himself. The Queen of Hungary rejected this appeal with contempt. Fleury then brazenly offered to abandon the puppet Emperor Charles VII if only Maria Theresa would allow Broglie to evacuate Bohemia. Again Maria Theresa refused. By August, when the Austrian generals Prince Charles of Lorraine and Königsegg were dining off well-stocked boards within sight of the doomed city, Broglie and Belle-Isle were eating horseflesh within the stony walls.

Maurice hurried to join Marshal Maillebois, who was engaged in bringing the army of the north down the Rhine with the intention of relieving Prague. He placed himself at Maillebois' disposal at Regensburg, and was chagrined at being given only an insignificant post on the staff of the duc d'Harcourt, although he was technically the latter's senior. If Maurice was piqued by the slight to his rank and reputation, Harcourt reacted more strongly still by complaining to Fleury that Maurice was a foreigner, a Lutheran, and the brother of a king who had just betrayed France.

These personal quarrels could not prevent Maurice from becoming the spearhead of the French counter-attack. As Maillebois' troops were unseasoned, Maurice ordered them to evade minor skirmishes with enemy irregulars. Unnecessary casualties must at all costs be avoided. He rightly considered that the immediate task was to free the passes through the mountains, and in August and September he succeeeded in accomplishing this operation with nominal losses. He seems to have been the only senior officer who acted with energy and a sense of urgency. 'I have never seen an army so ill-regulated as this,' groaned Prince Poniatowski, 'and if we lose Count Saxe, who is obliged to take everything upon his own shoulders, I do not know where we shall be.' It was Maurice who prodded Maillebois into entering Bohemia in October; it was Maurice who exorcized the general French fear of the ferocious Croat freebooters who were rampaging round the country-side; and it was Maurice who exterminated thousands of these blood-thirsty bandits in the autumn.

If Maillebois had acted as decisively as Maurice, Prague might still have been relieved. Its French garrison had fought off a major attack in August, though it had sustained nearly a thousand casualties in doing so. In October, exhausted by sickness and starvation, it was still holding on. At this juncture, Broglie decided to try a breakout at the head of twelve thousand men, hoping to link up with the advancing Maillebois. The plan was reasonably sound in conception, but it proved a complete disaster in practice. Broglie and Maillebois, after exchanging countless querulous despatches, finally agreed on a *rendezvous* for their respective flying columns. Both of them then failed to arrive at the appointed place on time. Maillebois had got cold feet, and had completely retreated after Fleury, wrongly informed that the Austrians were ready to conclude a peace, had given him permission to retire in order to save France's last intact army. While Maillebois was trailing homewards, with the vague intention of protecting France's exposed flank in Westphalia, Broglie added to the confusion by summarily deciding to leave his own column to its fate. He dashed ahead for safety, leaving his twelve thousand men to make their own way back to Prague as best they could, the stragglers being easily picked off by the encircling Austrians.

Maurice, who in the past had quarrelled with both the Marshals separately, now quarrelled with them simultaneously. He was com-pelled to watch Belle-Isle's agonizing ordeal inside Prague without being able to lift a finger to help him. Belle-Isle, who had indignantly rejected Fleury's appeals to surrender before he was annihilated, imagined that Broglie would still come to his rescue: after all, nothing less was at stake than the honour of France. But as week succeeded week, and autumn deepened into winter, it slowly dawned on him that he and his men would have to try to escape from Prague unaided. His troops were now dying in their hundreds, and ammunition was fast running out. How could he evade the vigilance of the Austrians and effect an escape?

He laid his plans skilfully. On December 16th, with the tempera-ture below freezing point, fifteen thousand Frenchmen suddenly debouched from the two main gates of the city in two columns. They carried with them provisions for twelve days and all the arms and artillery they could muster. Brushing aside the Austrian pickets, they stole a day's march on Prince Lobkowitz and marched hard for Bavaria. Behind them they left their sick and wounded, eighteen hundred crippled and starving men, with instructions to hold out as long as possible: a real skeleton garrison.

It was a fearful retreat. Contemporaries compared it to Xenophon's retreat to the sea after Cunaxa, while nineteenth-century historians likened it to the retreat from Moscow. Belle-Isle had to advance in full view of enemy cavalry; for ten nights his men slept in the snow. Wonderful work was achieved by the French master gunner, La Vallière, who kept the enemy horsemen at bay with thirty guns switched rapidly from flank to flank: the first recorded use of horse artillery. The commander of the rear, Biron, performed marvels worthy of Ney as the decimated columns tramped through Carlsbad and Elnbogen and finally, on St. Stephen's Day, emerged like a horde of ragged phantoms before the gates of Egra. Fully half of the original fifteen thousand had fallen by the way. Many more of them now perished as a result of pressing too closely round the bonfires prepared for their welcome.

The retreat represented a defeat, but it was a defeat that had salvaged the pride of France. With Belle-Isle's force there had marched a lieutenant who was one of the brightest spirits of the age, the young Luc de Clapiers, marquis de Vauvenargues. His sufferings during the march had been heightened by the fact that behind him at Prague had died his dearest friend, Hippolyte de Seytres, to whom all his principal works had been dedicated, and whom he had always regarded as the embodiment of the stoic ideal. Vauvenargues' own stoicism had been tested almost beyond the limit of endurance by the events of the Bohemian campaign. After a gay and sunny introduction to warfare in Italy, the frail philosopher of twenty-six had been cast into the ferocious squalor of the Danubian struggle of 1742 and 1743. Although the retreat from Prague failed to break his spirit, it destroyed his body. The consumption and frostbite which he contracted brought about his death four years later. As he tottered through the gate of Egra, one wonders if he recalled his own famous maxim: *Il n'y a pas de gloire achevée sans celle d'armes.*

It was part of Vauvenargues' misfortune that he regarded the career of arms as such a serious pursuit. He and Maurice de Saxe, in their different ways, were dedicated fighting men, soldiers by vocation, condemned to live their lives among those increasingly frivolous and unmartial people, the Parisians and Dresdeners of the age of reason. But while such men survived, eighteenth-century France was still warmed by the refulgence of its heroic age. Maurice was to be one of the last great men who gave meaning to the tarnished word *glory*, which in Vauvenargues' sense implied the exercise of unstinted energy and Roman will, breaking out at last into acts that reveal, in radiance, the full extent of human potentiality.

At the moment the feats which Maurice was called upon to perform were in no sense transcendental. In 1743 France asked for survival, not glory. The country was in a state of panic; Paris was packed with refugees; a law ordaining compulsory military service had hastily been drafted. He began by trying to run supplies through the mountains to Egra. He worked unsparingly: but in a matter of weeks he became aware that he had been rigidly excluded, through prejudice, from the higher counsels of the French army, counsels which his rank entitled him to attend. It also became clear to him that he was being deliberately hampered, to such an extent that he was driven to return for a while to Saxony, where he busied himself with raising a regiment of Uhlans for future use. Not that he lacked powerful supporters in France as a whole. Argenson, the new minister of War, and Noailles, who had replaced the exhausted and discredited Belle-Isle, thought highly of him, while Louis XV himself was intelligent enough to appreciate the need of able commanders in the field. The fissures which had begun to appear in the edifice of the *ancien régime* could no longer be concealed, even from the king. A victory or two were badly needed to restore a measure of faith in the monarchy.

In January 1743 old Fleury, the chief minister, had died. 'If the desire to please,' as a French historian observed, 'constituted the whole secret of the art of government, Fleury would have been a great minister.'[105] Now that the old gentleman's withered hands had at last been prised loose from the helm of state, it almost seemed possible that the tide of war might yet turn in France's favour, even at the eleventh hour.

The immediate task facing the new ministry was to prevent the junction of the Austrian troops in Bavaria with those of the 'Pragmatic Army', as the still non-belligerent British and Hanoverian force, now marching with great circumspection southwards from Brussels, was called. Whatever the ability and courage of the new ministers, their dilemma was formidable. Although the British had not yet formally declared war, and their army was taking elaborate care not to trespass on French soil, yet their ultimate target must be France. The ministers of Louis XV decided to call the British bluff. They intercepted their adversaries at Dettingen, a village south of Frankfort-am-Main, on June 16th 1743. The result was a bloody battle. Noailles, manoeuvring boldly, had thrust deeply into Germany and stationed his forces in an excellent position. He slipped neatly behind the Pragmatic Army and sundered it from its supply base at Frankfort. The

British and Hanoverians were not only numerically inferior to his own, but riddled with dissension at the top. The commander, until the arrival of King George II in person, was Lord Stair, who had once shared a Parisian mistress with Maurice, and had been a highly regarded pupil of Marlborough and Eugène. Unfortunately, Stair's military experience counted for little with George II and his young son Cumberland, both of whom took the comfortable view that the blood royal was born to command. While they wrangled with Stair, and their Hanoverian and British subordinates wrangled among themselves, Noailles skilfully penned the Pragmatic Army between a wide river and a dense forest, placing their lines of advance and retreat under direct fire from the French batteries under the celebrated La Vallière.

Yet, when the battle was eventually joined, George II contrived to snatch victory from the very jaws of defeat. It occurred much more by luck than by management, assisted by the fact that generals like Noailles, who fight by the book, are often incapable of coping with the unforeseen developments that are a feature of every battle. Noailles' judgement became completely paralyzed when a tragic blunder destroyed his neat dispositions right at the start of the engagement. His nephew, the duc de Grammont, prematurely and unaccountably led thirty thousand men, supposedly anchored on the village of Dettingen, into an exposed forward position. This rash action masked the French artillery and blocked the path of the cavalry. The British were commendably quick to see their opportunity, seized it, and swiftly routed their opponents.

The French poured back across the river in disarray. Hundreds of men were drowned or trampled to death in the mêlée. The British and their allies had only to charge in order to obliterate their enemies: yet somehow they allowed the French to withdraw with a loss of only four thousand men. The Pragmatic Army was denied a great victory for want of a final and decisive order. 'The King halted,' as a British officer wrote in his journal,

> and the scene of action and military ardour was suddenly turned into a court circle—His Majesty was congratulated by every military courtesan on horseback on the glorious event—the Hanoverian generals galloped up with their reports—questions innumerable were asked and reports made: the British generals returning lamented the loss of so interesting a crisis, and some of them ineffectually represented upon it, yet the enemy was suffered to quietly repass their bridge over the Main! although 6000 Hessians were at Hanau in perfect order for action! [106]

The truth was that George II had had enough exertion for one day. In his scarlet coat, waving a huge horse-pistol and brandishing an outsize sabre, the purple-faced king had expended much energy in riding along his lines. Once his horse had bolted, carrying him back towards the rear. It is not certain that he ever realized that only Grammont's error had saved him from the humiliation of surrender. That evening he pitched camp sedately on the ground vacated by the French, and rejected Stair's request to pursue Noailles. Five weeks later he got rid of Stair himself, when the general obtained his sovereign's 'permission' to resign from the British army.

The French were thrown into consternation by their unexpected defeat. When the news of Dettingen reached Bavaria, Broglie immediately withdrew his army, leaving the hapless Charles VII at the mercy of Maria Theresa. Broglie felt that he could no longer fight on the Danube when Noailles' army was no longer able to cover his flank. Not for the first time, he preferred to head for the shelter of his native country, whatever the consequences to his allies. Eastern France was thrown into a veritable uproar. The Austrians were pressing along the Rhine; Stanislas Leczinski fled from his palace at Lunéville; Hungarian and Transylvanian marauders were freely roaming round Alsace. Not since Oudenarde had France come so close to irretrievable disaster.

At the time of Oudenarde Maurice had been a juvenile spectator of France's trials. It now fell to him to be the principal agent of her salvation.

He had been summoned from Dresden in the spring of 1743 to assist Broglie in Bavaria. At first he was given charge of Broglie's rearguard, but was later ousted from that position by the young prince de Conti, a prince of the blood. Argenson fully appreciated the folly of Conti's appointment, but was unable, even as Minister of War, to prevent it. Nevertheless he managed to ensure that Maurice was soon given an even more important post, the command of the army at Spires in the Palatinate. 'They have given me command of the army of Alsace,' he told Augustus III in July: 'not bad for a German, and a Lutheran into the bargain.'[107] It was the first time that he had ever commanded an entire army. His main task was to keep the middle of the French line stable, while Broglie and Noailles operated on the wings.

A crisis was not long in coming. Broglie, repulsed after a half-hearted push into Bavaria, promptly ran for the shelter of the west bank of the Rhine. Once he was home and dry, he preferred not to stay with his army, and lost no time in handing it over to Maurice. The fate of France was in the hands of the Saxon.

Maurice was quick to see that his new forces were dispersed over too wide an area. The most resolute of the enemy generals, Prince

Charles of Lorraine, had also realized this, and was determined to profit by it. He declared his intention of crossing the Rhine and stripping France of his native duchy of Lorraine: and if Lorraine went, so would Alsace. Charles, brushing aside an amateurish challenge from Conti, established himself at Old Breisach and prepared to ferry his men across the river.

Old Breisach is west of Freiburg, forty miles distant from Strasbourg. Maurice forthwith took up his own position at New Breisach, on the opposite bank of the Rhine.[108] He made it plain that he intended to fight to the death to prevent a passage of the Rhine. He was not a Broglie nor a Maillebois.

His display of resolution halted Charles of Lorraine in his tracks. The Austrian general decided to turn aside and probe for a softer point of ingress further upstream. He should have remembered that Maurice was a master of this kind of manoeuvre. A man who had checked an attempt by Prince Eugène to ford the Rhine at Mannheim was unlikely to be outwitted by a less experienced commander. Wherever Charles halted, at once he became uneasily aware that he had been adroitly shadowed by Maurice's columns on the other side of the river. Below the dark silhouette of the Vosges lurked the lines of French musketeers. Maurice, now commanding the services of three lieutenant-generals and ten *maréchaux-de-camp*, reckoned that he had made the river virtually impassable from Basel on the south to Ettlingen in the north. He fortified the traditional outposts, built others, and devised a tight system of communications and intelligence to frustrate the armies of Maria Theresa.

As he wrote to Brühl from one of his temporary camps, during that late summer of 1743 he represented, quite incontestably, 'the shield of France against Prince Charles'.[109] And his reward was to be superseded. In September, with his task brought almost to a triumphant conclusion, he was ordered to surrender his command to the aged Marshal Coigny. Under the *ancien régime*, re-emergence of superannuated, practically senile commanders was a sure sign that a crisis was waning. In fact, the military situation was now quiescent. With exemplary obedience, Maurice rode away from his headquarters to join Noailles; and while Noailles marched his men into the interior of Alsace to establish them in winter quarters, Maurice was given charge of the rear. He placed himself in a pivotal position within the famous lines of Lauterbourg, facing the enemy camps at Ettlingen. He was permitted to remain there without molestation, for the Austrians decided not to try to cross the river that season.[110]

In November, at the conclusion of a rather unsatisfactory military year, Maurice was able to return to Paris. His homecoming—for Paris had long been his real home—was as triumphant in 1743 as it had been in 1735, when he had also been the man responsible for holding the Austrians at bay. Once again he was fêted; and once again he was invited to Versailles in order to give Louis XV a first-hand account of his exploits. The king, who had temporarily taken the government of the country into his own hands, did not conceal his personal admiration for Maurice. He found Maurice a congenial companion, a fellow huntsman of animals and women, a man never censorious of other people's pleasures. Louis also appreciated that Maurice was the only one of his generals who, in two major wars, had brought a much-needed measure of fame to France.

The big Saxon was clearly destined for higher things. At forty-seven, he had been a professional soldier for over thirty years, and had written the most seminal treatise on the art of war to appear in his time. The senior officers under whom he had served were compelled, even if some of them did so with reluctance, to recommend him. Noailles called him *mon enfant*; Belle-Isle had praised him in extravagant terms; Coigny testified to his tactical genius; Maillebois admitted that he had found his counsel invaluable. Even the atrabilious Broglie put in a good word for Maurice: and from distant Potsdam Frederick the Great bombarded his cousin of France with entreaties to entrust Maurice with supreme command.

By this time, even the officers who were his social superiors admitted that the foreigner was their master in the art of war. The ruffled pride of a Conti or a Harcourt could no longer be allowed to stand in the way of his advancement. France needed him, and needed him badly. She could not afford any longer to ignore or insult a general who was the tried pupil of Eugène and Schulenburg, a soldier with the strength and spirit of a Königsmarck.

Maurice would never again suffer the indignity of being superseded in his command in time of war.

CHAPTER X

DUNKIRK, 1743-1745

*'I wish,' quoth my uncle Toby, 'you had seen what
prodigious armies we had in Flanders.'*
TRISTRAM SHANDY

IN the winter of 1743-44, Maurice went often to Versailles to consult
with the King, Noailles and Argenson. Their deliberations were long
and anxious: France's prospects in the coming campaign were bleak.
The Austrians were encamped in full strength along the length of the
Rhine, and the expected invasion of Alsace and Lorraine could not long
be delayed. Effective counter measures hardly seemed possible, although
there was a slight chance that Frederick of Prussia might be persuaded
to relieve the pressure by resuming the war against Maria Theresa.
Before Frederick would consent to unleash his armies, he had to be convinced that France was willing to strike hard in the west. This, however, was a problem for the politicians. Maurice's immediate task was
to make sure that the holding operation on the Rhine was fool-proof.

To the north, in Flanders, the position seemed a little more promising. Here there was scope for making considerable military and diplomatic capital out of the political difficulties of the British Government.
The war was fast becoming unpopular in England, where it was now
suspected that formal intervention in the European conflict would
benefit Hanover rather than Great Britain. Malicious observers pointed
out that George II, as Elector of Hanover, had a peculiar interest in
Imperial elections which his British subjects did not share. Moreover,
the conduct of the late campaign had been heavily criticized, and the
ministry had come under sharp fire. There was inflammable material
here which the French could usefully work on.

There was obviously little advantage to be gained from policing the
northern frontier in the negative fashion adopted by Maillebois earlier
in the war. France would have to exert herself, if she wished to secure
the military prestige necessary to obtain an honourable peace.
Vigorous action alone could restore the morale of the troops, for
French soldiers have always been at their best in attack. Maurice
therefore urged the necessity of taking the offensive, and suggested an
immediate invasion of the Austrian Netherlands.

A CAVALIER

Plate from the first edition of Mes Rêveries
(Saxe's ideal notion of a cavalryman)

It was a startling and unorthodox suggestion. For France to go over to the offensive within a year of Dettingen, with the Austrians dominating the Rhine, would be risky in the extreme. Yet a bold strategy was clearly called for, and could hardly cause worse havoc than the prevailing strategy of *immobilisme*. Maurice was no advocate of the offensive for its own sake: the whole notion of *guerre à l'outrance* was abhorrent to him; but he knew very well that all war is hazardous, and that skill in waging it resides in accepting the calculated risk. The risks entailed in his most celebrated exploit to date, the storming of Prague by night, had been quickly and accurately calculated and gladly taken. The projected invasion of the Low Countries in 1744 was equally hazardous, but the stakes were even higher. If it succeeded, it would at one stroke restore French self-confidence and strike fear into the enemy; more important, it would further the strategic aim that Maurice would keep in the forefront of his mind from the very first moment that he was first summoned to supreme command. Like all sound strategic aims, it was simple: and like all good generals, Maurice clung to it despite repeated tactical setbacks. In a sentence, his aim was to drive a wedge between the forces of Great Britain and her continental allies. He would cut off Britain from Hanover and Prussia, and either intimidate or obliterate the Dutch. Further, whenever the British landed an army, he would not only move heaven and earth to prevent it from linking up with its allies across the Rhine, but would also try to isolate it from the Channel ports which were its lifeline.

Before embarking on any major schemes, Maurice paid a brief visit to Strasbourg. In February 1744, the regiment of Uhlans which he had raised the previous year arrived from Poland, and it was necessary to clothe it, arm it, appoint its officers, and impart to it the rudiments of his personal system of training [*c.f.* Plate 4]. The Volontaires de Saxe, as they were called, had been approved by a royal decree of March 30th, 1743. The regiment was to consist of six brigades, each of sixty-four 'volunteers' together with the usual number of servants. The men were to be

> Tartars, Wallachians, or Poles. They will be armed with sabre and lance, dressed in Tartar fashion, and provided with cuirasses. The servants will be armed with carbines and sabres. The regiment will be mounted on horses from Wallachia or from the Bessarabian province of European Turkey.[111]

Their uniform was to consist of a green coat and trousers, a red waist-coat, a red belt, and Hungarian boots. On their heads they were to wear gilded helmets adorned with horsehair plumes, and their saddle-clothes were to be of wolfskin. Even the servants were to be armed, for Maurice was alive to the potential usefulness of servants. At Prague he had permitted a warlike valet, called Fischer, to organize his fellow valets into a corps that performed excellent service. After Prague he made Fischer the captain of a company of one hundred men, and in less than four years the number of the *Chasseurs de Fischer* had risen to six hundred. In one of Maurice's later battles, the former valet's troopers were to act as Louis XV's personal bodyguard.[112]

Maurice was not the only foreign general in the service of France who had been asked to raise a regiment. In 1743 another remarkable soldier of fortune, Ulrich-Frederik-Waldemar von Löwendahl, had also been given permission to leave France to raise an Uhlan regiment. Löwendahl, a Dane whom Maurice had originally brought into the French service, was to play a great part in the remaining campaigns of the war, a part second only to that of Maurice. Three years younger than Maurice, he too had gone to war at the age of thirteen. He had been campaigning in Poland, as a youngster, when he first fell in with Maurice, though they parted company when the latter went to France to take up the brevet offered to him by the Regent. At the same time Löwendahl had entered the service of Saxony, and Augustus II had quickly made him a full general. As one who shared Maurice's advanced ideas on the training of troops, in 1730 he was seconded to Prussia to instruct the Prussian staff; and at the close of the War of the Polish Succession, in which he had defended Warsaw, he had accepted the post of general of artillery in the army of Maurice's former playmate at Mitau, the Tsarina Anna. After an adventurous career in the Ukraine and the Crimea, he had risen to the rank of Governor of Estonia at the time when Maurice prevailed upon him to accept a lieutenant-generalship in the French army.

Löwendahl was just the man Maurice needed as his principal lieutenant in the operations he was preparing to launch against the British and the Dutch. The Dane's appointment was not easily secured, in spite of his manifest brilliance, for the king and Argenson had to endure the usual ritual outbursts of indignation from the princes of the blood at the introduction of another foreigner and another Lutheran. But Maurice was now strong enough to be able to choose his own staff, and he knew that in choosing Löwendahl he was hastening a process near to his heart: revitalizing the outdated, fossilized routines of western European warfare. By introducing some of the more flexible techniques of the Great Northern War, in which they had both served, Löwendahl and Maurice would greatly enliven the new phase of the War of the Austrian Succession.

It was still too early to open the major campaign. In the meantime, Maurice went north to take charge of an entertaining military side-show.

As early as January 13th 1744, he had been commissioned by Louis XV to undertake the invasion of Great Britain. 'For this purpose,' ran the royal commission,

> we could not make a better choice than our well-loved friend Count Saxe, lieutenant-general in our armies. By reason of what we know of his valour, courage, experience in war, vigilance, activity and wise conduct, of which he gave ample proof during the last two campaigns in Germany, and on many other occasions in the different tasks which we have entrusted to him, we feel completely confident that he will enjoy a similar success in England.[113]

The invasion was to be launched to sponsor the cause of the Young Pretender, Princes Charles Edward. 'Bonnie Prince Charlie' was to sail to England with Maurice, depose King George II, and proclaim himself as regent for his father, the *soi-disant* King James III, with whom the French had secretly been negotiating for many years. Prince Charles Edward had earlier been invited to leave Italy, where he had been spending his exile, in order to discuss the project with the French authorities. After outwitting the spies paid to observe his every move, he sailed from Leghorn and landed at Antibes. When he reached Paris, however, he was received by Louis XV with unexpected and inexplicable coldness. He therefore left at once for Dunkirk to join Maurice.

The Duke-Elect of Courland and the would-be Prince of Wales had a great deal in common. If any man in France could sympathize with the young Pretender's predicament, that man was Maurice de Saxe. It was thus unfortunate that Maurice now proceeded, quite deliberately, to hoax and gull the unfortunate prince. The long-awaited invasion of England, so dear to Jacobite hearts, was never really intended to be much more than a charade. It is impossible to take the preparations for it seriously; the continual hesitations and delays of the French Government suggest that they were not acting in earnest. It is true that Maurice had won a reputation for being able to win great victories with slender resources; but even Maurice at his most impudent could scarcely have contemplated invading England with the ten thousand men now in camp at Dunkirk. Charles Edward eagerly assured the French that there would be a popular rising in Great Britain as soon as he landed. But the French were well aware that this was an inherited fantasy of the house of Stuart, and that the claims of the young prince's title, however acceptable in legitimist circles, were more than offset in the eyes of the British by his Roman Catholic faith and his foreign allies. Invasion, as Louis XV and his ministers knew, would only compel the British to rally behind the dynasty of Hanover.

Maurice, the confidant of Noailles and Argenson, also knew this.

He was aware too that the British army would swiftly destroy his force of ten thousand men, even if it escaped the vigilance of the British navy and actually landed. The whole project was nothing more than military vaudeville, which also happened to chime in very well with Maurice's general strategy: a concentration of troops at Dunkirk need only thrust north-east along the Flanders coastline to drive a wedge between Great Britain and her allies. Ten thousand men would never serve for a full-scale invasion of the British Isles: but they could very easily constitute the spearhead of a larger striking force. Furthermore, their mere presence at Dunkirk procured a useful advantage for the French, in that they frightened the British into withdrawing a substantial number of their regiments from the Continent in order to swell the garrison at home.

Maurice had inaugurated his career as a senior commander by devising a stratagem as inexpensive as it was successful. Less than a year after Dettingen, France appeared so little discouraged that she actually seemed on the point of carrying the war to the shores of Britain. There could scarcely be much wrong with an army so willing to assume the offensive. Maurice had put his men in good heart even before he led them into battle.

He paraded his ten battalions of infantry and fifteen companies of dragoons along the beaches of Dunkirk with great *élan*. To the accompaniment of beating drums and waving banners, they marched and counter-marched with the rataplan of a stage army. It was not without irony that over half of this expeditionary force, dedicated to the task of restoring the Stuarts to the throne of their ancestors, was composed of Swiss, Corsican and Monégasque mercenaries. They would have made a picturesque spectacle as they wound their way through the green lanes of Kent or Sussex.

Throughout February and March, long despatches were sent to Maurice by the king and Argenson, solemnly debating the best course to be adopted during and after the subjugation of the British Isles. Maurice's replies were equally solemn. Would it be better to land at Colchester or Maldon? Ought Admiral Barailh's squadron to sail further up the Thames than Blackwall? It is difficult to resist the conclusion that this portentous correspondence was undertaken solely to maintain the illusions of the Pretender and his entourage. The Jacobites in Dunkirk gleefully reported in the secret letters to England that Louis XV was showing a strong personal interest in the venture.

It was thus embarrassing for Maurice that at this delicate juncture the French fleet accidentally won a naval battle off Toulon. The French Mediterranean fleet was set upon by a superior British force under Admiral Matthews, the admiral who had so genially entertained Maurice aboard his flagship in the summer of 1740.

Matthews gave the French a severe mauling, but had bungled his pursuit, and the battle was hailed by France as a victory. As a result the Jacobite party became quite convinced that French superiority at sea was such that France must already command the Channel, and that Admiral Roquefeuille must already have bottled up Admiral Norris in Portsmouth. This piece of wishful thinking was hard to dispel; and a month later Prince Charles Edward was outraged when he heard that Norris had 'escaped' from Portsmouth and was marshalling his fleet off the Dunes.[114]

In fact, no French armada was likely to put out from Dunkirk with the British Channel Fleet at sea. True, a half-hearted process of embarkation was begun on March 1st, but was almost immediately disrupted by a week of violent gales. As in 1588, 'the wind blew, and they were scattered'. Many of the French ships sank at their moorings, and a number of men drowned. It was no great set-back. As far as the French were concerned, the invasion exercise had served its purpose; and the gales provided Maurice and Argenson with an excellent excuse for calling a halt. On March 11th, Maurice formally advised the Young Pretender that, on Louis XV's instructions, he had given orders to suspend the enterprise 'until a more favourable juncture'. He told the prince that the remaining troops were already being disembarked. 'I do not know, Monseigneur,' he observed, 'how to express my sorrow to Your Royal Highness for this delay, and how much it pains me.' Privately he softened tthe blow by suggesting ways by which the attack could still be pressed home. The prince wrote to him two days later to say that it was heartening to learn that Maurice 'was not in the least discouraged by all these tiresome misadventures that have befallen us', adding that 'your project of embarking 30,000 men in fishing vessels to make England sweat has given me infinite satisfaction'. Charles Edward ended his letter with a pathetic postscript: 'The court gave me to understand, before I left Paris, that you were in possession of a sum of money upon which I might draw at need. Would you therefore be good enough to give the bearer of this letter five hundred *louis d'or*?'[115]

It cannot have been pleasant for Maurice, of all people, to cheat a young princeling of his kingdom. He must have remembered Courland: and he must have felt some shame when Charles Edward had to be forcibly prevented, a little later, from setting sail for England with two or three faithful companions in a fishing-smack. And he was probably filled with admiration when he heard, in July 1745, that the prince, with only a handful of supporters and £5,000 in cash, had achieved a landing in Scotland. 'The Forty-five' was just the kind of madcap episode which would have delighted Maurice. If he had been twenty years younger, he might well have been tempted to join the Young Pretender's brigade himself.[116]

In 1744, Maurice was no longer a light-hearted adventurer, but one of the weightiest men in France. On Marsh 26th, 1744, the seal was finally set on his career of arms. To have been a lieutenant-general at thirty-seven had been a considerable achievement: but now, as a mere stripling of forty-seven, Maurice de Saxe was raised to the dignity of Marshal of France.

The Marshal of France had originally been, in feudal times, a great and unique officer of state. In the time of Francis I, the office had been divided between a pair of soldiers; then Henry III had raised the number of marshals to four; and Louis XIV had increased the number to twenty. But in 1744 there were only eleven men who bore this resounding title, and most of them were in retirement. Maurice's promotion as a twelfth marshal was all the more remarkable because he had not yet won a major victory in pitched battle. His main achievements, apart from minor skirmishes and a good deal of brilliant manoeuvring, had been the sieges of Prague and Egra, and the defence of the Rhine in 1743. Moreover he was a German, a bastard, and a Protestant. It was only to be expected that the French nobility should utter a concerted howl of outrage. Their sense of injury was not lessened when Louis decided to observe established precedent and address the new Marshal as *mon cousin*. The court had waited in a state of painful expectation for this crucial point of protocol to be settled: and its disgust when Louis eventually used the familiar term was almost universal. Louis had endured the sneers of many of these same courtiers when he had married his Polish wife, and so he cared little enough for their susceptibilities. It was now inevitable that Maurice should be given high command, and the spiteful twitterings in the eaves of Versailles were of no account.

For Maurice it was a wonderfully proud moment. He had reached his towering rank without crawling or making any concessions; he had won it fairly and squarely, and forced the French to accept him on his own terms. Some weeks earlier he had been privately advised that he could only hope to receive a marshal's *bâton* if he became a Roman Catholic: and although he had promised courteously to consider the matter, a Lutheran he had remained. When he was young he had refused to change his religion to please the Poles and gain a crown, as his half-brother Frederick Augustus had done in 1712. He was therefore unlikely, in middle life, to change his religious loyalties—faith is too strong a word—in order to please the French. He had thrust his way to the front by virtue of his record and his record alone. It was true that he had wooed Noailles, but at least Noailles was a moderately skilled commander and a man of integrity. Noailles had not hesitated to show his contempt for the Broglies and Coignys of this world.

As a Marshal of France, Maurice had at last equalled the achievement of Old Königsmarck, who had been a Marshal of Sweden, and his great-uncle Otto Wilhelm, who had been a Marshal of the Venetian Republic. The latter had commanded a single regiment for the king of France; Maurice would soon take command of the whole French army.

At the moment Maurice ranked as second-in-command to Noailles, the commander-in-chief. Coigny had been despatched to Alsace; Conti had been given charge of the army in Italy; and Maurice was deputed to assist Noailles in the north. It was to Noailles that Maurice principally owed his elevation in rank, for Noailles had no doubt realized that Dettingen might have ended differently had Maurice been at hand to assist him.

Early in May, the king left Versailles to join the army in Flanders. At thirty-four, Louis was possessed by a spasmodic thirst for military glory that was to desert him in later life. His martial ardour was being fanned by the most strong-willed of his many mistresses, the duchesse de Châteauroux, formerly Mme de Tournelles. Sponsored by Noailles and her uncle the duc de Richelieu, she was youngest of the five Nesle sisters, four of whom had already become Louis' mistresses. Her royal lover was far too indolent and easy-going to make a military commander; but he was nothing if not vain, and if he had no desire to fight a battle, he dearly longed to enjoy a triumph. In this uncommonly aggressive state of mind, he was persuaded by the duchesse de Châteauroux to set off in the spring for his northern frontier.

By May 12th he was at Lille, where his new marshal accorded him a magnificent reception. Maurice accompanied the king to Valenciennes for a conference with Noailles, to whom Louis was beginning to show a distinct coolness. Maurice's sense of theatre proved useful in organizing loyal demonstrations for the royal benefit. When they toured the fortresses of Condé, Douai and Maubeuge, Louis was received by wildly cheering crowds crying 'Long Live His Majesty!' and 'Now we have a real king at last!' At the climax of the demonstrations, Maurice's troops would break ranks and surge about Louis in a well-drilled impromptu. Louis found it very flattering, and some of his satisfaction communicated itself to the subtle Saxon at his side.

Privately, Maurice and Noailles were irritated by the arrival at Lille of the duchesse de Châteauroux and her female entourage. To men of Maurice's day, the company of women was by no means unknown during a campaign, but the presence of these great court ladies considerably lessened the martial effect of Louis' gesture. Kings do not acquire military reputations by trundling round the theatre of operations with their mistresses in the baggage-train.

At Valenciennes the final touches were added to a master plan whose authorship, since its principal feature consisted of a thrust along the Channel coastline, is not difficult to determine. The plan was designed to further Maurice's aim of isolating the British and cowing the Dutch.

Between the sea and the Meuse, the frontier between France and the Austrian Netherlands—the modern kingdom of the Belgians—ran from Dunkirk to Armentières, up to Menin, then southwards between Lille and Tournai, finally turning south-east to pass between Valenciennes and Mons [Fig. 5]. It was now decided that, as a first step, the enemy should be cleared from the territory between the rivers Lys and Yser. Maurice accordingly moved forward to establish an advance post across the border at Courtrai, while Noailles undertook the heavier task of reducing Menin. While Noailles applied himself to the siege of Menin, Maurice once again proved himself as much a master of the offensive as of defence, and was soon able to hustle the enemy back towards Bruges and Ghent in order to enable Menin to be reduced without interruption. It fell in a week, and the siege-train rumbled on to deal with Ypres, whose capitulation was quickly brought about by the marquis de Clermont-Tonnerre, an able descendant of Condé.[117] With Maurice fortifying Courtrai and masking the movements to his rear, Clermont-Tonnerre then completely switched the direction of the attack and marched directly for the sea at Furnes. Thus within a few weeks of succeeding to his command, Maurice had already come close to realizing his grand design of separating the British from their continental allies. His forces were already astride the Ypres-Nieuport canal, within striking distance of the key ports of Nieuport and Ostende.

It must be conceded that the spectacular success of the French so far was partly due to the inactivity of the enemy, who were content to withdraw and surrender the initiative. The British commander, Field-Marshal Wade, was one of the most mediocre generals ever to command a British army. Elderly and without the stomach for fighting, his only answer to the French manoeuvre was to place the river Scheldt between his forces and those of Maurice. By July he no longer felt secure even behind the broad riverline. Saxe's bewildering ability to change the direction of his attack was causing the British a great deal of apprehension. It dawned on Wade that his important forward bastion of Tournai was under threat, and even Bruges and Ghent as well. His rejoinder can hardly be classed as

FIG. 5. FLANDERS AND THE NETHERLANDS

warlike. He proceeded to remove his personal valuables and plate to Antwerp.

At the last moment, when the destruction of the British seemed certain, Maurice was to be baulked of his prey. News arrived that Prince Charles of Lorraine had eluded the somnolent Coigny and had slipped across the Rhine. The Austrians were already deep into Alsace. It was a serious crisis. A council of war was held at Dunkirk, at which Louis announced that he would expel the invaders in person. Noailles hurried ahead to confer with Coigny, while Louis set out for Metz, arriving there on August 4th.

Coigny's stupid blunder crippled the army of the north. Maurice was left behind with a reduced force to hold the line in Flanders single-handed against British, Hanoverians and Dutch. In the art of holding at bay a superior force with an inferior one, Maurice had no equal; but on this occasion a more modest man might have pleaded that his capabilities had been overestimated. By the time that Louis and Noailles had drawn off their massive reinforcements for Alsace, Maurice was left with a mere fifty to sixty thousand men, with which to defy an army comprising 22,000 British, 16,000 Hanoverians, 18,000 Austrians and 20,000 Dutch, a total enemy force of 76,000, soon to be augmented by another 20,000 Dutch. The odds against the French were nearly two to one. Maurice was to have a first-rate though unenviable opportunity to test the idea, propounded in *Mes Rêveries*, that a small army possesses a theoretical advantage over a large one.

For the moment Maurice's plight was obscured by more immediate perils. France was utterly absorbed in the danger to Alsace, and in a new danger to the king. Louis had fallen sick at Metz of a virulent fever. On August 13th it was announced that he was dying. The pantomime that had often been enacted during his many previous illnesses was now repeated with greater intensity. Two of his mistresses, the duchesse de Châteauroux and Mme de Lauraguais, rushed to his bedside, only to be forcibly removed by the assembled priests and bishops. Louis did not assist matters by the lachrymose self-pity to which he customarily succumbed on such occasions. He gave way to nauseating displays of repentance for his past self-indulgence, and enquired ceaselessly whether God would ever damn a king of France. He made maudlin promises to reform if his life were spared, and made public confession of his sins. His neglected queen arrived post-haste from Versailles, and in the course of a tearful scene heard Louis swear to be faithful to her henceforward. The queen and her partisans, scenting the reform of the prodigal or his removal to a better life elsewhere, prepared to usher in happier times. But Louis was restored to health not by prayer but by means of a powerful emetic; his contrition melted like snow in the sunshine; and the queen was promptly sent back to Versailles to resume her interrupted life of piety and good works.

Louis' survival did not mean the salvation of France. It was not Louis who rescued his country at this critical juncture, but Frederick of Prussia. For some time Richelieu and Mme de Châteauroux had been conspiring to bring Prussia back into the war on France's side: and at last their plans, successfully concealed from the agents of Maria Theresa, had borne fruit. When the Prussian army struck, the main Austrian army was with Charles of Lorraine on the French side of the Rhine, far from threatened Bohemia.

Frederick had impressed upon the French the necessity of destroying the Austrian army at the moment when it was most vulnerable. He pointed out that this moment would occur when the Austrians were re-passing the Rhine. He had envisaged the simultaneous invasion by the Franco-Prussian forces of Hanover, Bavaria and the Empire, and he had begged that Maurice should be given the opportunity of dealing with Hanover while Belle-Isle, now relegated to the status of a provincial quartermaster, should be restored to command in central Europe. Even Louis could see that here was his chance to deliver a devastating blow against the Habsburgs. He wrote from his sick-bed to remind Noailles that when Louis XIII was being carried to his tomb, Condé was giving the Spaniards the *coup de grâce* at Rocroi. He might have foreseen that Noailles and Coigny would let slip this incredible opportunity. They both dithered as feebly during Prince Charles' retreat as they had done during his recent advance. They allowed the Austrians to disengage without firing a shot, and watched them withdraw in excellent order across the Rhine. This piece of ineptitude finally brought about the eclipse of Noailles as a commander in the field. When he returned to Metz, he did his best to excuse himself to Louis, but his explanations were not accepted and his ascendancy was over. Although he continued to serve with the army for another year, he was eventually sent on embassy to distant Madrid.

At its sovereign's insistence, the main body of the French army began a clumsy advance. There was a promising moment when the comte de Clermont-Tonnerre rode forward with the van into Bavaria and stormed Munich, a daring action that should have been supported by the main force under Coigny. It was not. Coigny allowed his feeble attempt at an invasion to grind to a standstill not many miles beyond the French frontier. He halted his forces to besiege Freiburg-im-Breisgau, in the way that Berwick had halted to besiege Philippsburg in the previous war. It was one more classic instance of siege-mania, of the habitual reluctance to advance while a single enemy strongpoint remained in one's rear.

The king himself was present during the last three weeks of the siege, which ended with the governor's surrender to the French on November 5th. The campaign had hardly been more exacting for Louis than for Coigny. He had passed a few days at Lunéville with his father-in-law, now happily restored to his throne after the inglorious flight of a few months before, and had then moved on to Strasbourg, where he was welcomed by the *prêteur royal*, M. de Klinglin. Finally he consented to attend the siege of Freiburg.

Maurice also went to Strasbourg in 1744, and must have had official dealings there with Klinglin, the former lover of Adrienne Lecouvreur. Presumably Klinglin was obliged, by virtue of his position, to offer the marshal hospitality. It would be interesting to know how the two men behaved to one another.

While the French were in a state of suspended animation in Bavaria, Frederick had overrun the whole of Bohemia. In September he had emulated Maurice's feat by accepting the surrender of Prague from the hands of the luckless Count Ogilvie—but once again it proved a hollow victory. He attempted to invade Bavaria from the east in the hope of linking up with his French allies, but they were so slow to arrive that he was compelled to retreat. And a long and hard retreat it proved. At one stage Frederick was besieged in his own head-quarters, and almost taken prisoner. It was a neat and fitting reversal of the events of 1742, when he himself had abandoned the French to face the music in Bohemia. By the time he reached Silesia his army was in a pitiable state.

These distant alarms were of little concern to Maurice, who was still on the watch against Wade. He had managed to handle his little army so adroitly that the campaigning season was slipping by with unexpected quietude. He could not, with his depleted army, have risked a pitched battle; the enemy would have annihilated him by sheer weight of numbers. Indeed, when the news of the splitting up of the French armies had first reached London, even the politicians and armchair strategists had agreed that Britain had been presented with the opportunity for which she had waited for generations. Yet Wade vacillated. He dug himself in behind the barrier of the Scheldt, and special orders had to issue from London before he could be induced to cross the river. The old gentleman then led his vast army a few miles forward and pitched camp again. More orders came from London; another reluctant advance was made; and on July 30th he some-how found himself only four short miles from Lille.

Had Lille fallen to the British, a grave situation would certainly have developed for Maurice and the French. It is doubtful if in that case the onward advance of Wade's army could have been halted, even by Wade. Once the British were clear of Lille, they could set foot on the flat, rolling country of northern France. The compulsive dream of Marlborough and Stair of a direct march on the French capital could well have been realized. In the upshot, Wade fumbled his chance of taking Lille by failing to order up his artillery; and meanwhile Maurice, though taking every care not to expose himself by abandoning the shelter of the Lys, had reinforced the garrison of Lille with a sizeable force of militia. He was confident that the city was strong enough to fight off an assault, for it had been fortified by Vauban with fourteen bastions and a double ditch, and its seven gates had triple doors. True to form, Wade lingered immobile for weeks before the city.

The British general's brighter lieutenants were frantic. Some of them proposed a bold plan to swing south of Maurice, and shatter the remaining French defences by seizing Maubeuge and Landrécies. The plan was not unworthy of Marlborough, and its author was in fact the brilliant Ligonier, himself a Frenchman by birth, who had learned his trade under the great duke. Jean-Louis Ligonier, who was subse-quently to prove a thorn in Maurice's flesh, was a Huguenot who had left France after the Peace of Ryswick in 1697. He returned to France as a British officer to take part in Marlborough's major battles. In 1744 he was sixty-four and, if the British had had any sense, it would have been Ligonier not Wade who should have been entrusted with the command of the army in Flanders.

Wade could not be budged. When he complained that he could not advance because he lacked money to purchase horses for his guns, Ligonier and the Hanoverian General Somerfeldt, dazzled by the prospect of looting Paris, offered to pay £9,000 out of their own pockets. Wade was deaf to their pleas. Maurice, taking heart, encour-aged his cavalry to become bolder. 'In one of their raids,' observed an Englishman, 'the old Marshal was nearly carried off from his quarters, and they only discontinued, I suppose, on recognizing that such an enterprise, if successful, would have been prejudicial to themselves.'[118]

Neither the urging of his staff nor the instructions of the War Office could induce Wade to move nearer Lille. And since an army unemployed is an army in decay, his men began to rot and starve. After six frustrating weeks, the Dutch and Austrians drew off north-wards, to replenish their dwindling supplies. Their action marked the end of the year's campaign. Wade soon followed them, and later returned home to fight against Prince Charles Edward and his High-landers.

Maurice had been let off lightly. He had not even been called upon to sacrifice Courtrai. His reputation had already grown great enough, so it was said, 'to paralyze an enemy of allies who had no united command or agreed common war aim '.[119] A contemporary French historian has thus summarized his achievement:

> Posterity will scarce believe that an army which wanted for nothing, which was not fatigued by any expedition, and which was composed of more than 70,000 men, should be kept from daring to undertake anything against another, which had undergone the fatigues of five or six sieges, which was harassed by different motions that it had been obliged to make, which had been daily forced to do duty in many different places in order to guard them, and which was not composed of above 40,000 men.[120]

Posterity, of course, has more weighty matters to consider than Saxe's Flanders campaign in 1744. But the excellence of his achievement remains.

On November 13th, 1744, the king returned to Paris, and its citizens gave him a memorable reception. The streets were hung with banners, emblazoned with the legend: *Ludovico redivivo et triumphatori*. The early successes in Flanders and the later fall of Freiburg had revived heady memories of the triumphs of his great-grandfather. Despite the scandal of Mme de Châteauroux and her *coureuses*, the French king had at last shown himself, in Professor Cobban's words, as skilled in the combats of Mars as of Venus. France hoped that her handsome monarch would yet restore her to her former state as the first power in the world. To mark their concern for his illness at Metz, his people bestowed on him the affectionate sobriquet—which he was to outlive by many sad years— of *Le Bien-Aimé*. Riding down the thronged thoroughfares in his state coach, Louis is said to have murmured: 'What have I done, that they should love me so much?' It was a good question.

Soon after the king's return, Argenson wrote to Maurice to inform him that—

> His Majesty appears to have decided to entrust you again next year with the direction of the army which you have recently commanded to His Majesty's satisfaction and that of the troops. There is no time to be lost before devising the operations on which this army will be engaged; and I realize that you know more about the power and intentions of the enemy, and what we must do to oppose him, than anyone. If, as I assume, your winter dispositions are proceeding apace, and those of the enemy appear normal, let us devote the whole of January to our deliberations. You can then return to Flanders at the beginning of February to carry out the plans we will have worked out. If you agree with this I can then inform His Majesty, who, I can assure you, will be very pleased to see you.[121]

Louis certainly gave every sign of his pleasure in Maurice's company when his new marshal returned to court. Maurice was frequently closeted in private audience with the king. No doubt he exerted every ounce of his considerable charm in order to please Louis: but there is also no doubt that by this time the king regarded Maurice, quite simply, and without any qualification, as his best general.

During the winter of 1744-45, Maurice became an increasingly sick man. According to the Saxon envoy in France, his life was in danger. At one stage it seemed in the highest degree unlikely that, even if he survived, he would ever again be able to leave Paris on campaign. The king was in despair. 'His Majesty entertains so lively a regard for the marshal's experience and ability,' reported Count Loss, the Saxon ambassador,

> that he is convinced that his death would be irretrievable for France in the present circumstances; and although his kingdom swarms with general officers, none of them is considered capable of replacing him.[122]

A troop of doctors was called in to execute running repairs on Maurice's battered frame. His personal physician, Sénac de Meilhan, was soon reinforced by Roth, the physician to the *Régiment Saxe*. From Halle travelled the learned Professor Stahl, who prescribed draconian remedies for the unfortunate patient. At first glance they regarded the case as almost hopeless:

> *There is no cure for this disease,*
> *They murmured, as they took their fees.*

Maurice submitted to their ministrations with docility. He may have entertained some fleeting regret for those earlier excesses of bed, board and battlefield that now incapacitated him. The intensity of his debaucheries may be judged by the fact that he had originally been endowed with one of the most powerful constitutions of the age. Many regarded him as being even more remarkable in physique than his father, whom he so closely resembled in appearance. Yet Augustus the Strong, the 'Saxon Man of Sin' as Carlyle liked to call him, survived a life of riot and lechery until past his sixtieth year, whereas his favourite son began to break up before he was fifty. Maurice, driven by the dark impulses of the Königsmarcks, had early committed himself to a running fight with his own flesh. By now the breach had been effected, and the walls were crumbling. It was none the less an indication of his body's unusual strength that it could survive for so long the onslaught of disease, and the equally dreadful onslaught of the doctors.

He was suffering principally from dropsy, an affliction regarded in the eighteenth century as a fatal disorder, the culmination of a series of other disorders scarcely less fatal.[123] It was not until 1827 that Richard Bright established that dropsy, with albuminous urine, was the result of malfunction of the kidneys.[124] Earlier physicians could only shake their heads over the horribly swollen legs of their torpid and thirst-tortured patients, and prescribe for them time-honoured and useless remedies. These remedies, some of them no doubt swallowed by Maurice, included cantharides, elaterium, squills, gamboge, Rochelle salt, soluble tartar, and the juice of artichoke leaves steeped in hock. When these oral remedies failed to provide relief, as inevitably they did, recourse was then made to more drastic methods. Attempts were sometimes made to draw off the liquid in the calves and ankles by means of blistering: that is, by making burns on the limbs with a hot iron and puncturing the subsequent blisters. Fortunately this ugly technique was employed sparingly. But even when the legs were left alone, some action always had to be taken to relieve the quantity of water in the distended abdomen. In those days a doctor felt that it was a bad advertisement if his patient swelled up and literally burst before the eyes of his family and friends, so the sufferer was subjected to a process known as tapping. The abdomen was pierced, and the oppressive liquid allowed to drain away. In earlier centuries the emission of this fluid had been carefully regulated, but in the more flamboyant eighteenth century the abdomen was commonly emptied at a single operation, often with spectacular results. A single puncture of this type was often lethal: one of them had been sufficient to kill off Peter the Great; but cases were recorded of men and women surviving as many as thirty. But whether the patient lived or died, relief was in any case immediate.[125]

Beset simultaneously by the disease and by the doctors, Maurice was virtually under sentence of death. Neither he nor his entourage had any illusions about it. It was solely a question of whether his spirit and animal strength could propel his failing carcase through the gruelling days ahead. He must somehow find within himself a last reservoir of energy to overcome the tappings and the terrible lassitude which was the symptom of his ailment.

Voltaire has recounted the shock he felt at the pathetic appearance of his old friend when he went to offer him his good wishes on the eve of his departure for the coming campaign in Flanders. The dropsical Saxon seemed to him as a man *in extremis*. When Voltaire asked him whether he thought he would survive, Maurice made a reply which became famous. '*Il ne s'agit plus de vivre*' he answered, '*mais de partir.*' This evocative reply was not lost on Voltaire. Maurice,

ever the devotee of the drama, must surely have been echoing a line
from Racine's *Bérénice*,

Mais il ne s'agit plus de vivre, il faut régner.

Bérénice had been a favourite rôle of Adrienne.

Maurice set off for Flanders in a very sad condition. Nevertheless
the agony of his body did not subdue the habitual liveliness of his
mind. He had designed several items of special equipment to minimize
his physical disability. As it would have been impossible for him to
wear a heavy steel cuirass, he had invented a kind of breastplate of
quilted taffeta which could be clamped to his saddle. No doubt he
remembered how tough old Villars, when his knee was still suppura-
ting from his wound at Malplaquet, had ordered an iron clamp to be
made in order to hold his leg straight and enable him to sit in the
saddle. More, as Maurice wanted to husband his strength until such
time as the course of the action made it imperative for him to mount
his horse, he gave orders for a special two-wheeled vehicle to be constructed. It was a small, light, shell-shaped curricle of plaited osier, a
kind of miniature brougham. When eventually he limped off to the
wars, he must have looked not unlike the Knight of the Woeful
Countenance, perched on his stringy nag and crowned with a barber's
basin.

He left Paris on March 31st, 1745, to join the forces who had spent
the winter besieging Tournai. Every jolt of the coach must have sent
a shudder through his bloated frame. Beside him in the coach sat his
physician, Sénac de Meilhan, amusing him with his combative Gascon
patter; and at Sénac's feet rested the sinister leather case containing
the rows of surgical knives as keen and bright as the enemy's bayonets.
The marshal was determined not to allow his sickness to get the
better of him: he alone could be trusted to execute the plans which
he carried in his portfolio. After a week of swaying and bumping, he
reached Lille, where he penned the first of the obstinately optimistic
bulletins about his health which were to reach Paris and Versailles
regularly in the coming weeks. 'The trip did not tire me in the least,'
he assured Argenson: 'I am in even better health than I was before
my departure.'[126]

He was earnestly praying that he might be able to stave off physical
collapse for at least two months. Two months would be all he needed
to strike his decisive blow: the blow which he intended to bring not
only victory to France, but everlasting fame for himself.

CHAPTER XI

FONTENOY, 1745

*If they have the advantage of a wood, or you give them a
moment's time to intrench themselves, they are a nation
which will pop and pop forever at you.—There is no way
but to march coolly up to them,—receive their fire, and
in upon them, pell-mell—Ding, dong, added Trim.—Horse
and foot, said my uncle Toby. Helter skelter, said Trim.
Right and left, cried my uncle Toby.—Blood and 'ounds,
shouted the corporal;—the battle raged.*

TRISTRAM SHANDY

'THE question of the Austrian succession,' wrote Maurice to King
Augustus of Poland in March 1745, 'seems to me to be at the moment
of secondary importance.'[127] After five years of unrelenting en-
deavour, Maria Theresa had made good her claim to her paternal
domains. Now, with the realignment of the great powers, and the
formal declaration of war between France and Great Britain, the
struggle had entered a new and enlarged phase, and had become a
contest of brute strength in which the original cause of contention
had been forgotten. The French, encouraged by the emergence of an
outstanding general, had grown eager to recoup their losses and
recover their prestige.

They could not hope to win a great victory in Germany: the
rigours of the Bohemian campaign had cured them of any desire to
venture too deeply into Habsburg territory. The fire-eating Belle-Isle
had been consigned to limbo, together with his policies; and France's
pawn, the Emperor Charles VII, had conveniently died of gout and
discouragement at Munich early in 1745. As far as the French were
concerned, Bavaria was left to her fate.

It was in the north that the French hoped to achieve their success.
While Coigny and Maillebois sat tight in the east, Maurice would
attack in Flanders with a greatly augmented army. As a precaution,
he had planned foolproof dispositions for Coigny and Maillebois, and
incorporated them in an *aide-mémoire* which he had presented to the
king during the previous winter. The *aide-mémoire* was a tactful blueprint intended to prevent that lamentable pair of commanders from

146

committing the errors that they might otherwise perpetrate. Moreover, the cast-iron nature of these Rhenish dispositions would enable him to commandeer a considerable part of their forces for his own purposes. He asked for an army consisting of 120 first-line and 50 second-line infantry battalions; and he was not dissatisfied at receiving 89 first-line and 54 second-line battalions, even though the latter consisted mainly of militia and gendarmerie. Against this force of 65,000 infantrymen, of whom 40,000 were first-class, the enemy could muster 103 battalions, comprising 62,000 men. But although his infantry were numerically inferior to the combined infantry of the British, Hanoverians, Austrians and Dutch, Maurice made certain that he had a clear superiority in cavalry. He mustered 160 squadrons against only 107 of the enemy, and every one of the French squadrons was superbly trained and mounted. He was also supported by a number of companies of skirmishers and irregulars. He set great store by these unorthodox units, and had none of the prevailing prejudice against them. He was himself a man who had hacked his way out of an inn at Crachnitz, had organized an army of freebooters in Courland, and was in general familiar with the bands of predatory Poles, Croats and Hungarians which were a permanent feature of warfare in eastern Europe. If he had had his way, many more of these 'free companies', as he called them, would have been formed during the winter of 1744; but even the striking way in which he had employed them in Bohemia had not opened the eyes of the French high command to their worth. Here again Maurice was in advance of his time. It would be another thirty years before the American War of Independence brought home to the French and British the value of soldiers trained on semi-guerrilla lines.

The number and composition of his regular troops gave no cause whatever for disquiet, while their eagerness to attack gave rise to positive satisfaction. He was still confronted, however, with a difficult major problem. The quality of his subordinate commanders, particularly his junior commanders, was extremely poor. Two-thirds of them were frankly undependable. It was bad enough to have to fight the enemy when he was tormented by the dropsy, let alone being in conflict with his own lieutenants into the bargain. It was small comfort that the problem was at any rate not a new one. At Dettingen, Noailles had been quite unable to rely on his own brigadiers to bring their troops into action in a proper state of readiness.

Prominent among the social gadflies who were to plague Maurice were the princes of the blood. Because of their high birth, the princes of the blood automatically claimed the high rank of lieutenant-general. Maurice was cursed by the presence of a round half-dozen of them. They were the duc de Chartres, the duc de Penthièvre, the prince de Dombes, the prince de Pons, the comte de Clermont, and

the comte d'Eu. The incapacity of four of them was public knowledge. The comte de Clermont, for example, had been expressly forbidden by Louis to give orders to the troops whom he nominally
commanded. The comte d'Eu, the master of the royal artillery, had
been sternly warned not to interfere in any way with the functioning
of that important arm. None the less it was impossible for Maurice,
who valued his career and his standing at court, to be too strict with
these eminent nonentities. Chartres and Penthièvre, for instance, were
noted recipients of their sovereign's favour, and had been Louis' in-
separable companions during his tour of the Flemish front.

In addition, Maurice was hampered by a corps of unswerving
opponents, who criticized his every move, questioned his orders, and
joyfully prophesied disaster. This unregenerate and influential group
included the ducs de Richelieu, Grammont and Harcourt. Grammont
had been largely responsible for the *débâcle* at Dettingen; Harcourt,
at the same battle, had been in command of the *maison du roi*, and
had contributed to its disgraceful performance. Both of them had
every reason to be jealous of Maurice's unblemished record. Richelieu,
of course, was a special case, a law unto himself. Grand-nephew of the
great Cardinal, he was the most brilliant, most amusing, most brave,
most avaricious, most lascivious, most irreverent and most dandified
courtier of his time. He probably opposed Maurice as he opposed all
men—from sheer force of habit. A natural rebel, he had seen the
inside of the Bastille three times before he was thirty. It was a note-
worthy tribute to Maurice that, after a while, Richelieu was to modify
his attitude towards him.

It was fortunate for Maurice that he could count on the services of
at least a dozen officers of outstanding calibre. Foremost among them
was Löwendahl; and the official second-in-command, the sixty-year-old
marquis de Lutteaux, was of almost equal merit. Other lieutenant-
generals of proven reliability were the comtes de Danois, Chabannes,
Apcher and Clermont-Tonnerre, the vicomte du Chayla, and the
marquis de Clermont-Gallerande. All of them, like the majority of
princes of the blood, were older than Maurice, and all of them had
taken part in the distant campaigns of Louis XIV. Maurice was thus
far from being a paternal figure surrounded by youthful lieutenants:
on the contrary, some of his subordinates were old enough to be his
father. It was Maurice who was the *enfant terrible*, in spite of his
dropsy and his marshal's *bâton*. It was Maurice who, though trained
in the same hard school as his subordinates, was the military innovator, and the pioneer of novel manoeuvres.

He was also able to bring to the fore a number of younger men to
leaven the dough of the middle ranks. They included such men as
Louis-Hyacinthe de Crémille, his incomparable chief of staff, the
resourceful marquis de Brézé, and the dashing young duc de Biron.

And among his personal aides were his future biographers, the Chevalier Jean-Baptiste-Joseph de Sahueget d'Amarzit d'Espagnac, and the marquis de Valfons.

The primary objective was the city of Tournai. We have already made clear that the eighteenth century was still *par excellence* the epoch of sieges. For once paying lip-service to precedent, Maurice considered it advisable to take at least one of the three key fortresses, Tournai, Mons or Charleroi, before advancing into the lush pastures beyond. Mons and Charleroi were the outer bastions of Brussels, the capital of the Austrian Netherlands: and an assault on Brussels was the operation most dreaded by the British. On the other hand, the capture of Tournai offered a less spectacular but even more worthwhile advantage: it would consolidate and extend the line of advance that had been reached the previous year. It provided a natural link with Menin, Ypres and Furnes, and was within easy reach of the French headquarters at Lille.

Maurice was the least siege-minded general of the day, and his resolve to open the campaign in this manner was merely a cover for a much more original manoeuvre: the prompt engagement of the enemy at a time and place favourable to the French Army. Maurice had calculated that the British and their allies would not reach full strength before June: it would thus be wise to fight them in April or May. He knew that there was nothing more likely to provoke an early encounter than to threaten one of the largest of the enemy's Flemish fortresses, for in an age when military prestige largely rested on the process of siege warfare only a singularly acute and confident general could ignore a threatened attack on one of his key points. The British generals were also offered a further inducement, for Maurice managed to convey to them that if they arrived on the ground in time he would abandon the siege. The young Duke of Cumberland, the new British commander, swallowed the bait hook, line and sinker.

Of course, Maurice would not have been averse to snapping up a prize like Tournai quickly, if he could do so: and to put the enemy off the scent he first of all created the impression that his objective was not Tournai but Mons. A decoy force was sent off in the wrong direction, south-east to Maubeuge, and its progress was duly followed by Cumberland with the keenest interest. Meanwhile Maurice was keeping his main formations in a fluid state until the last possible moment. Only when he was sure that the enemy had been baffled by the artful manoeuvres of the decoy, did he suddenly wheel his main army round towards Tournai. At the same time he summoned his artillery to come up at the double, from Lille. The trap snapped shut. By May 1st the French were building pontoons and opening trenches before the great fortress.

The British and their allies had not been slow to move. Cumberland was not a man of the stamp of the dilatory Wade. On April 23rd he marched his combined forces out of Brussels, still suspecting that Mons was the real object of the French manoeuvres. It was not until he reached Soignies that he discovered that he had been fooled. He was on the wrong road, and he was now faced, as Maurice had intended, with an exceptionally exhausting cross-country trek to Tournai, along bad roads and across open countryside.

Had the British been led by a more experienced soldier, he would probably have halted to review the situation calmly. Some kind of outflanking movement, of the kind pioneered by Frederick of Prussia, might still have been possible. But Cumberland was only twenty-three, and relatively unfamiliar with the considerable art of warfare, and he kindly obliged Maurice by behaving in precisely the orthodox manner which the latter had envisaged. Cumberland was blind to all considerations except that Tournai was in danger and must be relieved. He did not pause to reflect that he was still on the end of the hook: that his army was not yet at full strength, and that a rapid and tiring march still lay ahead of it. He plunged off through brake and stream towards Tournai.

The young duke has had his apologists, and the muddle-headed march on Mons has even been represented as a master-stroke.[128] It is easy to condemn him: how could a youth of his little experience hope to prevail against Maurice at the height of his genius? Cumberland was convinced that the French would fall back before him, giving him the moral victory. If they chose to stand and fight, then he was equally confident that he would win, probably to the extent of capturing the French king himself. In truth, the British had been ill-advised to entrust so young a man as Cumberland with the supreme command, and with the proud title, once borne by the mighty Marlborough, of captain-general. His only qualifications were the fact that he was George II's favourite son, the record of his personal bravery at Dettingen, and the princely rank which enabled him to impose something like unity on his polyglot subordinates.

While Cumberland was preparing to place himself in the position that Maurice had previously chosen for him, Maurice himself was examining the ground with a view to delivering the *coup-de-grâce*. As early as April 28th he had ordered Löwendahl, Estrées, Apcher and Crémille to ride out and look for positions that would favour the

French forces in the battle to come. These *réconnaissances*, with their accompanying conferences, lasted a full ten days, and though Maurice had more or less already decided on the terrain he would select, he personally took part, despite his ailments, in these protracted forays. On April 27th he informed Argenson that his health 'was improving by leaps and bounds; yesterday I was four hours in the saddle, even though the ground was as hard as iron, without feeling the least ill effect'.[129] In fact, at Maubeuge the previous week, Sénac had punctured his abdomen and drained away five pints of fluid; but Maurice had enjoined the physician to keep the operation a secret. News of it only leaked out three weeks later, when Maurice was forced to admit to the king that a second abdominal puncture would be necessary. Yet immediately Sénac had knotted the bandages after this second operation, Maurice was holding a five-hour meeting with his staff at which his bearing was so natural that none of the officers who were present guessed that he had just emerged from so sickening an ordeal. He was grateful for the temporary relief from the pressure of the water, though by the eve of the battle his limbs had begun to swell again. It is a tribute to his phenomenal strength of will that he could so completely overcome the lethargy associated with his malady and undertake the hard planning and hard riding involved in the simultaneous preparation of a siege and a battle.

Most of the time, emulating Charles XII at Poltava, he was carried about in a litter. It was in this way that, accompanied by Sénac, he made repeated circumvallations of Tournai, and it was in this way that he was conveyed, in acute pain, along the interminable, dusty, uneven roads of Flanders and Brabant, which he had first known as a lithe-limbed boy.

Maurice's burdens were not lightened by the arrival at Tournai, four days before the battle, of the king and the Dauphin. Their arrival at the front may well have encouraged the rank and file, but to the senior officers of the army it was nothing less than a major embarrassment. Louis had brought with him an enormous retinue, all of whom had to be suitably encamped in proper style and order. They included chamberlains, gentlemen-in-waiting, Swiss Guards, almoners, provosts, masters of ceremony, *valets de chambre*, barbers, tailors, cooks, chaplains, physicians, surgeons, apothecaries, and even the royal clock-winders. This plague of *mouches de coche* buzzed ceaselessly round their royal master, many of them venturing to warn him from time to time of the obvious unsoundness of Maurice's military preparations. Their amateur criticisms were the least of the problems with which the royal presence presented Maurice, for he was now faced with the responsibility of ensuring Louis' safety. The possibility of the king's capture, which had already occurred to Cumberland, was even more serious than the possibility of his death in battle. His capture would have been little loss to his country in real terms, but it would have been a shattering blow to the prestige of France and the *mystique* of the monarchy. The person of a French king still possessed an almost pharaonic significance. In battle, Louis would be so hemmed in by his flunkeys, his courtiers and his baggage that the possibility of his being overtaken by some quick-witted detachment of enemy cavalry was a distinct possibility.

Of more immediate concern to Maurice were his arrangements for conducting the siege of Tournai while the preparations for battle were simultaneously under way. Whether Cumberland would approach Tournai from Mons or from Ath, the battle was bound to occur within half an hour's ride of the city walls. Maurice would therefore have to carry out complicated military operations on two fronts within a constricted space: and he had to take special precautions against any break-out, during the actual course of battle, by the 8,000 Dutch troops inside the city. He was therefore compelled to leave no less than twenty-seven battalions and seventeen squadrons in front of Tournai, in order to contain the garrison and secure the heads of the five pontoons which he had already thrown across the Scheldt.

On May 8th, he began to move his main army into position opposite the enemy forces, who after this gruelling march were at last enjoying a brief rest in a temporary camp. Cumberland was now in a rather thoughtful mood. He had rejected the advice of Ligonier and other more experienced members of his staff, and had persisted in his view that the French would retire on his approach. They had not done so. It was all very puzzling. His intelligence reports had also suggested that Maurice would not bring against him more than 35,000 men. He could now see only too clearly that here too he had been skilfully led into making an erroneous supposition. The gallant duke was left to reflect, as he inspected his footsore troops, that in war it is much wiser to overestimate than to underestimate the strength and courage of one's enemy.

On the battlefield of Fontenoy, Maurice was to base his dispositions on those of Villars at Malplaquet thirty-six years earlier. The only difference was that in the intervening years Maurice had acquired the experience to analyze Villars' mistakes and to correct them. Fontenoy was to be Malplaquet without the attendant bloodbath. In one sense Maurice was fortunate. Unlike Villars, he was not confronted by generals of the calibre of Marlborough and Eugène, but with

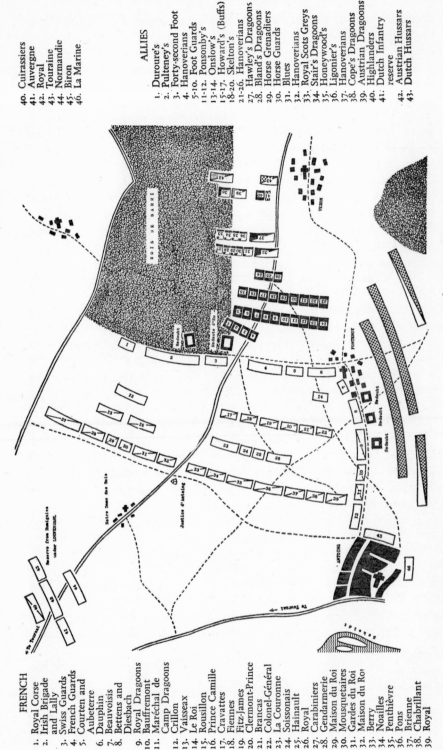

FIG. 6. THE BATTLE OF FONTENOY

Preliminary Dispositions

FRENCH

1. Royal Corse
2. Irish Brigade and Lally
3. Swiss Guards
4. French Guards
5. Courten and Aubeterre
6. Dauphin
7. Beauvoisis
8. Bettens and Diesbach
9. Royal Dragoons
10. Bauffremont
11. Maréchal de Camp Dragoons
12. Crillon
13. Vaisseax
14. Le Roi
15. Rousillon
16. Prince Camille
17. Cravattes
18. Fiennes
19. Fitz-James
20. Clermont-Prince
21. Brancas
22. Colonel-Général
23. La Couronne
24. Soissonais
25. Hainault
26. Royal
27. Carabiniers
28. Gendarmerie
29. Maison du Roi
30. Mousquetaires
31. Gardes du Roi
32. Maison du Roi
33. Berry
34. Noailles
35. Penthièvre
36. Pons
37. Brienne
38. Chabrillant
39. Royal

40. Cuirassiers
41. Auvergne
42. Royal
43. Touraine
44. Normandie
45. Biron
46. La Marine

ALLIES

1. Duroure's
2. Pulteney's
3. Forty-second Foot
4. Hanoverians
5-10. Foot Guards
11-12. Ponsonby's
13-14. Onslow's
15-17. Howard's (Buffs)
18-20. Skelton's
21-26. Hanoverians
27. Hawley's Dragoons
28. Bland's Dragoons
29. Horse Grenadiers
30. Horse Guards
31. Blues
32. Hanoverians
33. Royal Scots Greys
34. Stair's Dragoons
35. Honeywood's
36. Ligonier's
37. Hanoverians
38. Cope's Dragoons
39. Austrian Dragoons
40. Highlanders
41. Dutch Infantry reserve
42. Austrian Hussars
43. Dutch Hussars

commanders of the indifferent endowment of young Cumberland, the Dutchman Waldeck, and the Austrian Königsegg.

Yet he was by no means free from apprehension. It is a truism that in warfare nothing is certain, and he may have recalled Marlborough's words on hearing of Charles XII's defeat at Poltava: 'Ten years of unbroken success—and two hours of mismanagement!' Villars himself had been brimful of confidence on the eve of Malplaquet, a battle which Marlborough and Eugène had won only by crude expedients in the face of murderous fire. It was by no means unlikely that these crude tactics might now carry the day again. After all, it was less than a year since the English and Hanoverian infantry at Dettingen had swept the French guards out of their path with one of their famous and much-feared volleys of musketry. Why should they not do the same again on the present occasion? No one in the French camp, least of all Maurice, who had been in too many battles, supposed that victory would be easy.

When Maurice took up his final position [Fig. 6], he rested his left on the village of Ramecroix, protected by a wood and by swampy ground. On the extreme left he posted the little regiment of five hundred Corsicans which had been with him at Dunkirk. Next to them he placed his large Irish contingent, six battalions strong, behind wooden breastworks and equipped with eight cannon. The Irishmen would prevent the British from debouching from the woods in the early stages of the battle—if in fact they ever managed to make their way through the wood at all. At the worst, the Irish would form a reserve for the hard-pressed battalions in the exposed centre, for Maurice recalled that Villars had owed his defeat primarily to the fact that he had weakened his centre in order to reinforce his left wing. In the present battle that danger would at least be minimized: on what finer reserve could a general call in a moment of crisis than six battalions of the Wild Geese?

The brunt of the fighting, in the centre, would be borne by the seven battalions of the *Gardes-françaises*. Behind them, as reinforcements, or to stiffen their backbone, were placed a further five full regiments. The hinge of the French line consisted of the tiny hamlet of Fontenoy, which was to give its name to the coming battle. The little huddle of houses was turned into a fortress, and behind its walls crouched the flower of the French infantry. Armed men thronged the little grassy square where on more normal days the tall farmcarts were backed into the high dark barns.

After the bastion of Fontenoy, the French line turned at a right-angle and ran back towards Antoing, which had been transformed into another kernel of defence to protect the extreme right wing, which was thus anchored firmly on the banks of the Scheldt. Both wings were therefore secure: and to improve the situation still further, the ground fell steadily away from in front of the French position, which the enemy could only reach by climbing a slope in full view of sharp-shooters possessing an unimpeded line of fire.

Maurice knew that his left and left-centre needed to be particularly strong. By tradition, and by virtue of Cumberland's seniority, the British would take the right of the line, and the full weight of their onslaught would therefore fall on the French left. As additional insurance, Maurice had increased his already considerable reserve in this sector by creating another force, which later in the battle would play a vital rôle. On the high ground at Rumignies, a village as far away from Ramecroix as Ramecroix was from Fontenoy, he stationed a special detachment under the energetic Löwendahl. It consisted of four battalions of the *régiment-royal* and the *régiment de Normandie*. And near by, with a brief to watch over the bridgeheads on the river, waited seven battalions of the regiments of Auvergne and Touraine, together with four squadrons of cuirassiers. Between them these two small but important brigades were furnished with twelve of Maurice's sixty pieces of artillery.

Then, also on the French left, and the most piquant feature of all, there came the redoubts. The redoubts, forerunners of modern pill-boxes, were no sudden inspiration of Maurice, although they were new to warfare in Western Europe. He may have received the idea for them from the effective use which Peter the Great's generals had made of them in destroying the Swedish army at Poltava. Maurice would naturally be conversant with the minutiae of eastern campaigns. His own personal design for these structures had been first outlined in his *Rêveries* many years before, where there are three plans of the battle-field of Malplaquet with imaginary reconstructions of ways in which the French army might then have been deployed in order to avert defeat.

> 'I do not want to leave this section,' Maurice had written, 'without speaking of the affair of Malplaquet. If, instead of putting the French troops in wretched entrenchments, one had simply erected at the mouth of the Trouée breastworks constructed of three tree trunks, and had placed three or more of these "redoubts" in the Trouée, I believe that things would have turned out differently. What would the British have done? Would they have dared to attack the redoubts, backed as they were by numerous brigades? I believe that they would have been badly mauled had they done so; for they could not have captured them, and would have suffered fantastic losses.'[130]

At the same time, as Maurice explained, the purposes of these redoubts was not in the least defensive.

> The nature of the French nation is to attack. . . . One must seek every occasion to . . . take the greatest possible advantage of this

French audacity, which all nations and eras have known and respected.
To put them behind entrenchments is to deny to them the means of
conquest. It reduces them to the status of ordinary men.

The redoubts must be disposed so that the supporting infantrymen
could sally out through the gaps between them and fall upon the
enemy. As well as intimidating the foe, the emplacements would give
their own men confidence. They would feel that their retreat was
assured, and that the enemy would not dare to follow them, because
he would get caught among the redoubts.

According to Maurice, it had been Villars' deeply dug trenches
that had been the cause of his undoing. When his centre had started
to buckle, those well-constructed slits in the earth had become death-
traps. Maurice argued that in the case of tree-trunk redoubts the
lethal risks were considerably diminished. In essence, his redoubts
were to be nothing more than square wooden stockades for a self-
contained garrison with its own artillery. Trenches, which were so
inimical to the offensive spirit, would be utterly eschewed. Indeed, it
is remarkable that except for the redoubts, the heavily fortified salient
round Fontenoy, and the tip of each wing, Maurice had established a
line that ran through relatively open country. His single concession
in this regard was to establish his forward infantry in a sunken road,
long since metalled, that runs north-east from the hamlet of Fontenoy: and during the battle, this was a decision that he would
bitterly regret.

The redoubts thrown up by Maurice's corps of two thousand
pioneers were five in number. The two most important were situated
north and south of the Bois de Barri, and were manned by two regiments of the *Brigade d'Eu*, another formation which had served with
Maurice at Dunkirk and was imbued with his outlook. Each redoubt
was supplied with four cannon. One of them, the *redoute de Chambonas*, bore the name of the colonel who commanded it, and stood on
the edge of the wood. The trees round it had been cleared to permit
its occupants a free field of fire across the main track that led through
the wood and the open ground beyond.

The cannon in these two principal redoubts were so sited as to
enfilade the flanks of any advancing infantry. The principles of
enfilade fire were well known to Maurice, who had carefully studied
the technique of Gustavus Adolphus as exemplified in the deadly
formation of the 'Swedish Cross'. The plates of *Mes Rêveries* show
how thoroughly he understood the theory and practice of flank firing
along fixed lines.

The other three redoubts were smaller, and guarded the stretch of
line between Fontenoy and Antoing. In this sector, instead of the
usual practice of constructing the earthen entrenchments which were

repugnant to him, Maurice had ordered nineteen squadrons of dragoons and hussars to hold the line in place of the normal battalions of infantry. This was certainly a daring expedient for a general about to provoke the enemy to do the attacking.

Early in the afternoon of May 10th, the British broke camp and began to advance. They first seized the hamlets abandoned by the retreating French picquets, who burned the barns and cottages as they fell back. After a swift reconnaissance, General Campbell advised Cumberland to clear the French light infantry from the Bois de Barri. A whole day could quite profitably have been devoted to carrying out this difficult task. Maurice had sown the wood so thickly with his irregulars, or *grassins*, that Cumberland, perhaps remembering the horrors of the wood at Malplaquet in his turn, refused to involve himself there.

Nevertheless Cumberland was confident that the tactics of Dettingen would serve the British well a second time. The young duke's courage and tenacity were valuable qualities; but few historians have ever claimed that he possessed a profound insight into the art of war. Königsegg alone appreciated the magnitude of the problem which Maurice had set his opponents, and he seriously urged Cumberland to withdraw at once in order to try a flanking movement. Unfortunately, he was overruled: and at two o'clock in the morning of May 11th, Cumberland's footsore regiments took up their station for the frontal attack. On the right wing, Brigadier-General Ingoldsby was given five battalions and told to neutralize the twin redoubts in the Bois de Barri. Simultaneously the Dutch would strike on the left in all-out assaults on Fontenoy and Antoing. Once these wings were moving strongly the British and Hanoverian infantry massed in the centre would breast the slope and crush the French centre.

At dawn the French batteries opened fire. Although the early morning mists still obscured parts of the battlefield, the gunners did not lack for targets [see Plate 5]. In order to screen the British and Hanoverian infantry, as they stumbled through a maze of narrow tracks from the rear, Cumberland had deployed fifteen British squadrons of horse. These were now exposed to a furious fire that crackled out from the batteries at Fontenoy and from the *redoute d'Eu*. General Campbell was mortally wounded, and his leaderless squadrons remained dutifully in their exposed station, dumbly waiting until someone had the sense to grant them permission to withdraw. It was a full hour before Cumberland sent forward seven six-pounders to help them, and by that time the infantry forming up behind the cavalry were also being compelled to endure the same pointless ordeal. Their only consolation was a minor success recorded by one of the six-pounders, which managed to knock over a senior French officer in a magnificent uniform who was prancing about on a white horse. The dead man was the vainglorious duc de Grammont.

The artillery duel continued until nine o'clock. Maurice, who had bivouacked during the night among his first line of cavalry, was now galloping busily up and down in his wicker curricle. He knew that another hour or two would test the soundness of weeks and months of assiduous planning and preparation. Cumberland too was galloping hither and thither: not, like his Saxon vis-à-vis, to set the seal on a well-conceived plan of action, but merely to enquire why his orders were not being obeyed. What had happened to Ingoldsby? Why had the Bois de Barri not yet been captured? Why was his right wing immobilized? When eventually he made contact with Ingoldsby, he found the brigadier-general sheltering with most of his detachment in a hollow on the outskirts of the wood. They had been unable to enter the trees because of the grassins and the biting fire from the redoubts: so they simply cowered down beneath the lethal muzzles of the cannon in the redoute de Chambonas. Neither threats nor cajolery could induce Ingoldsby and his men to advance an inch. Cumberland, a young man of terrifying temper, cursed the general alternately in fluent German and broken English, but could make no impression. The men of the five battalions saw too clearly that if they attempted to obey instructions, and passed between the two redoubts, they would have been cut to pieces: and the survivors would have found themselves face to face with the embattled Irish on the slopes beyond the wood.[131]

Affairs were no better on Cumberland's left, where Waldeck was exhorting his Dutchmen to storm the three southerly redoubts. After a faltering movement towards Antoing, his eight battalions and forty squadrons had recoiled with the severe loss of four hundred and fifty men. Waldeck then joined up with the Austrians and made a more determined attempt to reach Fontenoy, only to be driven back with a further combined loss of a thousand men. The two generals can scarcely have hoped to succeed. Cumberland had failed to soften up the target by any kind of artillery bombardment, which meant that the task allotted to them was almost suicidal. On the Dutch and Austrian retreat, Cumberland had to digest the bitter fact that he had now suffered the total repulse of both his wings.

Undaunted, he tried to improve matters by pressing forward with his attack on the French centre. Here Ligonier had drawn up the British and Hanoverians in two disciplined lines. The young duke

THE BATTLE OF FONTENOY

Impression by a French artist during the opening exchanges, sketched from a vantage-point at Notre Dame des Bois

placed himself at their head beside Ligonier. The drums beat the advance. What followed was a magnificent, an altogether outstanding feat of arms. Seventeen British battalions, ten in the first rank and seven in the second, supported by the Hanoverian contingent on their left and the remainder of Ingoldsby's men on their right, advanced up the slope towards the enemy. The French artillery tore great gaps in their closely packed ranks with grape and canister. They kept coming on. Maurice had planned to compel any enemy units who advanced in this way to bunch together. He intended to make them march into a funnel of fire, a corridor of flame. His plan was realized. The advancing battalions were squeezed into one ever-narrowing front, until there was only room for six battalions to march abreast. The French cannon concentrated on them a terrific volume of fire. The red ranks closed up, closed up, and still closed up, denied even the satisfaction of firing back at their tormentors, since they had been given strict orders not to fire until they were within thirty paces of the French.

For a full half-mile they marched into the murderous cross-fire as if they were on parade. And eventually—

> they came abreast of village and redoubt, and the shot which had hitherto swept away files now swept away ranks. Then the first line passed beyond redoubt and village and the French cannon took it in reverse. The gaps grew wider and more frequent, the front grew narrower as the men closed up, but still the proud battalions advanced, strewing the sward behind them with scarlet, like some mass of red blossoms that floats down a lazy stream and sheds its petals as it goes.[132]

At last the ravaged formations clambered painfully on to the crest of the rise. There, about eleven o'clock, they halted. They were within forty yards of the blue ranks of the *Gardes-françaises*, the white ranks of Aubeterre and Courten, the red ranks of the Swiss. At the head of his grimed and sweaty men, Lord Charles Hay, colonel of the First Battalion of Foot Guards (now the Grenadier Guards), took out a silver hip flask, bowed to the French officers, drank with a flourish, and called out: 'I hope, gentlemen, that you are going to wait for us today, and not now swim the Scheldt as you swam the Main at Dettingen.' And one of my Lord's sergeants, finding himself staring down the barrels of the French muskets, murmured: 'For what we are about to receive may the Lord make us truly thankful.'[133]

The French muskets loosed off their volley. Unfortunately, it was ragged and ineffective.

> The turn of the British had come at last. . . . Now the British muskets, so long shouldered, were levelled and, with crash upon crash, the volleys rang out. . . . Down dropped the whole of the

French front rank . . . utterly shattered and broken. Even while the British were advancing, Saxe had brought up additional troops to meet them and had posted the Regiments Couronne and Soissonois in rear of the King's Regiment and the Brigade Royal in rear of the French guards: but all alike went down before their irresistible volleys. The redcoats continued their triumphant advance for full three hundred yards into the heart of the French camp and old Ligonier's heart leaped within him, for he thought that the battle was won.[134]

What had happened is clear from the *pièces justificatives* subsequently published by Colonel Colin. It was the French custom during this particular epoch to draw up their infantry in four ranks, while the British drew up theirs in three. The advantage of the British system was now made manifest. The three British ranks could each fire their weapons rapidly and economically and see what was happening ahead of them; but the fourth French rank had only a blurred impression of what was actually taking place up front. When the terrible British volley thundered out, almost the whole of the French front line fell, wounded or dead, and the fourth French rank simply panicked. Even the rear rank of the *Gardes-françaises* turned and ran, in spite of frantic efforts to rally them. The British and Hanoverians continued their march until they halted on the stretch of ground which the officers of the French guards had been using as their headquarters.

Cumberland and Ligonier believed that the day was already theirs. Most of the French officers thought so too. Maurice himself had advised the king and the Dauphin to retire two hundred paces in order to avoid flying bullets. They accordingly retired to Notre Dame des Bois, where Noailles then took it upon himself to ask them to leave the battlefield and cross the Scheldt without delay. They were dissuaded from doing so by the duc de Richelieu, whose caustic, incisive accents were heard above those of the plaintive courtiers who were urging the royal pair to flee for their lives. Maurice was grateful for Richelieu's intervention. He knew that the flight of the king at this juncture would have struck a further blow at the morale of his men. He had not wished the king to be present in the first place; but since he could not prevent it, the last thing he wanted was for his royal master to flee from the field. He expressed this view in French obscenities delivered with Saxon pungency. 'Who is the ——— ' he roared, 'who advised the king to do that?'

In spite of this momentary outburst, all accounts emphasize that Maurice kept admirably cool. A great hole had been punched in his centre; the most renowned regiment in the army was in flight; panic was spreading to other units. In such circumstances a certain loss of *sang-froid* was pardonable, but he kept his head. It is said that throughout the action he gave his orders precisely and energetically, as though he were in perfect health. The prince de Croy, who saw him dashing about in his curricle at the start of the battle, chewing a bullet to assuage his dropsical thirst, described him later in the day as 'passing alone on horseback at a gallop, looking more dead than alive, but always resolute'.

The French now had their backs to the Scheldt. If Cumberland could follow up his advantage, the French would be rolled into the wide, muddy, fast-flowing river. The result would be a massacre of appalling proportions.

Noon on May 10th, 1745, was the moment of meridian of Maurice's life.

It appeared certain that Cumberland had carried the day. In fact, however, there was little that his leading troops could do now but stand firm and be shot at. The cannon from the redoubts and the hamlet of Fontenoy were now taking them cruelly in the rear. For two hours the gallant infantrymen waited for their general to give the order for the final charge. It would be Dettingen all over again: the blunders of the senior officers had not prevented their long-suffering men from presenting them with an undeserved, miraculous victory. The French courtiers and their king cringed as they waited for the French formations to break up and flood back over them. Almost alone of the French commanders, Löwendahl, whose *coup d'oeil* was equal to Maurice's own, saw the true state of affairs. Galloping up from Rumignies, he saluted Maurice and begged to be allowed to turn the tide by bringing up the *Régiment de Normandie*, his dozen precious cannon, and the reserve cavalry. 'Well, monsieur le maréchal,' he said, motioning with a cheerful grin towards the British infantry, 'here is a great day for his Majesty! These fellows will never get themselves out of a fix like that.'

Not that the British and Hanoverians would yield tamely: they had won their slice of the slope at too heavy a price. Maurice's preliminary counter-attacks were rapidly beaten off. He then tried to interpose a cloud of cavalry between the two lines of infantry to provide a screen behind which his shattered regiments could reform and to dissuade Cumberland from further advance. The cavalry had strict orders not to charge: but the *maison du Roi*, as usual, obeyed its own insubordinate instincts and promptly indulged in repeated fiery attacks. Maurice fumed with rage as he watched their forty squadrons indulge in unauthorized assaults.

To beat off the French reply, the British took up a new and unusual position. They formed, not square, but oblong. This fresh formation consisted of six battalions in front and six in rear, with three facing outward on either flank. It is not known definitely whether Cumberland adopted this curious stance on purpose and of his own volition. The likeliest explanation is that his men were accidentally huddled into it by the fire smashing into them on all sides. None the less, for a time it enabled the British and Hanoverians to repel the French attacks with relative ease.

Cumberland was still determined to force his way into Fontenoy and thus knock out at least one of Maurice's bastions. He would then have a lever to use against the French flank. The Dutch had agreed to make a second attempt to storm the village, and if they succeeded they would give Cumberland a chance to extend to his left, relieve the pressure, and make another attempt to pierce the shaky French line. Maurice was wearily aware of the extent of the danger: and it must be admitted that, at this critical moment, Maurice was showing signs of wilting. He was awaiting the arrival of Löwendahl and his men with all the harried impatience of Wellington waiting for Blücher. His relief was indescribable when Löwendahl galloped up to ask permission to attack. 'Right!' exclaimed Maurice, taking fresh heart: and he added a favourite phrase: 'Now for the final heave (*le coup de collier*)!'

He waved his arm and sent every front-line regiment that still retained its steadiness into the grand attack.

As the French regiments ran down the slope, one regiment was ahead of the others. It yelled its ferocious battle-cry: *Remember Limerick! Remember Limerick!* The words echoed grimly in the ears of the English and the Dutch.[135] The Wild Geese of Ireland had many scores to settle, not least of them a failure at Malplaquet in face of Schulenburg, and a failure earlier that day at Fontenoy when Lord Clare had had to rally them after the first broadside of the English infantry. Now the Papishes were determined to be revenged on the Proddies. They advanced shoulder to shoulder, running with muskets levelled towards the bayonets of the English. A minute later the rival regiments had coalesced. The fighting was hand-to-hand. After a confused mêlée, it was seen that the Irish had achieved their ambition. They had sent the English reeling back. But the cost had been terrible. Thirteen of their officers, including the Chevalier Dillon, colonel of the *Régiment de Dillon*, and two hundred and sixty-one men were killed; fifty-nine officers and three hundred and twenty-four men were wounded. The Irish losses were higher in proportion than those of any other unit on the French side at Fontenoy. *Normandie* too, coming up with Löwendahl's brigade from Rumignies, charged heavily in the universal onslaught, and they also suffered heavily, although their casualties were mercifully lighter than those of the Irish Brigade. The Wild Geese had sacrificed themselves to compel an English retreat.

It was two o'clock in the afternoon before the British in the battered crimson parallelogram bowed to the inevitable. Yet they succeeded in crowning their superhuman advance with an equally superhuman withdrawal. Without confusion, without a trace of wavering, they tramped back stolidly to the shelter of their own lines. Every hundred yards they paused to turn round and deliver one of their paralyzing volleys. The leading squadrons of British cavalry, the Blues to the fore, galloped forward to distract their pursuers. Again and again the British cavalry charged home. Slowly the two armies disengaged. The battle, it was now conceded, had gone to the French.

This was the moment when matters might have been utterly and conclusively settled by the time-honoured expedient of a full-scale pursuit. Common-sense and precedent alike dictated that the French should maintain their momentum, remorselessly grinding back the enemy until they buckled and ran and were put to the sword. It was an obvious, well nigh inevitable process. But Maurice completely failed to initiate the pursuit. Apart from sending a corps of *grassins* through the wood to harry the British rear, he made no move to chase the retiring infantry. He later explained that the British cavalry was still comparatively intact, and was still spoiling for a fight, while his own squadrons had been severely decimated. The British also possessed an uncommitted rearguard, small, but fresh, and including a number of the formidable Highlanders. But there was more to his failure than that. At the close of the battle Maurice was physically exhausted, and the fact may have played a part in his apparent lack of resolution. Yet we ought to remember that in his youth Maurice had been horrified by the butchery of Malplaquet, and remained to his dying day something of a military sentimentalist. As it happens, he himself afterwards gave a characteristically honest and adequate reason for his aberration. 'Nous en avions assez,' he said. 'We had had enough.'[136]

In the last harrowing stages he was in as pitiable a state as the rest of his men. When the king and his courtiers hastened up to congratulate the man who had saved their skins and their sinecures, they found him lying on the ground in acute pain, with Sénac de Meilhan wiping the yellow froth from his lips.

The battle of Fontenoy had been quite bloody enough without the additional slaughter of a full pursuit. The total enemy losses in killed and wounded exceeded 10,000, including 4,000 British and 2,000 Hanoverians. The details of the French losses have not been clearly established, but a calculation from the regimental returns suggests that the toll on the French side was not much less, amounting to at least 7,000. For months afterwards the hospitals at Lille, Douai, Cambrai and Valenciennes were packed with the maimed and dying. There is something especially moving about the death roll of the Irish. Fathers, sons, brothers and cousins fell together, far, far from their native land: O'Neills and O'Briens, Burkes and Kellys, Sullivans and Nugents, Sweenys and Rourkes.

The 'other ranks' of casualty lists are the real casualties of history. Maurice did not forget them. Slumping to his knees before the king after the battle, he said with tears in his eyes: 'Sire, now you see what war really means.' He was as sedulous in visiting his wounded men in hospital as he had been in inspecting them in camp. He well knew that their bruised bones and pulped flesh were the bricks and mortar of which palaces were built.

On the morrow of battle he was gratified to receive a letter from Louis XV in acknowledgement of his services.

> Mon cousin, however great the success with which it pleased God to favour my arms during the last campaign, I have received a more striking mark of his puissant protection in the victory by which I have just vanquished my enemies. If I owe this trumph to the valour of my troops, and principally to those of my maison and my regiment of carabiniers, you also contributed to it no less by your steadfast daring, by your sage counsel and by your remarkable foresight.[137]

The royal letter was a generous gesture, and it pleased Maurice vastly, We may, of course, boggle at the sense of values which it reflects. We may recall that the king, personally, was incapable of leading a colour party, let alone an army; and we may have expected his letter to contain a little less about God and the king and a little more about Maurice. But nice customs curtsy to great kings; and in any event, no one more revered the institution of kingship than Maurice, himself the son and brother of kings.

It was not long before Maurice had written four letters giving detailed accounts of the battle for the benefit of various correspondents. One of them, enclosing a packet for his half-brother the chevalier de Saxe, was addressed to King Augustus at Dresden. 'That prompt courier Renown,' it begins,

> will already have informed you that we have achieved a complete victory over the duke of Cumberland and his army. I imagine that the setback will make the English sing small for a while. A large part of their infantry has been wiped out, and I doubt whether it can be reconstructed for several months. The engagement lasted nine hours, and although I was half-dying by the end of it, I resisted my fatigue as though I was in perfect health. It is very sweet to win battles. . . .[138]

Acknowledging the congratulations of his old mentor, the chevalier

Folard, he reported that the siege of Tournai was being prosecuted with renewed vigour. 'The battle,' he wrote,

> has not deterred us from pressing onwards with the siege, and I have concentrated my attack on the horn-work of the Gate of the Seven Fountains, in exactly the same place as I found myself with Schulenburg thirty-six years ago. We are now masters of the *demi-lune*.[139]

He favoured Folard, still at seventy-six his most informed admirer, with a careful dissection of the course of the battle. It was a full quarter of a century since Folard had first discerned the promise in Maurice, and he was the first to rejoice that the pupil had wholly outshone the master.

Maurice's carefully conceived master-plan had been brilliantly realized in the period between April, when he opened his campaign, and May, when he won the battle of Fontenoy. The shame of Dettingen had been avenged.

From the outset, he had chosen to employ as his principal weapon the device of the counter-punch: drawing his over-eager opponent on to a lethal and artfully concealed hook. His incidental errors were insignificant beside the major blunders of the Duke of Cumberland, an inexperienced and youthful general who favoured the old style of warfare in its most inflexible form. Cumberland would have been even more in his element at the third battle of Ypres in 1916 than he was at Fontenoy in 1745: and the generals on the western front in the First World War would have benefited from a study of Saxe's campaigns. It was only after Foch had lost 100,000 men of his Tenth Army in Artois, and 145,000 men of his Second and Fourth Armies in Champagne, that he began to appreciate the wisdom of a conclusion which might have been derived from a study of Fontenoy: 'It is a fact that infantry attacks always halt and fail at those points where preparation has been insufficient; once more we see that the power of organization is greater than the bravery of the troops.' The words were Foch's, but the sentiment belongs to Maurice. At Fontenoy, the power of French organization and its superiority over English bravery had been neatly demonstrated; yet in early twentieth-century Flanders a million French dead were to be sacrificed before the simple lesson had gone home. The changes in military tactics pioneered by Maurice and Frederick the Great had long since made *l'attaque à l'outrance* obsolescent; and the rapid development of armaments in the nineteenth century steadily shifted the advantage to the defence, until any but the most subtly devised attack became a free gift to those who resisted it.

As for the heroism of the British at Fontenoy, all that courage and anguish were to be a great disservice to those who came afterwards. It helped to create the legend of the invincible square, of the indomitable valour of British infantry. Reading subsequent British military history, in the Crimea, in South Africa, and in Flanders, one sometimes wonders whether some commanders did not march their men into death-traps for the pleasure of witnessing the devotion with which their orders were obeyed.

All this represented a world alien to Maurice. He hated *l'attaque à l'outrance*, and he valued his men. War to him was an art, and soldiers were individual human beings. The concept of cannon-fodder was anathema to him. This contention can easily be proved by a cursory reading of his great book. As he himself said, 'the starting point in all matters pertaining to warfare is the human heart'.

In a moment of sardonic self-doubt, however, he also said that 'war is a science shrouded in darkness'. Jomini, one of the greatest military commentators, later disagreed. To Jomini, 'there have always existed fundamental principles on which depend good results in warfare. These principles are unchanging, independent of the kind of weapons, of historical time, and of place'.[140]

What shall we do when doctors disagree? Both Jomini and Maurice were among the greatest academic exponents of the art—or science? —of war. But Maurice was not just a theorist, but also a great practitioner, and his achievement at Fontenoy seems to prove Jomini's generalization rather than his own. If there are indeed a number of basic and unchanging principles of warfare, it is not too much to claim that Maurice admirably demonstrated many of them on the battlefield of Fontenoy, and in his battles and campaigns of the next three years. But if it is also true that the science of warfare is shrouded in darkness, then no one did more than Maurice to help dispel it.

CHAPTER XII

ROCOUX, 1746

Condition de l'homme: inconstance, ennui, inquiétude.
                                              PASCAL

THE name of Maurice de Saxe was now on every Frenchman's lips.
He was a national hero. His latest victory, achieved in defiance of his
own threatened death from dropsy, was celebrated by Voltaire in his
Poème de Fontenoy.

The wily *philosophe* had been at school with Argenson; and six
weeks before the battle he had been given the post, at Argenson's
instigation, of historiographer-royal. His first official duty was to
celebrate the feat of arms of his old friend Maurice, and he naturally
found the task congenial. Apostrophizing Glory, he wrote:

> *Vous m'avez transporté sur ce sanglant rivage:*
> *J'y vois les combattants que vous conduisiez tous:*
> *C'est là ce fier Saxon qu'on croit né parmi nous,*
> *Maurice, qui, touchant à l'infernale rive,*
> *Rapelle pour son roi son âme fugitive,*
> *Et qui demande à Mars, dont il a la valeur*
> *De vivre encore un jour, et de mourir vainqueur.*
> *Conservez, justes cieux, ses hautes destinées;*
> *Pour Louis et pour nous prolongez ses années.*[141]

The prayer contained in the last couplet was echoed by Louis himself, who hastened to load his greatest general with honours. With his
own hand he signed a brevet on June 6th, 'making known, more and
more, the esteem and affection' which he entertained for his marshal.
'His Majesty thinks that he can give him,' the brevet sonorously
declares—

no marks of which he will be more sensible than by granting to him
and his descendants distinctions suitable to his birth, to the honour
he has of being brother to the king of Poland, and which may transmit
to posterity the memory of all the great qualities united in him. To
which end His Majesty has declared, and declares, wills and ordains
that M. de Saxe, and the lady his wife, should he marry again, may

167

enjoy during life entry into the Louvre in their coaches; and that the lady his wife shall be seated on a tabouret before Their Majesties and the Infants of France.[142]

It was enough to give the more acidulous souls like Saint-Simon the vapours. To these signal marks of the sovereign's personal regard for a German and a bastard—the exclusive *honneurs du Louvre*, or *grandes Entrées*—the king added a more material token of approval: an additional stipend of forty thousand *livres* a year.

Two months later, a second brevet bestowed on Maurice the château of Chambord, the most grandiose of the royal palaces. This gesture gave its recipient peculiar satisfaction. Chambord had been the home of Louis' father-in-law, Stanislas Leczinski, until his departure first for Warsaw and then for Lunéville. True, the vast edifice was a royal white elephant. Louis XV, who would not dream of living more than twenty miles from Versailles, and who could seldom be induced to make a tour of the provinces, had not the slightest intention of residing in it. The building had already remained empty for some years, and the king was glad to get it off his hands. Nevertheless he had chosen to grant it to a foreigner, and to a man whose own father had been often responsible for ousting Stanislas Leczinski from his revolving throne. It was exhilarating for Maurice to be so signally honoured, and to be treated almost as royalty, as befitted the legitimate Duke of Courland. At last, he could live in truly princely state. In the estimation of the Most Christian King, Maurice was a European ruler, and it scarcely mattered to him at that triumphant moment that he was a ruler in exile.

Maurice showed his gratitude to Louis by the ardour with which he urged on the royal armies to further victories. The city of Tournai surrendered to him on May 22nd, and the governor and garrison retired to the citadel. Maurice rode into the gilded triangular *Grand'-Place* of the beautiful city as a conqueror for the second time. As a boy he had accompanied Eugène and Marlborough when they had wrested it from Louis XIV: now he himself had captured it for Louis XV. The citadel held out for an additional month, putting him to the trouble of mounting regular siege operations; but once his cannon began to destroy the outer curtain, on June 19th, the governor quickly capitulated. The capital of the rich province of Hainault, key to the British forward defence system, was wholly in French hands.

He did not linger at Tournai. On July 1st he sent his men marching northwards in five columns. In the van was a specially selected striking-force of 5,000 troops under the command of Löwendahl, who had been ordered by Maurice to take charge of the striking-force at the last moment and to keep his identity secret. If the British got wind of the fact that the dangerous Löwendahl had been let loose, they would scent that something startling was afoot. The enemy, and the troops of the striking-force itself, supposed that they were destined for Oudenarde, a town ripe for investiture. This was only another of Maurice's feints. On the road to Oudenarde the column suddenly altered course and embarked on a tremendous forced march towards an unknown destination. Allowing his men only an occasional rest, and enforcing strict secrecy, Löwendahl unexpectedly appeared beneath the walls of Ghent, deep in British-occupied territory, and an important enemy base, on the morning of July 11th. The Danish General's Frenchmen were so full of fire that they would not wait for fascines to be brought up to fill the moat: instead they swam it, scaled the counterscarp, burst into the city, and broke open the gates to let the French cavalry through. In a matter of hours another ancient and renowned city was in French hands.

The loss of Ghent enhanced the confusion of the British. Only a week later, they staggered under another deadly blow. Bruges fell to the marquis de Souvre, at the head of another detached striking-force, without firing a single shot. And worse was yet to come. Maurice sent Löwendahl doubling back on his own tracks to effect a double-bluff by seizing Oudenarde, the town which had been ostensibly by-passed. It fell as easily as had Ghent; and by July 22nd Löwendahl was installed in the citadel, with a prize of no less than thirty-six cannon. Then, driving north-east again on Maurice's orders, Löwendahl added to the successes of a remarkable summer by sweeping Passchendael, Albert, Dendermonde, Nieuport and Ostende into the bag. The British position in the Lowlands was crumbling.

In three months Maurice had achieved his grand design. At very little cost to France, he had established himself on the shores of the Channel and the Scheldt, as far north as Bruges and Ghent. He commanded the Straits of Dover, and had captured two of the chief ports of entry into the German Ocean. Great Britain was perilously near exclusion from the mainland of Europe, and would find it hard to make contact with her continental allies. They would have to fight, and fight resolutely, to preserve what was left of their lines of communication and supply.

While his talented subordinates roamed abroad, Maurice himself had remained with the main French army besieging Ath. The garrison of this little town deserves special praise. It held out staunchly in the British cause long after the British armies had disengaged to the northward. It did not capitulate until October 8th, when it surrendered to Clermont-Gallerande, Maurice's deputy.

It was now late in the season. The campaign had been arduous, if highly successful, and Maurice therefore gave permission for the army to retire to winter quarters. It might have been expected that he himself would return to the capital, where a tumultuous reception awaited him. With the onset of the colder weather his disabilities had increased and he needed the most careful nursing; moreover, the news had recently leaked out that he had suffered a stroke and had temporarily lost the use of his right hand. None the less, he stayed in the north with his armies, even going so far as to take up his personal quarters at so advanced a point as Ghent, a fact which the enemy high command was quick to remark.

Maurice tried to lull their suspicions that he might be contemplating anything as unorthodox as military operations in midwinter by sending most of his senior officers on leave. He himself was too ill to return to France with them: but even his illness was promptly turned into a sly military advantage. He had it put about that he was much more ill than he really was: and when the enemy generals heard that he was at death's door, they were jubilant. They were told by their spies that he was designing a special carriage to whisk his ailing body to Paris, from which city he would never return. He was said to be in such a sad condition that he had sent for his favourite half-sister, Countess Orzelska, to minister to him. This lady, who was supposed to have been her father's mistress and had certainly been the mistress of her half-brother, Count Rutowski, was far from being the conventional type of ministering angel. Nevertheless the tales that were spread abroad were eagerly accepted at their face value.

Then, when he was eventually said to be recuperating, it was rumoured that he was neglecting his maps and despatches in order to spend his few remaining months in drinking, whoring and sponsoring cockfights. He may well have been doing all these things: but what he was also doing—and of this the enemy was completely ignorant—was planning the seizure of Brussels. And Brussels was the cornerstone of what remained of the enemy position in the Austrian Netherlands.

To invest Brussels in winter time was a bold plan, and it aroused inevitable opposition in high places. To reach this ancient and powerful city, Maurice would have to lead his men across four substantial waterways: the Scheldt, the Dender, the Vilvoorde canal, and the Senne. Argenson sent long, pompous, quavering despatches, voicing the general anxiety felt at Versailles. The legion of the Marshal's detractors hoped that he was at last about to over-reach himself. It was made crystal clear to him that he would have to stake both his reputation and his command on the coming siege. Characteristically, he agreed to take the risk.

He began by using the same diversionary gambit that he had employed at Dunkirk, two years before. Once again he started intense and well-publicized activity on his extreme left wing, at the point furthest from the destined scene of operations. Again he began to assemble a fleet, apparently for the same old purpose of invading England. This maritime manoeuvre was originally foisted upon him by the court, now roused to new efforts by the unexpected success of Prince Charles Edward's rebellion. At first he resisted a directive which would have meant sacrificing some of his best units in order to swell the ranks of the expeditionary force; but he changed his mind when he perceived the advantage of the hypothetical invasion in relation to his attack on Brussels: it would provide the perfect cover for his real intentions. He therefore agreed to permit Richelieu, Avaray and Contades to busy themselves at Calais and Boulogne. As in 1744, despatches flew backwards and forwards between Versailles, the coastal towns, and Maurice's headquarters at Ghent: and as on the previous occasion, some of them managed to fall, accidentally on purpose, into the hands of the enemy. Yet not a word, not a whisper, not the slightest hint of the great Brussels project was ever allowed to appear on paper. The secret was wonderfully well kept.

As the Young Pretender came marching southwards into Derbyshire, the news that twelve French men-of-war were fitting out at Dunkirk, and that a French force had been assembled at Calais, produced frantic excitement in London. There was even a false rumour that the enemy had landed in Kent. The uproar was at its height when, in January 1746, Maurice's troops began to steal not westwards, but eastwards, in five well-organized columns. The Marshal himself rode with the largest force. Before his departure he had been praying for clear skies and a good, hard, frost to give him an easy passage over the rivers and canals, but on the eve of the march it was cloudy and threatening to thaw. A Broglie or a Maillebois would have called off the whole enterprise. Not so Maurice. Recalling his own dictum, in his *Rêveries*, that 'a commander must often act on inspiration', he informed Argenson that: 'tomorrow I intend to embark on my enterprise, even if it is raining cats and dogs. My heart tells me that we shall have good luck'.[143]

His optimism was justified. Halle, Louvain, Malines and Vilvoorde fell with hardly a struggle. On the night of January 30th the *faubourgs* of Brussels were easily occupied and the French columns joined hands in a complete ring around the city.

Maurice had a compact force at his command. It consisted of forty-two infantry battalions, one hundred and two squadrons of cavalry, and five companies of irregulars. Against this total of 22,000 men the governor of the besieged city, Count Kaunitz, could muster a full 12,000, supported by a formidable tally of cannon. The garrison was amply provisioned, and expecting the early march to the rescue of the main Dutch army based on Antwerp. Moreover, although he was outnumbered, Kaunitz had the satisfaction of knowing that the French pioneers preparing the siege were suffering abominably, for the frosts had suddenly become so intense that their picks were splintering on the ground.

Maurice's men stuck to their task, confident that Brussels must soon be added to the list of cities that had already fallen to them. But for the Marshal himself, as day succeeded day and the artillery of the defenders thundered on, already bringing his casualties to almost a thousand, it was a trying time. He had hoped to capture the city quickly and with negligible losses; he had no desire, as he put it himself, 'to present the king with a bloody morsel'. He now saw that he had a fight on his hands, although not the slightest suggestion of anxiety clouds the *rusé* letter which he addressed to Kaunitz from his base at Laeken on February 11th. 'I have received the letter,' wrote Maurice,

which your Excellency did me the honour of sending yesterday. Under ordinary circumstances, your Excellency's propositions would be perfectly acceptable. I am aware of the respect due to a large and brave garrison, and would be delighted to accord it all the honours of war. But Brussels is an untenable city; any army which attempts to save it risks certain destruction; and I have all the resources necessary, and can augment them with artillery or anything else whenever I so choose. It requires only a little more time and effort on my part to compel you to ask for more realistic, and harsher, terms. It has never been my desire to turn Brussels into a battlefield; these great capitals, the adornments of their countries, should be declared to be open cities, as is Milan. But you have chosen to place a powerful garrison in the city; so what course is left to me? All the same, I have sent a fast courier to Versailles for instructions. I must confess that the factor that causes me most uneasiness is the high spirit of my men. They are fully conscious of their superiority, and if any of them should detect a weak point in your defences, which may have escaped the eyes of your Excellency or myself, then . . . they might break through, carrying their officers with them . . . and I should have to support them. Your Excellency may readily imagine the confusion and disorder that would result. It would be very sad if my career were to be marred by an incident of this kind: the destruction of a capital city.[144]

Kaunitz, hoping for relief from his allies, decided to hold on for another week. Maurice persisted with his siege operations, drew up plans for the assault, and began to hammer open a breach. On February 20th, after the French were seen to be carrying out an ostentatious dress rehearsal for the grand attack, Kaunitz suddenly hung out the white flag. The subsequent capitulation was abject. Seventeen battalions of infantry, eight squadrons of cavalry, and all the Austrian artillery fell to Maurice, together with two Dutch generals, an Austrian field-marshal, and sixteen Austrian generals, most of them former governors of the towns that had already surrendered to Maurice. The booty included the personal luggage of the Duke of Cumberland and Prince Charles of Lorraine, which Maurice promptly and courteously returned to its owners.

A consignment of fifty-two captured flags and three standards were despatched to Versailles, including the *oriflamme* of Francis I, lost to the Empire in the rout of Pavia. The court was suitably impressed. On February 23rd Maurice received from the king an unusually warm letter. ' *Mon cousin,*' it began,

> the conquest which my troops under your command have made of the city of Brussels, the most considerable city in the Austrian Netherlands, and the seat of government therein, is the happiest augury for the continued success of my arms, and will completely disrupt the plans of my enemies. Your abilities and experience have overcome innumerable obstacles :—the rigours of winter, the problems of transport, the resistance of a large garrison, and the propinquity of a relieving army. Your unshakeable resolution has been an inspiration to my troops.[145]

Maurice's decision to spend much of the winter in the field had been abundantly justified. Now he could take a brief and well-deserved rest, and enjoy a change of scene before the opening of the regular campaign in April. He had been in Flanders for eleven months without a break.

It was also essential that he should attend, in person, the councils of war which would be held at Versailles in the spring. No senior commander dare risk being absent from these meetings, otherwise some amateur and unworkable plan of campaign, drawn up behind his back by courtly noodles, would be duly approved by a noncombatant king. Maurice could not afford to neglect his connexions at court, and although he was no politician, he knew how vital it was for him to maintain his position there.

He had become involved in recent months in a head-on clash with the twenty-eight-year-old prince de Conti, a militarily inexperienced but clever and ruthless prince of the blood, distempered by personal ambition and jealousy. He had become the acknowledged leader of the faction opposed to Maurice. The Conti family had, as we have seen, detested Maurice ever since his first arrival in Paris in the days of the Regency; partly because of their thwarted pretensions to the crown of Poland; partly because Maurice had cuckolded a previous prince of their house; and most of all, because of their military ambitions. Young Conti was now lobbying the king to concede to him the right, accorded by immemorial custom to princes of his rank and name, of actively commanding an army in the field. He also had the temerity to insist that any plan of campaign which he saw fit to submit should be given equal consideration with that of Maurice. It was obvious that, if Louis were to accord to his cousin Conti the traditional military privileges due to a Bourbon, Maurice would be seriously embarrassed; moreover, if Conti gained his point, the whole princely tribe—Penthièvre, Clermont, Dombes—would soon clamour for equivalent favours. The king was naturally inclined, in this as in all matters except sex, towards a policy of judicious inactivity, and he contrived to keep Conti in suspense. But it was quite possible that in the end he would buy peace at court by placating his kinsman. Maurice knew that he must hasten to Versailles if he were effectively to counteract Conti's bid for power.

He entrusted the governorship of Brussels to Löwendahl, and on March 11th headed south. Once he had crossed the French frontier, his journey became a triumphal progress. At Lille a *douanier*, ignorant of the traveller's identity, came forward to search his coach for dutiable goods. 'Oaf!' snapped the captain of the marshal's escort, 'is there a tax on laurels?'

At the Opéra, on March 18th, these laurels were formally and literally tendered to him by the city of Paris. At a gala performance of Lully's *Armide*, Maurice, accompanied by the ducs de Biron and Villeroi, was given a fervent ovation. The director of the Opéra presented him with the *livre d'honneur*, a compliment usually reserved for royalty. In the prologue—*Armide* had originally been written to celebrate the military triumphs of Louis XIV—Glory, personified on this occasion by Mlle Demetz, advanced towards the great Saxon with a laurel wreath, singing:

> Tout doit céder dans l'univers
> A l'auguste héros que j'aime.

At this point Maurice, with unusual modesty, refused the wreath. The duc de Biron leant across the footlights, took it from the hand of Mlle Demetz, and to the deafening plaudits of the assembly insisted on Maurice accepting it. And so

M. le Maréchal de Saxe found himself crowned by Glory in person, during a public spectacle, and amid the most fashionable audience in Europe. Nothing could have been more flattering. It also seemed clear the gesture was made with the king's agreement and permission.[146]

To Maurice, with his strong histrionic bent and passion for the glittering surroundings of the theatre, this moment well may have been the proudest ten minutes of his career.

At court, the reception at the Opéra caused much heartburning. 'It is generally considered,' observed the waspish Luynes, 'that M. de Saxe should not have accepted this wreath.' He also hinted that the whole performance had been arranged with Maurice's knowledge: for there were rumours that, on the following morning, Mlle Demetz received from Maurice a pair of diamond earrings worth ten thousand livres.

The Bourbons no longer reign in France, nor the Wettins in Saxony; the diamond earrings may well be dust; and Maurice and his battles are almost forgotten. Yet that fragile, faded wreath has somehow survived the grinding revolutions of two centuries, and it may still be seen in the Musée de Carnavalet, in a vitrine filled with medals, snuff boxes and fans. It is made of metal, since the eighteenth century seldom resisted an opportunity to improve on nature, and it is wrought with all the careful and beautiful artifice of its age. The painted leaves are sere, and scarcely tinged now with green. Some green is still there, all the same. . . .

Once the public junketings in Paris were over, Maurice got down to serious business at Versailles. He had a definite, decisive plan of campaign in his portfolio—so he was aghast to learn that the king was already giving serious consideration to a plan devised by Conti. The young prince had had some easy successes in Italy in 1744, and a great deal of subsequent frustration in the backwater of Alsace in 1745, while Maurice was winning his victories in the Low Countries. He had therefore proposed a clever scheme under which, without attempting to deprive Maurice of supreme command, his own Alsatian theatre would supplant the Austrian Netherlands as the main seat of the war in the coming summer. He argued that the Queen of Hungary would certainly invade France, now that she had signed a new truce with Frederick of Prussia, and that France must prepare for immediate battle on the Rhine.

This argument, which was not wholly without justification, also chimed in with the views of Argenson, who had recently exchanged the post of war minister for that of foreign minister. Argenson was no longer the friend of Maurice that he once had been, except in the sense that Reldresal had been the friend of Gulliver at the court of Lilliput, and was already negotiating an end to the war. He was therefore against further offensive operations against the British and the Austrians. Ever timid and vacillating by nature, the new foreign minister seemed to have taken over at the point at which Fleury had left off.

Maurice was eager to finish the war by means of a final military success. Having already overrun the Austrian Netherlands, he now wished to invade the United Provinces. Argenson argued that this would merely spread the war, whereas there was still time, by employing the methods of diplomacy, to persuade the Dutch to declare their neutrality.

Although Maurice and Argenson were both almost personally incorruptible, in itself a fact to excite interest in the France of the *ancien régime*, neither of them was wholly guided on this issue by an impersonal judgment. Maurice had a clear vested interest in continuing the war, and Argenson's views were warped by the *naïf* trust which he reposed in the Prussia of Frederick the Great. Egged on by Voltaire, who had found favour at the court of Potsdam, the minister had recently conceived the idea that Frederick should be asked to act as mediator between an exhausted France and a harassed Austria. Unlike Argenson and Voltaire, Maurice distrusted Frederick the politician as cordially as he admired Frederick the soldier. In the past four years he had sent letter after letter to Brühl and Augustus at Dresden, urging them to be wary of the King of Prussia. He now argued that reliance on the good faith of Frederick would be as disastrous for France as it had already proved to have been for Saxony and Poland.

Maurice was able to count on the support of powerful allies in high places, including the brothers Pâris-Duverney and Pâris-Marmontel, the two leading financiers in France. The former, the Intendant-General of the Army, had been partially responsible for Maurice's success in Flanders, as a result of the efficient manner in which he had provisioned the troops. He was a wily old operator, who at one time or another had poked his fingers into every financial pie in France. Nearly thirty years before he had successfully supervised the liquidation of John Law's ill-fated 'system', and had gradually become the actual, if unacknowledged, controller of national finances. After the appointment of his brother as royal treasurer, his power was firmly consolidated, and he became by no means the least successful of the succession of bourgeois financiers who strove to shore up the tottering French monarchy. He had already acted as quartermaster to too many incompetent generals not to recognize the value of Maurice to the dynasty.

Argenson, who was as poor a judge of a man as Pâris-Duverney was a shrewd one, underrated both Pâris-Duverney and Maurice. He made an even more serious error, from the standpoint of his personal career, when he underrated the young woman who had become their protegée. Mme le Normant d'Etioles, *née* Jeanne-Antoinette Poisson, was soon to be raised by Louis XV to the dignity of marquise de Pompadour. Her father, François Poisson, had been a clerk in the employ of Pâris-Duverney. From this position of obscurity, his daughter had risen to the position of hostess to Voltaire and the other *philosophes*; and after the death of the formidable Mme de Châteauroux she eventually succeeded, after many months of scheming, in literally waylaying the king, when he was out hunting in the Forêt de Sénart, and offering herself as his mistress. She was ennobled a fortnight later.

Although the king was greatly in love with her, at this date the Pompadour's position at court was still precarious. Her plebeian birth was a grave handicap, and she needed allies. Maurice, the boon companion of Pâris-Duverney, was instantly captivated by her. She quickly realized that the Marshal could be of use to her at court; but her desire to utilize him was also reinforced by a genuine mutual esteem. Maurice, who had known all his life what it meant to occupy an equivocal position at great courts, sympathized with her predicament. If she was of common origin, his own birth in bastardy had made a similar outcast of him. He knew what it felt like to be secretly ridiculed and openly treated as an interloper.

The Pompadour was amused by the manner in which Maurice carried on a quaint and chivalrous flirtation with her. Although nearly fifty and very infirm, his manner still reflected the amorous glow of his famous uncle Philipp: and he was still lively enough to be the protector of a bevy of the most beautiful actresses in France. It was as instructive as it was entertaining to have him as champion and *beau*. They also shared, among other things, a love and knowledge of fine porcelain. Augustus the Strong had been the greatest collector of Chinese ceramics in Europe, and the founder of the Meissen factory; and Mme de Pompadour had quickly become the patroness of the rival establishment newly founded at Sèvres.

Their companionship soon attracted comment.

> *When the Maréchal Saxe and the proud Pompadour*
> *Were driving out gaily in gilt coach and four,*
> *Frelon spied the pair—'Oh, see them!' he cried,*
> *'The sword of our king, and his sheath, side by side'.*[147]

As yet, neither Mme de Pompadour nor the Pâris brothers were able to intervene decisively against Conti on behalf of Maurice. In fact he had to suffer the worst setback in his long career at court, and almost certainly the worst blow to his pride. He was able to persuade his superiors to reject Conti's original plan: but he was powerless to prevent Conti being placed in command of an independent army. This army would operate alongside him in Flanders, but would not be under his control. Further, the comte de Clermont, whom Broglie has stigmatized as 'a *bon vivant*, thinking of nothing but levity and self-indulgence',[148] was given command of a second army. The princes of the blood had gained field rank, and had made their point.

An even heavier blow was to come: Argenson had converted Louis to his conservative view of the international situation. There would be no invasion of the United Provinces: Maurice was given the strictest orders to confine his operations to the Austrian Netherlands. He had been forced into a sterile inactivity at the very moment when the French armies were poised to deliver the *coup de grâce*.

It was with heavy heart that he returned to Brussels on May 1st. Even the Pompadour had declared herself, for her own tactical reasons, in favour of a scheme whereby Conti was to be declared *generalissimo*. Maurice's deposition seemed at hand; but at the last moment the king summoned up enough courage and energy to draw back. The marquise hastened to explain to Maurice that she had only acted in this way in order to discharge an important debt of honour. Conti's mother, the disreputable old princesse de Conti, had been the only woman at court who had been willing to present Mme de Pompadour formally at court. Louis himself had bribed her to do so by promising to pay her losses at the gaming-table. Maurice probably sympathized with the Pompadour's predicament, but her temporary defection must have increased his depression.

The times were conspiring against him. He had been deliberately and viciously snubbed. It is doubtful whether the patent of naturalization which he had just received, making him a subject of the king of France and Navarre, can have been of much consolation to him at such a moment. 'We cannot too much express our satisfaction,' ran the royal decree,

> on account of the zeal and singular attachment which our most dear and well-beloved cousin, M. de Saxe, has manifested for our person and our crown, in abandoning the advantages and positions which he might have expected in Poland and Saxony, in order to come and serve with our armies in France. The superiority of his genius and the depth of his knowledge of the art of war, his many great exploits and continuous glorious service, engage us not only to acknowledge them, but also to anticipate the wishes of our cousin Marshal de Saxe, who hopes to dedicate the rest of his life to our service and to end his days in our kingdom, by permitting him to enjoy therein the advantages which our native subjects have, by now removing all the obstacles which might arise from his birth in a foreign country.[149]

Fulsome words. 'Superiority of his genius . . . Depth of his knowledge of the art of war. . . . His many great exploits.' True, he had
escaped being superseded in his command, as on an earlier and equally
bitter occasion; but he was now being asked, at the height of his
military powers, to share his position with the prince de Conti. It was
ridiculous. His new countrymen had chosen a very curious way of
demonstrating their confidence in his extraordinary qualities.

It was not surprising that he opened his new campaign listlessly
and without conviction. His first fumbling movements dumbfounded
his old mentor Folard. Maurice wrote to say that Folard did not realize
that he was no longer a free agent, and that 'this is a courtiers' army,
with all the drawbacks implied thereby. I have detached forty
battalions and fifty squadrons for the investiture of Mons: and the
siege is to be conducted by M. le prince de Conti, the Lord Almighty
bless him. Politics!—I refuse to discuss them. I leave them to those
more clever than myself.'[150] A few days later he wrote again in similar
vein to Frederick of Prussia, who by then had become as perplexed as
Folard. 'Your Majesty knows full well,' explained Maurice, 'that
military considerations are always sacrificed to political ones. I thus
flatter myself that your Majesty will not attribute to me any of the
grosser errors that may be made during the course of this campaign.'[151]
The next three tedious months were confined to minor siege operations. Maurice was more or less relegated to the rôle of serving as a
post-box for the florid despatches of the two princes, who now revelled
in their situation in the centre of the stage. He was compelled to
await the tardy onset of the enemy, whose empty threats had earlier
thrown Argenson into such a panic. His mood, as he watched the
antics of the princes, grew black. Soon he was warning Argenson that
'the pretensions of M. le prince de Conti may go too far'.[152] The
arrival of the king at Brussels merely postponed the inevitable explo-
sion; and Argenson himself had to hurry from Versailles expressly in
order to paper over the cracks which he had himself created in the
high command. As Frederick of Prussia later noted:

> The presence of the king and his ministers was extremely embarrassing
> for Count Saxe, and a strain on the resources of the army. The courtiers
> rent the camp with intrigues and generally thwarted the Marshal's
> intentions. So numerous a court required ten thousand daily rations
> of fodder for their horses.[153]

It was a signal boon to Maurice when Louis, who was finding life
among his soldiers dull, returned to Versailles in the middle of June.
Ostensibly the king had returned to attend the accouchement of his

daughter-in-law; but in reality he was pining for the *fêtes champêtres* at Choisy that Mme de Pompadour knew so well how to arrange.

His departure made imminent the fight to the death between Maurice and the princes. It was Clermont, however, who drew first blood. At first he had appeared tractable, even willing to learn, and unlike the more bumptious Conti, he was not above admitting that a prince of the blood might require a tip or two in the art of war. But at his lavish supper parties he was unable to suppress his natural flippancy. He would entertain his laughing guests with imitations of Maurice's thick German accent, earthy diction, and inelegant idiom, and would encourage them to make jokes about the Marshal's amatory prowess. He also shed crocodile tears at their laments that they had to subject their fine French natures to the commands of a boorish Saxon.

The prince had chosen the wrong victim, and the wrong moment. On one sly pretext or another, Maurice withdrew three of Clermont's four brigades of foot, and most of his horse and artillery. Clermont's once proud army looked ridiculous. The young man was enraged, and threatened to leave Flanders forthwith, declaring that it was altogether too humiliating for a scion of the house of Bourbon to have to obey the orders of a 'foreign bastard'.

The effect of the last phrase on Maurice was terrifying. Clermont had struck his dagger through the one chink in the glittering suit of armour which Maurice had spent a lifetime in perfecting. His sensitivity on the score of his birth had lessened with the years, as victory had crowned disappointment, and Chambord had replaced poverty. But few men had had the temerity to taunt him openly with the memory of his bastardy, and remind him that, whatever his military achievements, he could never finally escape the taint of original sin.

Clermont soon regretted his strong words, realizing that by uttering them he had played directly into Maurice's hands. Maurice could appeal to the king, and Clermont might be compelled to resign his command. An attempt at conciliation was indicated. As his rank made formal apology out of the question, he wrote to Maurice offering to explain the circumstances which had led to the 'misunderstanding'. The offending words, it seemed, had only been attributed to Clermont by troublemakers. But it was one thing for the prince to write a letter: he had next to deliver it: and Maurice might refuse to read it. Realizing the need for adequate preparation, Clermont therefore persuaded the young marquis de Valfons, the liaison officer between his army and that of Maurice, to act as his emissary. 'When I arrived at headquarters,' Valfons later recorded,

> the Marshal was lying on his bed in his boots. The door was locked. His chief of staff, Crémille, opened it, saw the letter in my hand, and asked: 'What's the matter? Has the enemy moved?' 'No,' I replied, 'this is a letter from M. le comte de Clermont.' 'Good God,' said

Crémille, 'don't you know that the Marshal is furious with the prince?' I went over to the bed, and said: 'M. le Maréchal, M. le comte de Clermont salutes you and sends you this letter.' He plucked the letter disdainfully from my fingers and threw it on the bed, saying: 'I may read it sometime or other.' 'If M. le Maréchal would permit me to open it,' I ventured to say, 'you could learn what really happened.' 'Nonsense,' was the reply, 'even though the man is a prince of the blood he has to learn to obey his superior officer.' 'M. le Maréchal, you are too great a general to listen to the gossip of trouble-makers.' 'But Valfons, you were there! You heard what was said!' 'Believe me, M. le Maréchal, whatever may have been said was said in jest. Everything else is pure exaggeration.' By this time I had opened the letter and had asked him if he would let me read its contents. 'Read it? What for? It is all lies!'

Valfons persisted, and read the letter; and as he had anticipated, its well-turned phrases had an emollient effect. Finally Maurice growled:

'If Clermont says the whole thing is moonshine, I suppose I shall have to believe him. I shall say no more.' I therefore suggested that when riding past the prince's headquarters on the morrow, the Marshal should stop and dine with him. 'I do not sup with those who ridicule me,' replied the Marshal. 'Still, I may call in on my way back. It will save me the trouble of writing a letter.'[154]

The meeting took place, and the two commanders were reconciled. Shortly afterwards Maurice formed a substantial reserve force of 12,000 men, and put Clermont in command of it. Honour was satisfied, and Clermont had learned his lesson. Henceforth his conduct was exemplary: and in any event, as Maurice well knew, he could do very little damage in charge of the reserve.

The clash with Conti was destined to be much more prolonged, and to be more intimately related to the general progress of the campaign.

Maurice was in command of an immense army, called the *Armée du roi*, to distinguish it from the smaller *Armée de Conti* and the *Armée de Clermont*. The *Armée du roi* numbered 200,000 men: but as we have seen, Maurice was forbidden to use it for offensive purposes, and in order to keep this great mass of men on their toes he was compelled to embark on a series of minor sieges which were little more than mopping-up operations to the successful exertions of the previous year. Meanwhile, Clermont and his army were engaged in taking Antwerp, which fell to the French in May, while Conti was busy reducing Mons, which surrendered to him in July.

By midsummer the character of the French campaign had changed.

Although the French were officially only marking time, their enemies could hardly be expected to stand by indefinitely while the remaining strongpoints in the Austrian Netherlands fell one by one. The British were slowly gathering their forces for a full-scale counter-attack; and in due course the interest of both sides became concentrated on the city of Namur, which was still occupied by the British and their allies. The British had at last understood that if Namur was taken the French would have no difficulty in advancing on Liége and Maastricht: and with Maastricht in Maurice's hands, the invasion of Holland would be so easy an undertaking that even the timid Argenson might be tempted to authorize the move.

The race for Namur began in earnest. Maurice was behind the Dyle and the Demer to the north of the city, with Conti an equivalent distance away to the west at Mons. The British and Dutch came marching down rapidly from the north-east, in the full heat of a blazing summer. The British were under the command of Ligonier, the Dutch under the command of Waldeck: and the commander of the Austrians, Charles of Lorraine, was already moving speedily with his army from the Rhineland.

Everything indicated that there would be a battle-royal in front of Namur, and Maurice was anxious to obtain the maximum number of first-class troops at the earliest possible moment. He knew that the enemy armies, though resolute, were small in size, and that their generals were dismally at odds. Their supplies were, moreover, said to be scanty, and their supply line badly organized. On paper Maurice's advantage was impressive. But whereas the enemy forces were concentrated, the French were scattered over a large area. Because of the necessity of wasting whole battalions on garrison and occupation duties, the effective, as distinct from the nominal strength of the *Armée du roi* was not greatly superior to that of its adversaries.

Maurice could have remedied this state of affairs swiftly and decisively by the simple expedient of adding a second French army to the *Armée du roi*. Obviously and logically this second army would be the *Armée de Conti*, now freed from the siege of Mons. Maurice therefore requested Conti to join him before Namur as soon as possible. He had not taken seriously an earlier discourtesy of Conti in failing to send a messenger with a formal report of the fall of Mons, which the Marshal had therefore heard of more or less by accident; nor did he suspect that Conti was about to commit an act for which the word treason, later used by Broglie, was hardly too severe. Maurice was wholly absorbed in a complicated manoeuvre which, when completed, would interlock the scattered French divisions under his command. He had advanced to Louvain, while units under Clermont-Gallerande and Löwendahl were sweeping round on his left in order to come down on the enemy line of march and cut off their retreat.

It was at this delicate moment that the prince de Conti decided to ignore the request of his senior officer. He had no intention of merging his army with that of Maurice. He preferred instead, in his oceanic ignorance of strategy, to invest and capture Charleroi. He did not see why Maurice and his staff should retain a monopoly of the glory.

Charleroi was a well-defended city of about the same size as Mons, and was therefore considered by Conti to be well within his capacities. But its gain or loss was irrelevant to the main issues of the campaign. Maurice was furious when Conti refused to abandon this new siege in order to join him, deigning only to send to Namur twelve battalions of infantry and ten cavalry squadrons; but he went quite mad with rage when, after giving a command to this miserable detachment, he was confronted with a written order from Conti forbidding its commander, the comte d'Estrées, from acting without Conti's express permission. Maurice had scanned so many insolent despatches from Conti that the mere sight of that final *L. F. de Bourbon* scrawled at the foot of the page drove him berserk. He calmed down sufficiently to write to Argenson:

> Here is a matter which warrants the closest attention of His Majesty and yourself. You will see from M. le prince de Conti's letter that if the enemy attacks me, which is in the highest degree likely, M. d'Estrées would remain a mere spectator of the battle. The prince's conduct is beyond comprehension. I have taken great care not to talk of the matter for fear the enemy should hear of it. As a loyal servant of His Majesty, I have not made any rejoinder; but to bring the prince to his senses, I have threatened to pull back my forces to Louvain.[155]

Argenson, utterly at a loss, returned a temporizing reply, and for a moment it seemed as though Maurice really would retire northward, leaving Conti to the tender mercies of the triple enemy army in his vicinity. The tension was partially resolved by the unexpected collapse of the garrison of Charleroi. The prince was therefore able to profess a hypocritical readiness 'to fly with all speed' to the aid of the Marshal. His subsequent tardiness belied his fair words. It also made nonsense of the proposals which he advanced at a council of war which was held on the following August 2nd. Conti, who had never been noted for offensive action, there had the audacity to propose an immediate attack on the enemy: an attack squarely opposed to the plan adopted by Maurice, who intended to refrain from headlong encounters until the completion of his preliminary manoeuvre before Namur. An open altercation ensued between the two commanders. They wrangled unrestrainedly in front of their embarrassed staff officers for two whole days. The truth was that Conti had divined that a large section of the army was eager for battle, and that Maurice was already incurring a certain amount of unpopularity by holding

his men in check. The senior officers had all reported that the enforced
inactivity was encouraging their men to brawl and loot. Although the
discipline of his own army appears to have been the worst of all, Conti
did not scruple to exploit the prevailing mood to the discomfiture of
Maurice.

It could not be denied that Maurice had been adopting the time-
honoured expedient of keeping the troops occupied by digging useless
trenches.[156] His enemies at Paris were not slow to put it about that
he was attempting to prolong the war for his own ends. Meanwhile,
in Flanders, Conti had received full backing for his nonsensical plan
from the influential chevalier de Belle-Isle, the great Belle-Isle's
brother, who five years earlier had led the opposition to Maurice's plan
for the seizure of Prague.

Maurice remained adamant. He insisted on making the issue one of
confidence between Conti and himself. He was rightly unimpressed
when Conti heatedly declared that 'a prince of the blood is subordinate to no one, not even a Marshal of France'. He cared not a rap when
Conti cited the example of his late kinsman, le grand Condé, who on
his last campaign had insisted that not only he himself but also his
son should take precedence over five marshals. Maurice knew very well
that in the final count neither Louis nor Argenson would dispense
with services of a Saxe in order to place the destinies of France in the
hands of a Conti.[157] After forty-eight vituperative hours, Conti
realized that Maurice would not budge. 'It is up to you to decide,' he
conceded, 'for it is you who have the biggest army.' The prince was
beaten. After such loss of face, he could no longer bear to remain in
Flanders, and he set out the following day for Versailles to tender his
resignation to the king.

When Conti failed to appear at the next conference, Maurice sent
a polite letter to speed him on his way. 'Have I had the misfortune to
displease you, monseigneur?' he enquired with ironic politeness.

> I flatter myself that there is no discord between us, and I certainly
> had no desire that you should resign. As your departure will leave a
> great many things to attend to, perhaps you would be good enough
> to indicate an hour when it would be convenient for me to await my
> orders and present my respects.

Conti's reply was curt.

> I was already on the road when I received your letter. I would have
> conferred with you with pleasure if I had not already set out. It is
> true that I have asked the king's permission to withdraw.

The prince added, au bout des lèvres:

> In view of our past relationship, I do not know why you should
> imagine that I should complain about you.[158]

On August 10th, the king and Argenson issued a noncommittal edict placing Conti's army formally under the command of Maurice. Within the general political framework laid down for his guidance, Maurice was free once more to conduct his campaign without further hindrance in the field. He had routed Clermont and Conti. He had now to deal with the enemy.

Most commentators on the campaign of 1746 appear to be unaware of the strategic strait-jacket, inspired by his interpretation of the political situation, which Argenson had imposed upon Maurice. Yet they unanimously describe his campaign of this year as masterly, thereby paying him a double compliment.

At the opening of the campaign there is none the less a suspicion that Maurice had lost his touch. He committed no error, but he was clearly not at his best—not the decisive, mercurial Saxe of happier years. Perhaps his responsibilities as commander-in-chief were tending to weigh upon him; perhaps he was chary of taking the kind of risk which, if it failed, might tarnish his new laurels. We cannot be sure. All we know is that the master of the bloodless campaign, the early exponent of the *Blitzkrieg*, had momentarily become the champion of the waiting game.

During the quarrel with Conti, the enemy had crossed the river Mehaigne (on August 1st). 'Saxe's main army,' observes an English commentator, 'remained inexplicably at Louvain.'[159] The French, for once, had allowed the British and their allies to outmarch and out-manoeuvre them. While they debated among themselves, they lost the chance to take Namur.[160] Maurice, his mind ever apt with military precedent, immediately recognized the strength of the enemy position. He realized that it now resembled the position enjoyed by the French themselves under Luxembourg at an earlier siege of Namur, in the reign of Louis XIV. At that time the Prince of Orange had wisely refrained from attacking the French, in spite of his superiority in numbers: and Maurice, now facing the same problem, decided to emulate the Prince of Orange. He was content to keep the enemy at arm's length, disregarding the restiveness of his troops. For three weeks the two armies fenced with one another along a broad front, suffering only slight casualties.

The enemy's hold over Namur was not so secure, however, as it had first appeared. The allies had won the opening trick, but they were playing from a poor hand, for Maurice had been informed by his indefatigable team of spies that the enemy supply system was extremely shaky. The British and Dutch position was not unlike that of the French in Bohemia in 1742, in that the closer they hugged their apparently impregnable lines, the taller grew the spectre of defeat. It was the elderly and experienced Ligonier who hit upon a way of escape from the predicament. He proposed a lightning cavalry attack at full strength on Antwerp: a startling and original notion, worthy of Maurice at his best. Such a confident *coup de main* might well have compelled the French to loosen their grip: but Ligonier's plan was firmly vetoed by the Dutch and the Austrians. As Ligonier had predicted, the allied army, starved of food and supplies, thereupon began slowly to disintegrate, and their withdrawal from their otherwise excellent position was merely a matter of time. Maurice hastened their departure by waging a war of nerves. He cannonaded the enemy positions, launched a succession of sallies led by small groups of infantry, and persistently spread rumours that he was about to cross the Mehaigne himself, in force. Finally he sent Löwendahl in a surprise dash to capture the town of Huy, at the junction of the Meuse and the Mehaigne, and on the direct route between the enemy and his bases at Liége and Maastricht. Löwendahl's slyly planned manoeuvre was at once economical and decisive. On the same day, August 29th, Prince Charles of Lorraine began to retreat, although he well knew that in doing so he was uncovering Namur and ensuring its eventual loss to the French. The discouraged and dissension-ridden allied armies began to trudge back to the Dutch border: and immediately Maurice moved forward to besiege Namur. The siege was entrusted to the now obedient and rehabilitated Clermont, with Löwendahl as his second-in-command, to prevent him from making a fool of himself. The city was invested on September 6th, the trenches were opened on the 12th, and by noon on the 19th the commander of the garrison was ready to surrender. It was a capitulation *à l'hollandaise*, for a sturdy and prolonged resistance had been expected. The French army, freed in so spectacular a manner from its boredom, was jubilant.

It is not only modern commentators who have admired Maurice's achievement. In spite of illness, rebellion among his officers, grumbling in the ranks, and criticism at Versailles, he had forced a well-placed enemy to make an ignominious withdrawal without exposing himself to the necessity of fighting a pitched battle. Espagnac was speaking for his contemporaries when he wrote that 'the manoeuvres of the Maréchal de Saxe, in obliging the enemy to abandon the Mehaigne and Namur, are a *chef d'oeuvre* of the military science.'[161] By his patient and skilful moves, Maurice had given the best answer possible to his detractors in Paris. After a few preliminary hesitations, he had ably demonstrated that the objects of Conti's much-vaunted plan of attack could be achieved without unleashing a single thunderbolt.

He had now pursued the enemy in earnest, and laid siege to Liége. He wanted to quarter his troops in the lush country around that rich city during the coming winter, rather than remain again in territory that was already exhausted by war and occupation.

Charles of Lorraine, knowing that the great town of Maastricht was also threatened, tried to adopt a posture that would protect Liége and Maastricht simultaneously. The result, as Ligonier despairingly pointed out, was merely to achieve a dilution of the strength of the allies, already badly eroded. When Maurice marched down from the north-west with the *Armée du roi*, Charles threw his men across the roads from St. Trond and Tongres in an effort to check them. But Maurice meant to have Liége, and he meant to have it before the end of the year's campaign. He therefore ordered a complicated and beautifully executed flank-march, which served the double purpose of foxing the enemy concerning his true line of advance, and also concealed his numbers by tucking one wing behind the other. He took up his position between the two roads on the afternoon of October 10th.

The weather was appalling. While Maurice rode from one part of the field to another, on a protracted reconnaissance, the heavens released a deluge. The downpour did not in the least depress the soaring spirits of the French. They had known for twenty-four hours that their commander was at long last on the point of joining the great battle they had been looking forward to for many weary weeks. Maurice announced the news in the theatrical manner which he knew would appeal to them. The previous evening, his troupe of players was preparing to perform in a marquee erected in the main square of Tongres. The director of the company, the playwright Charles-Simon Favart, was surprised and flustered when the Marshal unexpectedly entered the tent and beckoned him to a private conference. 'Tomorrow,' said Maurice, 'I intend to give battle. So far I have kept it to myself. I want you to announce it publicly this evening, at the end of your performance. You can write a few couplets for the occasion.'[162]

It was in this extraordinary but effective way that the news was broken. Justine Favart, the director's wife and the leading actress in the company, advanced to the footlights at the climax of the play and sang to Maurice's troops the following words:

> *Nous avons rempli notre tâche,*
> *Demain nous donnerons relâche;*
> *Guerriers, Mars va guider vos pas:*
> *Que votre ardeur se renouvelle:*
> *A des intrépides soldats*
> *La victoire est toujours fidelle.*

Demain bataille, jour de gloire,
Que dans les fastes de l'Histoire
Triomphe encore la nom français,
Digne d'éternelle mémoire!
Revenez après vos succès
Jouir les fruits de la victoire.

As she sang the words '*demain bataille*' a tremor of excitement ran through her audience. Finally she announced: 'No performance tomorrow, gentlemen, because of the battle: but the day afterwards we shall have much pleasure in giving you '*Coq du village*"!' At once there was a storm of cheering. '*Demain bataille! Demain bataille! Vive le maréchal!*'

Unlike the allies, the French endured the rainswept night without complaint. They had eaten a full supper and were light of heart. The following morning young Valfons, who had spent a busy night carrying messages from one battalion to another, made a hearty breakfast. Maurice, passing by, stopped and said to him with a smile: 'I like people who eat well before they fight. It is a good sign.'[163]

The enemy was in a sombre mood. British, Dutch, Hanoverians and Austrians had spent the night saddled up or standing to arms, soaked, shivering, wondering from which direction the blow would fall. Morning brought them depressing news. Liége, the mainstay of their left wing, had been betrayed by its citizens, who had opened their gates to the French during the hours of darkness. The allied left was therefore rendered untenable even before the opening shot was fired. Even worse, the allies were forced to thin out their centre in order to cover their exposed left flank, in a hurried last-minute redeployment that hardly helped to make them face the coming ordeal with equanimity.

The allied position was linked to three villages on the north-eastern outskirts of Liége, by name Liers, Varoux and Rocoux, the last named of which eventually gave its name to the battle [Fig. 7].[164] All these villages were held by the British and Hanoverians under Ligonier, while on the left were Waldeck and his Dutch, and on the right the Austrians under Prince Charles. Had Ligonier been granted sufficient time to fortify the villages in a proper manner, and dig himself in, he could have made them as impregnable as Maurice had earlier made Fontenoy. But everything had to be done in haste and muddle. Ligonier could do little more than site two batteries well forward in improvised redoubts in an attempt to close the gap between himself and Waldeck, and to make the best of such natural cover as the villages offered. To hold the villages and his front line he had only six Hanoverian and two British infantry battalions, which he put under the orders of a tough German general called Zastrow; and he kept under his own command an additional two Hessian and two British battalions, together with the Royal Scots Greys. They were very exiguous resources with which to stave off the full weight of the French army.

Maurice quickly decided on his plan of deployment. He had known since the opening of the campaign that the Austrian contingent was the largest; and he had learnt from his agents how, after protracted quarrels, the Austrians had been ceded the privilege of taking the

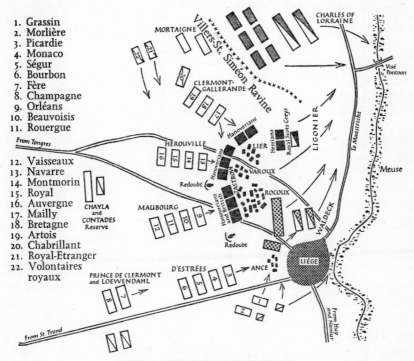

1. Grassin
2. Morlière
3. Picardie
4. Monaco
5. Ségur
6. Bourbon
7. Fère
8. Champagne
9. Orléans
10. Beauvoisis
11. Rouergue

12. Vaisseaux
13. Navarre
14. Montmorin
15. Royal
16. Auvergne
17. Mailly
18. Bretagne
19. Artois
20. Chabrillant
21. Royal-Etranger
22. Volontaires royaux

FIG. 7. THE BATTLE OF ROCOUX

coveted right of the line, on the grounds that, in the absence of Cumberland, the senior-ranking officer was Charles of Lorraine. Maurice reckoned that the Dutch could be counted on to give their usual poor performance; and after probing to make certain that they were indeed on the allied left, he angled his march in order to bring his main pressure to bear on the Dutch flank. He decided to aim at the weak spot between Dutch and British. While his infantry were hitting at this hinge in the line, he would simultaneously despatch a strong detachment of cavalry to take the unfortunate Dutch in the rear. He was also pleased to observe that his intentions against the allied left and centre were supported by the position of the Austrians on the allied right. They had cut themselves off from their allied comrades by aligning themselves behind the ravine of Villers-St. Simon, and would thus be unable to advance to the assistance of their Dutch and English comrades, behind whose backs rolled the broad, forbidding waters of the Meuse.[165]

'We were on the march at daybreak,' Maurice later reported to Argenson,

> and were in touch with the enemy about ten o'clock. If the attack had begun at noon, as it should have done, I could probably have destroyed the enemy completely. But it only began on my right, on the village of Ance, at three o'clock, and on my left-centre shortly afterwards. The affair was badly timed (*n'a point balancé*).[166]

Such frankness was characteristic of Maurice. Because his frontal attack was delayed, he was unable to exploit his advantages to the full. The reason for this error lay partly in the rawness and mistiness of the weather, partly in the late arrival of Löwendahl's contingent. (The comte de Clermont was nominally in charge of the right wing, but it had been decided in advance that the real task of shattering the Dutch would be entrusted to Löwendahl, technically Clermont's lieutenant.) Maurice, however, was too magnanimous to make Löwendahl the scapegoat that Napoleon was to make of Grouchy: and Löwendahl's success at Fontenoy more than atoned for his failure at Rocoux.

In mid-afternoon, battle was joined in earnest. Estrées took forward his column to attack Ance, a hamlet half a mile from Liége, and the linchpin of the Dutch left wing. The Dutch put up a surprisingly stiff resistance. At the same time the three other French columns on the right wing fell on Liers, Varoux and Rocoux. Maubourg made satisfactory progress at Rocoux; Hérouville did almost as well, after an initial reverse, against Varoux; but Clermont-Gallerande, the most gifted of the three commanders, could make little impression on Liers.

The French left remained stationary. Mortaigne, its commander, sat on his horse and gazed passively across the ravine at the immobilized Austrians, who could do nothing at all to reinforce their battered allies. Paradoxically, it was just as well for the allies that the large Austrian contingent stayed where it was. If the Austrians had been able to move down into the centre, the narrow strip of ground between their front line and the Meuse would have become intolerably congested, giving the English and Dutch little chance of escape. Prince Charles could only wait in order to cover the withdrawal of the left and centre when finally it took place.

From the start of the battle, the allied retreat was only a matter of time. Ligonier had only twelve battalions with which to keep at bay fifty-two French battalions that mounted attack after ceaseless attack.

'It must be said for M. de Saxe,' Ligonier said later, 'that his attacks were strong and without confusion, and as soon as two brigades had been repulsed at each village, a third came running in.'[167] When he saw that his initial attacks were being blunted by fire from Ligonier's makeshift redoubts, Maurice collected two spare regiments of cavalry from his left and personally led them into attack. Within half an hour of the start of the battle, Rocoux and Varoux had been overrun. Ligonier was soon forced to inform Waldeck that he could hold out no longer. The Dutch thereupon began to retire in good order 'to previously prepared positions': that is, to the pontoons across the Meuse at Visé. Ligonier next withdrew in his turn, his ranks torn open by the pitiless mobile batteries that Maurice had been moving skilfully round the field since the start of the action. The whole business of withdrawal was as gradual and orderly as the comparable retreat at Fontenoy; indeed Ligonier, who took part in both, considered the performance at Rocoux the more praiseworthy. It was managed so skilfully that it seems to have baffled the French and thwarted pursuit. Although Maurice's men swarmed round the beaten enemy as they trod their *via dolorosa* to the pontoons, they failed to cut the British and Dutch to pieces, as they might have been expected to do. The allies owed their ultimate preservation largely to the protective square which the British and Hanoverian rearguard formed round the end of the pontoons, an heroic square which not even the attentions of eight large cannon could deter.

Maurice, with commendable humanity, cut short his pursuit soon after the evacuation of the villages. It was nearly dusk; the enemy was in good order; and he hated bloodshed for its own sake. In the evening, irradiated by the crimson sheen of a westering sun, there occurred what Valfons termed 'a splendid moment'. In the fading sunlight, the Marshal rode back to his headquarters through the ranks of his victorious army, to thunderous shouts of '*Vivent le roi et le maréchal de Saxe!*' 'Each brigade,' recalled Valfons, 'offered him its captured flags, cannon and prisoners. It was the most grand and moving spectacle imaginable.'[168]

It was indeed *la gloire* made manifest.

Yet victory was incomplete. Maurice deserved full credit for the determination with which he had fought: and in terms of cold statistics his triumph seemed decisive. He himself put the enemy losses in dead and wounded at four or five thousand, which was probably a conservative estimate. He had captured nine flags and sixty cannon, and taken three thousand prisoners, a number far exceeding the total of his own killed and wounded.

But the victory of Rocoux lacked the finality of Fontenoy. The enemy had again got off lightly—perhaps too lightly. Maurice had brought 120,000 men into the field against 80,000; the enemy lines had been cramped in length and compressed in depth, and pushed up against a lethal river; and the Austrians were never properly deployed at all. Yet Ligonier, overwhelmed as he had been, had been allowed to fight a superb rearguard action and save the allies from destruction. For the second time Maurice had failed to follow through after winning in pitched battle. Again he had denied himself, and France, the traditional bloody fruits of victory.

The courtiers immediately began to chant, as on previous occasions, that he had spared the enemy in order to prolong the war to his own advantage. The truth was more creditable. The general who had watched Malplaquet as an impressionable boy was not by nature a bloodthirsty man. Indeed, he is said to have surveyed the grey wet landscape of the battlefield, before the French attack went in, with tears in his eyes and a line of Racine on his lips. Tired in mind, sick in body, he may well have thought that by gaining the day he had done all that was necessary, for honour and for France. He did not wish to go down to posterity as the butcher of a beaten foe. As the merciful darkness gathered, he may well have been content to echo his own words after Fontenoy: 'Nous en avions assez.'

The majority of Frenchmen did not share the opinion of the courtiers; they had no reservations about the magnitude of Maurice's success. When he reached Fontainebleau, on November 14th 1746, after settling his troops into their winter quarters, he received a warm welcome from the man who was now his king. Louis had already retired to bed: but on hearing that Maurice de Saxe had come, he rose and gave the weary marshal supper in the royal apartments. Later he placed in Maurice's hands a brevet bestowing on him an unusual mark of honour. 'The king,' it declared,

> desiring to give Count Saxe new marks of the satisfaction which His Majesty has in the great and signal services rendered by him, and in order to grant him a distinction which may perpetuate the memory of the famous victory obtained by him over His Majesty's enemies at Rocoux, has bestowed on Count Saxe six pieces of cannon, carrying three pounders each; three of which bear the arms of England and three those of Hesse; making a part of the artillery which the enemy lost in battle; and he has permitted Count Saxe to preserve and keep the said pieces of cannon at the royal *château* of Chambord, of which His Majesty has already granted him the enjoyment during his natural life.[169]

CHAPTER XIII

VERSAILLES, 1746-1747

Ce peuple fou, brutal et galant,
Superbe en sa fortune, en ses malheurs rampant.
FREDERICK THE GREAT

BARELY five weeks before Rocoux, while the feud with Conti was at its height, Maurice was tormented by an urgent problem of a more personal kind. He was too experienced a commander to let it interfere with his campaign: but it was of such magnitude that it must have caused him much lost sleep.

It was a matter far removed from the rough sphere of warfare, and concerned a projected betrothal. In July 1746, after the king had returned from Flanders in order to be present at his daughter-in-law's accouchement, the Dauphine had died in childbirth. The poor young girl, formerly the Infanta Maria Teresa, had left Madrid to become the Dauphin's wife only a year before. Her pious and prudish husband had doted on her, delighting in the modesty that had set her far apart from the bulk of the other women who graced his father's court.

The Dauphin was utterly heartbroken by her death: his grief was not lightened by the grisly ceremonial which accompanied her funeral. 'The black hangings,' writes Miss Mitford,

> over everything, even the furniture, and the courtyard outside; the professional weepers, the chanting of monks and nuns, the opening of the body (obligatory in the case of a royal person; the doctors said they found a great deal of milk in her brain) and the removal of its heart, handed on a salver to a lady-in-waiting; the lying-in-state, the struggling crowds and fainting courtiers, ceremonial visits to the baby, the endless torchlit visit by night to the royal mausoleum of St. Denis. Worst of all, what the French call *figures de circonstance*, suitable but fictitious expressions of grief on every face.[170]

The torches had scarcely been extinguished before the calculating minds behind the *figures de circonstance* began to speculate about the dead woman's successor. There were good reasons for haste in the matter. The baby who had survived the death of its mother was a girl, and had not therefore secured the succession. The Dauphin must therefore re-marry without delay. The candidates were duly short-listed, and finally reduced in number to three, of whom the most promising, despite her Lutheran faith, was a sister of Frederick the Great. Another princess of Prussia had recently been married to a future king of Sweden, and Louis XV's crucial need of European allies put Frederick the Great in high hopes of bringing off another matrimonial coup by matching his favourite sister Amelia with the heir to the throne of France.

The two Roman Catholic princesses who were also on the short list possessed claims that were considered to be almost as strong. One was the late Dauphine's younger sister, the Infanta Antonia; the other was Maria Teresa of Savoy, daughter of Charles Emmanuel III, King of Sardinia. All three ladies had powerful advocates at Versailles. The Prussophiles, headed by the belligerent Belle-Isle, were hoping for a chance to bind the elusive Frederick indissolubly to France; the Infanta's case was argued cogently by Noailles and seconded by the forceful Maurepas and by Huescar, the Spanish ambassador; while the cause of the princess of Savoy had been espoused by Argenson, who was busily intriguing to detach Sardinia from the Austrian cause and ally her to France, with the ultimate objective—so dear to French statesmen—of supplanting the Austrians in Italy.

It was only at a late stage in the contest, when the Dauphine had been dead a whole month, that a third Roman Catholic princess came belatedly to the starting line. At first the mention of her name was greeted with surprise, even derision, in court circles. This apparent outsider was the fifteen-year-old Maria Josepha of Saxony, eighth child of Augustus III of Poland, and a niece of Maurice de Saxe.

The Saxon bid had been engineered by Count Löss, the wily Saxon envoy at Versailles, assisted by his counterpart, the marquis des Issarts, the French envoy to the court of Poland. The two men knew that they had little time in which to act; there were many courtiers to be bribed, and many rumours to spread. Löss cast about swiftly for useful instruments, and naturally concluded that the chief among them must be Maurice. He promptly arranged to have himself attached to the suite of Louis XV, who was then considering another visit to his northern armies; but the wiles of Mme de Pompadour kept Louis at court, and Löss was forced to commit his plans to paper, although he would have preferred to broach so delicate a matter in person. 'You will know better than anyone,' he wrote to Maurice in September,

> that in order not to compromise our chances, I must handle the affair as discreetly as possible. It will suffice to say that the question is how

to make His Majesty regard our Saxon princess more favourably than her rivals. You can help immensely with your reputation, and by means of judicious hints.[171]

There was little need to enumerate the advantages of the match. The increase in prestige and security which it would bring Saxony and the precarious Polish throne was obvious. There would also be a corresponding increase in the prestige and security of Maurice de Saxe. Maurice's participation in the negotiations would firmly establish him as a person of consequence, and his ambiguous position at the French court would be transformed. Although still an outsider, a foreigner by birth, he would be linked, after the marriage of Maria Josepha and the Dauphin, to the royal family itself. The former soldier of fortune would become uncle to the Dauphine, and the head of a powerful Saxon interest at court.

It was with understandable gusto that Maurice joined in the fray. The buoyancy of youth seemed to have been restored to him by the prospect of the glittering prizes ahead. What might not the future hold were he once able to insinuate himself into the very centre of the royal power? By the second week of September, when he was manoeuvring in the neighbourhood of Namur, his couriers were already scuttling to and fro on romantic as well as warlike business. As early as September 10th, he opened his heart to his royal half-brother at Warsaw:

> I do not often importune Your Majesty with letters, for I well know how busy you are. It is the gravity of the situation that forces me to take the liberty of breaking silence.

He then enumerated the claims of the respective princesses, in the way they might appear to Louis XV, indicating just why His Most Christian Majesty might be tempted to favour a Saxon. His conclusion was that the prospects were good, adding:

> I am taking the liberty of enclosing a letter recently sent to me by Mme de Pompadour. It will show Your Majesty that I have the royal ear.[172]

The stock of the royal maidens of Prussia and Sardinia had already begun to fall. The main objection to the Prussian princess was not her Lutheranism: Louis XIV's own brother had married a Protestant. No, the main obstacle was simply the unreliability of the word of the king of Prussia. As for the Sardinian princess, the objection was precise: she came of unfertile stock, with a bias towards daughters. It was therefore clear that the chief challenge to the Saxon party would come from the swarthy and ill-favoured little Spaniard, the Infanta Antonia. The queen was known to be in favour of another

Spanish match, and Marie Leczinska's support became even more vigorous after she learned that a Saxon princess was in the offing. How could she possibly welcome to Versailles the daughter of a ruling house that had ousted her own father from the throne of Poland? Although the queen had long since made her private peace with the amiable and engaging Maurice, she had by no means learned to love the house of Wettin as a whole. And although her influence over her husband was slight, she possessed a powerful ally in the prince de Conti, whose opposition to Saxony was even more vehement than her own. Conti resisted the candidature of Maria Josepha and espoused the cause of the Infanta for two reasons: first, because of his personal hatred of Maurice; and secondly, because of the traditional partiality of his family towards the dissident nobility of Poland. Recalling the stillborn attempt of his grandfather to obtain the Polish crown, Conti had recently opened secret negotiations with a group of dissident Polish nobles. In this he enjoyed the support of Louis XV, the paladin of futile diplomatic conspiracies, and was on the point of receiving a firm offer from the Diet at Warsaw.

The Infanta also enjoyed the support of Noailles, who was at once a realist and a pessimist, and who had cogent political reasons for his attitude. At a time when the victories of Fontenoy and Rocoux were still fresh in everyone's minds, he had taken a long, cool look at the general situation of France and had not been reassured by what he had seen. 'In spite of Your Majesty's success in Flanders,' he told his royal master,

> and in spite of the glory which your armies have acquired, you would do well to review the fortunes of our country's allies. Charles VII had been twice deprived of his Empire, and was on the point of losing it a third time, when death put an end to his miseries. The Spaniards have been ejected from Italy. The Republic of Genoa has been invaded and is under the Austrian yoke. The king of the Two Sicilies is gravely threatened, and may well lose his throne. The Duke of Modena is a fugitive, and in dire straits. Charles Edward Stuart is a wanderer, most of his supporters dead on the scaffold. Even the king of Prussia, who has so far been lucky, has only been able to pay for his successes by his betrayals.[173]

It was a gloomy prospect: but in the prospect of a family compact with Spain, Noailles believed that he detected an expedient which might still repair the fortunes of France. In spite of the recent reverses of Spanish arms, he was convinced that Spain was on the eve of a spiritual renascence.

> The government of Spain was pro-French in the time of Louis XIV, and pro-Italian under Philip V. Now it is becoming Castilian and nationalist.[174]

If only France and Spain would link hands across the Pyrenees, another era of mutual prosperity might yet attend the Bourbon cousins who ruled at Paris and Madrid.

It was specifically in order to counter the influence of Noailles that Löss had enlisted the aid of Maurice. On October 27th, the latter told the king of Poland that he had been 'given the particular task of converting Noailles, who loves me more than his own children'. He also wrote about this time that Mme de Pompadour 'has been of great service to us, as she is now very friendly with the queen, who retains her little corner of *Stanislasisme*'.[175] Both Noailles and the queen were deeply religious, and the one aspect of the Spanish match which they viewed with reserve was the fact that it would mean the Dauphin marrying his deceased wife's sister, an action requiring special dispensation from Rome.

By November 1746, Löss and Maurice between them had all but won the contest. The king of France had written to Maurice to tell him that Issarts at Dresden had been instructed to make a tentative request for Maria Josepha's hand. Louis, suddenly turning against the Spanish connexion, had coldly informed Madrid that 'the French people abhor incest'. Maurice was elated. 'When I have seen the marriage celebrated,' he informed his royal half-brother,

> I shall descend into the empire of the shades without regret. My career will have been crowned. I shall have savoured all the delights of this world, and my destiny will have been fulfilled.

He also urged Augustus,

> to admit no difficulty, no delay. I do not wish to tie you down, but I hope you will act quickly.[176]

He knew only too well the fatal indolence of Augustus and his minister Brühl.

> The king of France desires that you will contribute towards the making of peace and league yourself with Prussia, even if only in appearance. These are his terms. There can be no serious objection to them. I dare to throw myself at your feet and to beg you to make no difficulty on any account.[177]

Louis had come to appreciate the value of a Saxon alliance. Thanks to Maurice's influence, Noailles too had fallen silent. 'Your Marshal has been storming at me,' he told Löss with rueful humour. He considered the military value of the Saxon connexion negligible, but acknowledged that Saxony was one of the richest countries in Europe, whose dynastic expectations were at least the equal of those of Prussia. Two of Augustus' numerous children had already married into the ruling families of Bavaria and Naples. The elder, Maria Anna, was the consort of the Elector Maximilian Joseph of Bavaria; and the younger, Maria Amalia, was married to King Charles of the Two Sicilies, later to rule Spain as Charles III. An alliance between Saxony and France would renew the historic links between Warsaw and Versailles: and it was possible that the Saxons might then prevail on their Austrian friends to grant France the peace she so urgently sought.

The main terms of the match had been concluded when Maurice reached Versailles in mid-November. His enormous popularity was now employed to offset the disadvantages of Louis' choice, and to dampen the ridicule which would attend the arrival at the court of France of yet another barbarous Polish princess. Maurice, more than anyone else, would be able to make the marriage acceptable in the eyes of the French [Table 3].

It fell to Maurice to help to seal the negotiations by sending his nephew Count Friesen to Dresden to assist the French deputation, led by the duc de Richelieu. Richelieu was so devious and fantastic that Maurice, who knew him well, could not be happy until the signatures were actually on the contract.[178] Maurice also wrote charmingly and at length to the young princess' mother, the former Archduchess Maria Josepha, who was pathetically anxious for her favourite daughter, and needed advice on her *trousseau*. Maurice, celebrated as a ladies' man, was able to offer expert guidance. He described in detail the entourage and wardrobe of the late Dauphine, and informed the queen of Poland:

> Of course, I know that Your Majesty will find it difficult to arrange the *trousseau* of *Mme la Dauphine* in such haste. Nevertheless you would do well to furnish her with some fine Dutch fabrics, if any are available, in satin or cloth-of-gold, in the style of Persia or the Indies. None are available here because of import restrictions. The Armenians at Warsaw will probably have some pretty ones. I have written to Debrosse at The Hague, and asked him to send off to Dresden whatever he has in this line, so that you can make a choice. I might also mention that, as there are no good furriers here, it might be an excellent idea to make the princess a present of a double sable wrap, such as is worn in Russia. They are warm and ample, and very attractive when furnished with a muff to match.[179]

In this letter we catch the voice of the old connoisseur of beautiful stuffs and lovely women. No doubt, in years gone by, the Armenians at Warsaw had supplied him with many a bolt of silk with which to delight the hearts of his own ladies.

After a brief visit to Chambord, which was being remodelled to suit his taste, Maurice returned to Versailles by the end of the year in order to confer with Noailles about another matter of great political moment.

Thanks to his own efforts, coupled with those of Noailles and the Pâris brothers, the days of the marquis d'Argenson at the head of affairs had long been numbered. When the marquis was ultimately given his *congé*, his younger brother, the astute comte d'Argenson, was confirmed in the post of war minister; but the post of foreign minister remained vacant. Maurice and his friends meant to secure the appointment of someone on whom they might rely. Their candidate was the marquis de Puysieux, whom Maurice described in a letter to Brühl as an intimate friend. Puysieux, still only in his forties, had previously been a soldier as well as a diplomatist, and had fought with Maurice in Bohemia. He was now appointed to the ministry of foreign affairs. Maurice had never exercised so much power and influence. He had won great battles: and now he was instrumental in joining together great dynasties, and in toppling statesmen of whom he disapproved.

On January 14th, 1747, Maria Josepha left Dresden. As protocol dictated, she made the bleak journey across central Europe alone in her coach. In spite of her thick French, she had passed the *viva voce* examination conducted by Richelieu with flying colours. The eye of the practised roué had surveyed her plump little person with approval. He reported as much to his crony Maurice, who well understood such matters. Although they often disagreed about politics, they took continuous pleasure in each other's company and that of the opposite sex. 'I found her really charming,' Richelieu confided to Maurice:

> She is not in any way a beauty, but she is enormously attractive. Picture to yourself a snub nose, ripe lips, and a pair of intelligent, laughing eyes. I tell you, if they have got girls like that at the Opéra, they had better trot them out quickly.

He was able to give her a clean bill of health.

> She has had smallpox, measles and chicken pox, and is not subject to colds or fluxions.

He added that on grounds of heredity she was also likely to prove fecund. France could count on having its heir by the end of the year.[180]

On January 27th, Maria Josepha reached Strasbourg. Her uncle Maurice had already received the first instalment of his reward for the part he had played in arranging her coming marriage. During a grand audience at Choisy, the king, who seldom raised his voice, and usually spoke in an expressionless monotone, addressed a remark to

Maurice which the latter failed to catch. Maurice turned to his old adversary but new admirer, the comte de Clermont, and murmured: 'What did His Majesty say?' Clermont had not heard either, but addressing the king he enquired: 'Sire, the comte de Saxe did not hear what Your Majesty was gracious enough to say to him.' The king repeated his words, this time more loudly. 'M. le comte de Saxe,' he announced, 'I create you Marshal-General of the Camps and Armies of France. Did you hear me this time?' Maurice bowed very low. The king continued:

> Since you have rendered the state the same outstanding services as M. de Turenne, it is only right that you should enjoy the same authority and the same distinction as he did. I trust you will follow—*in every way*—the example of M. de Turenne.

For Maurice it was a truly great moment. The king's words were tantamount to apotheosis. But, as usual, he kept his wits about him. He divined that by exhorting him to follow the example of Turenne, 'in every way', the king was advising him to do one of two things: either to embrace the Church of Rome, as Turenne had done in order to become Marshal-General, or to die in battle, as Turenne had done at Salzbach. The king was doubtless hinting at religious conversion: but in his courteous speech of thanks Maurice made it clear that he would not abandon his native Lutheranism. 'Then it only remains for me, Sire,' he said with graceful evasion, 'to *die* like M. de Turenne. . . .'

Louis XIV, who at the instigation of Louvois had abolished the ancient office of Constable of France, had made the new post of Marshal-General of the King's Camp and Armies the supreme military appointment, and had bestowed it on Turenne in 1660. It is often asserted that the office was not held by any other soldier between the death of Turenne in 1675 and the appointment of Maurice in 1747. This is not so, for Villars was appointed Marshal-General in 1733, shortly before his death. But its bestowal upon Maurice was in every way remarkable. In 1733 Villars was eighty, and had been a Marshal of France for thirty-one years. Maurice de Saxe was only fifty, and had been a Marshal of France for less than two. By that single inaudible remark, Louis had lifted the foreign-born Maurice from tenth to first place among his Marshals. Maurice now took precedence even over the aged duc de Biron, who had been *doyen* of the marshalate since 1740.[181]

More important, Maurice now possessed the absolute right to take charge of each and every royal army, not excluding an army commanded by a prince of the blood. Louis had hit upon an oblique and flattering way of preventing any recurrence of dissension among the generals of his high command. Maurice would have been less than human if he had not been secretly gratified by the presence at Choisy that day of Louis' favourite cousin, the prince de Conti. What price Conti's brevet now? When he wrote to tell Brühl the news, Maurice could hardly be blamed for a certain complacency.

> They have made me Marshal-General, the equivalent of the German 'General Field Marshal'. It makes me first general in the realm, above all the Marshals of France. Militarily, I cannot rise higher without falling and breaking my neck. . . . I only hope that peace will come soon enough to enable me to retire with honour.[182]

Maurice had already reaped substantial rewards for his efforts as a political intermediary. Not only had he been made a Marshal-General of France, but he had also managed, during the course of the negotiations, to squeeze out of Brühl a rise in his Saxon emoluments. The Minister had had little option but to surrender to Maurice's blackmail, and to pay up as pleasantly as possible.

The Marshal-General set out from Versailles to meet the child on whom he had helped to foist a husband. No doubt he shared the general view of the age that the sublime prospect which he had created for her, as a future queen of France, outweighed any unhappiness which she might encounter as the wife of the humourless Dauphin. When he had last played with her in her nursery at Dresden, she had been a mischievous imp of twelve. Now, at fifteen, she was within hours of becoming a bride.

When he rode out of Paris to embrace her at Nangis, he may well have felt a pang. Maurice knew what it meant for a woman to come to feel love's deeper satisfactions. But the Dauphin was a prig, a self-important bigot, and in his arms Maria Josepha would never experience the tempestuous pleasures and fructifying excitements of a woman whose passions had been genuinely aroused. She would probably be condemned to suffer the sterile frustrations that were the lot of Marie Leczinska.

Yet he may have told himself that, if anyone could capture a selfish and pleasure-loving court, it would surely be this lively, fair-haired girl. But on the very day that he greeted her, his heart was chilled by a prophetic incident. While the princess was at supper, a messenger arrived with a letter from the Dauphin. The duchesse de Brancas, who was waiting on the princess, recognized the Dauphin's infantile scrawl on the cover and handed it to Maria Josepha. Eagerly she tore it open and read it, then turned pale and ran sobbing from the room. The letter was no loving message to a young bride, but a lament, addressed to the duchesse de Brancas herself, in which the prince unburdened himself of his angry resentment at the way he had been treated. He declared that his love for his dead wife was inviolate and immutable. Although foolish, he was sensitive, and perhaps it was not altogether surprising that he should have been revolted at the matter-of-fact way in which a wife had been selected for him—and then duly apprized by that brace of satyrs, the duc de Richelieu and the comte de Saxe.

Maria Josepha bore up with uncommon courage. Next day she was ceremoniously welcomed on the road to Versailles by her future husband and future father-in-law. Eckstaedt tells us that she was 'gay, simple and natural: Louis XV was amused by the tricks she played to get the Dauphin to smile, and to stop gazing at her so fixedly and silently'.[183]

She reached Versailles on February 9th 1747, and was married the same afternoon. In the evening there was a state ball and banquet, after which she was called upon to face the traditional ordeals of the *toilette en publique* and the *mise au lit*. In the stern epoch of Louis XIV, these twin ceremonies had assumed an austere grandeur; at the marshmallow court of Louis XV they were merely indecent. Maria Josepha may even have been unaware, at first, of their real significance.

Maurice later wrote a circumspect account of these unsavoury proceedings to her mother, and a much franker one to her father.

> The princess has been wonderfully well received here; she is universally adored, and the queen loves her like her own child; the king is enchanted by her, and the Dauphin has been swept off his feet. She handles them with complete confidence, and I can only admire her. Your Majesty could hardly credit with what presence and dignity *Mme la dauphine* has conducted herself; her husband seems gawky by comparison. There has been nothing weak or childish in any of her actions, only a calm and noble resolution; and, believe me, there have been moments when a person called on to play that particular rôle has had need of such qualities. Among others I might mention the *mise en lit*, when the bed-curtains are drawn apart and the bride and groom solemnly deposited in the bed; a terrible business, for the whole court is present in the bedchamber. The king asked me to stay near *Mme la dauphine* to reassure her. She faced it with a tranquillity that astonished me. M. *le dauphin* held the sheet over his face, but the princess chattered away freely and paid no attention to the surrounding courtiers. I went over to her and told her that the king had asked me to stay close to her to prevent her from being nervous, and that it would not go on much longer. She thanked me, and I did not leave her and bid her goodnight until the curtains had been drawn and the spectators had left. They all went out in a mood that somehow seemed melancholy, for the whole thing had the atmosphere of a sacrifice and the princess had found a way to touch their hearts. Your Majesty

may smile when I say it, but the ceremony of blessing the bed, the priests, the candles, the pomp and glitter, the youth and beauty of the bride and my solicitude for her well-being—these things combined to make me more inclined to be pensive than to smile. In the room were crowded the king, the queen, princes and princesses, more than a hundred women draped in marvellous gowns and adorned with jewellery. It was a unique spectacle, and I can only repeat that somehow it seemed sacrificial.

Maurice then dropped his wistful, avuncular tone and became more practical:

Nothing in fact happened on that first night, in spite of M. *le dauphin's* exertions, and it all added up to a lot of fuss and bother without sleep. Since then there have been several days of pointless fatigue. One can only trust that they will soon be repaid by contentment and relaxation.

But before the letter was sealed, Maurice was able to add the necessary piece of intelligence concerning the royal couple:

The king summoned me to his apartments the day before yesterday. He whispered in my ear: 'It is done—she is Mme la Dauphine: it happened this afternoon.' I was later present at supper, when *Mme la dauphine* did not touch her food. M. *le dauphin* told me that she had not dined that day, nor eaten anything at dinner the previous day. It was extreme tiredness that was responsible. I said to the king that if she did not get some sleep she would fall ill. I really don't know how she stood it. I was weary enough myself! The heat in the apartments was killing, thinks to the candles and the press of people. In addition, her gown was of fantastic weight, and the formal presentations went on and on and on. She had to laugh and look charming the whole time, and was making a real effort to catch everyone's name. It was such a colossal task that I fail to see how she ever discharged it. The other day the king handed me one of her skirts from a sofa while she was at her *toilette*. It weighed at least sixty pounds. I do not know of a steel cuirass that weighs as much. Heaven knows how she manages to stay on her feet for eight or nine hours at a stretch in a monstrously heavy thing like that.[184]

The jaded girl; the twitching Dauphin, compelled to perform his ritual rôle in the very chamber and in the very bed where he had passed his first wedding night, and where his late wife had laboured and died not seven months before; the giggling and sniggering courtiers; the lecherous king, enjoying the part of *voyeur*: none of it was edifying. But the deed was done: and one result of it was that Maurice had become a key man at court.

CHAPTER XIV

LAUFELDT, 1747

*What satisfaction in this world, what pleasure can equal
that of vanquishing and triumphing over one's enemy?
None without doubt.*

DON QUIXOTE

LA *France, en ce moment, c'est lui.* At that moment Maurice was
France [*c.f.* Plate 6]. The verdict is Vitzthum d'Eckstaedt's, and it
may be maintained with a fair show of justice. Few historians of the
reign of Louis XV have treated Maurice as more than a minor and
meteoric figure, a brilliant general playing a peripheral rôle. But for
a few brief months, at the end of 1746 and the beginning of 1747, he
was one of the real rulers of his adopted country.

It is easy to see how this came about. Although Louis XIV had
been dead thirty years, the memory of the glories and sacrifices of his
age, wrought by commanders of the calibre of Maurice, had by no
means faded into oblivion. Lip-service was still paid to the Roman
virtues of the former reign, even though lotus-eating and *je-m'en-
ficheisme* were on the increase. It was true that the Contis, the
Richelieus, the Soubises and the Clermonts were now in the ascendant;
and it would not be long before Clermont would flounder about at
Crefeld, far gone in his cups, while an inferior enemy force carved his
army to pieces. But such humiliations still lay in the future: and in
the meantime Maurice, by winning the battles of Fontenoy and
Rocoux, had preserved the illusion that the France of the *Bienaimé*
was still worthy of the France of the *Dieudonné*.

Frenchmen could not know that Fontenoy and the victories that
immediately followed it represented the last triumphs of the *ancien
régime*, and that degradation, bankruptcy and revolution lay ahead.
Within ten years of Maurice's death, India and Canada would fall to
the British; but immersed in domestic troubles and in the folly of the
Seven Years' War, which was conducted after the style of a court
charade, France would fail to notice the terrible wounds inflicted upon
her. 'Monsieur,' Berryer would tell Bougainville, who came to plead
with him to save Canada, 'when the house is on fire, one does not

MAURICE IN MORE MATURE YEARS

A Pastel by La Tour

bother about the stables.' And Voltaire would say: 'I prefer peace to Canada. France can exist quite happily without Quebec.'[185]

While Voltaire and his friends were unconsciously undermining the *régime*, it was a mere hired mercenary, Maurice de Saxe, who was striving most valiantly to underpin it. Like Old Königsmarck, or the Swiss Guards who died almost to a man in defence of the Tuileries in 1792, he was faithful to the sovereign whose money he took. Had he lived only a few years longer, to steer the armies of France through the campaigns of the Seven Years' War, it is quite possible that the fate of the *ancien régime* might have been different. So much may great historical events turn on the life or death of a single man.

In the spring of 1747, the Marshal-General and his small group of gifted lieutenants were the only men capable of restoring the tarnished glories of the reign of the Sun King. If France were now to bring the War of the Austrian Succession to a favourable conclusion, and not merely accept the kind of peace acceptable to Vienna, it was clear that she would have to pursue her warlike policies to a vigorous conclusion. One final heave was needed. In the shadowy world of the court, the only man with the will and drive to provide it was Maurice, who almost alone had the qualities of candour, courage and stolidity which win wars.

Not that he was also devoid of guile. He had become the mainspring of a feverish bout of diplomatic activity that followed the retirement of the elder Argenson. In concert with Richelieu, he began secret negotiations with Vienna. Far from seeking to prolong the war, as his enemies at Versailles had supposed, he was eager to bring it to a close, provided only that France could obtain the favourable terms to which her unbroken victories in the Netherlands entitled her. The channel for the exchanges with Vienna had been established by Richelieu during his embassy to Dresden; and Löss and Puysieux were also privy to them. The secret was well kept, and ministers as highly placed as Noailles and Maurepas appear to have remained in ignorance of what was happening. The king, of course, with his emerging hobby of the *secret du roi*, must have personally blessed a course of action which was otherwise flatly treasonable.

Maurice's influence was so marked at this time that he was even able to nominate the new French representative to the seemingly endless negotiations at Breda. He successfully barred the departure of Saint-Séverin, whom he feared was weak, and secured instead the appointment of the more spirited Dutheil. Maurice saw clearly that France had nothing to hope for from the deliberations at Breda. The

British, Dutch and Austrians were happily prolonging the conference to their own advantage, while intensifying their preparations for the future conduct of the war. France must therefore show that she was not being duped. She must convince the enemy that she was still capable of delivering a final—and shattering—blow. Then, and only then, could she assume her place at the conference table, and dictate the peace from a position of strength.

The Dutch, for their part, were in an unusually combative mood. In the last campaign the line of battle had advanced dangerously close to their frontiers, and the imminent peril had served for once to unite them. If the Austrians and the British had ever doubted the willingness of the United Provinces to continue the war, their fears were swiftly allayed by the revival of the post of Stadhouder, originally created for William the Silent, and dormant since the death in 1702 of William III, King of Great Britain and Prince of Orange. The new Stadhouder, William IV, Prince of Orange, was a distant cousin of William III, and himself a son-in-law of George II of Great Britain and Hanover. It was clear that under his leadership the Dutch were determined to fight on. William's cousin, the Duke of Cumberland, was invited to spend the winter months at the Hague, training the Dutch army for their coming ordeal.

Cumberland's preparations revealed the determination with which he had returned to the fray. His earlier defeat at Fontenoy had been generally excused on the grounds of his youth and inexperience, and not even his sternest critics had suggested that he had borne himself in any way dishonourably on that occasion. Since Fontenoy, indeed, he had largely retrieved his reputation. At Culloden, in April, 1746, he had ruthlessly driven Prince Charles Edward's half-starved Highlanders from the field, after conducting a difficult campaign in a sufficiently brisk manner. His men trusted him. Their confidence was a reflection of the growing self-assurance of their country.

The British were dimly becoming aware that the hegemony of the world might well be theirs for the taking. Ten years earlier, the prescient Voltaire had confided to his Prussian hero, Frederick the Great, his sense of France's flagging destinies. 'I think the French are living in Europe on credit,' he said, 'like some rich man who is growing unconsciously poorer. Our nation needs a master to encourage it.'[186] The bills were now falling due, and it was the British, who were now about to embark on an era of imperial grand larceny, who were about to act the part of bailiff. An awareness of the coming shift of power was revealed even in a document as formal as Maurice's patent as Marshal-General, which spoke of the royal necessity:

> to support a war to oppose the ambitious views of the king of England, who, under pretence of a chimerical balance of power, seeks only to monopolize commerce, to the prejudice of all trading nations.[187]

Just as the *siècle français* had succeeded the *siglo español*, so now the world was moving into the century of the Anglo-Saxons.

Maurice was not, of course, to be 'the master whom France needed to encourage her'; but in his capacity of proud servant he would do his best. His impatience with Argenson's refusal to permit him to invade the United Provinces in 1746 had stemmed not only from the resentment of a soldier whose plans are being hampered, but also from the knowledge that the minister was casting away the one great advantage that the Flemish campaigns had brought to France. Yet, even without an attack on Holland, the war would have been worth fighting even if it was to produce no more tangible result than the expulsion of the Austrians from their Netherlands. We know from his correspondence with Brühl that Maurice was far-sighted enough at this time to champion the creation of an independent Belgian state, under a French guarantee, precisely as Louis-Philippe would do over eighty years later.[188] With this view Richelieu fully concurred; and certain circles in Vienna, sensing that the geographically unviable Netherlands could not be retained indefinitely, and preferring to transform the Habsburg domains into a compact Danubian realm, were by no means averse from evacuating Flanders and Brabant, in return for appropriate financial and territorial adjustments.

From the French viewpoint, the creation of an independent Belgium would confer three benefits. First, the existence of a weak client state to the north would effectively pacify an area as troublesome historically to France as it was to Spain and Austria. Secondly, such a buffer state would help to isolate the British from their continental allies. Thirdly, it would enable France to divert part of the immense army usually committed to Flanders to service elsewhere. Reinforcements were already urgently required not only in the French possessions overseas, but also in southern France itself, where the allies had now marched deep into Provence and had invested Antibes.

Maurice and his friends were putting forward an eminently logical policy; but it was not to be adopted. Ten years later it would again be advanced by Kaunitz, the most able of Metternich's predecessors at the Imperial Chancellery. (Kaunitz may, in fact, have discussed the plan with Maurice in 1746, when as Governor of Brussels he had held pourparlers with the French after the surrender of that city.) Unfortunately, Kaunitz was unable to persuade the Empress Maria Theresa to countenance any general settlement of the problem of the Netherlands which did not include Spain, without whom Louis XV refused to act. The plan was not in fact adopted by the great powers until 1830.

Maurice's tentative sorties into the diplomatic world came to little. It is a pity, for he had no lack of courage and imagination—virtues rare in French statesmen at that time. If he had been allowed to have his way at this juncture, then the Seven Years' War might never have broken out. In any case, had he lived, France might well have emerged from it victorious. There is something to be said for the view that it was a matter of: *Après Maurice, le déluge.*

'A glorious, ever-victorious Maréchal,' Carlyle observed in his most caustic vein:

> and has an army very high-toned, in more than one sense: indeed, I think, one of the loudest toned Armies ever on the field before. Loud not with well-served Artillery alone, but with playactor Thunder-barrels (always in itinerant Theatre attends), with gasconading talk, with orgies, debaucheries—busy service of the Devil, *and* pleasant consciousness that we are Heaven's masterpiece, and in perfect readiness to die at any moment;—our *elasticity* and agility (elan as we call it) well kept up, in that manner, for the time being.[189]

Carlyle was describing the spirit of Maurice's army before Rocoux. That spirit soared even higher when, in 1747, the French took the field for the third year in succession. The French army was fearful in mere numbers alone: Maurice now possessed 136,000 first-line troops to engage an enemy that even on paper would not muster more than 126,000. To give the all-conquering Marshal-General the initial superiority which he demanded, the other armies of France had been ruthlessly denuded, a fact which by no means lessened the dislike of his many ill-wishers.

In earlier years he had been the first to leave winter quarters; but in 1747 he nursed his excellent formations carefully, and did not stir from Brussels and Liége before the end of April. His troops were comfortably encamped along a line from Liége, Brussels and Ghent to Bruges. Cumberland, meanwhile, had clumsily tripped over his own feet in his haste to strike his tents. As early as February he had tried to move his forces into a threatening position before Antwerp, only to get himself bogged down outside Breda for lack of transport. The British then passed a miserable two months on exposed and wind-swept ground, while the French still lolled in their warm cantonments. 'When the Duke of Cumberland has sufficiently weakened his army,' said Maurice contentedly, 'I shall teach him that a general's first duty is to provide for its welfare.'[190] The allies were, as usual, bedevilled by internal dissensions. Cumberland and old Marshal Batthiany, the

Austrian commander who had replaced Prince Charles of Lorraine, agreed well enough with each other: but neither of them could co-operate with Waldeck, who was in any event unpopular with his own Dutchmen.

While Cumberland was pondering on ways to weld his polyglot army, which this year also included a Bavarian contingent, into a single unit, Maurice stole a march on him. Without disturbing his main force, he detached from the main army two flying columns, under a pair of his best officers, Löwendahl and Contades. The small columns penetrated deep into southern Holland, into the maritime province of Zeeland which lies between Antwerp and the sea. There they proceeded to snap up numerous unprepared fortresses on Dutch soil. Contades took Liefkenhock, and the fortress known as The Pearl to the north of Antwerp; Löwendahl captured Sas-van-Ghent, Ijzenijke and Eekels. Cumberland was frantic. With the French astride the south bank of the Scheldt, his communications were seriously menaced; and when Löwendahl came east to invest Hulst and Axel, the duke managed at last to make his first real move. He began a manoeuvre that suggested he was about to attack Antwerp, and Ligonier actually drew up a plan of attack on the city. But Maurice's defensive position there was so strong that the movement petered out, and Cumberland had no alternative but withdrawal from an exposed position. Hulst and Axel had not been long reprieved, and, by the middle of the month, both of them had fallen to sieges now directed by Contades.

In May, Contades was awarded a special annual increase in bounty of 2,000 *livres*, in appreciation of his services. Maurice himself was not forgotten in the new distribution of largesse. 'I have just been told by the king,' he was informed by the younger Argenson,

> that when Marshal Villars was appointed Marshal-General he was granted a salary of 30,000 *livres*. His Majesty wishes to accord you the same sum, dating from the day of your appointment. I have been ordered to pay into your account 15,000 *livres* every six months, payable at Paris. . . . And I take the liberty of pointing out, Monsieur, so that you may understand the effect of my participation in the matter, that Marshal Turenne enjoyed no more than 24,000 *livres*, and that it was only raised to 30,000 in favour of Marshal Villars.[191]

This money was not unwelcome, for Maurice's extravagances had increased in proportion to his rise in the world, and his personal finances were in as sorry straits as ever.

The military prizes of the new campaign did not lie among the fortifications of Zeeland. The great prize was the thriving city of Maastricht, to the east. Maurice and Cumberland both knew that the seizure of Maastricht might well make the defence of the United Provinces impossible. Cumberland was therefore willing to risk everything on a pitched battle, rather than allow Maastricht to fall as the cities of the Austrian Netherlands had already fallen. Maurice had already stationed his main army in his favourite position between Malines and Louvain, so Cumberland now moved up his own forces to the vicinity of Lier, about fifteen kilometres away. He simply dared not let Maurice out of his sight. Maurice had previously stationed a small army under Clermont on the Meuse to the south of Maastricht, and it now became Cumberland's obsessive preoccupation to watch for the moment when the two French armies would coalesce for the assault on Maastricht.

Cumberland had guessed accurately that Maurice would only venture against so powerful a stronghold as Maastricht when his strength was at its height. But there was always the nagging fear that Maurice might have used Clermont as a decoy, and that just when the British and Dutch were hastening south, the French main army would turn about and make a sudden dash for the flimsily guarded frontier of the United Provinces. Maurice could have it both ways. The duke's safest course was thus to stick to Maurice like a limpet, and to shadow his slightest move. This he did with a grim application, and during the whole of May and June the rival armies remained within striking distance of each other. Maurice was not at all incommoded by these tactics; he was content to lie low behind the river Dyle and bide his time. 'My aim,' he wrote in a subsequent memoir, 'was to ruin the enemy's army once I had taken Flanders. I would do it by adopting a suitable position and allowing time and circumstance to take their course.'[192]

This plan, as he later admitted, was not wholly successful. Cumberland did not oblige him by making any unconsidered moves. Maurice therefore began to tease his opponent by ordering Clermont's army to advance from its station to a more provocative position at Tongres, twelve kilometres south of Maastricht. At this, Cumberland naturally supposed that the union of the two French armies was about to take place: and he also saw that by a quick, bold stroke he might fall upon Clermont's modest force and destroy it. He slipped off with what he supposed was great secrecy, and marched southwards. As for Clermont and his second-in-command Estrées, when they learned that the whole enemy was bearing down on them, they were understandably alarmed. Clermont was actually on the point of withdrawing, after firing a volley of frenzied signals in Maurice's direction. And then, to his astonishment, the travel-stained Marshal-General himself came riding into his camp, and ordered him to stand firm. Reinforcements from the French main army were not only on their way—the whole of the French main army was itself at hand.

Maurice had started his parallel march to that of the enemy on the very day that Cumberland had moved. It was a brilliant manoeuvre. The result was that when, on June 30th, Cumberland supposed that he was confronted merely by the inferior army of Clermont, he found that he was up against the entire French first-line strength, much superior in numbers to his own. And moreover the French were extended in an excellent position on the crest of the wooded heights of Heerderen, calmly watching the allies as they struggled up the slopes towards them. It was a marvellous example of Maurice's guile, a really breath-taking gambit by an absolute master of the military chess-board.

The moment had come for Maurice to make another attempt at the destruction of the enemy army. The fate of Maastricht and of the United Provinces was about to be decided.

The battle of Laufeldt was fought forty-eight hours later, on July 2nd, 1747 [Fig. 8]. It took place in the plain two miles due west of Maastricht. The appearance of the line was at first almost exactly similar to that at the beginning of the battle of Rocoux. It remained to be seen whether Maurice could at last develop the initial advantages he had created for himself into an annihilating victory.

Rocoux and its dependent hamlets had been the hub of the allied position in 1746, and the village of Laufeldt and its surrounding villages were now to play a similar rôle. As at Rocoux, the enemy left rested on the fortifications of a great city, although the citizens of Maastricht were made of sterner stuff than the Liégeois, and did not open their gates at the sound of the first salvo. To provide the additional support, the enemy left was rested against the river Jaar, a tributary of the Meuse, in front of a village called Wilre. The British line extended westwards from Wilre, Laufeldt and Wiltingen, to the marshy terrain beyond the twin hamlets of Great and Little Spauwe. Laufeldt and Wiltingen were therefore at the centre of the enemy line, the former occupied by British and Hessians, the latter by the British Guards. The Dutch, Hanoverians and Bavarians were posted in the right-centre and right of the line. As at Rocoux, the Austrians were on the right flank and were once again entrenched behind a ravine. Once again it was destined to be the left and centre of the allied army which would bear the brunt of the fighting. The allied cavalry, under Ligonier, was massed in rear between Wilre and Laufeldt, astride the main road between Maastricht and Tongres.

Hours before the start of the battle, Ligonier had urged on Cumberland the necessity of putting troops into Laufeldt and Wiltingen.

Cumberland's inadequacy as a general was never better illustrated than by his original intention to ignore the existence of these natural bastions, and to range his army on the bare plain behind them in a single unwieldy fighting-line, four miles in length. Such an arrangement would almost certainly have led to disaster. Fortunately, Ligonier was able to persuade his commander-in-chief that the only way to blunt the fury of an all-out French onslaught, of the kind that he himself had had to endure at Rocoux, was to break it up by means of forward bulwarks. Unlike Cumberland, Ligonier had long since digested the lesson of Fontenoy, where it had been clearly shown that infantry who were sent to attack strongly-held villages would be in for a very lean time of it, while cavalry formations would not be able to attack them at all. Cumberland was not grateful for Ligonier's sound advice. He vacillated so much that Laufeldt and Wiltingen were occupied, evacuated, re-occupied, and again evacuated, before being finally occupied for a third time. Like the brave old Duke of York, Cumberland was much given to marching and counter marching. The final occupation of the villages was ordered only a bare hour before the first French attack; and the consequence of all this indecision was that there was no time to open suitable paths through the hedgerows along which reserves could reach the hard-pressed front line during the battle. At one stage Cumberland also issued confused orders that the two villages should be destroyed by fire, and torches were put to some of the houses before the orders were countermanded. The infantrymen therefore struggled back into the villages for the third time amid a choking blanket of smoke.

The morning of Laufeldt was misty.[193] There was heavy rain. From the heights of Heerderen, Maurice surveyed the incomprehensible evolutions in the enemy lines and strove, as an experienced tactician, to interpret them. He was baffled.

Beside him stood the king, who had journeyed from Brussels to be present at this crucial encounter. The two men correctly inferred from the chaos in the enemy position that Cumberland was in hesitant mood. No other inference was possible, unless Cumberland was indulging in some tortuous kind of psychological warfare. Maurice eventually came to the incorrect conclusion that Cumberland had declined the engagement, and was about to withdraw to Maastricht. As Valfons has said,

> For more than two hours, the Marshal believed that the enemy was manoeuvring to recross the Meuse; he was confirmed in this opinion when he saw that Laufeldt was on fire.[194]

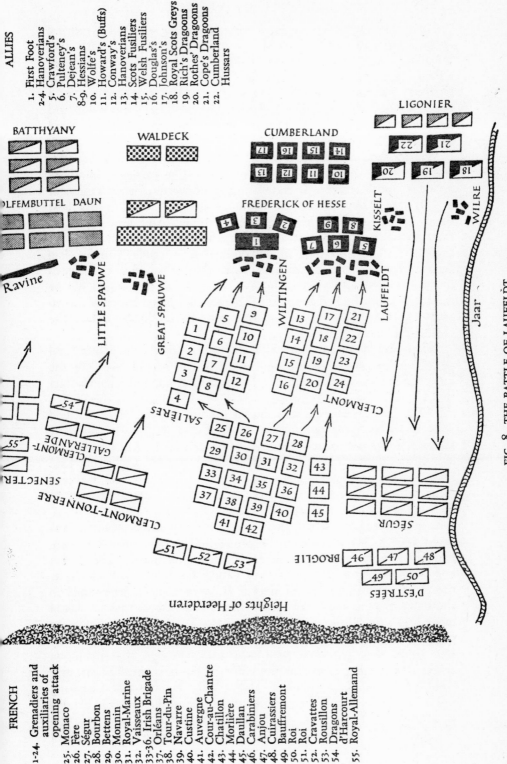

FIG. 8. THE BATTLE OF LAUFELDT

ALLIES

1. First Foot
2-4. Hanoverians
5. Crawford's
6. Pulteney's
7. Dejean's
8-9. Hessians
10. Wolfe's
11. Howard's (Buffs)
12. Conway's
13. Hanoverians
14. Scots Fusiliers
15. Welsh Fusiliers
16. Douglas's
17. Johnson's
18. Royal Scots Greys
19. Rich's Dragoons
20. Rothes' Dragoons
21. Cope's Dragoons
22. Cumberland Hussars

FRENCH

1-24. Grenadiers and auxiliaries of opening attack
25. Monaco
26. Fère
27. Ségur
28. Bourbon
29. Bettens
30. Monnin
31. Royal-Marine
32. Vaisseaux
33-36. Irish Brigade
37. Orléans
38. Tour-du-Pin
39. Navarre
40. Custine
41. Auvergne
42. Cour-au-Chantre
43. Chatillon
44. Morlière
45. Daulian
46. Carabiniers
47. Anjou
48. Cuirassiers
49. Bauffremont
50. Roi
51. Roi
52. Cravattes
53. Rousillon
54. Dragons d'Harcourt
55. Royal-Allemand

Maurice determined to tread on the heels of the supposedly retiring enemy with all possible speed. Clermont's grenadiers, with two brigades in support, advanced briskly on the supposedly deserted village of Laufeldt—to be greeted, to their surprise, by a busy musketry fusillade. The allied fire was nourished, furthermore, by a heavy battery that Ligonier had managed to hurry into a forward position, siting it with the skill with which he had sited the forward batteries at Rocoux.

Maurice was as disconcerted as the grenadiers to find Laufeldt crawling with troops. The battle was joined in earnest, almost by accident, and Maurice was grateful for some words of encouragement at this stage from the ardent young Valfons: 'Marshal, you beat them at Fontenoy, when you were dying. You beat them at Rocoux, when you were still a sick man. Today you will slaughter them!'[195] The fact was that Cumberland's crude blunder had been converted into a splendid *ruse de guerre*. Maurice seemed to have walked into a trap. He saw at once that this would not be the easy victory he had hoped for. There would be no leisurely investment of Maastricht, no lazy march into the fat hinterland of the United Provinces.[196]

What should he do? He could still pull back the grenadiers and withdraw his army; but it would mean fearful loss of face—for the king, for France, for himself. No, he must fight on, and seize the fact that the advantage still seemed to be overwhelmingly on the French side. Moreover, when he had drawn up his original plans, he had done so in the expectation that Laufeldt and Wiltingen would be manned, so he was merely required to prove that he had faith in his own dispositions. When the grenadiers came reeling back from Laufeldt, he promptly sent Clermont forward with a second wave of infantry to replace them. And at the same time he ordered the marquis de Salières to strike hard at Wiltingen.

A fierce struggle for the two villages now followed. Maurice was determined to break through the centre and cut the enemy in two. He would show them, once and for all, who was master. The British and Germans, under the purposeful Landgrave Frederick II of Hesse-Cassel, another son-in-law of George II, were equally determined to show Maurice, as they had shown him twice before, that he would never break the allied centre. Four times the British and Hessians were prised from behind the crumbling walls of the two townships; and four times they ploughed their way back through the rubble, to retake the burning houses at the point of the bayonet. The struggle went on for four bloody hours: and still the French came slithering towards Laufeldt and Wiltingen down the slushy slopes of the heights of Heerderen. There was no art or finesse in it: it was a brutal slogging-match. For the first time in his life, Maurice was afraid of finding himself at the centre of a battle which was slipping out of control.

The French had reached the point of no return. Maurice was now irrevocably committed to taking Laufeldt and Wiltingen, cost what it might. The only way he could justify the high price he had already paid was to go on and pay a higher one. Something he had always dreaded, since his boyhood experience of Malplaquet, had happened to him: he was compelled to fling in live battalions after dead ones, in the vague hope that he could impose his will. He could only mutter with Job: 'That which I feared is come upon me,' and pour in wave after wave of suffering men until the allies showed signs of weakening.

When Clermont's brigade was spent, it was the turn of the regiments of Monaco, La Fère, Ségur, Bourbon, Bettens, Monnin, Royal-Marine, Vaisseaux and Aubeterre. The colonel of the last named regiment, the comte d'Aubeterre, died with twenty-two of his officers beneath the blackened walls. The chevalier Dillon, commanding three regiments of the Irish Brigade, was mortally wounded and taken prisoner. This time, indeed, the Wild Geese were out of luck. Their cries of *Remember Limerick!* died in their throats. They were decimated by the hanging leaden curtain of shot. Cumberland's infantrymen were taking revenge for their own agonies at Fontenoy.

Maurice had now consumed forty of his battalions without achieving a breakthrough. As fast as he threw his men into the battle, Cumberland fed the garrisons of Laufeldt and Wiltingen with fresh battalions from his second line, even managing to bring nine battalions of Austrians across the ravine to fill the reserve. The British commander-in-chief had no cause for dissatisfaction. Ligonier's plan to exploit the two villages was paying dividends. It looked as though the French, under the command of the Apostle of the Redoubt, would this time be the ones to batter themselves to death against the enemy strong-points.

Laufeldt and Wiltingen had become the centre of an inferno. Both sides had thrust forward massed batteries of artillery, and were pounding each other at point-blank range. The *Régiment du roi*, one of cavalry regiments supporting the tormented infantry, sat steady in their saddles when thirty guns suddenly began to send shot tunnelling through their ranks, killing their colonel, the comte de Bavière, a half-brother of the late Emperor Charles VII. Another dozen French battalions were launched against Laufeldt, urged on by the indefatigable Salières, and by Maurice himself, whom came galloping up, sword in hand.

After receiving a frightful hammering, Salières at last managed to secure a tight toehold inside Laufeldt. Simultaneously the French infantry were also beginning to make some impression on neighbouring Wiltingen. Maurice then charged at the head of his cavalry regiments in an all-out assault on Wiltingen, which Cumberland immediately and properly countered by calling up units of the Dutch cavalry. The Dutch horsemen, unfortunately, failed him. Some of them took a good look at the Frenchmen who came galloping down the slope—and promptly fled. Worse, they bolted backwards through their own infantry, riding the footsoldiers down. And this unexpected mishap occurred at the most vulnerable sector of the line. Confusion broke out, the garrisons of Laufeldt and Wiltingen became isolated, the allied chain of command was snapped, and the line began at long last to cave in. The allied centre was punctured and crumbling. The French infantry started to stream in through the gap.

For five increasingly anxious hours Maurice had been waiting for this moment. Now he hastened towards the French right under Estrées, where he had massed the bulk of his cavalry. All day these troopers had waited, hunched in their saddles, helplessly watching the martyrdom of their comrades in the infantry. They cheered as they anticipated an order to charge.

Maurice's plan was to unleash them down the highroad in the direction of Wilre, with the object of turning the allied left flank and blocking the main escape route to Maastricht. He had already dragged up twenty guns and posted them on both sides of Laufeldt, to greet the enemy left as it came reeling back towards the centre in a blind *sauve qui peut*.

The apotheosis of Maurice's military career seemed at hand. He had only to wave his sword to Estrées' hussars to crown the achievements of nearly forty years of fighting. The battle of Laufeldt would go down in history as one of the most crushing victories that any general had ever won. It might have been one of the turning points in the history of Europe and of the world.

Ligonier, watching the French squadrons of horse as they came wheeling into position, was unaware that the struggle at the centre had gone so badly for Cumberland. All he saw from his post on the allied left wing was that challenging host of French cavalry. And Ligonier was a cavalryman born and bred. He could not resist the prospect of an all-out cavalry duel: or, as one writer put it, 'tempted by the occasion at last offered of opposing the French squadrons in a plain, he gave the order to advance upon them.'[197]

The result was one of the most spectacular cavalry contests in all the annals of war. To this day 'Ligonier's Charge' is justly regarded as one of the British Army's outstanding exploits. The Frenchmen suddenly found themselves on the wrong end of the charge, and were caught completely off balance. Ligonier sliced right into them. Sixty squadrons of British put to flight one hundred and forty squadrons of French cavalry, with hideous carnage. It was, of course, only a local success, and could not alter the final result of the battle, which the French had already effectively won. But by preventing Maurice from bringing his right wing into action at that critical moment, Ligonier had given the retreating British and Hessian infantry a few priceless minutes to collect itself. Overcoming their initial panic, the infantry in the allied centre now began to fall back in better order.

Ligonier's well-disciplined horsemen began to re-group themselves for a second charge against their demoralized opponents. And at this very moment Cumberland sent a galloper with the extraordinary command to cease any further attacks, since the loss of Laufeldt had made further activity superfluous. The duke added in his message that any unauthorized action by Ligonier would have to be accounted for after the battle. Ligonier instantly replied that another cavalry charge might well retrieve the situation. But the delay had given the French, in their turn, an opportunity to pull themselves together. By the time the indecisive Cumberland reluctantly authorized a second charge, the initiative was gone.

It was obvious to Ligonier's trained eye what Maurice now intended to do. The confused mass of British infantry was now shielded behind Ligonier's forward-thrusting cavalry as it went limping back towards Maastricht. If the French cavalry could burst at this stage through the ranks of Ligonier's horsemen, they could shatter the shield and emerge directly upon the stricken infantrymen. Court-martial or no court-martial, Ligonier deemed it essential, in the words of Espagnac, ' to sacrifice his horse in order to save the infantry'.[198] It was no longer a case of hoping to turn defeat into victory : it had become a matter of providing ten or twelve minutes' grace during which the fleeing infantry could scurry closer to the protective cannon of Maastricht. Old Ligonier drew his sabre and personally led his squadrons into the fresh attack. And again they skewered their way into the vitals of the enemy. For the second time in half an hour their charge was successful. Too successful. They galloped too far, and were shot down by a line of well-entrenched French infantry at the rear. Here they were quickly surrounded by the carabiniers, and by the régiment d'Anjou under Estrées and Armentières. Ligonier himself, easily identified by his star of the Bath, was taken prisoner.[199]

The cost of this quixotic charge had been high, but it had amply achieved its object. By the time Maurice could get ready to launch a general cavalry attack along the whole length of the enemy line, Marshal Batthiany was able to throw a screen of Austrians between

the retreating men and their pursuers, thereby enabling the main
body of the trapped army to scramble away from the battlefield.

Valfons—at heart, alas! something of a lickspittle—censures
Maurice, in his memoirs, for his conduct of the pursuit after Laufeldt.
He asserts that when, at Wiltingen, the Dutch cavalry broke, Maurice
could have started the rout by sending in Clermont-Tonnerre and his
dragoons. 'He thus proved to me,' Valfons says, 'that since he did
not wish to end the war, he could only half win his battles.'[200] This
is a very serious charge, and one which was frequently levelled against
Maurice. Yet it is surely nonsense. There would seem to have been
little doubt that, at least on this occasion, Maurice strained every
nerve to destroy the beaten enemy army. He knew that his failure to
do so would have serious personal and political consequences. But
what more could he have done? His right wing had been disorganized
by Ligonier's attacks; the Austrians had strongly and suddenly inter-
vened after the battle had already been raging for a full six hours;
the rain was still pouring down; the battlefield had been churned into
mud; and smoke was billowing thickly across the landscape from the
batteries and the burning villages. The battle

> had cost a good deal of blood. Never was anything more horrible seen.
> The plains and villages all round were covered with dead and wounded
> men. The loss on this day, on one side and the other, amounted to
> more than 20,000 men killed, wounded or taken prisoner.[201]

It was little wonder that Maurice eventually called off the hunt and
brought his lacerated squadrons and battalions back to camp. Of those
20,000 casualties, the enemy had suffered nearly 6,000, over 2,000 of
them British and nearly 2,500 Hanoverian. But the French, the
triumphant French, had suffered the horrible total of 14,000 dead
and wounded. Maurice had won his victory, but it was a pyrrhic
victory. He had lost the flower of his battalions, and lost a great part
of his own reputation.

Ligonier later told Prince Frederick of Hesse that the two French
carabiniers who had seized him had

> led me off towards the king, who was quite close, being in the thick
> of the fight. On the way some of the Household Provost guards, whom
> I recognized by their uniform, pressed in on me, and I thought, seeing
> my situation, they were going to kill me. But when I came to the king,
> he greatly reassured me, saying, with a charming smile, 'Well, general,
> we will have the pleasure of your company at supper tonight.'[202]

The British general had had good reason for his apprehensions. He
was still technically a citizen of France, and his captors could, if they
had wanted to, have treated him as a traitor. Furthermore, feeling was
running high in France over the recent executions of Prince Charles

Edward's supporters after Cumberland's suppression of the '45. It is little wonder that Ligonier was overwhelmed by the graciousness of his reception. The Franco-German Maurice is said to have introduced the Franco-British Ligonier to Louis XV with the words: 'Sire, I have the honour of presenting to your Majesty the man who has defeated all my plans by a single glorious action.'[203]

Ligonier's carriage and equipment, which had been captured when the battlefield was overrun, was restored to him. That evening he dined at the king's table. 'At the end, when I took leave of his Majesty, mustering all the French vocabulary I could still remember, the king said to me, "M. Ligonier, your captivity will not be harsh, for you know that I am a kind-hearted man". At that my heart swelled and I could only answer by putting a knee to the ground, and the king stretched out to me his beautiful gloveless hand, on which I planted, I swear you, a very warm kiss mingled with some tears. The king of France is a great and good king.'[204]

Maurice and Ligonier quickly became friends. They had much in common. Maurice had been for many years a member of the Royal Society of London, to which Ligonier, who also had a scientific bias, was shortly to be elected. Moreover both were notorious womanizers. Ligonier maintained at least two mistresses in London, and had recently, for all his years, been enjoying a high old time among the women of Holland. One of the Dutch women he had had to surrender to the Duke of Cumberland, in compliance with the *droit de seigneur*: but a few weeks later he reported to his friend Chesterfield that he had already recruited a satisfactory successor: 'volunteers come in apace, and I have lately taken one as handsome and younger.' He was a man after Maurice's own heart.

The two generals exchanged gifts. Maurice gave Ligonier four mules, and Ligonier, aware of his captor's passion for precious stones, gave Maurice three pairs of Brazilian diamonds. More important than such personal courtesies, the two generals were soon immersed in political negotiations which were to last for three months. Voltaire has recorded that, when Ligonier was first taken before Louis, the king had asked: 'Would it not be better to think seriously of making peace, instead of bringing death to so many brave men?' Louis had spoken sincerely, and he had spoken for the bulk of his subjects. He was anxious to exploit the unusual diplomatic opportunity offered him by the fact that the tent of Cumberland, the favourite son of the king of Great Britain, was at that moment within half an hour's ride of the French camp.

The civilians at Breda had not shown much enterprise as peace makers, and Louis saw no harm in finding out if the soldiers could do any better. On July 8th, Ligonier returned to Cumberland's headquarters on a four-day parole. He brought the news that France wished to make peace, and that the Maréchal de Saxe had been deputed by Louis XV to open negotiations. He brought with him a draft of outline peace terms drawn up by Maurice. Cumberland, who was suitably impressed, transmitted Maurice's proposals to London, requesting powers to negotiate a treaty.

This interlude in eighteenth-century diplomacy has seldom been treated seriously.[205] Historians have too often been misled by Maurice's bad French and worse spelling into thinking him a fool. It is also sometimes assumed that the idea of these particular negotiations were no more than his own private folly, and that he was surreptitiously attempting to steal the politicians' thunder. Nothing could be further from the truth. His letters to Ligonier and Batthiany were sent openly; within the prescribed limits of diplomacy they were quite above board. His main aims were perfectly honest, and it is obvious that Louis desired to exploit Maurice's reputation for plain dealing. 'Your Majesty may rest assured,' Maurice told his half-brother, Augustus of Poland, 'that I shall never lend myself to any plan that is not completely sincere.'[206]

Although the Ligonier mission was neither naive nor dishonest, it was unrealistic. By the time Ligonier returned to French headquarters, the politicians had already resumed their diplomatic prerogatives. The hour of the negotiating generals had been brief. All Maurice was now asked to do was to arrange a secret meeting at Liége between Puysieux, the French foreign minister, and Lord Sandwich, who had been the principal British envoy at Breda. These negotiations soon broke down, apparently because of Louis XV's refusal to renounce his support for the Young Pretender; and when the talks were eventually resumed at Aix-la-Chapelle, shortly before the end of the war, the final settlement was agreed without consulting Maurice. His brief attempt to establish himself as a politician and diplomatist had come to nothing.

In April 1747, Maurice had been one of the most powerful men in France; by July his influence was already on the wane. After eight years of war, France hungered for peace: and the nearer the inevitable settlement approached, the less need there was for Maurice's military skill.

In the spring of 1747, the court had still been sufficiently belligerent to relish the prospects of another long run of easy successes. Maurice had duly provided them. But the public at large had not been satisfied. Why, it had demanded, was Maurice's army hanging fire? Where was the devastating *coup de grâce*? Ironically enough, Maurice had fallen victim to his own propaganda. He had for so long fostered the image of himself as the speedy conqueror of Prague and Brussels, that he had let the public forget that probably his finest single achievement had been the infinitely slow delaying action that he had carried out in the summer of 1744. But a nation which applauded dramatic campaigns cared not a fig for river lines, fords, headwaters, defence in depth, fortress systems, lines of supply, and the rest of it. *La France s'ennuie.* The fribbles and tattles of Paris and Versailles attributed Maurice's military caution before Laufeldt to an obvious cause: the Marshal-General had a vested interest in warfare, and was trying to prolong the conflict. 'The Maréchal de Saxe,' wrote one of Frederick of Prussia's French correspondents, a fortnight before the battle,

> will only consider his personal interest. He loves the conquests he has made for the profit they bring him and his crony Count Löwendahl. He is practically the king of the Austrian Netherlands. He carries on there as he pleases, and his position is altogether too attractive for him to resign without being forced to. Those who envy him say that he does not want the war to end, and that he wants to prolong his brilliant situation for as long as possible before retiring to the obscurity of Chambord. There he will be a nobody, and anyone who wants to will be able to attack him. He will no longer be feared, and no one will have any further need of him.[207]

Admittedly, Maurice was only human. He must have enjoyed to the full the immense power which his military position in the Lowlands had given him. But he was also a soldier with a conscience, and he would never have prolonged a bloody campaign for his own ends. And then he had been confronted by the costly battle of Laufeldt, which had been to some extent thrust upon him by the presence of the king and the pressure of the politicians. 'This is what happens when you make generals hustle!' he is said to have growled to his friends. France had been horrified. After the carnage of Laufeldt, the longing for peace grew increasingly intense.

It cannot be denied that, while Maurice was an incomparably better generalissimo than Broglie or Noailles, he never quite managed to carry into the highest command the flair and *élan* he had shown in a subordinate capacity. His original disposition at Laufeldt had, for example, been excellent, yet he had made disconcerting mistakes during the course of the battle. According to Townsend, who was present, the enemy 'had in this battle every advantage we had ever wished for; the French found us uncovered by entrenchments, unsupported by batteries, in a plain and on the march.'[208] This may be Anglo-Saxon exaggeration, but it is first-handed testimony to the fact that Maurice had handled the phase leading up to the battle in his most brilliant vein, although when he actually arrived before Laufeldt he saw that his march had not quite brought him on to such favourable terrain as he had hoped. Yet he had then allowed himself to be fatally overruled by the court, and by the unseen pressure of public opinion, into fighting a battle in circumstances that he knew were unfavourable.

The roll of dead and wounded in this third great battle brought the French appetite for war to an abrupt end. At midsummer, the news of a terrible disaster to French arms in the southern theatre gave further impetus to peace. Belle-Isle, after making a splendid start to his operations in Italy, had then embarked on a mad project, in defiance of France's allies and without the approval of Versailles. He had allowed his brother, Maurice's old adversary the chevalier de Belle-Isle, to set off on a hare-brained dash through the Alpine passes to surprise Turin. Turin never was surprised at all: and the chevalier de Belle-Isle was. While marching his divisions through the mountains, he tumbled headlong into an ambush near the Col de l'Assiette. The Austrian and Piedmontese *montagnards* massacred his troops with savage thoroughness. The chevalier perished with his entire staff and 4,000 men. Even the impassive Louis XV was disturbed. 'My army has been decimated,' he was heard to murmur, 'as a result of the ambition of M. de Belle-Isle.' The fiasco in Piedmont, taken in conjunction with the casualties sustained at Laufeldt in the same month, brought French losses within a few weeks to over 18,000 men.

Maurice was also appalled by the Piedmontese disaster. 'You will have heard, Sire,' he wrote to King Augustus of Poland,

> about the Alpine affair, and that M. le chevalier de Belle-Isle has been killed. Ambition has always been the ruin of any scheme in which the Belle-Isle brothers have had a hand. It is the usual story. But what is surprising is that the court of France makes the same mistakes with the same people over and over again.[209]

Prophetic words. The court of France was indeed always repeating its mistakes; and in the next reign the desire of the ruling clique to use 'the same people' would lead to the enactment of a decree that would fatally reverse the reforms of Louvois and forbid men of common or bourgeois birth to hold military commissions. Even in Maurice's time, nearly half the officers in the French army were men of humble or relatively humble origin, and Maurice himself had always been the champion of merit against birth. But the decree of 1781 would perpetuate the practice of letting the same people commit the same mistakes, so apparent to Maurice in 1747, and would be one of the most stupid of the many errors that brought Louis XVI to the scaffold.

The morning after Laufeldt, Maurice understood why the allied officers were said to regard the battle not as a defeat but as a victory.

The French aim had been to invest Maastricht, the British aim to stop them doing so. And it was the British, not the French, who had achieved their object.

Maurice had long been seeking an opportunity not only to besiege Maastricht, but also to destroy the enemy army. By inducing the British to cross the Meuse, he had successfully lured them into un-favourable country on his own side of the river. But by failing to nail them to the ground at Laufeldt, he had allowed them to scramble back to safety, after subjecting his own army to a severe mauling. They were still strong enough to prevent the battered French from following them across the Meuse, and remained fully able to prevent the invest-ment of Maastricht, which was what the battle had been about. They could still oppose the expected advance of His Most Christian Majesty into Limburg. The tactical advantage lay unmistakably with the British.

Maurice did not dare to loiter, for fear that his badly shaken army would start to deteriorate. It seemed as if fortune and inspiration alike had temporarily deserted him. His ill-wishers rubbed their palms: had they not always insisted that his vast military reputation was highly inflated? The king had created him Marshal-General in order to advertise to Europe that France possessed the best soldier in the world. Very well then: let him prove it.

Maurice's rejoinder was swift. It took him less than forty-eight hours to decide on his next gambit. It was more startling than his critics could possibly have expected. Before the battle, he had stationed Löwendahl and 35,000 men at Tirlemont, midway between Maastricht and Brussels. He now ordered the adventurous Dane to march north-wards towards Bergen-op-Zoom, over one hundred kilometres distant. Löwendahl marched hard, and only ten days after Laufeldt, his little army emerged from the blue in front of the walls of Bergen.

The most remarkable of the many sieges engineered by Maurice and Löwendahl now began. Its secret purpose was not the capture of Bergen, but to draw the enemy strength northwards. 'The battle of Laufeldt,' Maurice later wrote frankly,

> was meant to enable us to besiege Maastricht. We made so many mistakes that we had to draw back. The only thing we could do to justify this sorry outcome was to besiege Bergen-op-Zoom. . . . M. de Löwendahl was sure that if the enemy marched to its aid he could withdraw his men and guns without the slightest risk. So we decided to proceed, less with the object of taking the town than with making a diversion that would encourage the enemy to . . . detach troops to help Bergen, thus giving us the opportunity to cross the Meuse and besiege Maastricht. The latter was the real target.[210]

The enemy's delight at having saved Maastricht duly changed to alarm at the threat to Bergen. The capture of Bergen would mean the closure of the entire Scheldt to British shipping. Maurice was already in possession of the Flemish coastline as far north as the southern bank of the Scheldt: he was now threatening to take the river's main port. In alarm, the Dutch began once more to make neutral noises, daunted by having the Frenchmen on their front doorstep. Maurice's move was thus proving politically, as well as militarily, effective.

Not that all the allied officers, however, shared the dismay of the Dutch. Some of them pointed out that in the past Bergen had resisted generals quite as energetic as Löwendahl. Parma had failed to take it in 1588, and the dreaded Spinola in 1622. And during the subsequent War of the Spanish Succession its defences had been made impregnable by the great Dutch engineer Cohörn, who had diverted the Scheldt so as to form a broad moat around the city.[211] Access was possible only by traversing a bog, and whereas Vauban would have emphasized the inner ring of fortifications, Cohörn's plan had been to concentrate upon the outer works. He had constructed a string of forts looming out of the water, making any attempt to invest the city in the traditional manner out of the question. Moreover the northern part of the town was embraced by the curve of the great river, completely beyond Löwendahl's reach. Throughout the siege, the town was freely supplied with munitions and troops, and on his arrival Löwendahl was greeted by the sight of sixty ships lying in the harbour, beyond the range of his guns. The confident Austrian garrison, commanded at first by Maurice's cousin, the Prince of Saxe-Hildburghausen, and afterwards by a sprightly ninety-year-old Swede called Crönstrom, consisted of 16,000 troops, well supplied with artillery.

The first week was passed in securing a suitable vantage-point from which to begin the parallels. The French sappers were sorely punished in the process, and there were lively sallies as the garrison attempted to prevent the cutting of the trenches. On July 19th, the French siege-train arrived, and Contades rode into camp with a column of reinforcements. On the Meuse, a battle of wits between Maurice and Cumberland was in progress. It took the form of the alternative and ostentatious despatch of units to both sides at Bergen. First Cumberland led off by detaching Waldeck with seven battalions and fifteen squadrons; then Maurice, who had set up his headquarters at Louvain, leaving Clermont in charge of the immobile main army, countered by sending to Bergen two regiments of foot and four of horse. Soon afterwards, a second allied detachment of 2,000 hussars and infantry left for the north; and Maurice's answer was the despatch of another regiment of infantry and two of cavalry. There was soon a sizeable allied army, under the command of Prince Schwartzenberg, in the neighbourhood of Bergen-op-Zoom, and Löwendahl's situation began to look increasingly unenviable. It would be no easy matter for him to maintain his siege and to fend off a relieving army at the same time. Accordingly, when Schwartzenberg advanced from Breda, Löwendahl decided to bluff him by moving out to meet him with such a show of hostility that the enemy backed down, and Löwendahl retired unmolested. And although a fresh reinforcement of eighteen battalions and sixteen squadrons now reached Schwartzenberg, the balance was swiftly redressed when Maurice hastily sent north a column of four infantry regiments, two brigades of cavalry, and the crack horsemen of the *Régiment Chabrillant*.

While he was executing this intricate pavane, Maurice was fully aware of Löwendahl's growing plight. As he told the king of Poland, a month after the siege began:

> Löwendahl is charged with a terrible commission. Bergen-op-Zoom is a well-defended place, garrisoned by an entire army, and it fights with admirable stoutness. Still, I hope the end is now in sight. . . . We have finished the *chemins couverts* and are about to start on the breaches. . . . Our fellows are sticking well to their task. There is not a house standing in the whole town. Both sides have exploded so many mines that it is hard to make out any longer where the *chemin couvert* actually runs. . . . As for Löwendahl himself, he is as firm as a rock. Now and again he has been a little shaken by the way in which the enemy have blotted out his trenches during the day, making him dig them all over again during the night. . . . But I hope that we shall be able to take the place by the end of the month.[212]

But Bergen did not oblige by surrendering so soon. When the month of July ended, the venerable Crönstrom was still in command of the city, and making quite as defiant a showing as his former master, Charles XII, had made at Stralsund.

The whole of Europe was watching the contest with breathless interest. The enemies of France had begun to crow over her threatened discomfiture, which could well be even more humiliating to her than the recent reverse in Piedmont. Maurice's reputation was in danger. It would be a poor season for the newly created Marshal-General if he were to close his campaign, after a dubious victory, with Maastricht and Bergen intact and still in enemy hands. His wider strategy was completely misunderstood. France could only see that the bulk of the French army was marking time on the Meuse while their comrades were floundering in the marshes of the Scheldt.

The mood of depression began to affect even the buoyant Löwendahl himself. He sent to Maurice for help, saying that he had tried everything he knew. He had mined, sapped, bombarded, and stormed, and all to no effect. Crönstrom merely sat tight and gave back as good as he got. One Frenchman in every three had trench-fever; winter was not so far off; and with every day Waldeck and Schwartzenberg were collecting the necessary force to relieve the city. Löwendahl begged Maurice to move the main French army nearer to the Dutch frontier, in order to be at hand when the relieving army marched on Bergen.

Maurice refused. He was resolved to remain where he was, in front of Maastricht. The whole object of the exercise would be frustrated if he abandoned his present station on the Meuse. Surely it could only be a matter of days before Cumberland's nerve snapped, and he marched northwards? And when Cumberland joined Waldeck and Schwartzenberg, Maastricht would be exposed. Maurice was sure that his plan was right. Yet court and camp were simmering with dissatisfaction. There were many in high places already exerting pressure on the king to countermand the orders of his Marshal-General. The *doyen* of French politics, Noailles, had turned against Maurice, and was tendering just such advice to the king. He had been in communication with Löwendahl, and as early as mid-August, he sent a portentous letter to Maurice to underline the implications of failure at Bergen. On the siege, said Noailles, depended 'the king's renown, the army's reputation, your own personal glory, the verdict of Europe, and the future of peace as well as of war'.[213]

To all this adverse criticism, Maurice was deaf. His own views were summarized in a memorandum:

> Any intelligent man must be dismayed at seeing his views generally repudiated. If uncertainty and indecision are a curse in private life, they are doubly so in war. To change one's mind in war would be to throw a whole army into confusion. Alterations in plan inflict damage on the original conception, and such conceptions are, after all, the fruit of spacious meditation. . . . True, the enemy has refused to be drawn; he has sent to Bergen only reinforcements proportionate to our own, and has thus saved Maastricht. . . . But politics, together with our losses and our vanity, have induced us to attach overwhelming importance to this siege, to a point where we are willing to sacrifice our army and the glory of our king. Men have become heated; they are blaming the commander for his slowness. . . . People argue with him, send him letters, pelt him with ideas, as though he had somehow lost interest in his own campaign; they want to lash him into action, and they plot and conspire to this end.

He then enumerated his principal reasons for standing pat before Maastricht. First, he confessed that he was 'not so sanguine about taking Bergen as to be willing to conduct my royal master thither to receive an affront'; it would make Louis a laughing-stock if he were to witness the repulse of his own army. Secondly, Maurice insisted that Löwendahl, respite his misgivings, in fact possessed enough resources to take the town, supposing it were humanly possible. Moreover, by leaving the vicinity of Maastricht, the army would move from rich to denuded territory, and would leave exposed the high road to France. Finally, if he once lost contact with Cumberland, he would have to split his forces into smaller units in order to guard the supply lines and maintain garrisons, whereas the key to salvation lay in keeping the army intact.

His critics seemed unaware that they were attempting to put him in the very dilemma in which he had so cunningly placed Cumberland. It had been Maurice's aim to induce the enemy to disperse his troops, and he was now being asked to scatter his own. In fact he was never unduly concerned about whether or not Bergen fell: his objective was always Maastricht. The closing sentences of the memorandum enshrined the kernel of his military philosophy.

> In war one often acts from inspiration. One would often be hard put to it to justify why one adopts one course rather than another. The circumstances of war are sensed rather than explained; and, if war depends on inspiration, it seems foolish to stick pins into the soothsayer.[214]

At first light on September 16th, the French mortar batteries in front of Bergen fired two heavy salvos. They were the prearranged signal for a surprise attack on the sleeping town. French formations dashed for the partial breach that had been gouged in the fortifications. With six companies of grenadiers at their head, three flying columns stormed the Pucelle and Cohörn bastions and one of the demi-lunes. They then fought their way inch by inch across the ramparts, and managed to claw open the gates for the rest of the army. Löwendahl's men stormed in and swept all before them. The garrison fled.

Löwendahl, who had maintained excellent discipline during the assault, lost control of his troops once they were across the wall. Soon a massacre was in progress. The Austrians and Dutch in Bergen were made to pay a fearful price for inflicting on the French assault groups a loss of two hundred killed and three hundred wounded. Two thousand of the enemy were stabbed or bayoneted to death, and another thousand were wounded in the orgy of insensate blood-letting. Espagnac asserts that a unit of Breton irregulars was responsible for most of these atrocities;[215] and Löwendahl, who told Maurice that he had 'sincerely wanted to save this unhappy town from pillage', spoke of the excesses of 'three hundred volunteers who reached me unexpectedly', who were probably these same Bretons.[216] It was a full twenty-four hours before order could be restored, and by that time Bergen was a graveyard.

The booty was immense. It included seventeen merchant ships and over two thousand prisoners. But the sacking had sickened the on-lookers. 'The warrior who had captured Ochakov in Tartary', Voltaire said of Löwendahl, in mock admiration,

> brought to the Dutch frontier new secrets of the arts of war, secrets beyond the ordinary rules of that art. With this conquest, which threw Europe into consternation and astonished even the victors, the world began to regard Louis XV as rather less easy-going than it had supposed.[217]

An officer of the *Régiment de Normandie* brought the news of the fall of Bergen to Maurice, who at once hastened to inform the king. There and then, without giving Louis time to ponder the implications of the massacre, he boldly demanded a Marshal's bâton on behalf of Löwendahl, who had genuinely deserved it. The courtiers began to fidget. Was it possible that two foreigners, two Protestants, two mercenaries, should be numbered at the same time among the Marshals of France? Maurice had his way; the patent was drawn up, signed, and dated that same day. The Marshal-General wrote off at once to his friend in his curious, phonetic French:

> I am delighted, my dear count, to be the first to salute you as Marshal of France. . . . The glory resides more in your achievement itself than in the recognition the king accords you. I shall say no more at this moment, when happiness shines for you in some faces and jealousy in others. You know what I am to you.[218]

According to other sources, the king is supposed to have spoken despairingly of Löwendahl when he learned of the brutal sack of Bergen, and to have asked Maurice what should be done with him. 'Hang him, or else make him a Marshal,' said Maurice. 'I can't stand half-measures.'[219]

Within a week Louis had bidden farewell to his troops and returned to his capital. He had performed all that had been expected of him. He had shown himself to his soldiers, and had encouraged them by his handsome presence. Before leaving, he bestowed on Maurice the post of 'Commandant-General of the Low Countries'. The flashy, hollow title cost Louis very little; nor did it satisfy Maurice, who was bitterly disappointed at failing to receive the viceroyalty which he felt was his due. He was also given to understand that once peace was signed the office of Commandant-General would lapse, and he could therefore scarcely expect to enjoy it for more than a few months.

He was ending the last full year of his fighting life with the taste of ashes in his mouth: the ashes of Bergen. Public opinion had grown more delicate since the terrible days of the Thirty Years' War, and this relatively minor catastrophe had produced a general shock of revulsion. Overnight, Maurice and Löwendahl were transformed into barbarian chieftains, and the French into a nation of savages. To Maurice, who had always been an outstandingly chivalrous soldier, the Bergen affair was especially mortifying. In four long decades of fighting, there had never before been any stain on his professional honour.

'It really seems,' wrote a later commentator, 'as though bad luck dogged Maurice's army, and deprived it of the fruit of its successes.'[220] For two more months he continued his attempt to force Maastricht. Without success. Cumberland continued to evade him. His two best generals, Löwendahl and Contades, fell sick. Everything appeared to be against him. There seemed little point in prolonging his inconclusive manoeuvres, so he gave reluctant permission for the army to go into winter quarters. After a tour of inspection, he set out for France, reaching Versailles on December 20th. He was low in body and low in spirits: but he was not the man to yield to ill-fortune tamely and without a struggle.

CHAPTER XV

MAASTRICHT, 1748

*La terre est une vaste théâtre ou la même tragédie se joue
sous des noms différents.*

VOLTAIRE

MAURICE'S reception at Paris and Versailles was not merely
apathetic: it was actively hostile. Those pleasant vices in his nature,
once regarded with general tolerance and affection, now became instruments to plague him. It was rumoured that he had reduced the cities
of the Netherlands to cinders for the sole purpose of lining his own
pockets. The name of Verres was bandied about: Flanders was compared with the Sicily that had groaned beneath the tyranny of that
rapacious proconsul. The conjectural amount of booty taken at Bergen
soared mountainously. It was whispered that Bergen had been by no
means an isolated example, and that other captured cities had equally
been subjected to systematic pillage.

There were no more triumphal appearances at the *Opéra*. Yet the
actors of Paris, to their honour, did not league themselves with his
detractors. They did not forsake him in his disgrace, but rallied round
their lifelong patron. On January 10th, 1748, the *Théâtre-français*
staged a new play, *Coriolan*.[221] It proved to be so hostile to the court
that it had to be banned by the authorities after five performances.
The parallel between Maurice and Coriolanus may well have been
apt and piquant, but Paris as a whole was unsympathetic. The
Marshal-General might well have been forgiven had he despaired of
his adopted country, and cried with Shakespeare's hero: 'There is a
world elsewhere.'

He preferred, as in the previous autumn, to ignore the vulgar
clamour, and to devote his efforts to having his new post of 'Commandant-General of the Low Countries' changed to 'Lieutenant-
General' or 'Lieutenant of the King'. He was still hankering after
the vice-regal status, and wanted to enjoy the same quasi-monarchical
power that his hero Prince Eugène had enjoyed at Brussels fifty years
before. It was the old recurring dream of royal authority: if he could
not hold Courland as a fief of Poland, then he would govern the

Austrian Netherlands in the name of France. He badgered his friends to support him. Pâris-Duverney was delegated to tackle the ministers, and Mme de Pompadour was persuaded to wheedle the king. The former reported that, according to Puysieux, the difficulties were insurmountable: Maurice was a Protestant, and the Austrian Netherlands were traditionally Roman Catholic. 'M. le marquis finished by saying, monseigneur,' reported Pâris-Duverney,

> that you ought to try and put yourself for a moment in the king's place. You would then perfectly understand the inner pain your request might cause him. He considers that he has already conferred on you a distinction sufficiently satisfying, and elevated in itself. This reflexion ought surely to sway your heart and mind.[222]

This was straight talking. It was plain that Maurice's stock had slumped heavily since the time of Maria Josepha's wedding. On January 12th his brevet as Commandant-General—and nothing more grand—was officially promulgated, under the shadow of the coming peace of Aix-la-Chapelle. As some slight compensation, he was entrusted with the nominal post of Governor of Alsace, the most Protestant province in France. The prizes were glittering, but they were empty.

In concert with Belle-Isle, who was only slightly more unpopular than he was himself, Maurice worked on the plans for the next campaign. The two men still hoped to bring off a bold stroke that would give France, even at this late stage, the initiative at the peace table. Maurice knew that, with his uncertain health, it might be the last military operation that he would ever undertake. He resolved to make it a good one.

The objective was still Maastricht, which it had become a point of honour to reduce. The plan of campaign was ingenious: a *coup de maître*: a dazzling demonstration of how to conceal one's preparations, how to move men and matériel across difficult terrain with the utmost speed, and how to switch one's angle of attack at the last possible moment. The time-table was complex: but it was essential that at the climax of the operation the intricate, artful, logistical elements of the pattern should slide smoothly into place. They did. As a military enterprise, the investment of Maastricht would be hard to surpass. No soldier could have desired a more impressive finale to a career of arms.

The plan had been taking shape in his mind before he left Brussels in the previous winter. In December he had discussed it with Noailles, who, whatever his shortcomings in the heat of battle, possessed a remarkably clear tactical brain. Together they shaped the necessary strategy.[223] The chief obstacle to investing Maastricht was how to devise a means of passing sufficient forces across the Meuse, in order to complete the city's encirclement from the rear. Maastricht stood partly on the west and partly on the east bank of the vast river, the two halves of the city being linked by bridges. There was no point in trying to besiege the western half, if troops and supplies could be fed to the defenders through the back door: and the enemy could be relied upon to foil any attempt to cross the river for the purpose of closing the ring. Maurice thought hard about the problem, and eventually decided that the best solution was to divide his forces. Somehow he must get a strong army on to the east bank of the river, at a point beyond the enemy's reach, with the aim of taking the eastern portion of the city in rear. But Maurice also realized that Maastricht would never be taken by means of a simple two-pronged attack, for the main enemy army might easily intercept the French on the eastern bank and annihilate them. It would therefore be necessary to organize one of the elaborate feints which were part of his stock-in-trade.

He decided to open his campaign by pretending that, so far from wishing to tie up his forces round Maastricht in the east, he was anxious to follow up the taking of Bergen in the west. He would therefore give out that his objective was not Maastricht, but Breda or 's Hertogenbosch. He would keep his attack high, like a modern boxer who jabs at his opponent's head to make him raise his guard and leave his body unprotected. It was the tactic which he had used three years before, when he had moved away from Lille to attack Mons, doubling back sharply when his opponents were off the scent.

Before Maurice reached Brussels on March 20th, he had already instructed the main French army to busy itself in the vicinity of Antwerp. Convoys of barges were being ostentatiously escorted towards Bergen. Maurice arrived at Antwerp with his staff at the end of the month, ostensibly to inspect the siege-train that was being noisily assembled there. Nor did it escape the enemy's attention that a vast artillery park had been established near-by. To keep the pot merrily boiling, Maurice sent out a skirmishing force under Estrées and young Broglie, and shortly afterwards another under Contades. On April 2nd he rode up to Bergen, again with his staff, to confer with the commandant and inspect the installations. All this diversionary activity to the north was carried out with such earnestness that the allies became convinced, as Maurice intended that they should, that Breda was about to be besieged. The allies therefore made anxious preparations to interpose a powerful screen of troops between Maurice and the apparently threatened city.

Meanwhile a secret French army, destined for the eastern bank of the Meuse, was being assembled far to the south in Luxembourg. It consisted of fifty-nine battalions and twenty-nine squadrons, with six hundred dragoons of the valiant ex-valet Fischer thrown in for good measure. It was a first-class, hand-picked force. As it was to march hard and fast, it had no more than six pieces of light artillery, and its baggage and supplies were cut to a minimum. Inevitably, the command had been entrusted to Marshal Löwendahl.

When Löwendahl's army stole out on its clandestine march, Maurice was holding the allied generals hypnotized in the vicinity of Breda and Tilburg. Löwendahl's divisions began their march independently from six towns spread out in an arc along the Luxembourg frontier. By April 7th, they had coalesced into a single unit at a pre-arranged point, Verviers, twenty-five kilometres east of Liége and forty kilometres south-east of Maastricht. The British and Austrians were utterly bemused by the unexpected appearance of a French army on their own side of the river. They wrongly concluded that it must be resting before resuming its march northwards to assist in the assault on Breda. They soon discovered their mistake. No sooner had Löwendahl concentrated his men at Verviers than Maurice began the most spectacular phase of his operation. At the word of command, the whole French main army about-turned and started a tremendous march from Antwerp to Maastricht. The four holding forces which he had placed between Antwerp and Liége, and which he had secretly enlarged and provided with special siege armaments, swung eastwards, either to join Maurice or to converge on Maastricht.

The enemy was completely surprised. On April 3rd, Flanders, Brabant, Limburg and Zeeland had been comparatively quiet, except for local manoeuvring in the north and the unexplained presence of a flying column at Verviers. Twenty-four hours later, the entire area was in turmoil.

As he marched southwards, Maurice produced a final feint to induce the main enemy army to remain in the north. He despatched Estrées' division eastwards across country to Bree, where Ligonier's principal arsenal was situated. The British could interpret Estrées' movements no more successfully than those of any other French division during this whirlwind week. Ligonier hastily pulled back to Roermond to protect his arsenal, putting himself in a position of defence. But there was no one for Ligonier to defend himself against. Maurice was already fifty kilometres away, investing the western half of Maastricht, while Löwendahl was swinging leftwards to encircle the eastern half of the city. The necessary artillery and siege equipment were sailing sweetly up the Meuse from secret depots at Namur. Pontoons were thrown across the river. On April 15th, two thousand labourers and sixteen pioneer battalions began digging entrenchments. Maastricht was surrounded.

The design which Maurice and Noailles had sketched out in the capital in midwinter had been realized three months later upon the banks of the Meuse. It is one thing to move troops on paper, but quite another to execute the blueprint on the ground. The entire operation had gone as planned. Only a very remarkable general, with the touch of the conjuror, could have evolved so masterly a stratagem, and only a very remarkable army could have carried it out. The troops of Louis XV, when properly led, were still capable of rising to the occasion. Moreover, at the outset, only four men had known the real destination of the French army: Maurice himself, Noailles, Crémille, and Pâris-Duverney. Not even Löwendahl had been privy to the original plan.

Maurice had no time to lose if he wanted to take Maastricht. The War of the Austrian Succession was in its dying hours. On April 30th, 1748, Saint-Sévérin reached provisional agreement with the British and Dutch plenipotentiaries for a cessation of hostilities. Aix-la-Chapelle, where the peace-makers were conferring, was a mere thirty kilometres east of Maastricht, a short ride for a fast courier. At any minute a galloper might bring the news that peace had been finally concluded: and Maastricht would be reprieved. Indeed, already the siege could only be mounted on the excuse of a mere technicality, in that the Austrians had not yet formally initialled the armistice, although they were imminently expected to do so. Maurice redoubled his exertions. By April 21st, he had brought his heavy guns into position, and he began to hammer at the fortifications with a battery of a hundred and fifty cannon.

The Prince von Aremberg, the Austrian commander, was a general of spirit. He made a night sortie with eight hundred men, and played havoc with the French lines. Next day the elements came to the aid of the Austrians. After a violent hailstorm, the French found themselves knee-deep in water in their own trenches. Maurice had to issue a special ration of brandy. The storm even swept away his pontoons, and for five days his own army actually lost contact with the army of Löwendahl.

Aremberg promptly launched another night attack. The Austrians swarmed over the French positions, spiking thirty guns before they were driven back. Next day the Austrian garrison was cheered by the news that Batthiany was advancing on Maastricht with a large army. Undeterred, Maurice pushed ahead with his *chemin couvert*, though it was not until May 4th that he was well enough placed beneath the enemy's outer works to order a general assault for that same night. But at noon, a few hours before the scheduled attack, the eventuality which Maurice had been dreading actually occurred. An envoy from Cumberland, the supreme enemy commander, arrived at the French camp with the momentous news that a general armistice had finally been signed.

Maurice was not to be baulked so lightly of his prey. He declared roundly that, armistice or no armistice, he meant to have Maastricht. He showed such bellicosity that Cumberland hastened to suggest a compromise. Maastricht would be delivered up to Maurice if the French would allow the garrison to march out with the honours of war. Maurice, knowing the delicacy and impropriety of his position, wisely consented. A forty-eight-hours' truce followed, during which the Governor of Maastricht sent a galloper to consult the Stadhouder. William IV agreed with Cumberland, and on May 10th, 1748, Maurice took the salute as the twenty-four battalions and six hundred horsemen of the Austrian garrison filed past him and marched away towards 's Hertogenbosch. Maastricht was in French hands at last.

Next day the war was over, and with it the military career of Maurice de Saxe.

When the black-and-silver ranks of Francis I and Maria Theresa had dipped their swords and flags to Maurice, they were saluting a soldier who had borne arms for five months short of forty years; who had risen from being an ensign in the Saxon army to being Marshal-General of the Armies of France; who had fought in the Great Northern War; at the siege of Belgrade; in the Wars of the Spanish, the Polish and the Austrian Successions. The last heir of the great Swedish family of Königsmarck, and a scion of the illustrious house of Wettin, he had fought under Schulenburg, Marlborough, and Eugène. As a commanding officer, he had never been worsted; had won three pitched battles; and had taken innumerable cities and fortresses. Finally, at the end of his long career, he had captured the great city of Maastricht and invested Marshal Löwendahl as its governor. *Magnus ad extremum.*

The Peace of Aix-la-Chapelle was ratified on October 18th, 1748, within a week of the centenary of the Peace of Westphalia which had closed the Thirty Years' War. Maurice was at Fontainebleau. He begged leave to retire to Chambord, having no desire to superintend the liquidation of his army and the evacuation of the provinces which he had won, at so great a cost, for France. Saint-Séverin, with the acquiescence of the king, had already agreed to relinquish the French grip on the Austrian Netherlands, the chief prize of the war.

From the French standpoint, the treaty was pitiable. Despite her setbacks in the south, France had ended the war in no worse a military position than her enemies, even if she was financially much weaker. She still had an army of 250,000 men under arms. But Louis XV wished, in a fine-sounding phrase, to go to Aix-la-Chapelle, 'not as a merchant, but as a king'. As a result, he was fleeced by the nations of mere shopkeepers, and the bargaining power secured by the last-minute seizure of Maastricht was thrown negligently away. The only territorial gain made by France was Cape Breton Island, off the Canadian coast, in exchange for which Louis surrendered not merely the Low Countries, but also the infinitely richer prize of Madras. He agreed to recognize the Pragmatic Sanction, by which Maria Theresa had secured the Habsburg domains; he agreed to recognize the succession of the electors of Hanover to the throne of Great Britain; and he agreed to allow the king of Sardinia to keep his various conquests. It was not exactly peace with honour.

The marquis d'Argenson summarized the general French reaction to the peace succinctly. 'The French,' he wrote,

> wanted peace, and their miseries added fuel to the fire. But they also love glory and honour; and so, after the first moments of joy that peace had been concluded, they were filled with consternation at the poor conditions which France had obtained. While in London and other British towns there was tumultuous rejoicing, in Paris and the provinces there was dismay. 'What'! they asked, 'have we really surrendered all our conquests? '[224]

Maurice and Löwendahl began to recover their former places in public esteem, although Maurice kept his private opinion strictly to himself, and only hinted at it in private letters. 'I am only a tyro when it comes to politics,' he wrote to Maurepas:

> and if I have sometimes been required to comment on political matters from a military standpoint, I have never pretended to be an expert. Nor do I understand about finance, or how we stand in that regard. But I cannot help noticing that money in England stood at 4 per cent at the end of the war, and is now at 14 per cent or 15 per cent. Credit was the only thing that kept the English and Dutch afloat: they were practically at rock bottom. With us it was different. We had an army in being, and even if we were low in funds, we could have continued for a long time. A sacrifice was well worth making in order to acquire a province with splendid ports and millions of people, which would have formed an impenetrable buffer. That, at any rate, is what I think, though I repeat that I know next to nothing about these damned politics of yours. All that I can see is that the king of Prussia has grabbed Silesia and is hanging on to it, and I do not know why we could not have done likewise in the Netherlands. After all, he is weaker

than we are, in a less tenable position, liable to attack on all sides, and is hemmed in by neighbours who hate him far more than our neighbours hate us.[225]

The surrender of the Austrian Netherlands was as much a private blow to Maurice as it was a public blow to France. The Generalissimo's occupation was gone. He no longer had an army to command nor territory to rule.

He was no longer even a serving officer. It was soon made abundantly clear to him that his active career had come to an end. Now peace had arrived, the plums of high command would be plucked by Frenchmen.

When the Uhlans of the *Volontaires de Saxe* returned from Flanders, Louis XV and the royal family reviewed them at Passy. All Paris flocked to behold the splendid spectacle. It was as though the king and his subjects sensed that they were witnessing the symbolic close of a great era, the end of the line of great commanders who had brought glory to the *ancien régime*.

The regiment was drawn up in battle order, and Maurice took his place at its head. The parade resembled the famous parades with which he and his men had delighted Paris thirty years before, when they used to flaunt themselves on the Champ de Mars. Maurice rode forward. He saluted his king for the last time. Afterwards he and his dragoons rode away, turning their horses' heads towards Chambord. Maurice was finishing his career as he had started it: as a plain regimental officer, like his Königsmarck forebears before him.

CHAPTER XVI

———

CHAMBORD, 1748-1749

Ay, your times were fine times indeed; you have been
telling us of them for many a long year. . . . All our
entertainment is your old stories of Prince Eugène and the
Duke of Marlborough. I hate such old-fashioned trumpery.
OLIVER GOLDSMITH

A MORE appropriate home for Maurice's retirement than the château
de Chambord could not have been found. The vast pile epitomized his
life: it was grand and spectacular, sad and eccentric. The courtiers of
François Premier had been mystified that the king had chosen to erect
so huge an edifice in so malodorous a stretch of the Loire, when he
already had a satisfactory residence near by at Blois. Nor had they
been pleased when he had uttered an arbitrary ' *allons chez moi* ', and
compelled them to leave Paris in order to inhabit his new folly.

The palace that Maurice might have built for himself at Mitau,
had he become the ruler of Courland, might well have resembled
Chambord. He would probably have shown the same reckless disregard
as François Premier for expenditure, and the same impulse towards
megalomaniac display. We are told that when François Premier was
a captive in Spain, and his treasury was so empty that he could not
pay his own ransom, and he was reduced to pillaging churches and
melting down his subjects' jewellery, even then he never allowed the
building of Chambord to be halted. It was at Chambord that he later
received his gaoler, the Emperor Charles V.

His successors could find little use for the immense palace, except
as a glorified hunting-lodge. It formed part of the comté de Blois,
bestowed by Louis XIII on his treacherous brother, Gaston, duc
d'Orléans; and it was up and down the echoing corridors of Chambord
that Gaston would play at hide-and-seek with his little daughter, the
Grande Mademoiselle. Not until the reign of Louis XIV was the
château fully reinstated in the royal favour. It offered the Sun King
a blend of grandeur and discomfort that he found irresistible. During
his regular sojourns there his entertainments were written by Molière,
and set to music by Lully.

CHÂTEAU DE CHAMBORD

Photograph by the author

Chambord [Plate 7] is second in size only to Versailles itself. It contains seventy-four staircases and four hundred and forty rooms. Yet it does not owe its impressiveness to bulk alone. Viewed from across the Cosson, the tributary of the Loire beside which it stands, it possesses a calm and radiant beauty. For all the solidity of its enormous façade, it has something of the quality of a palace seen in a dream. Its bulbous towers, its colonnades, its roofs crowned with the petrified glades of spires, its turrets, pinnacles and chimneys, lend it an oriental and fantastic air. Its setting too has the atmosphere of a fairy-tale. The dark woods stretch away, mile upon mile, to the distant horizon. Six great forest rides, ruled with the exactitude of Roman roads, radiate from the gay parterres. And towering above château and woods alike rises the stupendous central lantern, ornamented with its massive *fleur de lys*.

The lantern, and the central staircase of glistening white marble which the lantern crowns, are the twin glories of Chambord. The *escalier* is in the form of a double helix, and two people can ascend and descend simultaneously without ever seeing one another. Its monumental yet playful character is entirely in keeping with the spirit of this extraordinary palace, and with the spirit of Maurice.[226]

The retired Marshal-General began to remodel his domain with a fanatical zest unknown since the time of its founder. His first task was to provide for his regiment, and accordingly he built the handsome barracks which may still be seen beside the parade ground. The man who a few months before had commanded a quarter of a million men now devoted his energies to parading and housing six brigades of dragoons. These outlandish soldiers became his passion, his plaything. A year before, for example, he had approached Brühl about a new fancy that had seized him, the desire to add to his regiment 'six tartars, real mahometan tartars'. Brühl, who was to obtain them for him, was to ascertain that they were of the true 'mahometan persuasion' before Maurice's agent paid the expenses of their journey from Dresden to Strasbourg.[227] Months later, when he was immersed with the siege of Bergen, Maurice could still find time to inform Brühl that the Tartars had arrived. 'Captain Babac has been promoted lieutenant-colonel,' he wrote. 'I believe he is the first mahometan lieutenant-colonel who has ever served His Most Christian Majesty. You will see that I have given some justification to those people in France who have always said that we Saxons have a streak of the Turk in us.'[228] Outside the château he stationed the battery of cannon which the king had presented to him after Rocoux; and inside the *cour d'honneur* he mounted a twenty-four-hour guard. Sentinels patrolled the corridor outside the apartments of the Duke-Elect of Courland and Semigallia in the way that the King of France was guarded at Versailles; and in his antechamber were hung the English

and Dutch banners captured at Rocoux and Laufeldt. The display with
which he surrounded himself in peacetime exceeded the panoply with
which he had surrounded himself in war. The château rang with the
crash of boots, rattle of muskets, harsh cries of sentries, braying of
bugles, and sonorous boom of artillery.

As the weeks of inactivity grew into months, Maurice relapsed
increasingly into the world of make-believe. For men of his stamp,
with a strong histrionic bent, it is often difficult to tell where reality
ends and fantasy begins: or whether fantasy is not for them the true
reality. He began methodically to manufacture an artificial miniature
kingdom. If the princes of Europe had ejected him from Courland,
then he would create a personal duchy in this remote corner of France.
His hobby of breeding wild horses gave him an excuse to encircle
his park with the longest wall in France, thirty-two kilometres in
extent, making him the master of a battlemented area almost as large
as that embraced by the walls of old Paris. Here he ruled supreme,
ignoring the world beyond his wall: a feudal prince who owed no
more than nominal suzerainty to his liege.

At his death, a draft petition was found among his papers indicating
that after his retreat to Chambord he had considered applying to the
king for actual royal honours.

> The comte de Saxe, Marshal-General of the King's Camps and Armies,
> would humbly beg to remind his Majesty that he is the son of a great
> king, head of one of the most august sovereign houses in Europe, and
> that he has been legitimately elected Duke of Courland. It is true that
> the possession of this duchy has been torn from him by force and
> violence; but it is also true that no one can destroy a title based on
> the unanimous wish of a free people. Every European court, with the
> single exception of Vienna, including the courts of Poland, Saxony,
> Germany and Scandinavia, has always accorded the comte de Saxe the
> princely honours due to his birth, independent of his election to the
> dignity of Sovereign Duke of Courland. The comte de Saxe does not
> ask Your Majesty to recognize him as Duke of Courland. Although
> such recognition would only be his due, it would be attended by political
> embarrassment that the comte de Saxe would want to spare His Majesty
> even at the cost of personal justice. His Majesty has assured him, how-
> ever, in terms too flattering and glorious to bear repetition, that he
> has had the happiness of serving His Majesty usefully. Dare he hope,
> therefore, that he might be accorded the favour of enjoying the treat-
> ment, rank and honours possessed by the princes of the blood of France?
> The comte de Saxe feels less diffident in requesting such a favour in
> that he is the uncle of Mme la Dauphine.[229]

There is no record of whether the petition was ever actually submitted to Louis XV, or if it was, how it was received. Perhaps Maurice was dissuaded from submitting it by the candid friends who had earlier advised him not to petition for the rank of viceroy of the Netherlands. It is melancholy to record that, as Maurice's delusions of grandeur increased, so his real standing at court was diminishing. Within weeks of the signing of the Peace of Aix-la-Chapelle, the great war leader was no more than an honourable nonentity. Even his new connexion with the royal family counted for nothing. Writing to Augustus of Poland from Versailles, early in 1749, Maurice complained that the Dauphine 'had been a little short with him', and that her manner towards him, although polite, was cold. He blamed this coldness on her new circle of friends at court, most of whom were hostile to him and ill-disposed towards the king. He hinted that matters could soon be set to rights if Louis XV would 'root out of this clique two persons whom I and the rest of the world know well'. It seems more than likely that one of these persons was his old antagonist, Conti.[230]

The Dauphine was passing through a miserable period in her relationship with her resentful husband; and Maurice was paying the price for his part in sacrificing—the word had been his own—the little princess to dynastic necessity and his own ambition. There had been profit in the transaction for Maurice and Saxony, but none at all for Maria Josepha. She was prepared to do her duty, but no longer felt obliged to display affection towards the man who had been the main cause of her unhappiness. She could not forgive Maurice, whom as a child she had loved and trusted, for consigning her to the role of mindless fecundity that had already destroyed the queen. He had condemned her to bear the Dauphin twelve children, and to die at the age of thirty-five.

Excluded from the court of Versailles, Maurice became even more determined to create a court of his own. Circumstances in part mocked him. Four-fifths of the land encircled by his serpentine wall was forest: he was a monarch of the trees. And apart from his dragoons, his human subjects numbered no more than a hundred frightened peasants. Everything was at sixes and sevens. The peasants hated the dragoons, and the dragoons despised the peasants. His Turks, Tartars, Moslems and negroes were magnificent in braid and furs and shakoes: but they were men, not toys, and delighted to indulge their barbarous whims throughout the length of the valley of the Loire. What Maurice's troopers did not destroy was at the mercy of his horde of horses, the wild and beautiful creatures originally brought to France by his cavalrymen from the Ukraine, the Banát and the Hungarian hortobagy. It was small comfort to the victims of these fierce animals to be told that Maurice was helping to improve the equine bloodstock of France.

Maurice soon found it harder to discipline his regiment than he had formerly done to impose his will on the whole French army. Like their chief, the dragoons did not take kindly to inactivity; like him, they possessed unruly appetites. Looting and rapine gradually became the order of the day. Maurice had always been a lenient commander, but these infidels and blackamoors compelled him to instigate a régime that was harsher than any he had previously found necessary. On a great oak within sight of the château a number of malefactors were summarily strung up for looting and other offences.

Routine existence at Chambord settled down to a round of parades, manoeuvres, and extravagant entertainments. On one night a week Maurice, like Louis, dined in public. Plays, ballets and operas were regularly performed in his private theatre, where he would sit enthroned, just as the Sun King himself had sat when Molière and his troupe had performed at Chambord. The special theatrical displays which he staged when Mme de Pompadour visited him were especially lavish. His disappointments had not soured his love of the theatre— or of actresses.

In happier days, Maurice's companions had been the incomparable Adrienne and Mlle Cartou. Recent years had seen the ascendancy of the capricious Mlle Navarre and of the jealous Mlle Beauménard, who was one of the actresses in the company which Favart had taken to Flanders for the amusement of Maurice and his troops. This famous company had also included two attractive sisters, Marie and Geneviève Rinteau, daughters of a Parisian lemonade-maker. They had taken the high-sounding names of the Mesdemoiselles Verrières, and were moderately accomplished musicians.

The elder, Marie, was seventeen when she became Maurice's mistress, and when she was eighteen she bore him a daughter, the only acknowledged offspring of his innumerable *liaisons*. On October 19th, 1748, the child was baptized at the church of Saint-Gervais in Paris, her parents being described as Jean-Baptiste de la Rivière and Marie Rinteau. Marie was, of course, unmarried, and the name La Rivière was a *prête-nom*; no doubt the river in question was the Seine. The child was christened Aurore, after her famous grandmother, the Countess Maria Aurora von Königsmarck. In early childhood she was to be adopted by her royal cousin, the Dauphine Maria Josepha, and to become the grandmother of the novelist George Sand (who was born Armandine-Aurore-Lucie Dupin in 1804). George Sand, in her turn, was so proud of her Königsmarck descent that she called her son Maurice, while the elder of her granddaughters was named Aurore.[231]

Maurice gave Marie Rinteau, the mother of his child, a handsome allowance of fifty *louis* a month. Until the summer of 1749 their relationship ran smoothly; but then there was a fatal estrangement. The trouble was brought on by Marie's pathetic eagerness to please. Knowing his love of acting, and aware of her own limitations in this sphere, she decided to take advantage of his temporary absence to take lessons. Her aim was to surprise him on his return by being able to play major instead of merely supporting parts. Unfortunately she chose as her dramatic coach the successful young playwright Marmontel, whose lively reputation with women was well-known to Maurice, and who was himself not only a protégé but an amorous legatee of the Marshal-General. For example, when Maurice broke with Mlle Navarre she was passed on to Marmontel as his new mistress. 'M. de Saxe found Mlle Navarre too haughty,' Marmontel wrote in his memoirs,

> for she lacked abandon and the desire to please. Mlle Verrières, on the other hand, never bored him with tantrums about her rivals. She lacked artifice, but relied on her extraordinarily agreeable qualities. She was equable, good-humoured, and loved without reserve.[232]

Marmontel found the easy-going Marie an apt pupil. 'Her docility made me assiduous,' he recalled; 'but when word of my assiduity reached the Marshal, it was misrepresented.' Maurice's bellow of wrath was frightening to hear. Marie, unlike Mlle Navarre, was the *maîtresse régnante*—the mother of his child. It was as bad as being cuckolded. He cut off her allowance and vowed never to set eyes on her again. He ran round Versailles pouring out his woes to anyone who would listen, and even complained to the king about the wrongs done to him by 'that damned little poet'! The terrified Marmontel protested that he had 'only taken up with the ladies with whom the Marshal had finished'. Nevertheless Maurice had to be actively restrained by Sourdis and Löwendahl from physically chastising him. The whole court rocked with laughter at his discomfiture.

The uproar occasioned by the Rinteau affair was nothing compared to the tempest raised by Maurice's affair with another actress in his Flemish troupe, Mme Justine Favart, the wife of its director. At seventeen, Justine had been discovered by Favart at the court of King Stanislas at Lunéville, where her father was a resident musician. Under the stage name of 'Mlle Chantilly', Justine Duronceray had made her debut at the *Opéra Comique* in one of Favart's own plays. In December 1745, he married her.

In Flanders, where she went as the star of her husband's company, she made an immediate impression on Maurice. She was then twenty, and although she was no great beauty her vivacity was irresistible. Maurice had to have her. In 1746 he began to write gauche love-letters to her. 'Mlle Chantilly,' began one of them, 'you must release me; you are an enchantress more potent than Armide. I can already visualize myself draped with flowers and posies: quite the wrong attire for a devotee of Mars. What would the king say, if he found me clasping not the torch of vengeance, but a nosegay? '[233]

The events that followed the fifty-year-old Marshal-General's declaration of love were worthy of a Beaumarchais comedy. In a short while Justine was to be heard loudly bemoaning the loss of a virtue which she had lost several times before she had met Maurice, and would lose several times afterwards. As for her husband, he had a nose for publicity worthy of a true impresario. He played the part of injured husband for all it was worth, both during Maurice's lifetime and after his death. He probably realized that Justine's liaison with Maurice would immortalize him far more certainly than any of his trivial plays. Maurice had offered the histrionic Favarts the fattest parts of their lives.

The comedy began when Favart was unexpectedly dunned for a huge sum of money which he owed to the lessees of the largest theatre in Brussels, where he had begun to present his plays after being paid off by Maurice. He promptly went into hiding, whereupon Maurice wrote to Justine a letter which he was later to regret. Dated from Paris, on June 7th, 1749, it begins:

> I have been informed, madame, that the Mesdemoiselles Myesses are pursuing Favart as the result of a decree which they obtained against him at Brussels. I expect that you will now want to leave that city; and as your situation is painful, I should like to offer you some assistance in the shape of 500 *livres* a month, payable until your circumstances take a turn for the better. Let me know what is happening, and where you and Favart are living. You know, madame, how I feel about you.[234]

Obviously, this was not pure disinterested generosity. Maurice was not above taking advantage of the Favarts' misfortunes; but it does not follow, as the champions of the Favarts would have us believe, that he was necessarily the author of them. Two weeks later he wrote from Dresden to Justine's mother:

> I have received, madame, the letter which you wrote to me on June 11th. I shall be very glad to help your son-in-law. He would find here in Dresden a safe asylum for as long as he desires. The king of Poland has several French pensioners, and I could, if your son wished, secure him honourable employment here. Men of a talent far inferior to his have made fortunes in Saxony. You may assuredly count on my lending him all the support in my power.[235]

This has been construed as a ruse on Maurice's part to get Favart out of France. Favart had, meanwhile, gone to earth in Strasbourg, where he began to issue furtive complaints of 'persecution' and 'tyranny'. After a pregnant pause, he finally named Maurice as the source of all his woes. It was a more romantic plea than bankruptcy.

Justine was so little persecuted at this time that she had completed a successful season at the *Comédie-Italienne*. As late as September, she was still unconcerned by Maurice's attentions, and wrote to tell her lurking husband:

> The Marshal is still furious with me. I do not care. There is talk of harming me, but I laugh at it. I would gladly come and beg in the streets with you. I told your mother and sister that the Marshal has offered to break off his affair with little Rivière, and indeed, he declares that he loves me more than ever.[236]

Soon afterwards, however, she was suddenly seized by two police agents and thrown into prison. It never occurred to her to blame Maurice for this. Indeed, sincerely convinced that it was her father who was at the bottom of this latest disaster, she appealed to Maurice for help.

She did not regard Maurice in any way as a persecutor. He had offered her a monthly allowance, presumably to induce her to become his mistress, and had offered to secure a post at Dresden for Favart, presumably to get him out of the way. This was not persecution: it was the well-known amatory combination of generosity and self-interest. It is highly unlikely that Maurice had bothered, as was later alleged, to seek out Justine's obscure parent and persuade him to apply for the *lettre de cachet* by which she had been detained. Such pettiness and personal deviousness was not in his nature; and besides, at this time he was still tolerably happy with Marie Rinteau. He was much too lacking in finesse to mount so sustained a conspiracy against a mere director of musical comedy: yet if Favart is to be believed, he was prepared to devote to the seduction of Justine the high abilities normally reserved for the overthrow of a Bergen or a Maastricht. He was manifestly incapable of such refinements in his personal affairs. In any case, Justine had never been any impregnable fortress.

It appears very likely that, while Favart was in hiding in Strasbourg, Justine became Maurice's mistress in Paris. Marmontel tells us that at this time the Marshal's favourite mistresses were two actresses, Chantilly (i.e. Justine) and Beauménard. He complained that their rivalry, jealousy and tantrums gave him 'more trouble than all the queen of Hungary's hussars'. Maurice, said Marmontel, soon 'grew angry with Chantilly', and the lady retired to Lunéville. Whether or not she had really sacrificed her virtue in order to save herself and her husband from Maurice's persecution will never be known: but it is true that the *lettre de cachet* was now revoked, and that Justine was permitted to go into exile at Issoudun, a town less than a hundred kilometres from Chambord. Next she was granted a series of monthly permits to allow her to absent herself from Issoudun: and it is easy to speculate where she spent this freedom. We also know that she sought her family's, even her husband's, sanction for her cohabitation with Maurice.

Everyone concerned was having a splendid time. Maurice had succeeded in enthroning his *petite fée*, as he called her, in his palace; the Favart family was enjoying the outrage to its honour; and Justine was probably queening it among the young officers at Chambord. The historians of the nineteenth century paid heavy-handed tribute to the bourgeois rectitude of the Favarts. '*Quel instinct des choses pures,*' exclaimed Taillandier of Justine: '*quel respect des devoirs et des émotions de la famille!*'[237] Assuredly Maurice was no saint, and does not come out of this unsavoury affair very well: but if one thing is equally certain, it is that Favart was not only hysterical, but a humbug. The real cause for regret is that Maurice, who in his youth had been the lover of Adrienne Lecouvreur, should have stooped in his declining years to the pursuit of Justine Chantilly. He had slithered down the slope from the sublime to the ridiculous. In his own person, he typified the emotional transition that had brought Frenchmen from *La Princesse de Clèves* to *Les Liaisons Dangereuses.* Maurice, like Don Giovanni, had come to see love as a vulgar act of conquest, a crude matter of numbers. Everything he had—his health, his reputation, his peace of mind—was sacrificed to the accumulation of a satisfactory tally. He was a collector. It did not matter to him that, in the words of Lord Chesterfield, 'the position is ridiculous, the pleasure momentary, and the expense damnable'. Like all collectors, he could never admit that his collection was even partially complete: he was driven onward by the ceaseless urge to acquire further specimens. And once the specimen had been deposited in the collection, it no longer interested him. It was the next, the unacquired piece, that aroused the anticipatory lust.

Many years before, François Premier had scratched with a diamond on the window of his study at Chambord—the room below Maurice's bedroom—the words: *Souvent femme varie, bien fol est qui s'y fie.* No woman could have been more inconstant than François Premier— or Maurice de Saxe.

Maurice's next visit to Dresden, in June 1749, was to be his last. He did not stay long. Prematurely old at fifty-three, enfeebled by ill-health, he was still restless and still ambitious: and still unemployed.

Shortly afterwards he went to Potsdam, where he stayed at Sans-Souci as the guest of another great soldier, Frederick of Prussia. Carlyle, no admirer of Maurice, has painted a characteristic picture of the last meeting of the two outstanding commanders of the age, adding his own jaundiced reflexions on Maurice's career.

In summer 1749, Maréchal de Saxe paid Frederick a visit; had the honour to be entertained by him three days (July 13-16, 1749) in his royal cottage of Sans-Souci seemingly, in his choicest manner. Curiosity, which is now nothing like so vivid as it then was, would be glad to listen a little, in this meeting of two Suns, or of one Sun and one immense Tar Barrel, or Atmospheric Meteor really of shining nature, and taken for a Sun. Of Saxe's Generalship, which is now a thing fallen pretty much into oblivion, I have no authority to speak. He had much wild natural ingenuity in him; cunning rapid whirls of contrivance; and gained Three Battles and very many Sieges, amidst the loudest clapping of hands that well could be. He had perfect intrepidity; not to be flurried by any amount of peril or confusion; looked on that English column, advancing on Fontenoy with its *feu infernal*, steadily through his perspective; chewing his leaden bullet: 'Going to beat me then? Well!' Nobody needed to be braver. He had great good nature, too, though of hot temper and so full of multifarious voracities; a substratum of inarticulate good sense withal, and much magnanimity run wild, or run to seed. A big-limbed, swashing, perpendicular kind of fellow; haughty of face, but jolly too; with a big, not ugly strut;—captivating to the French Nation, and fit God of War for that susceptible People. Understood their Army also, what it was then and there; and how, by theatricals and otherwise, to get a great deal of fire out of it. Great deal of fire;—whether by gradual conflagration or not; on the road to ruin or not; how, he did not care. In respect of military 'fame' so-called, he had the great advantage always of fighting against bad Generals, sometimes the very worst. To his fame an advantage; to himself and his real worth, far the reverse. Had he fallen in with a Friedrich, even with a Brown or a Traun, there might have been different news got. Friedrich is profuse in his eulogies, in his admiration of Saxe; amiable to see, and not insincere.[238]

Frederick the Great penned one of these eulogies in a letter to Voltaire the day before Maurice's departure.

I have been entertaining the hero of France, the Turenne of the age of Louis XV. I have derived much instruction from my conversations with him, not in speaking French but in the art of war. The Marshal should be the tutor of every general in Europe.[239]

Exactly a year later, Voltaire was himself a guest at Sans-Souci, and wrote to Argental that he was 'ashamed to have been given the apartment formerly occupied by the maréchal de Saxe. I do not know why a mere historian should be put in the room of a hero'.[240]

To most Europeans at the time, the meeting of these two German commanders, aglow with their respective applications of French polish, represented the communion of the two greatest military minds of the day. To Carlyle, with his passion for all things Prussian, it represented an unequal meeting between a true military genius, the serious Friedrich, and a military lightweight, the frivolous Saxe, who had set his army on 'the road to ruin'. Those of us who have survived into the second half of the twentieth century may perhaps be forgiven for finding the Saxon Tar Barrel rather more congenial than the Sun of Prussia.

CHAPTER XVII

STRASBOURG, 1750

Que du pauvre soldat, déplorable est la chance!
Quand la guerre finit, son malheur recommence.
FIN DES TRAVAUX DE MARS

ON his return from Berlin in 1749, Maurice resumed his life as ruler of Chambord. There remained to him only seventeen more months of life. These he proceeded to squander with the prodigality with which he had always consumed time, strength, talent and money.

To the very last, the cheerful but decrepit old Marshal never despaired of gaining an earthly crown. Kingdoms far more distant and fantastic than Courland continually beckoned to him. In 1748, as we know from Argenson's journal, he had petitioned Louis XV to grant to him the island of Madagascar, which he proposed to populate with German peasants. His request was seriously considered, and was not dismissed out of hand as impractical; but unfortunately Maurice ruined his chances by asking the hard-headed Compagnie des Indes for too much money and too many ships.

Undeterred, he next applied for the gift of the West Indian Island of Tobago. Once again, there was a real chance that the king might grant his request. Now that the war was over, there were many courtiers at Versailles who were only too eager to advise Louis to seize any opportunity of hastening Maurice's departure from the soil of France. In peacetime he was a nuisance, a standing reproach to a foolish treaty and an incompetent ministry. Once more, however, there were snags; and eventually Tobago, which had been by turns Spanish, British, Dutch and French, was restored to the United Provinces under the terms of the Peace of Aix-la-Chapelle, while Maurice's request was still on the *tapis*. Thus that very Peace which had already deprived him of his active command, and of his Commandant-Governorship of the Netherlands, now also robbed him of a chance of reigning in the Caribbean.

His questing mind then turned to other, no less fanciful projects. He planned an invasion of Corsica. He put forward the bizarre suggestion that he should transport a band of dispossessed Jews to the

New World, and there form them into a French colony under his control. It was a curious notion: but no one knew better than Maurice how often strange dreams can be translated into sober reality. The nineteenth century would see Portuguese emperors ruling Brazil, an Austrian archduke perched on the imperial throne of Mexico, and a family of English rajahs reigning in Sarawak. Was there therefore no scope, in the Americas of the 1750s, for a Jewish community ruled by the Lutheran Maurice de Saxe?

While he hared after these elusive prizes, the daily round at Chambord continued at the same dizzy pace. Sick though he was, Maurice did not brood on his imminent dissolution. He had always held to the view that life was for living, and he accordingly spent his last summer on earth in a manner worthy of his great father, Augustus the Strong. He threw himself into a frothy vortex of hunting parties, amorous debauchery, and extravagant amusements.

Valfons has left us a vivid glimpse of Maurice in the last months of his life. 'In 1749,' he records,

> I passed some time at Chambord. The Marshal lodged me in the room once occupied by Marie de Médicis, and for four days in succession the great man came to sit beside me, while I was still in bed, and recounted his campaigns in great detail, with all the charming frankness that was peculiarly his own. The château which the king had bestowed on him was altogether worthy of him. There he lived in princely style on the revenues of his rank and regiments, amounting to more than one hundred thousand *écus.* . . . His mental and physical activity required varied and continuous distraction, and while nursing vast and often chimaerical enterprises, he gave himself up to ceaseless diversions. He hunted, he supervised his estates, and above all he drilled the regiment which the king had allowed him as garrison, and which he kept on a war-footing, as though his château was indeed a fortress. This illusion was completed by the presence of captured cannon and standards draped over the doorways. There were ceaseless concerts and plays, either on the lake or else in his apartments. The Marshal was only fifty-three, and in spite of the physical pain which I often saw him endure with heroic courage, his vigorous will still made him brisk and indefatigable. No one would have believed, on seeing him so robust and active, so filled with the joy of being alive and still bursting with grandiose plans, that he was on the verge of the grave.[241]

In his capacity of elder statesman, Maurice was still occasionally consulted by the War Ministry. In March 1750 he went to Paris, and was lodged in the *Invalides,* in order to examine the various methods of drill that had been adopted by certain enthusiastic young colonels. The Ministry wanted to establish a reasonable degree of uniformity, and units which practised contrasting styles were paraded for Maurice's inspection. The *Gardes-français,* the regiments of the comte de Maillebois and the duc de Broglie, and the *Régiments de Beauvoisis* and *d'Alsace* performed their various evolutions before him. Afterwards he submitted his verdict in a report to the comte d'Argenson. All the detachments, he said, had adopted some practices which might with advantage be copied throughout the army. The traditional drills employed by the *Gardes* and the *Régiment de Beauvoisis* were impressive, but in the last analysis, Maurice considered, the newfangled methods of Broglie's regiment and the *Régiment d'Alsace*, both adopted from the Prussian model, were most to be commended. His only criticism of the latter was that both regiments had discarded the long musket, which he liked, for the new short model.

He prepared two further reports for Argenson.[242] The first set out to challenge, in an unequivocal manner, a cherished tradition against which he had long battled in vain. This was what he termed the 'obstinate practice', stemming from the victorious campaigns of the previous century, of compelling the French front rank to remain motionless while the enemy advanced towards it and fired the first volley. It was still an article of faith with French commanders that this display of cold courage struck a fatal fear into the hearts of the enemy. 'Good God!' commented Maurice, 'what a way to win a battle, when you have to pay for your laurels with so much blood!' He argued that it was downright stupid to suppose that the French infantry would be any less brave if they were allowed to fire first. He insisted that they were being cruelly sacrificed to a ridiculous tradition. Writing with feeling, for this foolish practice had nearly cost him the battle of Fontenoy, he urged the adoption of a tactic already successfully employed by the Prussians. The infantry could advance and fire an initial volley, then advance and fire again. This system could exploit to the full the pugnacity of the French footsoldier. He added as a rider that it was absurd to compel regimental officers to stand out in front of their men when volleys were exchanged, a practice which was doubtless impressive, but which turned them into sitting targets. Maurice wanted to see the officers take their place in the line, in direct control of their men.

It is interesting that Maurice should have ended his life as an admirer of the school of Prussia. He had been forced to admit that his friend Frederick the Great had been able, by his combined authority as king and commander-in-chief, to introduce many of the reforms that had been dear to his own heart, and which had been stoutly resisted in France. Although he was always more cautious than such uncritical Prussophiles as Belle-Isle, he knew that a major reform of the French army, along Prussian lines, was long overdue. He foresaw that France's enemies would be mightily disconcerted if, when the next war broke out, they found the French advancing upon them in full possession of modern techniques of warfare instead of the antiquated techniques which their enemies had come to expect. And what, by contrast, would happen if the French army, in its present form, were to encounter a Prussian-trained enemy using just the kind of devastating rolling fire which he was himself advocating? The Prussian army of 1750 undoubtedly deserved Maurice's praise. Frederick had pioneered a number of masterly gambits, including the use of horse-drawn artillery, and the celebrated order of march by which he could bring his men into battle-line simply by turning his column to the right and executing a left-wheel by platoons. Above all, Frederick had introduced the famous oblique order, by means of which, on three occasions, he had thrashed a far superior enemy force. This oblique order has best been described as essentially an advance of one wing by échelons with refusal of the other, the second covering the withdrawal of the first. It was this manoeuvre which had often enabled Frederick to fall with all his force on the chosen flank of the enemy, establishing a local superiority before going on to roll up the entire enemy line. This novel practice, which reproduced in brilliantly concentrated form the laborious processes of the old out-flanking movement, had eliminated much of the butchery associated with conventional frontal attacks. It therefore had a powerful appeal for 'economical' generals of the stamp of Maurice, and it was in a spirit of humanity as much as of efficiency that he tried to commend it to his French *confrères*.

In August 1750, Maurice paid his last visit to Versailles, to attend the *accouchement* of his niece, the Dauphine. She brought her first child, Marie-Zéphirine, into the world with much pain, and at one stage was not expected to live. Writing afterwards from Chambord, Maurice reported to her father that:

> her gentleness, constancy and courage drew upon her the affection of the king and the whole court. The king held her hand during the delivery, and one might almost say that she gave birth in his arms. He sweated profusely. It was a very hot day, and the number of people in the room made the atmosphere intolerable. I persuaded the king and queen to banish everyone from the room for nine days, which greatly relieved madame la Dauphine. None the less, there was a general outcry against it, as it was against etiquette, and had never been done before. My principal thought was of the danger of infection to a woman in childbirth, as everyone smelled to high heaven in a greater or lesser degree. Everyone's clothes were impregnated with odours, even though they swore to the contrary. However, God be thanked, madame la Dauphine is now quite well, and still able to give France a great number of princes and princesses.[243]

Maria Josepha was in fact to present France with eleven more infants, including three future kings, Louis XVI, Louis XVIII and Charles X.

In the same letter, Maurice informed King Augustus of his amusements in recent weeks. He gave news of the two French dancers whom the king had sent back from Dresden to Paris 'to improve their skill'. 'I saw,' confided Maurice,

> Little Rivière dance at the Comédie-française. She was accorded a splendid ovation. In the short time that she has been here, she has already made perceptible improvement, as Your Majesty will find; Maltoire is the best coach imaginable. If Your Majesty lets her stay here this winter, she will make an admirable dancer. . . . As for Mlle Favier, I do not know how she is faring, and her mother is an idiot who undoes all Maltoire's good work. She is discontented, dislikes work, and wastes time.

Maurice then proceeded to describe what was to be his last house-party at Chambord.

> Mme de Sens has come to spend part of the autumn with me here at Chambord. She has brought with her a selection of ladies from court. I shall entertain them with hunts, plays and balls. I have waylaid the troop of performers who have been playing at Compiègne, and will feed them forcibly on venison and boar. I imagine that the ladies will be tolerably happy here. My officers are all handpicked; they are young, handsome, and have been shut up like monks. One would really have to go a long way to find things more satisfactorily arranged. The scandal-mongers have already begun to talk. Let them say what they like: the women are already on the way! I suppose Your Majesty will think that I am only behaving in the way which one would expect. So be it! It is the fate of an old coachman to love the sound of the whip. Pity all sinners! If I desire pleasure, why should it be wrong? But I write in this strain only to make Your Majesty chuckle. The women are wise enough. They enjoy laughter, nothing worse.

The Duke of Wellington, who was godfather to Queen Victoria's third son, liked to toboggan round the corridors of Stratfieldsaye on a tea-tray, drawn by a team of young women. Maurice de Saxe preferred more spectacular performances. We will never now know the precise forms which his indulgences with Mme de Sens and her court beauties assumed, but we do know that his consequent exertions killed him. In the very middle of a protracted orgy, in which copulation alternated with military parades, the old coachman finally dropped off the box. Towards the end of November, 1750, he was confined to bed with a severe chill, after what may well have been a stroke. He refused all food, dosing himself instead with his remedy for all physical ills: copious potations of rough cider. But the chill grew worse, and eventually turned into a 'putrid fever'.

Alarmed, his regimental doctor hurriedly sent to Paris for the faithful Sénac de Meilhan. When the latter arrived at Chambord, he realized at once that the case was hopeless; there was nothing to be done. Löwendahl arrived hot on Sénac's heels, and in his excitable manner contrived to raise the temperature in the sick-room even higher. Even as the princesse de Sens was shepherding her frightened flock away from the stricken château, Marshal Löwendahl was marching up and down at the foot of Maurice's bed, urging him to repent his sins and to be received into the Roman church. The facile Löwendahl had always made a practice of adopting the religion of his current paymasters, easily convincing himself on each occasion that he had finally found the one true faith. He had been a Lutheran in Saxony, a Moslem at Constantinople, a member of the Orthodox Church in Russia; and when Louis XV had indicated that it might strengthen his prospects in France if he became a Roman Catholic, the amiable Dane had promptly complied. He now regarded Romanism as a panacea on a par with rough cider, and during the course of this unusual death-bed scene played a vigorous Leporello to Maurice's equally vigorous Don Giovanni.

Even on his death-bed, Maurice refused to take the road to Rome. He rebuked his former lieutenant with good humour, observing that since they had never quarrelled before it would be a great pity to fall out at so late a stage in their friendship. He clung fast to his own brand of Lutheranism to the very end; but as he had not shown any very remarkable piety during the years of his health and good fortune, he thought, like the gentleman he was, that it would be unbecoming to make a display of religion at the last.

In any case, the old hedonist's mind was fixed less on the life to come than on the life which he was about to leave. He had led a rich life. The world had furnished him with almost all that he had desired; and he may have feared that the next world, in which there would probably be no place for either fighting or fornicating, would be far duller than this one. His only expression of regret on his death-bed was characteristic of a man who had devoted most of his life to the pleasures of the flesh: he remarked that he was sorry that he had been unable to cram in a few more bouts of pleasure before death claimed him at a relatively early age.

Life had been sweet; it had been good to him; and he was most reluctant to leave it. There were only two personal ambitions that he had not achieved. As a foreigner and a Lutheran, he had been unable to extract from Louis XV the order of the *Saint-Esprit*; and he had been unable to gain a crown. For a kingdom in this world, he would gladly have traded the kingdom of Heaven. But he was in no way discontented. As death approached, he turned and murmured a few graceful and dignified words to Sénac: '*Je vois que la vie,*' he sighed, '*n'est qu'un songe; le mien a été beau, mais il est court.*'

He died on November 30th, 1750, between six and seven in the morning. The officers of his regiment promptly broke their staffs of office, and the six cannon outside the *cour d'honneur* began to fire a salute at intervals of fifteen minutes. The thudding tribute continued day and night for thirty days.

When the news reached Versailles, the pious queen, Marie Leczinska, paid a generous tribute to the son of her father's old enemy. 'It is a pity,' she remarked, 'that Catholic France cannot say a *De profundis* for the repose of the soul of one who has so often caused the nation to sing a *Te Deum.*'

The Pompadour's reaction fitly expressed the rough tenderness of ordinary people. 'Poor Saxe,' she said, 'has died in his bed like any old woman, believing nothing and hoping for nothing.'

The French people may well have thought that the manner of Maurice's death was something of an anticlimax. He should have died like Turenne. But they must have consoled themselves with the thought that, after all, he had finally succumbed, as the editor of his despatches was to put it, from *un excès avec des femmes*. It had been an end only a shade less glorious to a Frenchman than death in action —a very acceptable second-best. Some people, indeed, sceptical that so perturbed a spirit could yield up the ghost so peaceably, actually put it about that Maurice had been killed in a duel. Argenson hinted as much in his journal only three days after Maurice's death; and according to a story which was still circulating in the neighbourhood of Chambord a century later, Maurice had been slain at a chance encounter in the woods by his old adversary Conti. Such *canards* were patently absurd, and were probably invented by local wiseacres to explain the muffled and mysterious goings-on that concluded Maurice's individual tenancy of the great château. The events of his last days had been so extraordinary that it would hardly have been surprising if the women at Chambord had behaved, after his death, as the kitchen maids at the château in which Casanova died were reputed to have done—crept up the back-stairs to his bedroom and, giggling and greatly daring, rolled up the dead man's nightshirt to see for themselves what the lifelong fuss had all been about.

The marble-topped table on which Maurice's body was laid out may still be seen at Chambord in the room in which he died. The château was looted by the mob at the Revolution, and nothing now survives of the Marshal-General's régime except this table and a vast stove of Meissen ware in the *cour d'honneur*.

The king and his ministers were hard put to decide what to do with the body. No doubt some of Maurice's enemies would have liked, now that he was at last at their mercy, that his remains should share the fate of those of Adrienne Lecouvreur. His friends, on the other hand, ignoring the religious issue, urged that his bones should be brought to Paris to lie beside those of Turenne.

Louis hit upon a judicious compromise between anonymous burial and apotheosis. He directed that Maurice's body should be buried, according to Lutheran rites, in Protestant Strasbourg, the capital of that province of Alsace of which Maurice had nominally been the governor for the past two years. And so it was. There has never been any adequate memorial to Maurice in the Paris that he loved so much, and served so well, other than the walk from the *Invalides* along the *avenue de Loewendahl* to the *avenue de Saxe* and the *place Fontenoy*.

Maurice had directed in his will that his body should be buried in quicklime, 'so that in a short time nothing more of me may remain in the world but my memory among my friends'. His request was ignored, for it was not fitting that so great a man should be buried in so poor a fashion. Moreover the penniless military adventurer had died in unexpected affluence, despite the reckless extravagance of his entire life, and his testamentary bequests were both lavish and extensive. To his Saxon executor, the cup-bearer to the king of Poland, he left his famous diamond ring 'Prague', which later came into the possession of his nephew Friesen. To his French executor he bequeathed a thousand *louis d'or*, and he also gave a similar sum to each of the four principal officers of his regiment, all of whom 'had followed my fortunes for a long time'; the colonel, indeed, was that same Dieskau who had once risked his life for Maurice before the Polish Diet at Grodno. His faithful valet Beauvais, who had served him for over thirty years and had escaped with him from Courland, inherited five hundred *louis*. Altogether, over twenty people received substantial legacies, including his grooms, his drum-major, his surgeon, and the gentleman of his horse. The residuary legatee was a certain Louise de Metzerat, about whom nothing is known.[244]

For five weeks the body remained at Chambord. Then the heart was removed and embalmed and placed in a silver-gilt box, and the entrails were extracted for separate interment. The corpse was next placed in a triple coffin of lead, copper and wood. On January 8th, 1751, Maurice de Saxe crossed the parade-ground at Chambord for the last time, his body drawn by six black horses and escorted by a hundred Uhlans. Owing to bad weather, the journey to Strasbourg lasted almost a month. Finally, on February 7th, the cortège made a ceremonial entry into the ancient capital of Alsace.

There was much characteristic eighteenth-century funereal pomp. Cannon thundered from the ramparts, church bells tolled, the streets were lined by soldiers. The garrison of the city, the Clermont dragoons, who had fought well for Maurice in Flanders, turned out to accompany the Governor of Alsace to his castle.

> The Counts Friesen and Löwenhaupt, nephews of M. de Saxe, were in long cloaks; M. de Saint-André, and several other general officers, attended in the court of the castle to receive the body, and remained there till it was placed by ten gunners on a bed of state dressed on purpose for it . . . with a grand imperial of black velvet faced with gold and silver, and adorned with fringes of the same. . . . The hall was hung with black from top to bottom, and adorned with different emblems, military trophies, death's heads, tears and marshals' staffs, tied salterwise with a ribbon of the White Eagle and the arms of Saxony and Courland. Under the Imperial, at the head of the coffin, were placed a ducal crown, on a cushion of black velvet, the marshal's staffs set across and tied with the ribbon of the White Eagle, his sword with a gold hilt, with the scabbard salterwise and the whole covered with fine crêpe.[245]

Strasbourg spared no expense to honour its dead governor and co-religionist. The birthplace of Kléber, Kellerman and Desaix has always had a rare appreciation of a good soldier. No more fitting resting-place for the Marshal-General could have been decreed. Many of those who had served in his two regiments had been Alsatian in origin; and the citizens of Strasbourg, like Maurice himself had always held fast to their Lutheran faith, their splendid city, Erasmus' *urbs omnium pulcherrima*, being an early outpost of the Reformation. Maurice had always had a special affection for Strasbourg, not merely as a favourite recruiting centre, not because the unique love of his life had been the most celebrated actress who had ever adorned its stage, not even because he had lately been Governor of Alsace, but because it had been from Strasbourg that he had once set out, across the *pont de Kehl*, on the first of his major campaigns.

Next day, his body was taken from the castle to the church of St. Thomas. The funeral was an impressive ceremony. The coffin was borne by twelve sergeants and preceded by two of Maurice's officers, one of them bearing the ducal crown of Courland, the other the casket containing his heart. Behind the coffin walked noblemen, magistrates and other provincial dignitaries, among them that same Klinglin who had also once loved Adrienne. Inside the church, even the ceiling was hung with black, and the windows were blacked out

in order to create an impression of night. The gloom was illuminated
by a vast number of tapers.

> In the pulpit, behind the preacher, were placed the arms of Saxony
> and Courland. A great black velvet carpet was spread on the altar,
> likewise laced with silver. At the head of the catafalque was the rep-
> resentation of Death with a scythe; and at his foot stood Saturn. Four
> virtues were at the four corners, with Genii who wept. The whole
> adorned with casques, bucklers, cuirasses and laurel-branches.[246]

The service itself included anthems, 'two elegant discourses', and
a 'doleful symphony'. Twelve great cannon boomed out three separate
salvoes; the assembled troops let fly a crackling volley of small-arms
fire; and to the sound of gunfire the coffin was lowered into its grave.

Maurice lies buried near the heart of the old city, not far from the
quais. The church of St. Thomas is close to the quarter known as *La
Petite France*, and today this district is especially remarkable for its
excellent eating-places; its restaurants are filled with the sound of
music, with the odour of *choucroute garnie*, with the tang of
foaming *chopines*. Maurice would have approved of all this. He might
even have been amused to learn that his tomb is within a stone's
throw of the headquarters of the Society for the Redemption of the
Victims of Intemperance.

Maurice's fame was not diminished in France until the extinction
of the social order of which he had been so distinguished an orna-
ment. As late as thirty years after his death, a large congregation
drawn from all corners of France assembled at Strasbourg, in the
church of St. Thomas, to pay tribute to his memory. The occasion
was the unveiling in 1777 of his huge marble tomb, on which
France's leading sculptor, Pigalle, had long laboured. Pigalle was
still young when Maurice had died, but by the time his master-
piece had at last been finished and transported from his studio in
Paris to its resting-place at Strasbourg, he was already an old man.
Towering and ornate, the monument occupies the central position in
the church, as often happened in Protestant churches at that time.
It completely dwarfs the altar, which stands modestly before it. The
spectator may be forgiven for supposing, when he first enters the
shrine, that a Christian shrine has been converted into a temple of
Mars. Maurice, clad in armour and adorned by the sash of the White
Eagle of Poland, stands at the apex of the monument, his right hand
negligently holding the baton of a Marshal of France. At his feet
crouches an ample-bosomed wench, appropriately symbolizing
Marianne, who is striving to prevent death from opening the tomb

MAURICE DE SAXE

Enlargement of a medal probably struck to commemorate the unveiling
of his monument by Pigalle at Strasbourg in 1777

which, as yet, the Marshal-General does not deign to enter. Beneath her Hercules, symbolizing Maurice's almost legendary strength, leans on his knotty club; while a plump Cupid hovers behind, understandably overcome by sorrow. The emblems of Maurice's defeated enemies, the English leopard, the Dutch lion, and the Austrian eagle, tumble and writhe among their tattered banners. At the foot of the monument, an achievement of arms bears testimony to Maurice's origin.

Under this great pile of masonry the *ancien régime* finally disposed of Maurice, one of its most ardent and embarrassing champions. It only survived him by forty years.

Contemplating that boldly erect white figure, one may recall Baudelaire's description of Don Juan's voyage to the shades:

> *Tout droit dans son armure, un grand homme de pierre*
> *Se tenait à la barre et coupait le flot noir;*
> *Mais le calme héros, courbé sur sa rapière,*
> *Regardait le sillage et ne daignait rien voir.*

MES REVERIES, 1757

*'Is this a fit time,' said my father to himself, 'to talk of
Pensions and Grenadiers?'*

TRISTRAM SHANDY

THE eccentric voluptuary who had been buried in 1751 was not the
whole man. In spite of his odd notions and fantastic ambitions, his
flamboyance and extravagance, he had been one of the greatest
generals of the eighteenth century.

In death, as in life, he suffered his detractors. Carlyle was one of
the most remorseless of them. 'It is certain,' thundered the Sage of
Chelsea,

> that the French army reaped no profit from its experience of Marechal
> de Saxe, and the high theatricalities, ornamental blackguardisms, and
> ridicule of life and death. In the long run a graver face would have
> been of better augury. King Friedrich's soldiers, one observes, on the
> eve of battle, settle their bits of worldly business; and wind up, many
> of them, with a hoarse whisper of prayer. Oliver Cromwell's soldiers
> did so; Gustav Adolf's; in fact, I think all good soldiers.[247]

Carlyle was wrong. Plenty of foul-mouthed, blasphemous, hard-
drinking, cynical and cruel men have made good soldiers. Maurice
was freer, perhaps freer than Carlyle's King Friedrich, from the worst
of these qualities. But it is true that he was a very showy kind of
general. On the other hand, he indulged in the high theatricalities
that displeased Carlyle for a sound and deliberate reason: because he
knew that they inspired and appealed to the French armies that he
led. The colourful nature of his methods ought not to make one suppose that they were therefore superficial. He knew that his men
fought not for the glory of God, but for the glory of France. More
important, he was able to communicate to them the sense that he,
like themselves, had a direct personal stake in the outcome of each
campaign. He fired them with his own personal conviction that glory
was not an abstraction, but a visible, tactile, golden substance to be
picked up only within the muddy ambit of a battlefield.

He also gave them the feeling that he cared about them. He did not strike them as the sort of man who would cast an indifferent eye on the mounds of dead, as Napoleon did after Eylau, and remark: *Ces sont de la petite espèce.* He had a paternal figure, and lived among them, joining them early in the season and leaving them late, if indeed he left them at all. He knew, with the Comte de Ségur, that 'miseries seem light to a soldier if the chief who imposes hardships on him also volunteers to share them'.[248] Not only did Maurice share their hardships, but their dangers also: and he had wounds on his body to prove it. Nor did his lust for pleasure lessen his prestige in the sight of his men. It seemed to them a positive virtue, a guarantee that he was on the side of life and not death. He was a virile, prodigal, hard-living and hard-dying man of their own stamp.

His concern for the welfare of his men was as old as his experience of warfare. The opening chapter of his *Rêveries*, written when he was in his early thirties, though not published until seven years after his death, contains two long sections devoted to the clothing and feeding of the infantryman alone.

In his ideal army, the diet and apparel of the footsoldier were to be revolutionized. 'Our present dress,' he wrote,

> is not only too expensive, but inconvenient, no part of it being made to answer the end required. The love of appearance prevails over a due regard to health, which is one of the major points demanding our attention.[249]

He recommended that, instead of the towering headdresses of the period, infantrymen should wear light helmets, proof against sword blows. They were to be given Prussian-style doublets and Turkish-style cloaks which, hooded and reaching to the calf, would be waterproof and could easily be carried in a knapsack. The familiar white leggings of the period were to be abolished as 'inconvenient, hurtful, of no real use, and very expensive'. Maurice also advocated supple, tallow-greased shoes, supplemented by wooden galoshes for the winter season. And he had strong views on the elaborate military coiffure then in vogue, arguing that it encouraged disease and dirt. In its place, he wished to introduce close-cropped hair covered by a small wig of wiry Spanish wool.

His projected reforms in cavalry dress were also prompted by efficiency rather than appearance. He had specially designed a light cuirass, weighing less than thirty pounds; and, as with the infantry, he again advised that a sensible lightweight helmet should be introduced. This strangely shaped helmet seems to have been modelled upon the mediaeval Polish *Flügelhelm*, a specimen of which had certainly been preserved in the royal armoury at Warsaw.[250] It will be seen from Plate 4 that the cavalryman of his dreams closely resembled one's notion of the appearance of Don Quixote; although his ideas of dress were taken less from the Knight of the Woeful Countenance than from the lean and speedy horsemen whom he had led or fought against on the wide flat plains of eastern Europe. He proposed to arm his cavalrymen with a type of short-barrelled, rifled carbine with which he had been experimenting, with twelve-foot lances, and with swords designed for pointing and not cutting.

Every paragraph of the *Rêveries* testifies to a powerful intelligence trained in a severe and practical school. Why, then, should its author have chosen to call so down-to-earth a treatise by so whimsical a name? The answer is that the word *rêveries* did in fact denote his cherished dreams: dreams which one day he hoped to clothe with reality. The book enshrined those flights of fancy which were never wholly divorced from his diurnal activities. The reader may recall that the book was written in the winter of 1732, during a period of temporarily enforced idleness. In May of that year his father, Augustus the Strong, had consulted him in the most flattering terms with regard to a number of technical points concerning the use of cavalry, no doubt as the result of one of the periodical attempts which the King made to woo him back into Saxon service. Accordingly Maurice spent the following August in Poland in an intensive investigation into the state of his father's army. It seems likely that he wrote an official report at the end of his tour of inspection, and later, on his return to Paris, worked it up into the vivid and prophetic pages of *Mes Rêveries*.[251] The vestigial remains of such a report can still be discerned within the bulk of the book.

The Polish report had been useful; *Mes Rêveries* was a military classic. But Maurice was never to be given the opportunity—in Poland, in Saxony, or in France—to put together his new model army. As a relatively humble regimental commander, the owner of the *Régiment Greder* and of his own cavalry regiment, he was able to make certain minor alterations in dress and drill;[252] but once he had risen to the rank of general he was automatically prohibited, by the dead hand of military tradition, from tampering with the time-honoured practices of the armies of France. The number and composition of the French regiment and squadron remained the same during his thirty years of service, until the warning note sounded by the Seven Years War tempted Broglie and Choiseul to pioneer the concept of the division, and Gribeauval, following Lavallière, to overhaul the theory and practice of the artillery. Had Maurice been a native Frenchman like Louvois, or an autocrat like Frederick the Great, he would have stood a greater chance of being given his head; but as a foreign mercenary, dependent at every stage on the favour of the court, he discovered that even a Marshal-General was not free to carry out any far-reaching reforms. All his life he was fettered by the 'slavish adherence to custom' of which he complained, at the outset of his career, in *Mes Rêveries*. After his death, it was the precepts of his fellow German, Frederick of Prussia, whom his adopted country-men would follow in making radical changes in their military manual. Although Maurice had given certain aspects of the Prussian system his qualified approval during his lifetime, for the French as for most European armies the benefits of that system were to prove somewhat mixed. Indeed, it seems fair to say that the achievements of Frederick himself were not, on balance, notably more startling than those effected by Maurice with the obsolescent means at his disposal.

The first section of *Mes Rêveries* is devoted to Maurice's conception of the perfect army. As his basic formation he chose the Roman legion, a predilection no doubt inspired by the *Epitome rei militaris* of the celebrated Flavius Renatus Vegetius. This seminal work greatly influenced Machiavelli's *Arte della Guerra*, and provided the frame-work of the important military reforms of Francis I and Maurice of Nassau. By the time that Maurice de Saxe began to study the *Epitome*, it had already been thumbed through by European com-manders for over three hundred years, losing none of its potency in the process. In fact the ground plan of *Mes Rêveries* seems roughly to conform to the five books of the *Epitome*, a sure indication that Maurice privately nursed the highest ambitions for his own work and was not ashamed to invite comparisons with that of the renowned Vegetius.

His regiment or legion was to consist of four centuries of infantry, a half-century of light-armed foot, and half a century of horse. It would total eight hundred and eighty-two men. On the parade ground it would be drawn up in the customary four ranks: but the arrangements for its disposition in the field were highly unconven-tional. Maurice's diagrams show the heavy infantry placed in single or double rank with half-centuries of light skirmishers grouped in front to cover them. Gaps would be left in the lines of heavy infantry in order that the skirmishers, after they had blunted the edge of the enemy attack by opening fire at three hundred paces, could fall back safely to the rear. This plan, which scrapped the hitherto sacred doctrine of the single continuous line of infantry, was little short of revolutionary.

Further, Maurice decided to break up his infantry formations even more drastically by placing units of light artillery at intervals between them. The light guns, nine feet in length, were like modern bazookas, and were his own invention. He called them *amusettes,* and each of his four centuries in the regiment were to be provided with one of these handy and deadly little 'toys' or 'playthings'. They could fire a half-pound shot at a rate of nearly four to the minute and had a range of over three thousand paces— three times as far as that of any existing artillery. Finally, small groups of infantry were to be placed thirty paces behind the main body, whose flanks would be protected by bristling hedgehogs of pikemen formed in square, each of them a kind of human redoubt.

The object of this unorthodox formation was to provide every soldier in the army with the sense that he was firmly supported, whether in advance or in retreat. 'I am persuaded,' wrote Maurice, 'that unless troops are properly supported in action, they will be defeated': a military truism, but one too often forgotten, even in more recent times. Every unit was to gain confidence and cohesion from a sense of mutual reliance. In particular, the half-centuries of horse would consist of seasoned, hand-picked men whom the infantry could trust to stand firm in any emergency. 'As a fortifier of morale,' observes Liddell Hart,

> an immediate and visible form of support is infinitely more efficacious than a distant and unseen one. Few have grasped more clearly than Saxe how delicately is poised the balance between the will to go forward and the instinct to seek safety in flight, and that confidence and its decline is most often the deciding factor in the scales. Nothing strengthens confidence more than the feeling of close support. His solution, in those pre-tank days, was to place small bodies of heavily-armed cavalry close *in rear* of the infantry between his cavalry wings— a strong contrast to the practice of his age, which was to place all the infantry in the centre and all the cavalry on the wings, each sustained only by itself.[253]

In this desire to take into account the functioning under the pressure of combat of the minds and emotions of his men, Maurice was far in advance of his age. 'The human heart,' he affirmed, 'is fundamental in all matters pertaining to war.' Long before Clausewitz or Ardant du Picq, Maurice had pondered deeply on the mysterious, often fatal, shifts of an army's collective will during battle. In this respect he would have found himself able to agree with Clausewitz that the task was to kill the opponent's nerve, not his men, that 'the will is central, standing like an obelisk towards which the principal streets of a town converge'.[254] Maurice had discussed with Villars and Schulenburg (both of whom had had painful experience of the problem) the nature of those disturbing psychological spasms which can throw into utter confusion an army seemingly poised on the brink of victory. The disposition of forces which he evolved in *Mes Rêveries* was his principal solution to this fundamental problem, and the way in which he formed up his regiments at Fontenoy showed how prepared he was to translate his theory of 'close support' into effective practice. It can indeed be argued that it was precisely this disposition of his forces, based on psychological considerations, that enabled the French to survive the paralysing moment when their centre caved in beneath the pressure of the British and Hanoverian infantry. At that point in the battle the enemy assumed that the day was theirs, that the French were about to break and flee. Yet there had been no general panic of the type that had turned Dettingen into a rout. When the crisis occurred, Maurice's hard-tried infantry, unlike their predecessors on the previous occasion, sensed that they were being adequately shielded by the battalions to the left and right of them. Secure in that knowledge, they were able to summon up a reserve of courage and determination.

Machiavelli had argued that a commander's ability to maintain discipline was directly related to the size of his army. He had suggested that 50,000 was the optimum number. Maurice concurred in this view. He had often seen small armies conquer far larger ones, particularly during his campaigns against the Turks. The Turkish army, he asserted, was defective neither in 'courage, numbers, nor resources, but only in discipline and order'. At this epoch, it was unusual to view the contribution of the Turks to warfare with such respect.

> 'At the battle of Peterwardein,' said Maurice, 'the Turks had above 100,000 men; we had only 40,000, and defeated them. At the battle of Belgrade, they had more than double their former number; we not 30,000, but won again. This will always be the result of their battles as long as they depend on mere numbers instead of skilful management.'

It was doubtless this overriding desire to command compact and controllable units of men that led to his advocacy of the compactly designed legion. He once declared that he could have subjugated the whole of Poland with a force of only forty thousand soldiers.

The use of the word 'legion' by Maurice was, of course, figurative. His legion was to consist of less than nine hundred men, whereas the classic Roman legion in the time of Julius Caesar was three thousand strong, and in the late imperial period often swelled to twice that number. What Maurice sought to re-capture was the legion's essential structure: a self-contained infantry force supported by its own cavalry formation. In fact, although his model was ostensibly classical, his interpretation of the legionary formation and his predilection for a small army were influenced less by the ancient Romans than by the Swedes of Gustavus Adolphus' day. There is a striking resemblance between the formations advocated by Maurice and the formations

perfected by Gustavus Adolphus at the beginning of the Thirty Years
War. In 1625, the great Swede adopted a regiment of 1008 men, consisting of eight companies of 126 men apiece. His rivals clung to
regiments of two to three thousand men apiece, and although the bulk
of such regiments was certainly more classical in practice, they were
infinitely harder to manoeuvre than their new Swedish counterparts.
Maurice's legion was smaller even than the legion of Gustavus, consisting of 882 men in four centuries of 184 men. To this total must
be added the supernumerary horse. Gustavus' cavalry regiment had
consisted of eight companies of 66-72 men, 528-576 in all; Maurice's
proposal was for four squadrons of 134 men, totalling 536.

Maurice was intimately acquainted with all the phases of Gustavus'
career. Had not Old Königsmarck been one of Gustavus' most
illustrious marshals? The only two authorities whom Maurice
explicitly acknowledged in *Mes Rêveries* were Gustavus and the Im-
perialist general Montecucculi (1609-1681), Turenne's famous
adversary. Gustavus was the more significant. His success with a
small, sternly disciplined army, fired by an indestructible *esprit de
corps*, had provided a fresh point of departure for military thinking.
The part which Gustavus' techniques played in winning the Great
Rebellion for the English Parliamentarians is very well known. By
the late seventeenth century, however, they had largely fallen into
desuetude on the orderly battlefields of western Europe, although
they still held sway on the more fluid battlegrounds of the east, where
they were practiced in his youth by Charles XII and his generals,
from whom Maurice had a direct experience of them.

It was not lost on Maurice, even in his prentice years, that the
Swedes, adhering to the methods of Gustavus, had twice succeeded
in subjugating half Europe. And although Gustavus had not brigaded
part of his cavalry with his foot regiments, as Maurice was to advocate, he had anticipated Maurice's desire to provide 'close support'
by forming his infantry in the so-called 'Swedish Cross'. His aim had
been to mingle musketeers and pikemen in such a way that the fire
of the former protected the latter. The 'Swedish Cross' was the first
systematic application of the principle of enfilade fire, and it quite
clearly served as the starting point for much of Maurice's military
theorizing. Ironically enough, it was Schulenburg, a worshipper of
Gustavus' memory, who practised this same system with devastating
effect against the Swedes themselves, when he was putting up such
a splendid fight against Charles XII on behalf of Augustus the Strong
when Maurice was a boy at Dresden. At Fontenoy, it was to be the
enfilade fire from the *redoute d'Eu*, and from the heavily fortified
village of Fontenoy itself, that eventually overwhelmed the British
and Hanoverian infantry.

It might not be too much to claim that it was Maurice who reintroduced into the western theatre of war the fructifying principles of Gustavus. We also have Frederick the Great's personal testimony that it was Maurice who taught him most of what he knew about the art of waging war. Thus we can discern the importance of Maurice de Saxe as the link between the two outstanding military figures of the seventeenth century (in which he was born) and of the mid-eighteenth (in which he died).

We cannot leave *Mes Rêveries* without mentioning Maurice's conception of the rôle in warfare of the redoubt, which he championed with truly fanatical enthusiasm against the contemporary dogma of the entrenchment. Entrenchments he regarded as absolute death traps. He claimed that he owed his insight into the infinitely richer potentialities of the redoubt from studying the clever way in which the Russians had used them at the battle of Poltava. Before Poltava, the Russians fought from entrenchments in the usual manner: and Maurice pointed out that it was nothing for ten or twelve thousand Swedes to assault trenches held by fifty to eighty thousand Russians and quickly overrun them. At Poltava, however, the Russians tried a new gambit. The night before the battle, they erected seven stout wooden redoubts in front of their main body of infantry, and furnished each of them with a garrison of two battalions. They thus made it extremely hazardous for the Swedes to try to charge in among the enemy infantry without first carrying the redoubts, which could neither be avoided nor circumvented because of the nature of the terrain. 'The King of Sweden and his generals,' stated Maurice, 'remained totally ignorant of this disposition, till the moment when they saw it; but the machine, as it were, having been once put in motion, it was now impossible to stop it.' After colossal efforts, the Swedes managed to carry three of the redoubts, but failed to take the other four. As a result, they were unable to break through and come to grips with the Russian centre. They were finally defeated.

Maurice calculated that one of his legions could throw up an impregnable redoubt in a matter of five hours. His treatment of a closely related subject, that of the fortress, was really a logical extension of his attitude to the redoubt. He detested the traditional reliance, exemplified by practically all the generals of his generation, on the fortified town, and advanced invincible arguments to show that such reliance was foolish. He pointed out that fortified towns were often wrongly sited from the strategic viewpoint; that they were usually under-provisioned; and that they were always handicapped by the presence of a large civilian population. In demonstrating how few of them were constructed to withstand long sieges, he did not scruple to criticize the two most venerated military architects of the day.

'I am not to be imposed upon,' he declared, 'by the exalted names of Messieurs de Vauban and Cohörn, who have consumed immense sums in the fortifying of places without having made any addition to their strength; at least, any that was material or proportioned to what might have been expected, as is evident in the circumstances of their being taken with so much ease and expedition.'

These sentiments might have been taken to be gross conceit in a young man writing in 1732: but in his campaigns of the late 1740s Maurice justified his words to the hilt. The facility with which, under his orders, Löwendahl and Contades snapped up whole chains of fortresses should have dealt a death blow to the 'fortress mania' of the age. One of the least inspired features of the campaigns of his disciple Frederick the Great was the emphasis which the King placed on maintaining fortresses and conducting sieges. He himself recognized this trait as retrogressive and out-of-date: but the political necessities of his policies of aggrandizement compelled him to regard fortresses as 'the mighty nails that hold a ruler's provinces together'. Napoleon, however, conducted only two sieges in twenty years of fighting.

Instead of permanent fortresses, Maurice urged the erection of temporary forts, larger versions of his redoubts. They were to be constructed as the progress of the campaign dictated, at such genuine strategic points as the junction of rivers. Once again he brought into play the principle of enfilade fire, and aimed to provide his forts with an interlocking series of casemates. He also poured out his usual profusion of subsidiary notions—ingenious suggestions for floating batteries, for masked cannon, and so forth. He estimated that one of his legions could construct a solid fortress in a month: but though he was able to give practical expression to his theory of the redoubt, he was never given an opportunity to test this idea of the temporary fortress. Until the latest and most hopeless stage in their colonial wars (e.g. in Indo-China), the French army ignored the possibilities of the temporary fort. Eventually (with some contribution from the experience of the Foreign Legion), they borrowed the idea from the practice of Wingate in Burma and from that of the Germans during the retreats of 1944 and 1945. They could have taken it earlier from a book published by one of their own Marshals-General. In metropolitan France itself, the emphasis unfortunately remained on the continuous lines of permanent fortresses advocated by Vauban as early as 1678; and although there once existed genuine political and geographical reasons for the policy of couverture, they led eventually to the disastrous defensive systems of Rivière and Maginot.

Maurice strove continually to banish artificial tactical aids in favour of those afforded by nature. He was the exponent of day to day, even hour to hour exploitation of the natural advantages of the terrain. This was a lesson instilled into him by the lively and perspicacious Folard. Few generals of the age possessed such a striking insight as Maurice into the potentialities of the landscape. Wellington once remarked that he 'had spent most of his life guessing what the other fellow was doing on the other side of the hill'. At this vital guessing-game Maurice too was singularly adept.

Among minor matters, Maurice argued strongly in favour of conscription. He wanted a five-year term for men between the ages of twenty and thirty. 'It is necessary,' he asserted.

> that no sort of distinction should be admitted, no rank or degree whatsoever excluded, and the nobles and rich rendered, in a principal manner, subservient to it; this will effectually prevent all murmur and repining, for those who have served their time will look upon such as may betray any reluctance or dissatisfaction at it with contempt; by which means, the grievance will vanish insensibly, and every man at length esteem it an honour to serve his term.

Once again his views are reminiscent of those of Gustavus Adolphus. Gustavus had actually introduced universal and non-discriminatory conscription of this type, his sole concession to the nobility being that their sons could choose to serve, if they so wished, in the cavalry instead of the infantry.

Maurice was also in favour of paying enlisted men handsomely, and of offering them the prospect of immediate and unlimited advancement if they exerted themselves. This applied particularly to men of humble birth, who usually found that the path to the top was blocked by their social superiors. 'I would not,' Maurice said,

> be understood to argue that princes, and other persons of illustrious origin, should be denied all marks of preference and distinction; but only that some regard should be had to their abilities; and the privileges of birth required to be supported by those of merit.

This was a remarkable, not to say proto-jacobin, suggestion in its day. Such a practice would have been unthinkable in the French and Saxon armies of the period. One is reminded of the great mercenary Wallenstein, who prided himself on promoting for merit alone, and who disdained to show favouritism even to the son of the Holy Roman Emperor. Maurice's words, moreover, assume an added poignancy when we realize how they foreshadowed the bitter clashes with Conti and Clermont which he sustained in later life.

He had no liking at all for new regiments. He preferred his formations to be battle-hardened and possess their own sense of tradition, and he always made it a practice to sprinkle the ranks of new levies with veterans. On the other hand, he was strongly opposed to the French custom of concentrating the flower of the infantry into a small number of crack regiments. These regiments naturally tended to bear the brunt of the fighting, with the result that a high proportion of the army's best men were often disabled in the course of a single campaign, sometimes even in a single battle. His policy was to distribute his trained men as evenly as possible.

He suggested that every private soldier should wear a brass shoulder-plate with the name or number of his regiment engraved on it, an idea later taken up by Napoleon; he also threw out the suggestion that as an aid to identification, and a deterrent to deserters, the right hand of every man—colonels included—should be marked 'with the kind of composition used by the Indians' (i.e. indigo): a slightly less drastic alternative to the Roman custom of branding. He was also in favour of labelling regiments not by a number or by the name of their colonel, but by their place of origin. He knew the power and value of an appeal to local loyalty.

He also borrowed from the Romans the trick of adding a few drops of vinegar to his drinking water when he was on active service. 'The use of vinegar,' he claimed, 'was the grand secret by which the Romans preserved their armies.' The sudden disablement of entire armies through a plague of typhus or dysentery was a familiar phenomenon in the eighteenth century; Maurice himself had witnessed it at Belgrade. Another item of diet which he would have liked to have brought into general use was biscuit in place of bread. Army bread was uniformly atrocious in quality; it was unwholesome; it would not keep; and it required many waggons to transport. As the forerunner of iron rations, the use of biscuit was not without merit; yet every soldier or sailor knows the loss of appetite and gloom of spirit which descends on him when confronted by this obnoxious comestible, which possesses the lowest barter value of any military or naval article. Here, for once, Maurice's insight failed him. When Napoleon crossed the Alps, he took Maurice's advice and issued biscuit to his men; they had nearly starved to death long before they crossed the bridge at Lodi.

Napoleon professed to have small regard for Maurice's capacity as a general, rating him among the commanders of the second rank. This is not surprising. The Corsican subaltern was not renowned for the amount of praise which he doled out to his military predecessors, particularly those who had successfully commanded the armies of France. His poor opinion of Maurice was offset by the esteem in which the memory of Maurice was held by Wellington, who as a young general in India had included in his travelling library a copy of *Mes Rêveries*.

The indifference of Napoleon prefigured the neglect into which Maurice's reputation was to fall during the course of the nineteenth century. To some extent this was merely the result of the oblivion which was swift to overtake the memory of the soldiers of the *ancien régime*; but Maurice, in any case, was perhaps too restrained and too humane a commander to make an impression on the thickened consciousness of post-Revolutionary Europe. His career had already been diminished in retrospect by the cruel and spectacular aura of the career of Frederick the Great, while Napoleon and his followers were unprepared by temperament to understand the delicacy of touch which had characterized the better generals of the eighteenth century. In the age of Bach and Couperin, warfare had been intricate, formal and shapely; in the age of Wagner and Berlioz, it had developed into a bloated exercise in turgid metaphysics. Napoleon progressively exhausted his country and his empire in order to feed the moloch of his army, the *levée en masse* becoming the *Grande Armée*. The notion that warfare was a contest which involved select bands of professionals became increasingly unreal. The *Grande Armée* was deliberately *Grande*: an arrogant, all-embracing, megalomaniac extension of the personality of its author, a machine not only for fighting but for the propagation of terror. With Napoleon is ushered in the age of the mass man, of the cult of numbers. It was all very far from the poised and lucid world of Maurice and his contemporaries. It was far, too, from the world of Wellington, who, although he mastered Napoleon, remained at heart an eighteenth-century grandee. Neither Maurice nor Wellington would have understood the maxim of Clausewitz: 'War is an act of violence pushed to its utmost limits.'

Many of the battles of the eighteenth century had none the less been bloody enough to suit even the taste of a Clausewitz. The casualty lists of the major engagements in which Maurice fought— Malplaquet, Gadesbusch, Fontenoy, Rocoux, Laufeldt—demonstrate that they were fought out in grim earnest. Warfare, once unleashed, cannot always be controlled by even the most scrupulous of generals; but the severity of the main battles of the eighteenth century does not detract from the fact that most of the soldiers and politicians of that period, mindful of the recent horrors of the Thirty Years War, made a genuine and honourable effort to minimize the extent of the damage. The one great exception to the rule was Charles XII, who manifested a serious interest in the possibilities of total war: and it is significant that he was regarded in his day as something of a savage. What else could one expect of a man who cropped his hair like a barbarian and spread his butter with his thumb? The eighteenth century was not sympathetic to what Delbrück, in discussing Clause-witz, defined as *Niederwerfungsstrategie*: the strategy of annihila-tion: the strategy of Alexander the Great, of Julius Caesar, of Charles XII and Napoleon. The eighteenth century was the classic age of *Ermattungsstrategie*: the strategy of attrition: the code of limited hostility which Delbrück associated with Pericles and Belisarius, with Gustavus Adolphus and Maurice de Saxe.[255] It will be remembered that, when Löwendahl's troops slipped the leash at Bergen-op-Zoom, the news of the subsequent massacre was received with horrified disbelief. It was regarded as a disaster to the reputation of France and her king; and Maurice, as commander-in-chief, was profoundly morti-fied. Sixty years later, when Davoust brutalized Hamburg, or Mac-donald the city of Frosinone, or Victor the city of Madrid, their actions were accepted by their Emperor as a matter of course. The world had changed.[256]

An assessment of Maurice's standing as a commander is made diffi-cult by the fact that he often fought against indifferent adversaries. True, his antagonists were not always, in the scornful words of Carlyle, 'the very worst': they had, after all, included Prince Eugène; but it is true that his abilities had not been fully stretched by a Cumberland or a Wade.

It is certainly not true that he could only work satisfactorily with a small army. He liked small armies, but in his time achieved striking results with large and unwieldy ones. Indeed, in the arts of arming, provisioning, and inculcating a sense of purpose into enormous bodies of troops he was possibly without a superior in his day.

His very artistry, however, could be a source of weakness. At times his handling of a campaign could become slightly self-conscious. His preference for the rapier rather than the sabre probably accounts for his successive failures to institute proper full-scale pursuits, although in his *Rêveries* he had declared himself in favour of such a manoeuvre. To some extent, although brimming with *élan*, he was too thoroughly a representative of his century to possess the full and naked instinct of aggression. He won three mighty and protracted pitched battles: but in each of them one senses that he enjoyed the dazzling pre-liminaries much more than he relished the eventual trial of brute force. Yet it is precisely this moderate bias that makes him so attractive as a man, and which made him such a splendid exponent of the subtle-ties of *Ermattungsstrategie*. He wrote that he was 'far from approving of general engagements', and was 'fully persuaded that an able general might avoid them, and yet carry on the war as long as he pleased. Nothing reduces an enemy so much as that method of conduct.' He liked to stalk his enemy with the apparent aim of provoking a clash, but always maintained throughout a faint air of hesitancy; and it is revealing that as rule he was content to play the rôle of a counter-puncher, a fighter who waits for his more impetuous opponent to lead. It was by temperament as well as by conviction that he would have endorsed the words of du Picq in his *Études sur le Combat* that 'manoeuvres are threats; he who appears most threatening wins'.

His methods, like those of Gustavus, were based on the Roman model to a more profound extent than he may have realized. Like Gustavus, he substituted a Roman conception of warfare for the Grecian model that had preceded him. Gustavus, a master of artillery tactics, had long ago pointed out that the use of cannon had rendered the disposal of regiments in close formation, after the manner of the Greek phalanx, totally obsolete. After Lützen the lesson was forgotten, and was not recalled to mind until the advent of Maurice, himself a gifted exponent of the employment of artillery. After his death, to the bitter cost of several generations of European infantrymen, the majority of commanders reverted to the old crude tactics. Few of them remembered the two outstanding items that Gustavus and Maurice had contributed to the military repertoire: the effective use of fire-power, and the sensible dispersal of forces in face of the fire-power of the enemy.

In many ways, Maurice is very close in spirit to some of the generals of our own day. He would, for example, have made a magnificent panzer general. Like the better commanders of World War Two, his approach to military problems was essentially flexible. We are probably in a better position to appreciate him now than we would have been a generation ago, bogged down in memories of the *millionenheeren* and the lines of static entrenchments of the Western Front. The genuine achievements of eighteenth-century warfare may be due for an intelligent reappraisal. Maurice was also the pioneer of the modern conception of the general staff, perhaps the most important single military innovation in the past two hundred years. Crémille is the first instance of a real chief-of-staff in the modern sense, and Maurice's relationship with his immediate subordinates suggests that he regarded them not as messenger boys but as responsible lieutenants. He expected Crémille and his colleagues to relieve him of the daily *minutiae* of command—what he himself referred to as 'the alphabet of the troops'. He saw only too clearly that the work of an able commander may be ruined if he allows himself to be swamped by the humdrum details of routine administration. He asserted that 'it is necessary that a general officer should preserve his judgment quite free and disengaged from trivial circumstance'. It was a highly original view for a man of his time, and it explains why he was so much the superior of the pedantic Broglies and Noailles of the day. He was a man of unusual imagination: he decided to give it rein.

'War,' said Foch, 'is a simple art: its essence lies in its accomplishment.' Few men have mastered the simple art as thoroughly as Maurice de Saxe. If Velasquez can be called a painter's painter, or Stendhal a novelist's novelist, then Maurice can rightly be called a general's general.

BIBLIOGRAPHY

Publication is at London or Paris unless otherwise indicated

Adlerfeld, G. *Military History of Charles XII* (1740).
Argenson, René Louis de Voyer de Paulmy, marquis d'. *Journal et mémoires* (1859-67).
Argenson, marquis d'. *Adrienne Lecouvreur: Lettres à Maurice de Saxe* (*Revue des Deux Mondes*: Vols. 36 & 37).
Babeau, A. *La Vie Militaire sous L'Ancien Régime* (1889).
Bain, R. N. *Charles XII and the Collapse of the Swedish Empire* (1895).
Barbier. *Journal* (1861).
Beaumont, G. du Bosc de. *Correspondance de Sophie-Dorothée, princesse électorale de Hanovre, avec le comte de Königsmarck* (*Revue des Deux Mondes*, 1914).
Bégard, Yvonne. *Lettres de Guerre sous Louis XV* (Fontenoy) (*Revue des Questions Historiques*, 1927).
Bilmanis, Alfred. *History of Latvia* (Princeton, 1951).
Boindin (attrib. to). *Première Lettre, sur la Comédie française* (1719).
Boissy, Desprez de. *Lettres sur les spectacles* (7th ed., 1779).
Boussanelle. *Histoire de la cavalerie* (1756).
Bottée. *Etudes militaires: Exercises de l'Infanterie* (1731).
Broglie, J. V. Albéric, duc de. *Frederick the Great and Maria Theresa* (1883); *Maurice de Saxe et le marquis d'Argenson* (1891).
Bülau, M. *Die Grafen von Koenigsmarck* (in *Geheime Geschichten und rathselhafte Menschen*, Leipzig, 1860).
Burne, A. H. *The Art of War on Land* (1944).
Burg, P. *Die schöne Gräfin Königsmarck* (Brunswick, 1919).
Carlyle. *History of Friedrich II* (1894 ed.).
Carré, H. *La France sous Louis XV* (1891); *La marquise de Pompadour* (1937).
Charnois, le Vacher de. *Costumes et annales des grands théâtres de Paris* (1788).
Charteris, Hon. Evan. *William Augustus, Duke of Cumberland* (1913).
Churchill, Winston. *Marlborough* (1933-38).
Cohörn, Baron de. *Versterkinge des Vijfhoeks* (Amsterdam, 1682); *Nieue Vestingbouw* (Amsterdam, 1685).
Colin, Col. J.: *Campagnes de Maurice de Saxe* (1901-06).
F. Cramer. *Denkwürdigkeiten der Gräfin Maria-Aurora Königsmarck and der Königsmarck'schen Familie* (Leipzig, 1836).
Crevellier, J. *La Vie Romanesque d'Aurore de Koenigsmarck* (1929).
Dally, A. *La France Militaire* (1900).
Dangé, C. *La Bataille de Fontenoy: Lettres d'un Témoin* (Bull. de la Soc. acad. de Bordeaux, 1926).
Delahache, P. *Strasbourg* (1923).
Eckstaedt, comte C. F. Vitzthum d'. *Maurice comte de Saxe, et Maria-Josèphe, dauphine de France* (Lettres et documents inédits des Archives de Dresde. Leipzig-Paris-Londres, 1867).
Espagnac, Baron d'. *Histoire de Maurice, comte de Saxe* (1773).
Favart, C. S. *Correspondances* (1808).
Fieffé. *Histoire des troupes étrangères* (1834).
Fortescue, Hon. J. W. *History of the British Army* (1910 ed.).
Gozlan, Léon. *Mme. Favart et le maréchal de Saxe* (1853).
Grimoard, comte P. H. de. *Histoire des conquêtes de Gustave Adolphe* (1789).
Haake, Paul. *August der Starke* (Dresden, 1927).
Hart, B. H. Liddell. *Great Captains Unveiled* (1927).

Histoire de la dernière guerre de Bohême (Amsterdam, 1750).

Histoire de la guerre de 1741 (Amsterdam, 1755).

History of Maurice Count Saxe, The. By an Officer of Distinction. Translated from the French. (1753). (N.b. This is a translation of the book by Néel, *vide infra*. It is referred to in the references as H. of M.C.S. It should not be confused with the book of the same title by Espagnac (*vide supra*), which is referred to in the references as Esp.).

Lachesnaye des Bois. *Dictionnaire militaire* (1745).

Lacour-Gayet. *La Marine militaire sous la Règne de Louis XV* (1902).

Lémontey. *Oeuvres* (1829).

Liv- Est- und Curländisches Urkundenbuch (Riga, 1853).

Luynes, duc de. *Mémoires* (1861).

Malleson, G. B. *Eugène of Savoy* (1888).

Malo, Henri. *La Vie Ardente de Maurice de Saxe* (1928).

Marmontel. *Mémoires* (1804).

Mauvillon, E. de. *Histoire du prince Eugène de Savoie* (1790).

Montandre and Longchamps. *Etat des troupes en 1748* (1748).

Monval, G. *Lettres de Adrienne Le Couvreur* (1892).

Mouillard, L. *Res Régiments sous Louis XV* (1882).

(Néel). *Histoire de Maurice, comte de Saxe* (Mittaw—i.e. Mitau—1752; Dresden, 1755 & 1760). (N.b. This is the French original of the *History of Maurice Count Saxe* (vide supra), speedily rendered into English after its appearance at Mitau. Néel acknowledges his debt to conversations with d'Alençon, Maurice's friend and tutor).

New Cambridge Modern History (Cambridge, 1957).

Noailles, duc de. *Mémoires* (ed. Millot) (1777); *Correspondances de Louis XV et du maréchal de Noailles* (ed. Rousset) (1865).

Nouveaux Amusements, Les (1736).

Orgeval. *Le Maréchalat de France* (1932).

Parnasse françois (Supplément) (1743): *Eloge historique d'Adrienne Lecouvreur*.

Pompadour, madame la marquis de. *Letters* (1772).

Pougin, A. *Madame Favart* (1912).

Preedy, George R. (pseud. Marjorie Bowen). *Child of Chequer'd Fortune* (This biography of Maurice, like Malo's (*vide supra*), is slight and riddled with inaccuracies; but it is written with all Miss Bowen's grace and skill, and would appear to have suggested most of the raw material for her two magnificent historical novels, *The Rocklitz* and *General Crack*.)

Preedy, George R. (pseud. Marjorie Bowen). *Sundry Great Gentlemen* (1928). (One of seven studies.)

Richelieu, duc de. *Mémoires* (1818).

Rousset, C. *Histoire de Louvois* (1860).

Sainte-Beuve. *Lundis* (1851-62).

Sain-Geniès, R. de. *Art de la guerre pratiqué* (1754).

Sand, George. *Histoire de ma Vie* (1856).

Saxe Galante, La. Histoire des Amours d'Auguste I (scil. Frederick Augustus II) *Roi de Pologne* (Amsterdam, 1736). (A scandalous but amusing chronicle).

Saxe, Maurice, comte de. *Histoire de Maurice, comte de Saxe* (Author's name not given, but actually by Néel: see (Néel) supra. The French edition of the work is useful for the carefully engraved plans in Vol. II of the battles of Fontenoy and Laufeldt).

    History of Maurice Count Saxe. See separate entry.

    Mes Rêveries. Ouvrage posthume de Maurice comte de Saxe, Duc de Curlande et de Sémigalle, Maréchal général des Armées de sa Majesté très-chrétienne: Augmenté d'une histoire abrégée de sa vie, et de différentes pièces qui y ont rapport, par M. l'abbé Pérau. (Two vols., Amsterdam and Leipzig, 1757.) (134 pp. Intro.; 410 pp. text; 84 engraved plates, those in Vol. 1 finely coloured by hand.)

    Reveries, or Memoirs upon the Art of War, by Field-Marshal Count Saxe, Translated from the French (London, 1757). (No biographical introduction; text complete; 40 uncoloured engraved plates).

BIBLIOGRAPHY

Lettres et Mémoires, choisis parmi les papiers originaux du Maréchal de Saxe (Paris, 1794). (40 pp. biographical notice; 5 vols. letters, despatches and memoranda).

Schnath, Georg. *Der Königsmarck-Briefwechsel* (Hildesheim 1952).

Schulenburg, Johann Matthias, Graf von der. *Leben und Denkwürdigkeiten* (Berlin, 1834).

Spanheim, F. *Le soldat suédois* (1633).

Sorel, Cécile. *La Vie Amoureuse d'Adrienne Lecouvreur* (1925).

Stryienski, Casimir. *The Eighteenth Century* (London, 1916); *La Mère des trois derniers Bourbons, Marie-Josèphe de Saxe et la cour de Louis XV* (1904).

Taillandier, Saint-René. *Maurice de Saxe* (1865).

Taylor, Frank. *Wars of Marlborough* (1921).

Thomas, *Eloge de Maurice, comte de Saxe* (1756; second, revised ed. 1774).

Touchard-Lafosse. *La Loire* (Tours, 1851).

Townshend, C. V. F. *The Military Life of Field Marshal George, First Marquess Townshend* (1901).

Urch, R. O. G. *Latvia* (1938).

Valfons, Charles Mathei de. *Mémoires* (ed. Maurin) (1906).

Vauban. *Traité des sièges* (1705).

Voltaire. *Candide* (trans. Aldington, 1939).
    Histoire de Charles XII (1891 ed.).
    Histoire de la Guerre de 1741 (1755).
    Histoire de la Russie sous Pierre le Grand (1891 ed.).
    Oeuvres Complets (Garnier, Paris, 1880).
    Siècle de Louis XV (1891 ed.).

Weber, Karl von. *Moritz, Graf von Sachsen* (Leipzig, 1863).

Whitworth, Rex. *Field Marshal Lord Ligonier* (1958).

Wilkins, W. H. *Love of an Uncrowned Queen* (1900).

Wolframsdorf, Jean Frederic de. *Portrait de la Cour de Sa Maiesté le Roi de Pologne, Electeur de Saxe* (MS, 93 pp.; formerly in the possession of Mr. H. D. Lyon, vide Intro. This document, secretly circulated by one of the King's chamberlains, gives a venomous account of the personalities and circumstances affecting Maurice during his childhood years at Dresden; Wolframsdorf was subsequently savagely punished by the King for his indiscretion).

NOTES AND REFERENCES

ABBREVIATIONS

DPR=*Différentes Pièces Relatives* (printed at end of first French edition of *Mes Rêveries*)
Eck.=Vitzthum d'Eckstaedt
Esp.=Espagnac
H. of M.C.S.=*History of Maurice, Count Saxe*
L. et M.=*Lettres et Mémoires du Maréchal de Saxe*
M. Rêv.=*Mes Rêveries*
Taill.=Taillandier
Volt. H. of C.XII=Voltaire, *History of Charles XII*
Volt. OC=Voltaire, *Oeuvres Complets*
Volt. R. of L.XV=Voltaire, *Reign of Louis XV*
(N.b.: Publication is at London or Paris unless otherwise indicated)

PROLOGUE

1. Acton, *Lectures on Modern History* (1906), p. 267.
2. Wilkins, *Love of an Uncrowned Queen* (1900), II, p. 538.
3. Wilkins, II, p. 540.
4. George Sand, *Histoire de ma Vie* (1856), I, Ch. II, pp. 41-57.
5. H. of M.C.S., I, p. 14.
6. Wilkins, II, p. 486.
7. Usual refs. to a journey to Dresden by the 'three beautiful Königsmarck sisters' are inaccurate. Hübner, *Genealogische Tabellen* (No. 1324) (Leipzig, 1733), shows conclusively that Maria Aurora possessed only one sister, Amelia Wilhelmine.
8. H. of M.C.S., I, p. 154; see also *Saxe Galante*, p. 200.

CHAPTER I

9. G. P. Gooch, *Catherine the Great and Other Studies* (1954), p. 205.
10. Volt., H. of C.XII, Ch. II, p. 51.
11. Volt., loc. cit., p. 64.
12. Frank Taylor, *Wars of Marlborough* (1921).
13. Volt., loc. cit.
14. Mid-nineteenth century travel guides (e.g. Murray and Baedecker) give interesting descriptions of the decor and contents of the Dresden palaces.
15. For history of the Saxon crown jewels, see Joan Evans, *History of Jewellery* 1953). The 'Dresden Green', the most famous green diamond, was looted by the Red Army in 1945 and has disappeared.
16. H. of M.C.S., I, p. 34.
17. Taill., p. 13.

CHAPTER II

18. Taill., p. 14.
19. Taill., p. 15.
20. Taylor, *Wars of Marlborough.*
21. H. of M.C.S., I, p. 37.
22. Churchill, *Marlborough* (1933-38), IV, p. 127.
23. Churchill, loc. cit., p. 171.

CHAPTER III

24. Taill., p. 59, quoting a letter of Madame de Pompadour to the duchesse d'Estrées.
25. Taill., p. 35.
26. Boswell's *Life of Johnson*: April 10th, 1778.
27. Taill., p. 40.
28. Taill., p. 40.
29. Taill., p. 46.
30. *History of the Four Georges* (1910), p. 6.
31. M. *Rêv.* (Fr. ed.), I, p. 24.
32. Taill., p. 48.

CHAPTER IV

33. Taill., p. 63.
34. Since the death of Lt. Gen. Greder in 1716, the regiment had been commanded by a Swede. There were four French recruiting stations openly and permanently established on German soil. By the end of Maurice's life the number of foreign regiments in French service had risen to forty. Maurice's descendants were to be particularly associated with the Royal-Bavière. See A. Babeau, *La Vie Militaire sous l'Ancien Régime* (1889), p. 230 ff.; A. Dally, *La France Militaire* (1900), p. 113 ff.
35. Taill., p. 65.
36. Hyacinthe Rigaud (1659-1743); most celebrated portrait painter of his day; painted Augustus the Strong. I cannot trace the original of his portrait of Maurice: not listed in Bénézit, *Dict. crit. et doc. des Peintres* (1954). Nägler, *Künstler-Lexicon* (1843), lists portraits of Maurice by Petit, Chereau, Sornique, Dupin and Haid. Further portraits are listed in *Allgemeiner Bildniskatalog*, XI, (1934), pp. 5-6. The well-known portrait by Lefort, almost certainly painted by his protégé Jean-Marc Nattier (1685-1766) is now at Dresden; so is the pastel by Maurice Quentin Latour (1704-1788) (Plate 6 in text). A second pastel by Latour is on view in the Musée Carnavalet. Also at Paris is the excellent portrait by the famous Swiss painter Jean-Etienne Liotard (1702-1790).
37. Folard, *Commentaires sur Polybe*, III, Bk. II. 11, Ch. XIV, Para. 4.
38. Brunet, quoted in Monval, *vide infra.*
39. G. Monval, *Lettres de Adrienne Le Couvreur* (1892), p. 179. The following quotations from Adrienne's letters, for which no further references are therefore necessary, are taken from Monval, who gives them in chronological order. Use is also made of a parallel series published by the marquis d'Argenson in *Revue des Deux Mondes* (Vols. 36 and 37: 15th Dec. 1926; 1st Jan. 1927; 15th Jan. 1927), under the title of *Adrienne Lecouvreur: Lettres à Maurice de Saxe.*
40. Adrienne caused a sensation by playing the court scenes in Thomas Corneille's *Le Comte d'Essex* in actual court dress. For an account which her acting made on her contemporaries, see the article published in the *Mercure de France* soon after her death and reproduced in *Les Nouveaux Amusements* (1736); also Titon du Tillet's *Supplément aux Parnasses françois* (1743).
41. Cécile Sorel, *La Vie Amoureuse d'Adrienne Lecouvreur* (1925), p. 7.

42. See Delahache, *Strasbourg* (1923), p. 110 ff., for Klinglin's subsequent glittering rise and spectacular fall. He died in gaol in 1752 after being tortured and tried in secret for massive peculation while serving as Royal Praetor. *L'affaire Klinglin* made a sensation throughout France. Adrienne was evidently attracted to men accustomed to playing recklessly and for high stakes.

43. *Première Lettre sur la Comédie française* (anon., attrib. to Boindin, 1719), p. 21.

44. Lémontey, *Histoire de la Régence* (1829), III, p. 328.

45. *Lundi*, Dec. 24th, 1949.

46. *H. of M.C.S.*, I, p. 90.

47. Taill., p. 57.

48. *L. et M.*, I, p. xi (Intro.).

49. *H. of M.C.S.*, I, p. 91.

50. Conti or Conty is the name of the cadet branch of the great house of Bourbon-Condé.

51. Maurice to the duchesse de Luynes, Dec. 23rd, 1745. Quoted in Valfons, p. 155. But Maurice's prose style could also be brief and incisive: Voltaire compared to the *brevitatem imperatoriam* of the ancients a note from Maurice to the marquis de Courtivron, who in 1742 was holding at bay 4,000 Croats with 600 Frenchmen: 'No need to write long messages to a good soldier. Fight on. I am on my way. Maurice.' (Volt., OC, XXXVII, p. 551.)

CHAPTER V

52. DPR *M. Rêv.*, II, p. 174.

53. Taill., p. 102.

54. Taill., p. 103.

55. Taill., p. 110.

56. Taill., p. 117.

57. Taill., p. 123.

58. Taill., p. 136.

59. Taill., p. 130.

60. Taill., p. 131.

61. DPR, p. 185.

62. Taill., p. 141.

63. Taill., loc. cit.

64. DPR, p. 181.

65. Taill., p. 143.

66. Cramer, *Denkwürdigkeiten der Gräfin Maria-Aurora Koenigsmarck und der Koenigsmarck'schen Familie* (Leipzig, 1836), II, pp. 112-123.

67. Cramer, loc cit.

68. Cramer, loc cit.

CHAPTER VI

69. Taill., p. 175.

70. *H. of M.C.S.*, I, p. 152.

71. *History of Friedrich II* (1894), Vol X, p. 6.

72. Volt., loc. cit.

73. *Don Quixote*, Bk IV, Ch. III (Motteux trans.).

74. The anecdote is in *Lettre à M. Rousseau, au sujet de sa lettre à M. d'Alembert* (1759).

75. Monval, loc. cit.

76. *Tableau du siècle* (anon., Geneva, 1759), p. 220.

77. Desprez du Boissy, *Lettres sur les spectacles* (7th ed., 1779), I, p. 53; II, p. 182.

78. *Candide* (trans. Aldington, Nonesuch Press, 1939, p. 96): 'Candide asked the little abbé from Perigord how queens were treated in France. The abbé replied: "In the provinces we take them to a tavern; in Paris we respect them when they are beautiful and throw them in the public sewer when they are dead." "Queens in the

public sewer!" said Candide. "Yes, indeed," said Martin, "I was in Paris when Miss Monime (n.b. *Monime* was one of Adrienne's favourite rôles) departed, as they say, this life; she was refused what people here call *the honours of burial*—that is to say, the honour of rotting with all the beggars of the district in a horrible cemetery; she was buried by herself at the corner of the Rue de Bourgogne; which must have given her extreme pain, for her mind was very lofty." "That was very impolite," said Candide. "What do you expect?" said Martin. "These people are like that."' Sixty years later 'these people' threw into the common ditch the body of the Queen of France. See also Voltaire's poem *La Mort de Mlle Lecouvreur, Célèbre Actrice*, first printed in Vol. I of his *Oeuvres* (Amsterdam, 1732). He asks what future generations will think about cruel priests being allowed to throw into ignoble ground 'the immortal remains of this beloved body'.

CHAPTER VII

79. H. of M.C.S., I, p. 5 (Intro.).
80. *Eloge historique d'Adrienne Lecouvreur (Supplément au Parnasse françois,* 1743), p. 806 ff.
81. *Saxe Galante*, p. 413.
82. *Manon Lescaut*, ed. F. C. Green, see Introduction.
83. *M. Rêv.*, II, pp. 194-211.
84. *Lundi*, Sept. 16th, 1830.
85. Casimir Stryienski, *The Eighteenth Century* (Nat. Hist. of France, 1916), p. 77.
86. Henri Carré, *La France sous Louis XV* (1891), p. 164.
87. H. of M.C.S., I, p. 164.
88. *New Cambridge Modern History*, Vol. VII (1957), p. 378.
89. H. of M.C.S., I, p. 168.
90. *Pont de Kehl*. Franco-Prussian War: Left wing of Prussian Third Army enters Strasbourg across bridge. World War I: Bridge scene of bitter fighting in last days of 1918, when fifty years of German occupation ends with beaten Imperial troops raising the red flag in the streets of Strasbourg. World War II: Bridge twice completely destroyed, first by retreating French, then by Germans as Leclerc's Second Armoured Division enters Strasbourg on September 27th, 1944.
91. Noailles, *Journal*: Entry for May 5th, 1734.
92. *L. et M.*, I, pp. 8-9.
93. See *Anthologie des Ecrivains français du XVIIIe Siècle* (Larousse, ND), p. 48.

CHAPTER VIII

94. Horace Walpole, *Memoirs of the Reign of George II* (ed. Lord Holland, 1847), 11, p. 393 ff.
95. Taill., p. 194.
96. Volt., OC, XXXIV, p. 232.
97. H. of M.C.S., I, p. 220. Matthews was undeservedly disgraced after the fiasco at Toulon in Feb. 1744.
98. *M. Rêv.*, II, p. 212, as trans. in H. of M.C.S., I, p. 230.
99. Taill., p. 199.
100. Taill., loc. cit.
101. Taill., p. 213.
102. Taill., p. 214.
103. Eck., p. 459.

CHAPTER IX

104. Eck., p. 413.
105. Broglie, *Frederick the Great and Maria Theresa* (1883), II, p. 184.
106. Townshend: *Military Life of First Marquess Townshend* (1901).

107. Taill., p. 242.

108. Old Breisach is now known simply as Breisach, New Breisach as Neuf-Brisach. The latter is a small, symmetrical, militarized town, built by Vauban. Its octagonal enceinte and bristling complex of curtain walls are solidly built of beautifully cut stone. It is entered through a fine archway and its streets are laid out in neat rectangular blocks. The crossing of the Rhine at this point was as important as at Kehl, and in the winter of 1945 the town was the scene of pitiless fighting as the Germans frantically resisted de Lattre de Tassigny's drive to clean up the 'Colmar pocket'. But in spite of the shell-holes and the blackened buildings—or perhaps because of them—the township still affords the visitor a remarkably evocative glimpse of the circumstances of seventeenth- and eighteenth-century warfare.

109. Taill., p. 243.

110. The Lines of Lauterbourg fronted the Lines of Ettlingen and were of equal strategic importance. The possession of the little town of Lauterbourg had been hotly contested in Marlborough's time; but its greatest trial occurred in 1870, when Abel Douay and most of his 8,000 men laid down their lives in an attempt to beat back the oncoming Bavarian divisions.

CHAPTER X

111. See Mouillard, *Les Régiments sous Louis XV* (1882), p. 91.

112. Mouillard, loc. cit.

113. L. et M., I, p. 44.

114. See Lacour-Gayet, *La Marine militaire sous la Règne de Louis XV* (1902), also Rear-Admiral H. W. Richmond, *The Navy in the War of 1739-48* (1920), for detailed discussion of the abortive invasion. The naval historian Cyril Hughes Hartmann, in his *The Quest Forlorn* (1952), recounts the developments in question with admirable clarity; he assumes, however, that the invasion exercises were intrinsically serious, a point of view not shared by the present writer.

115. L. et M., I, p. 69.

116. It seems probable that Maurice may have had a further reason for sharing personally in the Prince's keen disappointment, in that the duchesse de Bouillon who had fallen so passionately in love with him was Prince Charles Edward's aunt (see Chapter VI). She was also a daughter of one of Maurice's idols, Prince James Sobieski. Their mutual attraction through a shared Polish link is therefore understandable. See Brian Fothergill, *The Cardinal King* (1959), a life of the Jacobite 'King Henry IX', p. 16.

117. Gaspard, marquis and later duc de Clermont-Tonnerre, although a Condé, was a needy aristocrat who fought his way slowly up the ladder of professional promotion. He was fifty before he gained the rank of lieutenant-general, and was a full ten years older than Maurice. He must not be confused with the equally able and equally professional comte de Clermont-Gallerande. And neither of these first-class soldiers should be confused with their inept but influential kinsman, Louis de Bourbon, comte de Clermont, who was to cause Saxe such infinite trouble in his later campaigns (see Chapter XII).

118. Townshend, p. 49.

119. Rex Whitworth, *Field-Marshal Lord Ligonier* (1958), p. 88. Here, as elsewhere in his masterly study, Col. Whitworth pays generous tribute to Saxe's military genius.

120. H. of M.C.S., II, p. 56.

121. L. et M., I, p. 156.

122. Taill., p. 257.

123. 'A dropsy is very rarely an original distemper, but is generally a symptom of some other, which is too often incurable': William Heberden (b. 1710), in *Commentaries on the History and Cure of Diseases* (3rd ed., 1806), pp. 216-224. When M. Argan, in *Le Malade Imaginaire*, shies away from M. Purgon's enormous clyster, he is warned of the succeeding ills that will inevitably overtake him: 'Bradypepsia, dyspepsia, apepsia, lientery, dysentery—and finally hydropsy.' 'Then,' explains Argan, 'I am a dead man!'

124. See Douglas Guthrie, A History of Medicine (1945), p. 290 ff.

125. For an account of the operation, see Kurt Sprengel, De la Ponction du Bas-ventre, in Histoire de la Médecine, Vol. IX (1832).

126. Broglie, Maurice de Saxe et le marquis d'Argenson (1891), loc. cit.

CHAPTER XI

127. Eck., p. 479.

128. See Lt. Col. A. H. Burne in Art of War on Land (1944): a spirited but sadly confused account.

129. Broglie, loc. cit.

130. M. Rêv., II, p. 95.

131. Ingoldsby was no coward: he was wounded at Cumberland's side later in the day. Afterwards he was court-martialled for disobeying orders, and Cumberland gave him three months to leave the army.

132. Fortescue, History of the British Army, II, p. 114. He should have written Redoute de Chambonas for Redoute d'Eu; and in using the term entrenchments he was technically incorrect, for reasons to be shown in the Epilogue.

133. The celebrated story about Lord Charles Hay inviting the 'gentlemen of the French Guards' to fire first, related by Voltaire (Reign of Louis XV, Ch. XV), is apocryphal; the actual words are as given here.

134. Fortescue, p. 116.

135. On a large Celtic cross erected by 'the Irish people' in the centre of the hamlet of Fontenoy is the inscription: 'Limerick, le 3ème Octobre 1691; Fontenoy, le 11ème Mai 1745. A la mémoire des soldats de la Brigade Irlandaise qui sur le champ de Fontenoy se vengèrent de la violation du traité de Limerick.' The monument was erected in 1907; Irish memories are long.

136. L. et M., I, p. 231. The letter to Argenson in which the words occur is also quoted by Colin, Campagnes du Maréchal de Saxe (1901-6), p. 218.

137. Colin, p. 434.

138. Broglie, loc. cit.

139. Broglie, loc. cit.

140. Traité des Grandes Operations Militaires, III, p. 335.

CHAPTER XII

141. Volt., OC, VIII, p. 383.

142. H. of M.C.S., II, p. III.

143. Broglie, I, p. 36.

144. L. et M., II, p. 86.

145. L. et M., II, p. 140.

146. Barbier, Journal (1861), March 1746.

147. Quoted in Thomas Mann's Buddenbrooks, Pt. I, Ch. 8.

148. Broglie, I, p. 337.

149. H. of M.C.S., II, pp. 119 ff.

150. L. et M., II, p. 90.

151. L. et M., II, p. 200.

152. L. et M., II, p. 208.

153. Frederick the Great, in Histoire de mon temps.

154. Valfons, Mémoires (ed. G. Maurin, 1906), pp. 147-156.

155. L. et M., III, p. 6

156. Esp., II, p. 242.

157. L. et M., III, p. 22. Maurice here sets out his own arguments and those of Conti in a temperate letter to Argenson (Aug. 6-7th, 1746).

158. L. et M., III, pp. 33-35.

159. Whitworth, p. 128.

160. L. et M., III, p. 23.

161. Esp., II, p. 263 (note).

162. C. S. Favart, *Mémoires et Correspondances* (ed. Dummollard, 1808), I, p. xxv.
163. Valfons, p. 169.
164. *Rocoux* is variously spelled *Racoux, Roucoux, Raucoux,* etc. *Rocoux* is preferred.
165. For French dispositions, see Esp., II, p. 290 ff., supplemented by H. of M.C.S., II, p. 133 ff.
166. *L. et M.,* III, p. 267.
167. Whitworth, p. 141.
168. Valfons, p. 176.
169. H. of M.C.S., II, p. 137.

CHAPTER XIII

170. Miss Nancy Mitford, *Madame de Pompadour* (1954). See Ch. VI.
171. Eck., p. 32.
172. Eck., p. 34.
173. *Correspondance de Louis XV et du Maréchal de Noailles* (ed. Rousset, 1865), II, p. 271.
174. Broglie, I, p. 355.
175. Eck., p. 63.
176. Eck., p. 65.
177. Eck., p. 64.
178. Voltaire, who owed his lucrative sinecure of Historiographer Royal to the good offices of the duc de Richelieu, was careful to over-praise his patron in his official account of the battle of Fontenoy. Maurice reacted strongly to Voltaire's hint that Richelieu had pulled his chestnuts out of the fire for him. There had therefore been bad blood and a marked degree of jealousy between the two men. See also *Mémoires authentiques du maréchal de Richelieu* (ed. Boislisle, 1818), pp. 98-111; Paul d'Estrée, *Le Maréchal de Richelieu* (1917), pp. 204-207.
179. Eck., p. 100.
180. Eck., p. 138. For an entertaining account of Richelieu's grand and raffish embassy to Dresden, see *Vie privée du maréchal de Richelieu* (attributed to Faur), II, p. 92 ff.; Marcel Pollitzer, *Le Maréchal Galant* (1952), pp. 202-203.
181. The anecdote is in Luynes, *Mémoires,* VIII, p. 83. For details of the marshalate, see Orgeval, *Le Maréchalat de France* (1932), II, p. 259. The last French soldier to hold the rank of Marshal General was Soult, who was appointed to it in the post-Napoleonic epoch.
182. Broglie, p. 159.
183. Eck., p. 159.
184. Eck., pp. 161-164.

CHAPTER XIV

185. See Octave Aubry, *Histoire de France* (1947), p. 266.
186. Letter to Frederick the Great, May 27th, 1737.
187. H. of M.C.S., II, p. 147.
188. Eck., pp. 170-177.
189. Carlyle, op. cit., VII, p. 138.
190. Broglie, loc. cit.
191. *L. et M.,* IV, p. 149.
192. *L. et M.,* IV, p. 160.
193. *Laufeldt* is variously spelled *Lafeld, Laffeldt, La Veld,* etc. *Laufeldt* is preferred, although Larousse favours *Lawfeld.*
194. Valfons, p. 206.
195. Valfons, p. 207.
196. The best and fullest account of the battle is in Esp.
197. Whitworth, p. 153, quoting a contemporary account.
198. Esp., II, p. 374.

199. The regiments taking part in this heroic cavalry action were the Royal Scots Greys, Cumberland's Hussars, a regiment of Hanoverians, Rich's, Rothe's, and Cope's Dragoons (the last named afterwards becoming the 6th (Inniskilling) Dragoons).

200. Valfons, p. 210.

201. H. of M.C.S., II, p. 165.

202. Whitworth, p. 158. The Household Provost Guards were the *Maison du Roi*.

203. Whitworth, loc. cit.

204. Whitworth, loc. cit.

205. The basic material of the exchanges is outlined in Broglie, II, 337 ff. See also Chesterfield, *Correspondence*, III, p. 209; *Marchmont Diary*, II, p. 210.

206. Eck., p. 505.

207. Broglie, II, p. 231. Chambrier to Frederick the Great, June 16th, 1747.

208. Townshend, p. 115.

209. Eck., p. 504.

210. *L. et M.*, IV, p. 161.

211. Menno, Baron de Cohörn (1641-1704). Vauban's great rival. Principal works on fortification appeared in 1682 and 1685.

212. Eck., p. 305. See also Weber, *Moritz, Graf von Sachsen* (Leipzig, 1863), p. 241.

213. *L. et M.*, IV, 230-237.

214. *L. et M.*, IV, pp. 159-164.

215. Esp., II, p. 433.

216. Broglie, II, p. 367.

217. Volt., R. of L.XV, Ch. XXVI, p. 148.

218. Broglie, II, p. 367.

219. *Dictionnaire biographique française*: see entry *Saxe*.

220. Broglie, I, p. 366.

CHAPTER XV

221. The author was Mauger.

222. *L. et M.*, IV, pp. 237-242.

223. *Mémoires de Noailles* (ed. Millot, 1777), VI, p. 242 ff. See also *L. et M.*, IV, pp. 21-34.

224. Argenson, *Mémoires* (1863), V, p. 277.

225. *L. et M.*, V, p. 269.

CHAPTER XVI

226. The staircase figures in Vigny's *Cinq-Mars*; see also Chateaubriand's *Vie de Rancé*.

227. Eck., p. 179.

228. Eck., p. 509.

229. *L. et M.*, V, p. 291.

230. Eck. loc. cit.

231. A mine of valuable information concerning Aurora von Königsmarck and the other ancestors of George Sand is contained in the *Bulletin du Musée Carnavalet* (Year 7, No. 2; December 1954).

232. See Marmontel, *Mémoires* (1804).

233. Favart, p. xi.

234. Favart, p. xiv.

235. Favart, p. xlvi.

236. Favart, pp. lii-liv.

237. Taill., p. 370.

238. Carlyle, op. cit., VI, pp. 161-163.

239. Volt., OC, XXXVII, p. 32. See also Frederick the Great's eulogistic letter to Maurice, signed 'with great esteem, your affectionate friend', in *L. et M.*, III, pp. 260-262.

240. Volt., OC, XXXVII, p. 147.

CHAPTER XVII

241. Valfons, p. xxx.
242. *L. et M.*, V, p. 299 ff.
243. Taill., p. 389.
244. The details of the will are in H. *of M.C.S.*, II, p. 231. ff.
245. H. *of M.C.S.*, II, p. 241.
246. H. *of M.C.S.*, II, loc. cit.

EPILOGUE

247. Carlyle, op. cit., VI, p. 162.
248. *Mémoires*, quoted in Maurice Marshal, *L'Autorité* (1958), p. 95.
249. This and subsequent quotations from *M. Rêv.* are either translated from the first French edition or taken from the first version (see Bibliography).
250. See *Zeitschrift für Historische Waffen- und Kostümkunde* (1929), III, 10, p. 246 (with illustration).
251. See *M. Rêv.* (Fr. ed.), II, whole of Ch. III; also ibid. p. 196.
252. It may be of interest to detail the subsequent career of Maurice's two personal regiments. *Régiment Greder*: Raised in 1667 by the Landgrave of Fürstemberg, it remained in the hands of the Fürstembergs until 1685, when it passed into the hands of M. Greder. (It should not be confused with the regiment subsequently known as the 55th Infantry, which earlier had also been owned by the Greder family.) The regiment passed to M. Sparre, a Swede, in 1716, who sold it to Maurice in 1720. Maurice commanded it until his death, when it was purchased by M. Bentheim. In 1759 it was bought by M. Anhalt, and in 1783 became the Régiment de Salm-Salm. In 1791 it was commanded by a French colonel for the first time, and served throughout the nineteenth century, becoming the 62nd Infantry. Honours: Wagram, 1809; Lützen, 1813; Sebastopol, 1855; Matchuala (Mexico), 1864. *Volontaires de Saxe Dragons*: At Maurice's death, Count Friesen paid off the uhlans, who had become unmanageable, and reduced the regiment's strength to 240. In the Seven Years War it was augmented with men recruited at Phalsbourg, and fought under the name of the Volontaires de Schomberg. In 1791 it became the 17th Dragoons; in 1814 the 12th Dragoons; and the 17th Dragoons again in 1815, when it was disbanded. Honours: Le Moskowa, 1814; Bautzen, 1813; Dresden, 1813; Champaubert, 1814. It also fought with distinction at Valmy, Austerlitz, Eylau, Friedland, Albuhera and Vittoria. *Vide* MS book, *Noms, Drapeaux, Devises des Régiments français*, by Lt. Col. Pichot, in the library of the Invalides.
253. *Great Captains Unveiled* (1927), p. 52.
254. See *On War* (trans. Graham, 3rd ed., 1918).
255. See Delbrück, *Die Strategie des Perikles erläutert dürch die Strategie Friedrichs der Grossen* (1890).
256. N.b. Clausewitz's apostrophe of Napoleon as the 'God of War'. Clausewitz himself has been aptly described as 'the Mahdi of the Mass'.

INDEX

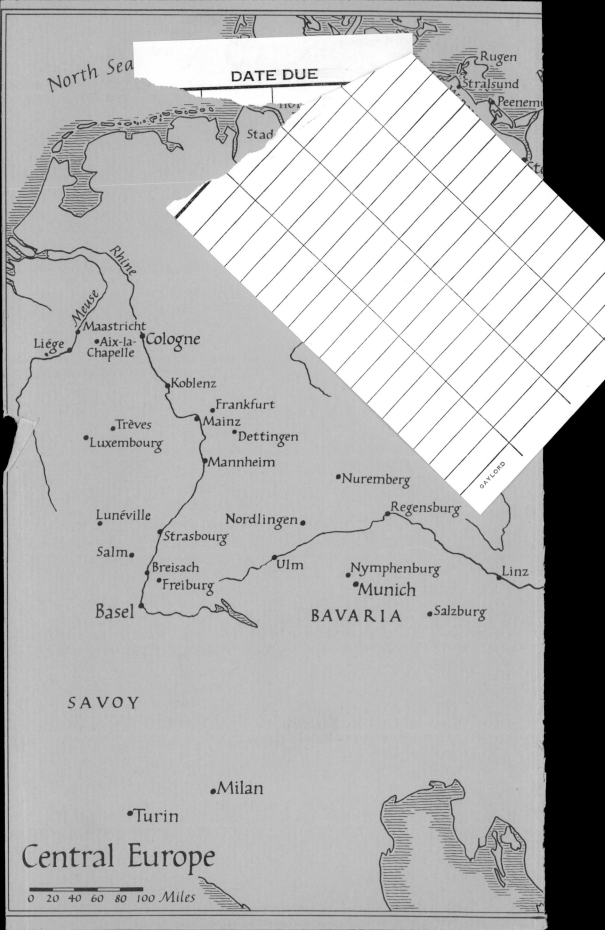

North Sea

Rügen
Stralsund
Peenem[...]
Sta[...]

DATE DUE

Rhine

Meuse

Liége
Maastricht
•Aix-la-
Chapelle
Cologne

Koblenz

Frankfurt
Mainz
•Dettingen

Trèves
•Luxembourg

Mannheim

Nuremberg

Regensburg

Lunéville
Nordlingen•

Strasbourg

Salm•
Breisach
•Freiburg

Ulm
Nymphenburg•
•Munich

Linz

Basel

BAVARIA
•Salzburg

SAVOY

•Milan

•Turin

Central Europe

0 20 40 60 80 100 Miles